MARX'S THEORY OF CRISIS

Also by Simon Clarke

KEYNESIANISM, MONETARISM AND THE CRISIS OF THE STATE

MARX, MARGINALISM AND MODERN SOCIOLOGY

ONE-DIMENSIONAL MARXISM

THE FOUNDATIONS OF STRUCTURALISM

WHAT ABOUT THE WORKERS? Workers and the Transition to Capitalism in Russia

Marx's Theory of Crisis

Simon Clarke
Reader in Sociology
University of Warwick

M
St. Martin's Press

© Simon Clarke 1994

All rights reserved. No reproduction, copy or transmission of
this publication may be made without written permission.

No paragraph of this publication may be reproduced, copied or
transmitted save with written permission or in accordance with
the provisions of the Copyright, Designs and Patents Act 1988,
or under the terms of any licence permitting limited copying
issued by the Copyright Licensing Agency, 90 Tottenham Court
Road, London W1P 9HE.

Any person who does any unauthorised act in relation to this
publication may be liable to criminal prosecution and civil
claims for damages.

First published in Great Britain 1994 by
THE MACMILLAN PRESS LTD
Houndmills, Basingstoke, Hampshire RG21 2XS
and London
Companies and representatives
throughout the world

A catalogue record for this book is available
from the British Library.

ISBN 0-333-54282-7 hardcover
ISBN 0-333-54283-5 paperback

Printed in Great Britain by
Mackays of Chatham PLC
Chatham, Kent

First published in the United States of America 1994 by
Scholarly and Reference Division,
ST. MARTIN'S PRESS, INC.,
175 Fifth Avenue,
New York, N.Y. 10010

ISBN 0-312-12035-4

Library of Congress Cataloging-in-Publication Data
Clarke, Simon.
Marx's theory of crisis / Simon Clarke.
p. cm.
Includes bibliographical references and index.
ISBN 0-312-12035-4
1. Business cycles. 2. Depressions. 3. Marxian economics.
4. Marx, Karl, 1818–1883. I. Title.
HB3714.C57 1993
338. 5' 42—dc20 93-37978
CIP

Contents

1	**Introduction: Marxism and the Theory of Crisis**	**1**
	Political Economy and the Necessity of Crisis	1
	Marxist Theories of Crisis	5
	The Impasse of Contemporary Marxism	7
	Marx and the Marxist Theory of Crisis	9
2	**The Theory of Crisis in the Marxist Tradition**	**14**
	The Theory of Crisis in the Second International	14
	The Marxist Heritage: Engels's Theory of Crisis	17
	Kautsky and the Historical Tendencies of Capitalist Accumulation	21
	Kautsky's Theory of Secular Overproduction	23
	Kautsky's Theory of Crisis	25
	Bernstein's Challenge — Reform or Revolution	29
	Tugan-Baranowsky and the Necessity of Crisis	33
	Hilferding and the Disproportionality Theory of Crisis	39
	Rosa Luxemburg's Underconsumptionist Theory of Crisis	53
	Crises Associated with the Falling Rate of Profit	58
	The Reformulation of Marxist Crisis Theory in the 1970s	63
	Class Struggle and the Rate of Profit	70
	Is There a Marxist Theory of Crisis?	72
3	**Overproduction and Crisis in the Early Works**	**77**
	Engels's Theory of Crisis	77
	Marx's Early Development of Engels's Analysis	81
	The Dynamics of Capitalist Production and the Tendency to Crisis	84
	The Theory of Crisis in the Communist Manifesto	90
	The Early Theory of Overproduction and Crisis	92

4	**Production, Circulation and Global Crisis after 1848**	**95**
	The Politics and Theory of Crisis after the 1848 Revolutions	95
	The Historical Development of Capitalist Crises	97
	Money, Credit and Crisis in the Notebooks of 1851	102
	The Theory of Crisis in 1853	110
	Revolutionary Hopes and the Crisis of 1857	113
5	**Money, Capital and Crisis in the Grundrisse**	**120**
	Production and Circulation	122
	Money, Crisis and Currency Reform	124
	The Money Form and the Possibility of Crisis	127
	The Transition from Money to Capital	129
	The Self-Expansion of Capital and Overproduction	131
	Production and Realisation	134
	Marx's Theory of Crisis: One Theory or Three?	136
	Disproportionate Production and General Overproduction	138
	Competition and Disproportionality	141
	Underconsumption and the Tendency to Crisis	144
	Disproportionality and the Valorisation of Capital	150
	The Tendency for the Rate of Profit to Fall	158
	The Dynamics of Capitalism and the Tendency to Crisis	167
	The Methodology of the Grundrisse and the Theory of Crisis	173
6	**Underconsumption, Disproportionality and Overproduction**	**176**
	Underconsumption Theories: Malthus and Sismondi	180
	Overproduction and Crisis: Say and Ricardo	187
	Capitalist Reproduction, Disproportionality and Crisis	201
7	**The Falling Rate of Profit and the Tendency to Crisis**	**208**
	The Critique of Political Economy and the Falling Rate of Profit	209
	Is There a Tendency for the Rate of Profit to Fall?	213
	The Falling Rate of Profit and Relative Surplus Population	220
	The Concentration of Capital, the Rate of Profit and Crisis	224
	Internal Contradictions of the Law	227
	What is the significance of FROP?	240

8	**Crises and the General Law of Capitalist Accumulation**	**246**
	The Theory of Crisis in Capital	246
	Politics and the Theory of Crisis	247
	The Theory of Crisis in the First Volume of Capital	249
	The General Law of Capitalist Accumulation	251
	The Necessity of Crisis and the Periodicity of the Cycle	260
	Fixed Capital and the Periodicity of the Cycle	261
	Fixed Capital and the Problem of Reproduction	268
	Credit and the Investment Cycle	273
9	**Conclusion**	**279**
	Bibliography	**287**
	Index	**290**

1

Introduction: Marxism and the Theory of Crisis

Political Economy and the Necessity of Crisis

With every boom the apologists for capitalism claim that the tendency to crisis that has plagued the capitalist system since its very beginnings has finally been overcome. When the boom breaks, economists fall over one another to provide particularistic explanations of the crash. The crisis of the early nineteen nineties was the result of the incautious lending of the nineteen eighties. The crisis of the early nineteen eighties was the result of excessive state spending in the late nineteen seventies. The crisis of the mid nineteen seventies was the result of the oil price hike and the inflationary financing of the Vietnam war ... the crisis of the nineteen thirties was the result of inappropriate banking policies .... Every crisis has a different cause, all of which boil down to human failure, none of which are attributed to the capitalist system itself. And yet crises have recurred periodically for the past two hundred years.

Bourgeois economists have to deny that crises are inherent in the social form of capitalist production, because the whole of economic theory is built on the premise that the capitalist system is self-regulating, the principal task of the theoretical economist being to identify the minimal conditions under which such self-regulation will be maintained, so that any breakdown will be identified as the result of exceptional deviations from the norm.[1]

Even the most apologetic of economists cannot fail to notice that recurrent crises occur, but, developing the traditions of classical political economy, the economists explain such crises as contingent phenomena. The normal operation of the forces of supply and demand ensures

---
[1] There are professional as well as ideological reasons for such an assumption. The economists' claim to their role of scientific soothsayers depends on their possession of models with determinate and quantifiable solutions.

that there is always a tendency towards equilibrium. This means that crises can only arise as a result of external shocks, which temporarily disrupt equilibrium, or internal disturbances, which impede or subvert the processes of market equilibration.

Within the framework of general equilibrium theory capital moves between branches of production in response to variations in the rate of profit which arise from imbalances between supply and demand.[2] This movement of capital is the means by which competition maintains proportional relations between the various branches, so that disproportionalities which might disrupt accumulation are evened out by the smooth interaction of supply and demand. Any crisis of disproportionality, such as that of the mid nineteen seventies, is then attributed to market imperfections, in this case the monopoly powers of the oil producers.

Within neo-classical theory the overall balance of supply and demand is maintained by the interaction of the rate of interest and the rate of profit. If there is a shortfall of investment the demand for investment funds will fall, leading to a decline in the rate of interest which will stimulate renewed investment. A stable monetary policy will ensure that equilibrium is maintained. In the classical world of the gold standard a deficit on the balance of international payments provided the prime indication of overheating, the outflow of gold and currency reserves forcing the monetary authorities to tighten monetary policy to rectify the imbalance. Similarly, the onset of recession led to an inflow to the reserves which permitted a more relaxed monetary policy. In the modern world the indicators of inflationary and deflationary pressures are more complex, but the principle remains the same. A crisis of overaccumulation, such as that which struck at the end of the nineteen eighties, is then the result of lax monetary policies which have stimulated inflationary and speculative over-investment.

For all their mathematical sophistication, the explanations of crises offered by today's economists are no different from those that were being put forward at the beginning of the nineteenth century. It was always recognised that a large external shock, such as a war or harvest failure, might precipitate a temporary disruption in the relations between branches of production, or in the international economic relations of the national economy, but the cause of such a crisis lies

---

[2] Even within the framework of general equilibrium theory the conditions of stability of the equilibrating mechanism are very restrictive and unrealistic.

outside the capitalist system, and it was assumed that stability would soon be restored by the normal processes of market adjustment. Apart from such external shocks, the principal cause of crises was traditionally identified as the discretionary intervention of the government in the regulation of the economy. In particular, if the government sought to stimulate the economy artificially by printing money to finance its excessive spending, it would promote over-investment, which would lead to an inflationary boom. Eventually the boom would collapse as unsound and speculative ventures failed, requiring a period of recession to purge the excesses from the system. The cyclical alternation of boom and bust which has marked the history of capitalism is not, therefore, inherent in the capitalist mode of production, but is the result of the folly and irresponsibility of politicians.[3]

Keynes questioned the stability of the classical macroeconomic adjustment mechanism, but otherwise his work remained largely within the classical framework. Keynesian theory was able to explain the cyclical alternation of boom and slump that comprised what was known as the 'trade cycle' or the 'business cycle', but only to explain that this cycle was by no means inherent in the capitalist mode of production, but could be remedied by appropriate government policies. The implication of Keynes's critique was that stabilisation required the more active intervention of the government in pursuing contra-cyclical fiscal and monetary policies in order to maintain a macro-economic balance, but the fundamental purpose of Keynes's critique was to re-assert the harmony of liberal capitalism in the face of the threat of communist and fascist corporatism. For Keynesians, as for the classical economists, the tendency to crisis is not inherent in the capitalist mode of production, but is a result of the inadequacy of institutional arrangements and policy responses. The tendency to crisis can accordingly be overcome by appropriate institutional and policy reforms. After Keynes, as before him, the persistence of crises is testimony not to the deficiencies of capitalism but to the ignorance and irresponsibility of politicians.

After two hundred years of repeating this nonsense one would have expected that the economists would have begun to smell a rat. The economists' explanation of crises is as if a scientist were to deny that the recurrence of the seasons was a natural phenomenon, attributing the return of spring each year to the whim of a supernatural force.

---

[3] Of course in practice stabilisation is by no means as simple as it is in theory, particularly once the economy has established a cyclical pattern of development, which tends to be self-reproducing.

The theoretical problem is not to explain the particular causes of this or that crisis, any more than the task of the scientist is to explain the precise date on which spring arrives in any particular year. The task is to explain the regular recurrence of economic crises as a normal part of the developmental tendencies of the capitalist mode of production. This has been the task that Marxism has taken upon itself, in trying to prove that crises are not merely superficial dislocations of capitalist accumulation, but that the tendency to crisis is inherent in the social form of capitalist production.

The distinctive feature of Marxist theories of crisis is their emphasis on the *necessity* of crisis as an essential and ineradicable feature of the capitalist mode of production, that defines the objective limits of capitalism and the necessity of socialism. Rosa Luxemburg provided the classic statement of the role of Marxist crisis theory in her reply to Bernstein. 'From the standpoint of scientific socialism, the historical necessity of the socialist revolution manifests itself above all in the growing anarchy of capitalism which drives the system into an impasse. But if one admits, with Bernstein, that capitalist development does not move in the direction of its own ruin, then socialism ceases to be *objectively necessary*.' If reforms can 'eliminate or, at least, attenuate the internal contradictions of capitalist economy, ... the elimination of crises means the suppression of the antagonism between production and exchange on the capitalist basis. The amelioration of the situation of the working class ... means the attenuation of the antagonism between capital and labour. ... There remains only one foundation of socialism — the class consciousness of the proletariat ... [which] is now a mere ideal whose force of persuasion rests only on the perfections attributed to it' (Luxemburg, 1899/1908, 58).

It is the Marxist theory of the *necessity* of crisis, of crisis as a necessary expression of the inherently contradictory form of capitalist production, which marks the dividing line between 'reform' and 'revolution', between social democracy, which seeks institutional reforms within a capitalist framework, and socialism, which seeks to create a fundamentally different kind of society. If crises are purely contingent, or if they merely mark the transition from one phase, 'regime' or 'social structure', of accumulation to another (Aglietta, 1979; Bowles, Gordon and Weisskopf, 1984), then socialism has no objective necessity and the socialist movement has no social foundation. If a reformed capitalism can meet the needs of the working class, the class struggle loses its objective foundation and socialism is reduced to an ethical ideal, which has no particular connection with the needs and aspirations of the working class, expressing a particular set of moral values which have no privileged class basis and have no more validity than any other.

The theory of crisis has a central role to play in the ideology of Marxism, and cannot be understood outside that ideological context. However it is hardly sufficient to defend the Marxist theory of crisis on ideological grounds. The Marxist claim to set socialism on 'scientific' foundations rests unequivocally, as Luxemburg so clearly realised, on the scientific status of its theory of crisis. If the theory cannot claim such a status, it becomes merely an ideological prop to a variant form of ethical socialism. Thus, while an *understanding* of the Marxist theory of crisis can never be disengaged from its ideological and political context, it is equally important that it be evaluated on strictly rational *scientific* grounds. This book is concerned exclusively with the scientific evaluation of Marx's theory of crisis, but in full knowledge of the political and ideological significance of the issue.

Marxist Theories of Crisis

The theory of crisis has played a central role in the Marxist tradition, but at the same time it has been one of the weakest and least developed areas of Marxist theorising. The tendency to crisis provided the starting point for the early economic studies of Marx and Engels, and it was with the problem of crisis that Marx resumed his economic studies in 1857, but nowhere in his own work does Marx present a systematic and thoroughly worked-out exposition of a theory of crisis. At various times Marx appears to associate crises with the tendency for the rate of profit to fall, with tendencies to overproduction, underconsumption, disproportionality and over-accumulation with respect to labour, without ever clearly championing one or the other theory.[4] Engels consistently referred both to the contradiction between the tendency for capitalism to develop the forces of production without limit and the limited consumption power of the mass of the population, and to the anarchy of the market, in his explanation of the crisis tendencies of capitalism.

---

[4] It is difficult to see how Dobb could substantiate his bold assertion that 'undoubtedly for Marx the most important application of his theory was in the analysis of the character of economic crises' (Dobb, 1940, 79).

Crisis theory played a limited role in the Marxism of the Second International until the movement was split by the revisionist debates at the end of the nineteenth century. Karl Kautsky, the leading theorist of the Second International, separated the two aspects of Engels's account to provide a theory of the secular tendency to overproduction linked to a theory of crisis based on the anarchy of the market. This theory came under challenge from Bernstein, who denied the inevitability of capitalist breakdown and argued that cartels would overcome the anarchy of the market, and Tugan-Baranovsky, who denied the necessity of underconsumption.

In response to Bernstein's challenge the Marxists of the Second International tried to set the theory of crisis on more rigorous foundations. Although most participants in the debate did little more than reassert established orthodoxies, Rosa Luxemburg and Rudolf Hilferding laid the foundations for the subsequent division of Marxists into the camps of 'underconsumption theorists' and 'disproportionality theorists' of crisis. Initially the two theories were not incompatible, with underconsumption being considered to be a particular, and privileged, form of disproportionality. However, the division between the two grew progressively wider through the 1920s, until by the end of the 1930s Marxist orthodoxy had become unequivocally underconsumptionist, with disproportionality theory being condemned as a social democratic reformist deviation. In the Soviet Union Varga emerged as the high priest of underconsumptionist orthodoxy.

In the West the most sophisticated exposition of orthodox Marxist crisis theory was Paul Sweezy's *Theory of Capitalist Development* (1942), which surveyed the earlier debates, categorised the various theories, and developed a stagnationist theory which drew on Marxist underconsumptionism. This approach was brought to fruition in Paul Baran and Paul Sweezy's *Monopoly Capital* (1966), which synthesized Marx and Kalecki, and linked the 'Keynesian' stabilisation of Western capitalism to imperialism, militarism and waste through which the growing surplus was absorbed or destroyed.

The dominance of Marxist underconsumptionism was eroded during the 1960s as new crisis tendencies emerged which could not be counteracted by Keynesian measures or accounted for by Keynesian or underconsumptionist theories. One feature of these new crisis tendencies was a distinct fall in the rate of profit in the metropolitan centres of capitalist accumulation. Within classical Marxist crisis theories, whether based on 'disproportionality' or 'underconsumption', a crisis arose as a result of a breakdown in the relation between production and consumption, expressed in the accumulation of unsold stocks, and the fall in the rate of profit in the crisis was then a result of this overproduction of commodities. However, in the late 1960s it appeared that the fall in the rate of profit was not a result but a cause of the crisis, and this led Marxists to try to explain the crisis tendencies of capitalism on the basis of this fall in the rate of profit.

During the 1970s Marxist debate raged between those who believed that the fall in the rate of profit that precipitated the crisis was the result of the erosion of profits by rising wages, and those who linked it to Marx's 'law of the tendency for the rate of profit to fall', with the latter explanation eventually emerging as the dominant Marxist orthodoxy.

The Impasse of Contemporary Marxism

The Marxist crisis theory of the 1970s developed in the context of a deepening economic crisis of capitalism, and an associated political crisis of social democracy, which had hitched its waggon to the prosperity of the post-war boom. The immediate theoretical aim, which Marxism shared with bourgeois theorists, was to explain this crisis. The distinctiveness of the Marxist approach was the attempt to establish that this crisis expressed the contradictory foundations of the capitalist mode of production, and that the resolution of the crisis could not be achieved by reform, but only as the outcome of an intense class struggle. The ideological expectation was that the deepening crisis would shatter the reformist illusions of social democracy and precipitate a political and ideological polarisation. While few believed that the forces of socialism would necessarily emerge triumphant from such a polarisation, there was a widespread belief that socialism would move back onto the historical agenda, in both the capitalist and the 'socialist' countries.

The reality proved very different from the optimistic expectations of the 1970s. Certainly the crisis unleashed the expected class struggles, but, far from thrusting the working class into the arms of the socialist movement, the experience of defeat shattered the hopes and aspirations of the organised working class, and fostered demoralisation and division throughout the working class movement. Large sections of the radical intelligentsia lost their socialist faith in the 1980s as rapidly as they had acquired it in the 1970s. In particular they abandoned the Marxist theory of crisis, seeing the crisis of the 1970s not as an expression of the inherent contradictions of the capitalist mode of production, but as a transitional phase from the 'Fordism' of the post-war boom to the 'post-Fordism' of the age of information. This abandonment of the theory of crisis was closely linked to the dissociation of the 'political' struggle for socialism from the 'economic' development of capitalism, and equally from the struggles of the organised working class, which were relegated to the 'Fordist' pre-history of the new era (Clarke, 1988).

The set-backs suffered by the socialist left cannot be explained in terms of the betrayal of the left intelligentsia, nor in terms of the deficiencies of its theoretical analysis. They have to be explained by the defeats suffered by the organised working class, which may have been ideologically ill-equipped for a socialist offensive, but more importantly was organisationally and politically far less well-prepared for the intensification of the class struggle than were capital and the state. Not only did the working class not advance towards socialism, but even its reformist attempt to realise its most modest material and social aspirations met with often brutal defeat. Nevertheless the fact that such defeats have led, by and large, not to the advance of the socialist left, but to its increasing isolation from the organised working class, indicates the gulf that existed between socialist theory and the everyday reality of the class struggle. While Marxist theory had correctly anticipated the capitalist crisis, it provided little guidance for the struggles that the crisis unleashed.

The fact that socialism has suffered such a comprehensive political defeat does not mean that the socialist critique of capitalism has lost its validity. The alternation of boom and slump, the coexistence of overwork and unemployment, of staggering wealth alongside devastating poverty, of concentrations of power alongside hopeless impotence is as much a feature of capitalism today as it was a century and more ago. The sense of a world beyond human control, of a world driven to destruction by alien forces, is stronger today than it has ever been. The gulf between the bland reassurances of the bourgeois economist and the reality of life for the mass of the world's population has never been wider. The failure of Marxism has not been the inappropriateness of its scientific project, but the inadequacy of its ideological and political realisation, its inability to connect its theoretical diagnosis of the capitalist condition with the everyday hopes and aspirations of ordinary people. If we are to learn from this failure we have to re-examine not only the forms of working class and socialist politics, but also the theoretical foundations of our analysis of capitalism. In this book I hope to make a small contribution to this project, by focusing on what has long been the weakest part of Marxist theorising, the theory of crisis.[5]

Marx and the Marxist Theory of Crisis

It is a remarkable feature of the history of Marxist crisis theory that orthodoxy should shift so fundamentally, and yet so unselfconsciously. At the turn of the century the orthodoxy was a rather vague disproportionality theory, with crises being attributed to the anarchy of the market. By the 1930s Marxist orthodoxy had become rigidly underconsumptionist. During the 1970s the theory of the falling rate of profit had become the canonical theory of crisis. At each stage it was generally assumed that the dominant theory was the authentic theory of Marx, a claim backed up by selective quotation from Marx's works, and that the alternative theories were heinous deviations. Yet, despite the centrality of the theory of crisis to Marxism, there has been no serious study of the development of the theory of crisis in Marx's own works. It is generally assumed that Marx never developed a systematic theory of crisis, an assumption that has left his successors free to construct their various interpretations of Marx's crisis theory from scattered, and not entirely consistent, fragments.

The main purpose of this book is not to provide a survey of Marxist theories of crisis, since the secondary literature in this field is already reasonably comprehensive, while the theories themselves are unfortunately not very sophisticated.[6] The main purpose of the book is to develop an understanding of the role of the theory of crisis in Marx's

---

[5] The project of writing this book came out of my work on overaccumulation, class struggle and the state, which resulted in my book *Keynesianism, Monetarism and the Crisis of the State*. The latter was based on a theory of crisis which I took to be that of Marx, but which I could not find developed systematically either in Marx or in the Marxist tradition. This led me back to the exploration of the theory of crisis in Marxism (Clarke, 1990), and then to the role of the theory of crisis in Marx's own work.

[6] The best introductory account is still that of Sweezy (1942). The most comprehensive recent textbook account is contained in Howard and King (1989, 1992). Kühne (1979) explores various by-ways of the debate. Day (1981) provides an excellent account of the Soviet tradition from Lenin to Vargas. While Soviet theorising had little to do with Marx, Day's account makes it clear that in the 1920s much the most advanced theorising of the dynamics of capitalism was to be found in Moscow.

own work, by situating his writings on crisis in the context in which they originally arose. This task is made much easier today by the publication of Marx's notebooks from the 1850s, and of the manuscripts written over the period between 1857 and 1863, making it possible for the first time to follow the development of Marx's economic thought from his first encounter with political economy in 1844 right through to the publication of *Capital*, and so to set his discussion of the theory of crisis in its full context.

The reason for this return to Marx's own works is not simply an antiquarian interest in chronicling what Marx actually said about crises, nor is it a belief that a close reading of Marx's writings on crisis will provide the key to understanding that has eluded subsequent Marxists. In themselves Marx's writings on crisis are indeed fragmentary and confused. In isolation from his work as a whole they are not of any great interest, and they certainly do not provide a consistent and rigorous theory of crisis (although their originality and insight in relation to the state of economics in Marx's day, and in ours, should not be underestimated). However, looking at Marx's work as a whole through the prism of his writings on the problem of crisis does provide a new perspective on Marx's work, which brings to the fore its distinctiveness in relation to bourgeois theories of political economy, and which provides a foundation on which contemporary Marxism can build an understanding of the contradictory dynamics of capitalism in the modern world.

Looking at Marx's work in this way brings out not only its distinctiveness in relation to the apologetics of bourgeois economics, but also in relation to what has come to be known as 'Marxist political economy' (something of a contradiction in terms, since Marx always referred to his work as a 'critique of political economy'). The impasse of Marxist crisis theory has arisen primarily because it has tried to establish itself on bourgeois theoretical foundations, and in particular the theoretical foundations of general equilibrium theory, neglecting the critical dimension of Marx's theory. This erosion of the critical foundations of Marxist crisis theory is not only a feature of contemporary academic Marxism, but can be observed even in the earliest stages of the development of Marxism in the Second International, laying the Marxist theory wide open to the revisionist critiques of Bernstein and Tugan-Baranovski.

In the first chapter of the book I will outline the principal contributions to the classical Marxist theory of crisis, those of Engels, Kautsky,

Hilferding and Luxemburg, before briefly summarising the positions adopted in the debates of the 1970s that defined the new orthodoxy of Marxist political economy. This survey will then provide a reference point for the remainder of the book, in which I will turn from Marxism to Marx, and explore in some depth the role of the theory of crisis in Marx's critique of political economy.

The presentation of Marx's theory of crisis raises difficult problems. The first problem is that Marx does not offer us a theory of crisis as such. The theoretical discussion of crisis in the works published in Marx's lifetime consists of no more than brief epigrammatic comments. Virtually all the extensive theoretical discussion is contained in Marx's voluminous notebooks, but even there it is never brought together as a discussion of crisis as such, but is embedded in discussion of other issues. This makes it impossible simply to extract and present 'Marx's theory of crisis'. This is hardly surprising, since for Marx the tendency to crisis was the culmination, and in one sense the most superficial expression, of the historical tendencies of the capitalist mode of production. Marx's theory of crisis therefore has to be presented as a part of his wider characterisation of the dynamics of the capitalist mode of production.

The second problem is that of the significance to attach to different elements of Marx's theory. Marx's method of working was to follow through various trains of thought to see where they would lead him, then to go back over his notebooks to try to bring some order to his ideas, before starting again from the beginning trying to fit everything into place. The basic framework of his analysis of capitalism was laid down in the 1840s, and presented in *The Communist Manifesto*. He then spent the first half of the 1850s reading intensively, before working out his own ideas in more detail in the most creative period of his life, from 1857 to 1863. The following four years were spent re-working the material of those notebooks, culminating in the first volume of *Capital*, which is the only systematic text that Marx completed. Marx returned to his theoretical work briefly in two spells in the 1870s, during which he wrote most of the material incorporated by Engels into the second volume of *Capital*. Volume Three of *Capital* was put together by Engels from Marx's notebooks of 1864–5, which were a re-working of the manuscripts of 1861–3. However, unlike the first volume of *Capital*, this re-working was confined largely to the rearrangement of existing material, without any systematic conceptualisation of the analysis as a whole. We are therefore left with a large number of fragments in which Marx works through his ideas in different ways, sometimes reaching conclusions, sometimes abandoning a train of thought, and sometimes losing his way (usually in a thicket of arithmetical examples), without providing any indication of the systematic significance of his observations. Any attempt to present Marx's theory of crisis therefore necessarily includes a substantial element of interpretation and reconstruction.

The third problem in the presentation of Marx's theory is that virtually all his discussion of crisis is deeply embedded in his critical commentaries on political economy. This means that the form of Marx's exposition of the theory of crisis is dominated by its role in his critique of political economy, which is not necessarily a guide to its role in his own diagnosis of capitalism. It is therefore necessary to present Marx's theory of crisis not only in the context of an interpretation of Marx's wider analysis of the dynamics of capitalism, but also in the context of his critique of political economy. Moreover, although much of the detail of Marx's critique of classical political economy is only of antiquarian interest, the most fundamental issues remain alive today, since modern economics retains the conceptual foundations of its classical ancestry. Thus we have to consider Marx's theory of crisis and of the dynamics of the capitalist mode of production not only in the context of classical political economy, but also of contemporary economics.

These problems mean that any discussion of Marx's theory of crisis is bound to involve a compromise between exposition, interpretation and contextualisation. In the course of writing this book I have been conscious of the need to try to maintain some balance between these three elements. For the first draft of the manuscript I read through all the relevant works of Marx and Engels to present their discussion of crisis strictly chronologically and contextually, while trying to keep the interpretation to a minimum. I then divided the material into five parts, corresponding to the periodisation of Marx's work into the early works (up to 1848); the period of re-evaluation after the revolutions of 1848; the foundations of the critique of political economy in the manuscript of 1857–8; the development of the critique of political economy in the manuscripts of 1861–5 (which comprises two chapters in the final version of the book); and the mature works from the first edition of the first volume of *Capital*. I then re-organised the material in each part thematically, within the framework of an interpretation which I nevertheless tried to root as closely as possible in Marx's texts, and which I modified in the light of a re-reading of most of the significant texts. Finally, I reworked the whole text, in an attempt to clarify the exposition and set it in the context of an interpretation of Marx's work as a whole. One thing that I have not done is to relate Marx's work explicitly to issues and debates in contemporary economics, although I hope that the connections will be obvious to those familiar with such debates. The significance of Marx's work is not the contribution it can make to bourgeois economics (although virtually all the significant advances in economists' understanding of the dynamics of capitalism have been derived from, or anticipated by, Marx and Marxism), but the contribution it can make to its dissolution.

I have tried to make the final text as clear as possible, but have also tried to avoid over-simplification. The issues are complex, and some of Marx's discussion is confused. While I have tried to steer around the confusion, I have not tried to avoid the complexity. If parts of the book still make difficult reading I can only apologise, and invite the reader to return to Marx's original text rather than simply abandon the attempt at understanding.

My aim in writing this book is not to present a closed interpretation of Marx's theory of crisis, but to provide one building block for the development of a more adequate analysis of the dynamics of capitalism by laying before the reader the insights and originality of Marx's work which, although written more than a century ago, still has a devastating theoretical significance. The political economy that Marx annihilated with his critique did not lie down and die, nor was it depassed by the birth of neo-classical economics. Marx's critique of political economy is as relevant to the critique of contemporary economics as it was to the critique of Ricardo (Clarke, 1991). My hope is that this book offers both a clear and consistent interpretation of Marx's theory of crisis, and a sufficiently open presentation of Marx's own writings to allow the reader to use Marx's work as the basis of alternative interpretations, or as the basis on which to build in other directions.

In this book I only indicate the wider significance of Marx's work in the hope that others will build on this exposition as part of a collective project to create a radical theoretical critique of capitalism and its ideological mis-representations, which can engage with the everyday experience of resistance to capitalist exploitation and despoliation, and so develop as a part of an ideological critique and a liberatory political force. Whether or not Marx's name is attached to such a movement is neither here nor there. What matters is that we should take full advantage of the insights that Marx's work has to offer.

2
The Theory of Crisis in the Marxist Tradition

The Theory of Crisis in the Second International

The failure of Marxism in the 1980s was essentially the failure of the Leninist tradition which had dominated Marxism since the 1930s. The supremacy of Leninism owed something to the fact that Stalin and Hitler between them physically exterminated the leading exponents of alternative traditions, but was primarily determined by the political defeats suffered by the Social Democracy of the Second International, above all in Germany. The triumph of Leninism led to the dismissal of the Social Democratic tradition of Marxism, yet this was a tradition which, for all its failures and defeats, had been forged in the experience of the crisis-ridden and struggle-torn development of the capitalist mode of production, by intellectuals who were neither academics nor state functionaries but were the builders of a mass socialist movement.

The conventional Leninist view was to write off the orthodox Marxism of the Second International as being marked by a vulgar economistic conception of politics and a crude underconsumptionist theory of crisis, according to which economic collapse would precipitate the inevitable revolution. For Kautsky the inevitability of a terminal crisis legitimated a political passivism, for Luxemburg it legitimated a revolutionary spontaneism, neither of which was able to pose an effective challenge to revisionism, and which degenerated into reformism, on the one hand, and ultra-leftism, on the other.

While there is an element of truth in this caricature, it is a caricature. The theoretical analysis and political strategy of the Second International was not inappropriate for its time, and was certainly not unsophisticated. The failure of the strategy was not inevitable, and could not have been foreseen. Although the Marxism of the Second International had a fundamental theoretical weakness at its core, this weakness was as much an expression of the political barriers that it confronted as of any lack of theoretical insight.

The theoretical weakness of the Marxism of the Second International lay primarily in the growing divergence between its analysis of the historical tendencies of capitalist accumulation and its political programme for the transition to socialism. Its analysis of the former tendencies was remarkably prescient, and certainly far more incisive than anything that could be offered by the bourgeois economists of the day. However its belief that these historical tendencies would inevitably lead the working class movement to encompass the vast majority of the population, and to embrace the politics and ideology of social democracy, prevented the leaders of the social democratic movement from facing up to the problem of the relationship between theory and practice, between reformist practice and revolutionary ambition, between immediate tasks and ultimate goals. The result was an increasing divergence between a socialist rhetoric and a reformist practice which ultimately underlay the split in the movement with the outbreak of war in 1914. However, the very fact of the disintegration of the movement once its practice moved into flagrant contradiction with its ideology made it clear that the theoretical weakness was only an expression of the political ambiguity of the social democratic movement.

Social democracy before the First World War owed its strength above all to the theoretical and ideological pragmatism that enabled the leadership to maintain the unity of the movement. The belief in the inevitability of socialism as the necessary culmination of the historical tendencies of capitalist accumulation derived directly from Marx and Engels, whose account in this respect was faithfully developed by the leading theorist of the Second International, Karl Kautsky, and which seemed to be fully vindicated by the rapid advance of German Social Democracy in the last quarter of the nineteenth century. The theoretical weakness of the analysis only came to the fore when it had to confront the political consequences of new developments in the world capitalist system which emerged in the 1890s, but these developments were themselves in part a response to the challenge presented to capitalism by the forms of class struggle on which the theory and politics of the Second International had been built. The theoretical weakness of the movement was not so much a matter of the failure of the intellect, as the expression of the political limitations of the movement.

The political limitations of the Social Democracy of the Second

International had a direct expression in the role of the theory of crisis in the analysis of capitalism. The inevitability of socialism was linked to the secular tendencies of capitalist accumulation, which underlie the polarisation of classes and the development of the class struggle. The account of these secular tendencies derived from the only works of Marx which were generally available at that time, the *Communist Manifesto* and Volume One of *Capital*.[1]

In both of these works Marx linked the theory of crisis closely to the theory of the secular development of the capitalist mode of production, the role of crises being to accelerate the development of the secular tendencies and to bring the inherent contradictions of capitalism to a head. For Marx crises were not exceptional periods in which a normal, uncontradictory, pattern of accumulation breaks down, but the most dramatic expression of the inherently contradictory foundations of accumulation, crises being 'always but momentary and forcible solutions of the existing contradictions. They are violent eruptions which for a time restore the disturbed equilibrium' (CIII, 244).

Although Marx did not rigorously conceptualise the continuity between the secular tendencies of capitalist accumulation and the crisis which brought those tendencies to a head, such a continuity is politically crucial in linking the tactics of the everyday struggle, which is linked to the cyclical fluctuations in the level of capitalist economic activity, to the strategy of the development of a mass socialist movement, which is linked to the secular tendencies of capitalist development. The political weakness of the Marxism of the Second International was reflected in the increasing gap which opened up between these two aspects of its politics and its theory. Politically the gap was marked by the growing discontinuity between a revolutionary strategy and a reformist tactics. Theoretically it was marked by a growing dissociation between the theory of the secular tendencies of accumulation and the theory of cyclical crises.

---

[1] The *Communist Manifesto* was re-published in 1872, and a revised edition of Volume One of *Capital* in 1873. Kautsky's *The Economic Doctrines of Karl Marx*, first published in 1887, provided a relatively faithful popular exposition of Volume One of *Capital*. Of Marx's other theoretical works only *The Poverty of Philosophy*, *The Holy Family* and *The Critique of Political Economy* were published in Marx's lifetime, and they were only re-issued in the 1890s. Volume Two of *Capital* was published in 1885 and Volume Three in 1894.

The Marxist Heritage: Engels's Theory of Crisis

The orthodox Marxist account of the crisis tendencies of capitalist accumulation derived primarily not from Marx, but from Engels, whose *Anti-Dühring* was the textbook of Marxist orthodoxy, through which the majority of the leaders of the Second International had been converted to Marxism.[2] Engels firmly rejected the underconsumptionism of Lassalle and Dühring in favour of an overproduction theory of crisis.

Although formally the distinction between 'under-consumption' and 'overproduction' may appear to be a fine one, there was a fundamental difference between the kind of underconsumptionism espoused by the Lassalleans and the Russian populists, which essentially argued for the impossibility of sustained accumulation on the grounds of the 'iron law of wages', and that of Engels, who offered a dynamic theory, based not on the absolute poverty of the masses, but on the contradictory form of capitalist production, which led accumulation constantly to run ahead of the growth in demand. Engels noted that under-consumption is a 'thousand-year-old phenomenon', whereas crises only arise in the capitalist form of production. Thus under-consumption is 'a pre-requisite condition of crises, and plays in them a role which has long been recognised. But it tells us just as little why crises exist today as why they did not exist before' (AD, 394).

For Engels the tendency to overproduction was not absolute, but was closely linked to the 'anarchy of production', supply and demand only being equalised 'by means of a storm on the world market, by a commercial crisis' (CW26, 'Marx and Rodbertus, 23.10.84). However, for Engels the 'anarchy of production' was not simply a matter of the capitalist misjudgement of the market, as it came to be for Kautsky. The anarchy of production derives from the fact that production and consumption are determined by quite different laws, so that the divergence between the two is systematic. This leads us immediately to a fundamental difference in the conceptualisation of

---

[2] Dühring had been the dominant theorist of the German workers' movement in the 1870s. His work reproduced Lassalle's stress on the primacy of politics, but gave a much greater importance to the organised working class than did Lassalle, calling for political trade unions. Although Dühring reserved some of his most splenetic outbursts for Marx and Engels, even the Marxists acclaimed his philosophical system. Only Liebknecht stood out against the trend, and it was Liebknecht who appealed to Marx and Engels to reply to Dühring, and to provide a popular exposition of their own ideas. Bernstein and Plekhanov were both followers of Dühring and, like Kautsky, were converted to Marxism by Engels's critique.

the process of competition between Marxism and political economy.

According to political economy capitalist competition ensures that production is adapted to the consumers' need for the product as supply is adjusted to demand in response to fluctuations in market prices. For Marx and Engels, however, the dynamics of competition are quite different. The capitalist does not respond to competitive pressure by passively cutting prices or curtailing production, and accepting a lower rate of profit, but by driving his workers to greater efforts, or by installing new methods of production, in order to cut costs. Meanwhile, the capitalist with a competitive advantage does not sit back and enjoy his share of the market, but expands production in order to capture the market of others. Far from passively adapting production to the limits of the market, the tendency is for competition to compel the capitalist to develop the forces of production without regard to the limits of the market. The 'anarchy' of production is therefore the source of a systematic overproduction.

In *Anti-Dühring* (1878) Engels argued that the 'anarchy' of capitalist production 'forces the individual industrial capitalist always to improve his machinery, always to increase its productive force. The bare possibility of extending the field of production is transformed for him into a similar compulsory law. The enormous expansive force of modern industry ... appears to us now as a *necessity* for expansion, both qualitative and quantitative, that laughs at all resistance. Such resistance is offered by consumption, by sales, by the markets for the products of modern industry. But the capacity for extension, extensive and intensive, of the markets is primarily governed by quite different laws that work more or less energetically. The extension of the markets cannot keep pace with the extension of production. The collision becomes inevitable'. According to Engels, this tendency to overproduction is a cyclical rather than a secular tendency, the basis of the periodic crises which have recurred since about 1825.[3] These crises are the inevitable result of the 'contradiction between socialised production and capitalist appropriation ... *The mode of production is in rebellion against the mode of exchange*' (CW24 316).

Engels had always seen a direct and immediate connection between the crisis tendencies of accumulation and the coming revolution. In his 'Condition of the Working Class in England' (1844–5) Engels had re-

---

[3] The secular tendency is defined by the concentration and centralisation of capital, the pauperisation of a growing mass of the population, and the polarisation of classes, discussed by Marx in *The Communist Manifesto* and Volume One of *Capital*.

ferred to commercial crises as 'the mightiest levers for all independent development of the proletariat' (CW4, 580). This was a view which Engels and Marx reiterated through the 1850s, as they expected the next crisis to herald the revolution which had been aborted in 1848, and to which Engels returned in the 1880s.

Engels' theory of crisis was a straightforward overproduction theory, according to which the expansion of production necessarily ran ahead of the growth of the market so that eventually the result must be a crisis, which is likely to be all the more devastating the longer it is postponed. Although at times he argued that the outcome might be a state of chronic stagnation, he nevertheless saw stagnation as paving the way for the apocalyptic crisis.

Engels had anticipated the cyclical form of accumulation giving way to stagnation as early as 1850, when he argued (on the eve of the mid-Victorian boom) that 'the English industrialists, whose means of production have a power of expansion incomparably superior to that of their outlets, are rapidly approaching the point where their expedients will be exhausted and where the period of prosperity which now still divides every crisis from its successor will disappear completely under the weight of the excessively increased forces of production ... The proletarian revolution will then be inevitable, and its victory certain' ('The English Ten Hours Bill', CW10, 299).

It was thirty years before Engels returned to the theme, in the middle of the 'Great Depression' in July 1881, noting that now that capitalism had developed machines which could make machines it had become possible to expand production all the faster, so leading to chronic overproduction. Every captain of industry 'increases his plant irrespective of what his neighbours do' so 'recklessly expanding the productive power of the country beyond the power of absorption of the markets.' The increase 'has been out of all proportion to what it was in former periods of expansion, and the consequence is — chronic overproduction, chronic depression of trade' lasting several years (CW24, 412).

Three years later, just after Marx's death in 1884, Engels noted that since 1876 there had been 'a chronic state of stagnation in all dominant branches of production. Neither will the full crash come; nor will the period of longed for prosperity to which we used to be entitled before and after it. A dull depression, a chronic glut of all markets for all trades, that is what we have been living in for nearly ten years.' This is because capitalism is running out of markets, and competition is increasing, while 'capitalist production *cannot* stop, it must go on increasing or it must die ... Here is the vulnerable place, the heel of Achilles, for capitalist production'. As the depression inevitably gets worse the English workers will lose even their limited privileges, and socialism in England will be reborn (CW26, 300).

However, Engels stressed the following year that despite the stagnation, a general crisis would still inevitably come. 'By thus delaying the thunderstorm which formerly cleared the atmosphere every ten years, this continued chronic depression must prepare a crash of a violence and extent such as we have never known before.' (Engels to Danielson 13.11.85, c.f. Engels to Bebel, 28.10.85, Marx-Engels, *Selected Correspondence*, 389, 86–7). Engels's rather confused wishful-thinking is well summed up in an article that he wrote in 1892, when he asserted simultaneously the impossibility and the inevitability of a giant crisis. He noted that the absence of a crisis since 1868 was 'also due to the expansion of the world market, which distributes the surplus English, respectively European, capital in transport investment, etc., *throughout the world* and also among a whole mass of other *branches* of investment. This has made a crisis impossible ... but small crises, such as the Argentinian, have become possible for the past three years. But all this proves that a *giant crisis* is in the making' (CW27, 324–5).

In 1894 Engels was still awaiting the big crash. In one of his footnotes to Volume Three of *Capital* he noted that 'the acute form of the periodic process, with its former ten-year cycle, appears to have given way to a more chronic, long drawn out, alternation between a relatively short and slight business improvement and a relatively long indecisive depression – taking place in the various industries at different times. But perhaps it is only a matter of a prolongation of the duration of the cycle ... is it possible that we are now in the preparatory stage of a new world crash of unparalleled vehemence? Many things seem to point in this direction.' The world market has opened up and capital is more widely spread 'so that it is far more widely distributed and local speculation may be more easily overcome. By means of this, most of the old breeding-grounds of crises and opportunities for their development have been eliminated or strongly reduced. At the same time, ... protective tariffs are nothing but preparations for the ultimate general industrial war, which shall decide who has supremacy on the world-market. Thus every factor, which works against a repetition of the old crises, carries within itself the germ of a far more powerful future crisis.' (CIII, 477-8 n.).

Kautsky and the Historical Tendencies of Capitalist Accumulation

The classic statement of the theory of the Second International was the 1891 Erfurt Programme, written jointly by Eduard Bernstein and Karl Kautsky. Kautsky published his commentary on the programme, *The Class Struggle* (hereafter CC), in 1892, and this became the basic text of Marxist orthodoxy. *The Class Struggle* provided a popular application of Marx's account of the historical tendencies of capitalist development in *The Communist Manifesto* and Volume One of *Capital*, and applied it to the development of the class struggle in contemporary Germany.

The focus of Kautsky's analysis was the secular tendencies of capitalist development as the basis for the formation of the proletariat, the development of the class struggle, and the inexorable growth of the revolutionary movement. In the course of capitalist development independent small producers are destroyed, intermediate strata are proletarianised, and small capitalists are swept aside, leading to the progressive polarisation of capitalist society into a dwindling class of capitalists and the growing mass of the proletariat.

These tendencies are intensified by the mechanisation of capitalist production. The application of machinery does not lighten the burden of labour. On the contrary, the introduction of machinery compels the capitalist to increase the intensity and duration of labour, as the capitalist has to recover his capital and realise his profit before new machines render his own obsolete. The application of machinery increases the insecurity of capitalist production as 'new inventions and discoveries are incessantly made which render valueless existing machinery and make superfluous, not only individual workers, not only individual machines, but often whole establishments or even whole branches of industry' (CC, 70). Moreover, the application of machinery progressively increases the scale of capitalist production, narrowing the ranks of the capitalist class and widening the gulf between it and the proletariat. In sum, the capitalist monopolisation of the means of production 'means increasing uncertainty of subsistence; it means misery, oppression, servitude, degradation and exploitation. Forever greater grows the number of proletarians, the more gigantic the army of superfluous labourers, and sharper the opposition between exploiters and exploited' (CC, 8).

Industrial crises 'which are periodically brought on, with the certainty of natural law' reinforce these secular tendencies and increase the uncertainty facing both capitalists and workers (CC, 71). 'The abyss between propertied and propertyless is further widened by industrial crises. These have their causes in the capitalist system and, as the system develops, naturally occur on an increasing scale. They make universal uncertainty the normal condition of society and so prove that our power of production has got beyond our control, that private ownership of the means of production has become irreconcilable with their effective use and development' (CC, 8).

However crises do not play a significant role in Kautsky's account of the development of the socialist revolution. The crisis merely intensifies the secular tendencies of capitalist development, and brings to the fore the limitations of the capitalist system. 'It is at such seasons that the fact becomes most glaring that the modern productive powers are becoming more and more irreconcilable with the system of production for sale' (CC, 80). Although crises have a conjunctural importance as periods in which the class struggle intensifies and becomes generalised, and periods of stagnation might be periods in which the evils of capitalism are more apparent, the political development of the working class is a long-drawn-out process, building up to the revolution which will not occur until the great mass of the population has been won over to the socialist cause. While crises might accelerate the process, they are neither a necessary nor a sufficient condition for revolution.

The inevitability of the revolution derives from the secular tendency of the capitalist mode of production to create the social force which will overthrow it. 'We consider the breakdown of the present social system to be unavoidable, because we know that the economic evolution inevitably brings on conditions that will compel the exploited classes to rise against this system of private ownership. We know that this system multiplies the number and strength of the exploited, and diminishes the number and strength of the exploiting, classes, and that it will finally lead to such unbearable conditions for the mass of the population that they will have no choice but to go down into degradation or to overthrow the system of private property.' (CC, 90)

This does not mean that socialism is a desperate reaction on the part of a pauperised and degraded proletariat. Kautsky stressed that 'the recruiting ground of socialism is the class of the propertyless, but not all ranks of this class are equally favourable' (CC, 165). The demoralising and corrupting influence of pauperism, the exclusion of the pauper from any functional role in society or any direct experience of exploitation, and the dependence of the pauper layers on the charity of the rich, underlie the paupers' humility and servility and deprives them of any motive for wishing to put an end to the existing system.

'The victory will not be born out of degradation, as many have believed' (CC, 215), but out of the moral elevation of the proletariat above its degraded state, which is achieved through the development of the labour movement. 'The elevation of the working-class is a necessary and inevitable process. But it is neither peaceful nor regular. ...But fortunately for human development there comes a time in the history of every section of the proletariat when the elevating tendencies gain the upper hand.' (CC, 173)

Kautsky's Theory of Secular Overproduction

The focus of Kautsky's account of the secular tendencies of capitalist development is the polarisation of classes which Marx and Engels had emphasised in the *Communist Manifesto*, and in this respect he faithfully follows Marx and Engels. However, Kautsky also believed that there were objective limits to the continued existence of the capitalist mode of production inherent in the secular tendencies of the capitalist mode of production. In this shift in emphasis from cyclical crisis to secular tendency Kautsky was departing from both Marx and Engels.

Kautsky considered the possibility that the limits to the capitalist system might be set by the secular tendency for the rate of profit to fall.[4] He notes that, even after considering the counteracting factors, the rate of profit can be expected to fall, although 'this, of course, holds good only on the average and during long periods of time' (CC, 60), citing the steady fall in the rate of interest as evidence for the falling tendency of the rate of profit. He notes that this tendency for the rate of profit to fall, while the rate of exploitation rises, 'is one of the more remarkable contradictions of the capitalist system of production — a system that bristles with contradictions' (CC, 61), and notes that it is made more serious by the growing burden of rent and taxation, which ultimately falls on the capitalist class. But he then clearly rejects the idea that this has any significance for the fate of the capitalist system. 'Some there are who have concluded from this sinking of profits that the capitalist system of exploitation will put

---

[4] Kautsky clearly saw this as a *secular* tendency, and did not connect it in any way with the tendency to crisis.

an end to itself, that capital will eventually yield so little profit that starvation will force the capitalist to look for work. The conclusion would be correct, if, as the rate of profit sank, the quantity of invested capital remained the same. This, however, is by no means the case. The total quantity of capital in all capitalist nations grows at a more rapid pace than the rate of profit declines. The increase of capital is a prerequisite to the sinking of profit ... The decline of the rate of profit ... in no way implies a reduction of the income of the capitalist class, for the mass of surplus that flows into its hands grows constantly larger.' (CC, 61) What the fall in the rate of profit does mean is that it requires a larger capital to free the capitalist from the need to labour, so that 'the decline of profit and interest does not bring on the downfall, but the narrowing of the capitalist class' (CC, 62).

For Kautsky the limits to the capitalist system lie in the tendency to overproduction, which is attributed to the fundamental contradiction between the tendency to develop the productive forces without limit, on the one hand, and the tendency to restrict the consumption power of the mass of the population, by forcing down the value of labour power and by creating a relative surplus population, on the other. However, for Kautsky this tendency to chronic overproduction is not a cyclical tendency, as it was for Engels, but a secular tendency. It leads not to violent eruptions, but to ultimate destruction.

'Along with the periodical crises and their permanent manifestations, along with the recurring periods of overproduction and their accompaniments of loss of wealth and waste of force, there develops chronic overproduction and waste of energy.' (CC, 81–2) In addition to the periodical pressure of overproduction, 'there is a permanent pressure in this direction inherent in the capitalist system of production itself. This pressure, instead of being brought on by the extension of the market, compels the latter to be pushed constantly further' (CC, 82–3). This is the pressure of competition, which compels capitalists to develop the forces of production without any regard to the development of the market, and so compels them to find outlets for their growing product. 'But there is a limit to the extension of the markets ... Today there are hardly any other markets to be opened' (CC, 83). The capitalist expansion of the market is self-defeating, for the penetration of new territories by capitalist production destroys indigenous production, and so lowers the purchasing power of the population.[5]

---

[5] Kautsky had already stressed the capitalist need for colonies as an outlet for the surplus

Moreover, it also lays the foundation for the extension of the capitalist mode of production, with its chronic tendency to overproduction, to new parts of the world. 'Thus capitalist large production digs its own grave. From a certain point onward in its development every new extension of the market means the rising of a new competitor ... the moment is drawing near when the markets of the industrial countries can no longer be extended and will begin to contract. But this would mean the bankruptcy of the whole capitalist system. For some time past the extension of the market has not kept pace with the requirements of capitalist production. The latter is consequently more and more hampered and finds it increasingly difficult to develop fully the productive power that it possesses. The intervals of prosperity become ever shorter; the length of the crises ever longer' (CC, 84–5).

'The capitalist system begins to suffocate in its own surplus; it becomes constantly less able to endure the full unfolding of the productive powers which it has created. Constantly more creative forces must be idle, ever greater quantities of products be wasted, if it is not to go to pieces altogether.' (CC, 85–6) Private property in the means of production has changed, 'from a motive power of progress it has become a cause of social degradation and bankruptcy' (CC, 87).[6]

Kautsky's Theory of Crisis

The theory of overproduction was adopted by Kautsky as a theory of the secular tendency of capitalist development, and although it was not well developed, its implicit foundation was clearly underconsumptionist. However Kautsky makes no reference at all to underconsumption in his discussion of industrial crises in *The Class Struggle*. He notes that 'the great modern crises which convulse the world's markets arise from overproduction', but relates this not to underconsumption, but to the 'anarchy of the market'. Moreover, the anarchy of the market is not related to the laws of capitalist production, as was the 'anarchy of

---

product in 1884, stressing the need for capitalists to find 'a market outside the sphere of their own production' so that 'as a sales market the colonies have become a condition of existence for capitalism' ('Tongking', *Die Neue Zeit*, 2, 1884, 157 quoted Howard and King, 1989, 92).

[6] Ironically, it was only in 1927, on the eve of the Great Depression, that Kautsky repudiated his theory of chronic depression, arguing that 'the expectation that crises would someday become so extensive and long-drawn-out as to render the continuation of capitalist production impossible and its replacement by a socialist order unavoidable finds no support today' (*Materialist Conception of History*, quoted Sweezy, 1946, 208).

production' for Engels, but simply to 'the planlessness that inevitably characterises our system of commodity production' (CC, 71–2), so that cyclical overproduction has become, as it was for political economy, a normal part of the trade cycle, as prosperity encourages overproduction, leading to crisis and depression.

In *The Economic Doctrines of Karl Marx* (EDKM), first published in 1887, Kautsky had treated crises very briefly as an aspect of the business cycle, which he saw as being driven by the successive conquest and saturation of new markets. This 'Keynesian' formulation is quite different from the account of secular overproduction, in that the cyclical expansion of production is not an expression of an inherent law of capitalist production, but is stimulated by the growth of the market. Kautsky noted that the only limits to capital accumulation are to be found in 'the supplies of raw materials and markets for its products', and continued, 'hence the continual and feverish incentive to open up new markets to furnish fresh raw materials and fresh buyers for the manufactures. Every important extension of the market is followed by a period of feverish production, until the market is surfeited, whereupon a period of stagnation ensues'. (EDKM, 170). Similarly in *The Class Struggle* the trade cycle, with its associated commercial crises, is derived from 'the periodical incentives to increase of production brought on by the periodical extensions of the market' (CC, 82).

The origins of the tendency to crisis for Kautsky lie in the producers' ignorance of the demand for their products, since 'it is left to each producer to estimate for himself the demand there may be for the goods which he produces'. An imbalance of supply and demand in one branch of production then precipitates a crisis as the complex network of purchase and sale breaks down because 'no one except the producer of coinable metals can buy before he has sold. These are the two roots out of which grows the crisis' (CC, 72).[7] The problems of estimating demand have become increasingly difficult in modern society, with its world market, and efficient transport and communications, which 'render more and more uncertain the work of estimating the demand for, and supply of, commodities' (CC, 75).

The growing complexity of the system of interdependence also means that the risk of crisis is becoming much greater. 'The economic

---

[7] The 'Keynesian' character of this explanation is reinforced by the example Kautsky gives, where a crisis arises because one person withdraws money from circulation.

Kautsky's Theory of Crisis

machinery of the modern system of production constitutes a more and more delicate and complicated mechanism; its uninterrupted operation depends constantly more upon whether each of its wheels fits in with the others and does the work expected of it. Never yet did any system of production stand in such need of careful direction as does the present one. But the institution of private property makes it impossible to introduce plan and order into this system' (CC, 50).

Finally, credit, which gives an unprecedented spur to capitalist development, also increases the likelihood of crisis. 'Next to the great development of machinery and the creation of the reserve army of unemployed labour, credit is the principal cause of the rapid development of the present system. Credit is, however, much more sensitive than commerce to any disturbance. Every shock it receives is felt throughout the economic organisation.' (CC, 47)

The speculative activity of the merchant capitalist 'helps to bring some order into the chaos of the planless system of production', 'but he is liable to err in his calculations, and all the more as he is not allowed much time to consider his ventures' (CC, 75–6), and if he makes a mistake his failure can easily precipitate a commercial crisis. Trusts also represent an attempt of capitalists to bring some order into the system, but they cannot overcome the tendency to crisis, because to do so they would have to cover all branches on an international scale. 'With regard to overproduction the principal mission of the trust is not to check it, but to shift its evil consequences from the shoulders of the capitalists upon those of workmen and consumers.' Moreover, trusts only sharpen competition between groups of capitalists, leading to the formation of 'hostile groups, who would wage war to the knife against one another ... Only when all trusts are joined into one and the whole machinery of production of all capitalist nations is concentrated in a few hands, that is, when private property in the means of production has virtually come to an end, can the trust abolish the crisis.' (CC, 80–1)

Kautsky offers neither an underconsumptionist nor an overproduction theory of crisis, but a 'proto-Keynesian' theory of the business cycle, which has no distinctively Marxist features. The flexibility and expansibility of modern production, the elasticity of credit, and the availability of a large reserve army of labour means that capital can respond rapidly to a favourable stimulus by expanding production. When a leading branch of production, such as iron or spinning, receives a boost, 'not only does it expand rapidly, but it imparts the impetus it has received to the whole industrial organism', so a boom gathers momentum. 'In the meantime, production has greatly increased and the originally increased demand upon the market has been satisfied. Nevertheless production does not stop.' (CC, 78–9) Even if capitalists know that it is getting out of hand, they must still try to profit by the opportunity rather than be left behind in the race. But then one capitalist fails, precipitating a chain of bankruptcies and the inevitable crash.

The business cycle for Kautsky plays an important role in sustaining capitalist accumulation in the face of the secular tendency to overproduction, as the opening of new markets stimulates a renewed burst of capitalist activity that develops capitalist production to new heights. The alternative to the business cycle is not, therefore, stable and sustained economic growth, but chronic stagnation as the limit of the market permanently restrains the accumulation of capital.

Kautsky's separation of the theory of crisis from the theory of secular overproduction, and subordination of the former to the latter, is politically very significant. For Kautsky the political priority was the methodical work of building a movement ready and able to seize power when the decisive hour comes. The theory of the secular tendency to overproduction underpinned Kautsky's revolutionary rhetoric in defining the ultimate inevitability of the revolution, while his downplaying of the significance of crises underpinned his caution, which prevented him from committing his political forces before the decisive hour struck. Although crises might have a conjunctural importance as periods in which the class struggle intensified and became generalised, the political development of the working class was a long-drawn-out process, which expressed the secular tendencies of accumulation, building up to the revolution which would occur when the great mass of the population had been won over to the socialist cause. Against this, the crisis tendencies of accumulation which underlay the cyclical fluctuations in trade were quite beyond the realm of working class experience, to be found in the limits of the world market, located in the further recesses of empire.

For Kautsky the necessity of crises, and the deepening of successive crises, implied the ultimately necessary breakdown of the capitalist system, and so the ultimate necessity of socialism. Kautsky's caution led him to downplay the significance of crises, but the dominant mood in the revolutionary movement in the 1890s was closer to the view of Engels, with a widespread belief that the collapse of capitalism was imminent, and that with this collapse political power would fall into the hands of the proletariat.[8] Although collapse was not seen as purely economic, but was understood in moral and political terms, there is no doubt that the basis of that collapse was the anticipated terminal crisis of capitalism. This belief in the apocalypse underlay a degree of political passivity within the Social Democratic movement which threatened to degenerate into political paralysis as the anticipated breakdown did not come. It was this apocalyptic vision that Bernstein challenged.

Bernstein's Challenge — Reform or Revolution

Bernstein's revisionist critique focussed particularly on the supposed inevitability of capitalist breakdown, which he saw as the key to the revolutionary critique of reformism. His main target was Kautsky's belief in a secular tendency to overproduction as the basis of a general economic crisis and of the inevitability of socialism. Bernstein argued that the growth of the domestic market with the rise of the middle class and the 'labour aristocracy', and the opening of foreign markets with the rise of imperialism, had reduced the dangers of general overproduction. Moreover, while Bernstein recognised that the tendency to crisis was inherent in capitalism, he argued that the rise of joint-stock companies and the formation of cartels had reduced the risk of crisis inherent in the anarchy of the market, while raising the rate of profit by cutting unproductive expenses and rationalising production. Meanwhile the modern credit system, improved sources of information and means of communication, harnessed speculation to the adjustment of markets towards equilibrium.

Far from intensifying, the secular tendency to overproduction and crisis was countered by the growing market and by the progressive socialisation of production. The growing scale and extension of capitalist production made it likely that crises would in future be localised or confined to particular branches of production, so that the general crisis would be a thing of the past. Bernstein welcomed these developments, because he doubted that Social Democracy could handle

---

[8] At the 1891 SPD Congress Bebel claimed that 'bourgeois society is working so vigorously towards its own destruction that we need only wait for the moment when we can pick up the power which has already dropped from its hands' (quoted Guttsman, 1981, 274). A resolution of the London Congress of the Socialist International of 1896 stated that 'economic development has now reached a point where crisis could be imminent', calling on workers to be 'in a position to take over the management of production'.

the consequences of a catastrophic crisis. The dispersion of property means that 'Social Democracy could not abolish capitalism by decree and could not indeed manage without it, but neither could it guarantee capitalism the security which it needs to fulfil its functions. This contradiction would irrevocably destroy Social Democracy; the outcome would only be a colossal defeat' (Tudor and Tudor, 1988, 167). The necessity and inevitability of socialism could not be based on the objective dynamics of accumulation, but only on the progressive growth of a reformist movement based on socialist moral values.

Bernstein's critique of Marxist orthodoxy was empirically acute, but was as theoretically unsophisticated as was the theory which was the object of his critique. The relative prosperity of capitalism and the growing strength of reformism, on which Bernstein based his critique, could not be denied. However the Left took issue with Bernstein's claim that the apparent stabilisation of capitalism was a permanent feature.[9] According to the Left, the penetration of capitalism on a world scale, the formation of cartels and the expansion of credit did not mark a qualitative change in capitalism, but merely marked the new stage in the socialisation of the forces of production that Marx himself had already anticipated, which further developed the objective conditions for socialism.

In his reply to Bernstein Kautsky did little more than deny that Marxism had a catastrophist theory of breakdown, and reiterate his belief in the secular tendency to overproduction and stagnation, which was not undermined by the occurrence of occasional periods of prosperity. Nevertheless, Kautsky did insist that crises necessarily recurred, and he related the tendency to crisis directly to the tendency to overproduction much more clearly than he had in his previous accounts, playing down the 'anarchy of the market' that Bernstein claimed was being overcome by cartels. Kautsky's insistence that he did not hold to an apocalyptic view of the revolution was not as disingenuous as most subsequent commentators have supposed. As we have seen, Kautsky's political passivism was not underpinned by a belief in a terminal crisis, but rather by his view of the revolution as the culmination of a

---

[9] Parvus was the first to point out the significance of Bernstein's revisionism: 'What would be the point of striving to achieve political power if it only led to a "colossal defeat"? What would be the point of opposing capitalism if we could not manage without it? Instead we would have to *encourage* capitalist development, since, if it is *not interrupted by general trade crises*, it must eventually lead to the prosperity of all!' (Parvus: 'Bernstein's Statement', *Sächsische Arbeiter-Zeitung*, 09.02.1898. Tudor and Tudor, 1988, 195).

political process underpinned by the secular tendencies of capitalist development. While Kautsky expected that socialism would be won long before any terminal crisis which might spell the breakdown of capitalism, he also noted that the existence of an ultimate limit is still important in bringing the ultimate goal within sight.

The most vigorous response to Bernstein's apostasy came from Rosa Luxemburg. Rosa Luxemburg was one of those on the Left of the German SPD who came closest to the catastrophist view of revolution that Bernstein condemned.[10] At the 1898 Party Congress she boldly laid out her view of capitalist society as 'caught in insoluble contradictions which will ultimately necessitate an explosion, a collapse, at which point we will play the role of the syndic who liquidates a bankrupt company.' (quoted Tudor and Tudor, 1988, 28).

Luxemburg took up the issue of crisis in a series of articles in the *Leipziger Volkszeitung*, subsequently published as a pamphlet, *Reform or Revolution*. Her central argument was that the credit and cartels, which Bernstein saw as alleviating the crisis tendencies of capitalism, serve only to postpone the crisis, at the price of intensifying it. In her first article she immediately took up Bernstein's challenge, and developed Parvus's argument that Bernstein's revision of Marx had revised away both the necessity and the possibility of socialism. 'Up to now socialist theory has assumed that the point of departure for the socialist revolution would be a general and catastrophic crisis' ('The Method' 21.09.98, Tudor and Tudor, 1988, 250).

In her first article Luxemburg explained the necessity of crisis only by reference to 'the growing *anarchy* of the capitalist economy, leading inevitably to its ruin.' However, in her second article Rosa Luxemburg linked the tendency to crisis to the tendency to overproduction in denouncing Bernstein's claim that the growth of the credit system provided a mechanism for the alleviation of the crisis tendencies of capitalist accumulation.

> If it is true that crises arise from the contradiction between the capacity, and tendency, of production to expand and the limited capacity of the market to absorb the products, then, in view of the above, credit is precisely the means whereby this contradiction is brought to a head as often as is possible. In particular, it vastly increases the rate at which production expands, and it provides

---
[10] As she baldly stated in her response to Bernstein's *Evolutionary Socialism*, 'the theory of capitalist breakdown ... is the cornerstone of scientific socialism' (Howard, 123).

the inner driving force which constantly pushes production beyond the limits imposed by the market. But credit cuts both ways. Having brought about overproduction (as a factor in the productive process), it then, in the subsequent crisis, assumes its character as a means of circulation and demolishes all the more thoroughly the very forces of production it helped to create. ... Put in very general terms, the specific function of credit is none other than to remove the last vestiges of stability from the capitalist system ... credit reproduces all the main contradictions of the capitalist world. It pushes them to the point of absurdity, it convicts capitalism of its own inadequacies, and it hastens the pace at which capitalism speeds towards its own destruction, the collapse. (Tudor and Tudor, 1988, 252–4)

Luxemburg was equally dismissive of Bernstein's faith in the stabilising role of trusts and cartels. 'cartels, like credit, appear as particular phases of development which ultimately serve only to increase the anarchy of the capitalist world and to express and bring to fruition all its immanent contradictions. ... Finally, they intensify the contradiction between the international character of the capitalist world economy and the national character of the capitalist state by bringing in their wake a general tariff war, thus pushing to extremes the antagonism between individual capitalist states' (Tudor and Tudor, 1988, 255).

Finally, Luxemburg asked whether the absence of a general trade crisis for two decades might be 'an indication that the capitalist mode of production has indeed "adapted" itself to the needs of society ... and has thus rendered Marx's analysis obsolete?' (Tudor and Tudor, 1988, 256)

She answered her question by developing the distinction, implicit in Kautsky's work, between the cyclical crises of capitalism's past, which are explained essentially in terms of the anarchy of the market, and the terminal crisis which lay in the future, which is explained by the final exhaustion of the market. She argued that past crises have not been 'the crises of capitalism's old age ... but of its childhood', arising 'from *restructuring* the social economy in various forms and from laying new foundations for capitalist development ... We are at a stage in which crises are no longer a symptom of the rise of capitalism and not yet a symptom of its demise. ... Once the world market has more or less reached its limit and can no longer be enlarged by sudden expansions while labour relentlessly increases its productivity, then sooner or later the periodic conflicts between the forces of production and the limits of exchange will begin.' ('The Adaptation of Capitalism', 22–3.09.98, Tudor and Tudor, 1988, 256–8)

Tugan-Baranowsky and the Necessity of Crisis

Bernstein's critique of Marxist orthodoxy was theoretically unsophisticated, and it elicited a theoretically unsophisticated response, which did little more than restate established positions. The theory of overproduction of the Second International was intuitively plausible, but it rested on no more than intuition. Moreover this intuition rested on a fundamental fallacy. The limited consumption power of the mass of the population would indeed be a barrier to the sustained accumulation of capital if it were the case that consumption was the driving force of accumulation. However, for Marxism the driving force of capitalist accumulation is not consumption but profit. Moreover, this is not merely an aspect of the subjective motivation of the capitalist. It is imposed on the capitalist by the pressure of competition.

The capitalist does not invest because there is an additional demand already in existence, the capitalist invests in order to reduce his costs of production and increase his rate of profit, and thereby to gain a greater share of the existing market at the expense of his competitor. However, the result of this investment is an increase in the total demand for labour power and means of production, and so an increase in the demand for the means of production and subsistence. So long as the surplus appropriated by the capitalists is either consumed or re-invested by them (or lent to others to re-invest), then capitalists' consumption and investment spending will provide the growing demand to match the growing supply of products.

The limited consumption power of the mass of the population is only the other side of the growing mass of profit appropriated by the capitalists. Provided that there is a reserve of labour power, and that necessary means of production and subsistence are available in the appropriate proportions, there is no reason why the growing mass of profit should not be reinvested productively, and the greater is the rate of profit the more rapid will be the accumulation of capital. Provided that this reinvestment takes place, there is no reason why capital accumulation should be held back by the limits of the market, because the extension of the market is only the other side of the development of the productive forces. The limited consumption power of the mass of the population is no barrier to sustained accumulation because the driving force of capitalist accumulation is not consumption but the production and appropriation of surplus value.

Underconsumptionism was powerful in Germany, drawing on the traditions of Dühring and Lassalle. The Marxist critique of underconsumptionism was most powerfully developed in Russia, against the populists who argued that the limited home market made the development of capitalism in Russia impossible. The Russian Marxists argued that the tendencies to overproduction inherent in capitalist accumulation did not imply that capitalist development was impossible. On the contrary, such tendencies dictated that capitalism would constantly seek to expand the home market by destroying the peasant production on which populism pinned its political hopes. Any tendencies to overproduction would accordingly only come to the fore as pre-capitalist forms of production were destroyed.

The most influential critic of the underconsumptionist theory of crisis was Tugan-Baranowsky, who was not himself a Marxist, but who drew on the 'reproduction schemes' which Marx had developed in Volume Two of *Capital*. These schemes were developed specifically to explore the inter-relations of production and consumption in order to identify the source of the demand for the increased product corresponding to the growing surplus value appropriated by the capitalist. Marx showed that the source of increased demand lay in the purchase of means of production and labour power by the capitalist as the capitalist sought to expand his capital by reinvesting his surplus value. The conclusion which Tugan drew was that capital would not face any barriers to the realisation of its expanded product, provided only that the appropriate proportional relations between the various branches of production were maintained.[11] A crisis might arise if the branches of production producing the workers' means of subsistence expanded beyond the limits of the consumption demand of the working class, but this was merely a special case of disproportionality, whose causes lay not in the limited consumption of the working class, but in the

---

[11] Expanded reproduction also implied the existence of an adequate reserve of labour power, but this was created by the destruction of backward forms of pre-capitalist and capitalist production. This was the other side of the rising organic composition of capital that accompanied the rise in the rate of surplus value. Thus, the diminution in the proportion of capital laid out as variable capital simply corresponded to the increase in the proportion laid out for the purchase of means of production.

over-expansion of the production of means of subsistence. Tugan concluded that sustained accumulation depended only on maintaining the appropriate proportional relations between the various branches of production, the implication being that the only possible cause of crises was disproportionality between the branches of production. 'If social production were organised in accordance with a plan, if the directors of production had complete knowledge of the demand and the power to direct labour and capital from one branch of production to another, then, however low consumption might be, the supply of commodities could never outstrip the demand' (M. Tugan-Baranowsky, *Studien zur Theorie und Geschichte der Handelskrisen in England*, G. Fischer, Jena, 1901, [1894], 33, quoted Sweezy, 1946, 166). '*If social production is proportionately organised, there is no limit to the expansion of the market other than the productive forces available*' (p. 231, quoted Luxemburg, 1971, 313). This implies that production can expand indefinitely, however restricted may be the market for consumption goods, by expanding the production of means of production.

Tugan did not believe that proportionality would necessarily be achieved, for the anarchy of the market meant that there were no guarantees that new investment would be appropriately distributed among the various branches of production. Accumulation could be sustained for a period, despite growing disproportionalities, by the expansion of credit, but credit could not sustain such disproportionalities indefinitely.[12]

Tugan's critique did not undermine Engels's overproduction theory of crisis, but it undermined the belief that overproduction and underconsumption are 'opposite sides of the same coin', as Sweezy described them (Sweezy, 1946, 183), and destroyed the foundations of the theory of secular overproduction. The important point about Engels's theory was that production and consumption in each branch of production were determined independently, by different laws. However, this did not necessarily imply an overall tendency to overproduction, provided that credit was not expanded excessively, since over-

---

[12] The Russian Marxist S. Bulgakov developed a similar critique of underconsumptionism in *On the Markets of Capitalist Production. A Study in Theory*, Moscow, 1897, replacing the underconsumptionist hypothesis with the claim that the collapse of capitalism will result from the secular decline in the rate of profit, although he did not challenge the orthodox objection to such an argument that the fall in the rate of profit is consistent with the continued growth in the mass of profits.

production in one branch of production might well be matched by 'underproduction' in another.

Tugan's critique made it clear that the outcome of the tendency to overproduction was not underconsumption, but disproportionality, as some branches grew more rapidly than others. A crisis would then arise first in a particular branch of production, where overproduction had reached its limits, with the possibility that the collapse would then be generalised in a chain-reaction. There was no particular reason to expect the branches producing means of consumption to be especially prone to tendencies to overproduction, and so no particular reason to stress underconsumption as a form of disproportionality. In short, the orthodox Marxist theory of overproduction did not imply that there was an underconsumptionist tendency inherent in the capitalist mode of production.

Tugan's theory of disproportionality leads not to a theory of a secular tendency to growing underconsumption but to a theory of the business cycle, as crises restore proportionality and secure the conditions for renewed accumulation. In the absence of any theory of the secular tendencies of accumulation, there was no reason to believe that such crises would get progressively worse. Moreover, since Tugan attributed disproportionalities to ignorance, rather than to the tendency to overproduction, his theory implied that the planning of investment and appropriate regulation of credit could in principle ameliorate or eliminate the cyclical tendencies of accumulation.

The general Marxist response to Tugan's use of Marx's reproduction schemes was to denounce his work as a formalistic exercise of no theoretical significance, since it abstracted from the specific features of the capitalist mode of production which underpinned the contradiction between the tendency to develop the forces of production without limit, and the tendency to depress the consumption power of the mass of the population. Thus the Left dismissed Tugan's critique and re-asserted the orthodox theory of overproduction/underconsumption, the disproportionality between production and consumption being no accident, but an essential feature of capitalist production.[13]

Most Marxists simply ridiculed Tugan's argument that accumulation could be sustained regardless of the growth of consumption, by asserting that it was consumption alone that could provide the driving force of capitalist accumulation. Conrad Schmidt insisted that 'The

---

[13] These debates are well surveyed by Sweezy in his *Theory of Capitalist Development*.

"purposes of production"...are purposes which in the final analysis ...proceed from the demand for consumption goods. ...Definitive or consumption demand is the enlivening force which, throughout the entire economy, keeps the huge apparatus of production in motion' (Conrad Schmidt, 'Zur Theorie der Handelskrisen und der Überproduction,' *Sozialistische Monatshefte*, V, 2, 9, 1901, 673, quoted Sweezy, 1946, 170), a view which was reiterated by Kautsky, Boudin, Luxemburg, Bukharin and, with qualifications, by Lenin.

Kautsky simply restated the orthodox theory against Tugan, emphasising that underconsumption is not an accidental feature of disproportionality, but a necessary tendency of capitalist development, although he did not confront the fundamental issues. 'In the proletariat, however, there exists a class whose underconsumption is a necessary result of its social circumstances. The underconsumption is not however to be understood in a physical sense, a bit like undernourishment, but in social terms, as the consumption of a class which falls behind its production' (Kautsky, 'Krisentheorien', *Die Neue Zeit*, 20, 1901–2, 78–9, quoted Howard and King, 1989, 83) In this sense underconsumption is a feature of all class societies, but in precapitalist societies luxury consumption avoided the problem. However the capitalist restricts his own and his workers' consumption in order to devote all his resources to the expansion of production so that capitalists 'must seek an additional market outside their own sphere in occupations and nations not yet producing capitalistically'. However, this does not solve the problem because these markets do not have the needed elasticity. 'This is, in short, as far as we can see, the generally accepted "orthodox" Marxist theory of crisis, established by Marx.' Kautsky agreed that disproportionality was a 'factor which from time to time can ... engender crises of its own accord or further sharpen a general crisis' already in existence (ibid., 79–81, 110–8, quoted Howard and King, 1989, 83) , but in the final analysis 'the extension of *human* consumption exercises the decisive influence over the expansion of production ... Production is and remains production for human consumption' (ibid., 117, quoted Sweezy, 1946, 170).

Rudolf Hilferding realised that Tugan's position was in keeping with Marx's analysis of the 'formal economic categories of capitalist production', leading to 'the curious conception of a system of production which exists only for the sake of production, while consumption is simply a tedious irrelevance. If this is "madness" there is method in it, and a Marxist one at that, for it is just this analysis of the specific historical structure of capitalist production which is distinctively Marxist. It is Marxism gone mad, but still Marxism, and this is what makes the theory so peculiar and yet so suggestive.' (Rudolf Hilferding, *Finance Capital*, n. 4, 421–2).[14]

Tugan's critique opened up a gap in Marxism between those who re-asserted the underconsumptionist orthodoxy, and those who took up Tugan's challenge to develop a disproportionality approach to crisis, although this division was not altogether clear-cut. On the one hand, disproportionality theorists usually paid lip service to underconsumption theory by noting underconsumption as a privileged case of disproportionality, while underconsumption theorists admitted the possibility of crises of disproportionality. On the other hand, the distinction between disproportionality and underconsumption was closely bound up with the distinction between the cyclical and secular tendencies of capitalist development. We have already seen that Kautsky combined a theory of the business cycle that rested on the 'anarchy of the market' with an underconsumptionist theory of the secular tendencies of capitalist accumulation, and Luxemburg had similarly distinguished cyclical fluctuations from the secular trend. Thus it was quite possible to maintain a disproportionality account of the business cycle alongside an underconsumptionist account of the secular tendency and ultimate limits of capitalist accumulation.

The theory of crisis was extensively debated and became a focus for the most fundamental divisions in the Social Democratic and Communist movement in the first three decades of the twentieth century, not only on its own account, but also because the theory of crisis provided the foundation for the theory of imperialism. The most fundamental issue was that raised originally by Bernstein of whether the historical tendency of capitalist development was towards increasing stability or towards inevitable breakdown. These debates were wide-ranging and politically important, but theoretically they did not offer any fundamental advance on the foundations laid down in the first decade of the century by Rudolf Hilferding and Rosa Luxemburg in their responses to the revisionist critique.

---

[14] Sweezy also recognised that Tugan's logic was in accordance with Marx's insistence that the purpose of capitalist production was not the production of use-values, but the expansion of surplus value, but Sweezy insisted that there is a contradiction between 'the ends of production regarded as a natural-technical process of creating use-values, and the ends of capitalism regarded as a historical system of expanding exchange value', characterising this contradiction as 'the fundamental contradiction of capitalist society from which all other contradictions are ultimately derived' (Sweezy, 1946, 172).

Hilferding and the Disproportionality Theory of Crisis

Although Tugan developed his argument as a critique of Marxism, his work was perfectly consistent with the kind of disproportionality theory of crisis, based on the 'anarchy of the market', that had been espoused by Kautsky. Although Kautsky had retreated from this theory towards underconsumptionism in response to Bernstein's critique, the disproportionality theory was developed by Rudolf Hilferding, whose *Finance Capital* (FC) provided much the most serious and rigorous attempt to develop Marx's analysis of capitalism in the light of developments in the quarter century since Marx's death. However, while Hilferding provided a rich and complex analysis of the dynamics of capitalist development which was vastly superior to the analyses of his bourgeois contemporaries, his account was essentially based on a model of 'imperfect competition' which made no specific reference to the social relations of capitalist production, so that in the last analysis it was not clear what (if anything) was specifically Marxist in his theory.

Hilferding reiterated Tugan's criticism of underconsumptionism, that underconsumption is only a special case of disproportionality.[15] 'The term underconsumption ... has no sense in economics except to indicate that society is consuming less than it has produced. It is impossible, however, to conceive how that can happen if production is carried on in the right proportions ... the narrow basis of consumption is only a general condition of crises, which cannot be explained simply by "underconsumption". Least of all can the periodic character of crises be explained in this way, since no periodic phenomenon can be explained by constant conditions.' (FC, 241–2) 'It does not follow at all, therefore, that a crisis in capitalist production is caused by the underconsumption of the masses which is inherent in it. A crisis could just as well be brought about by a too rapid increase in consumption, or by a static or declining production of capital goods' (FC, 256).

---

[15] Hilferding makes a concession to underconsumptionism in arguing that the contradiction between production and consumption in a capitalist society defines a source of disproportionality which lies 'in the nature of capital', because 'if consumption could be readily expanded, overproduction would not be possible. But under capitalist conditions expansion of consumption means a reduction in the rate of profit' so that 'one necessary precondition of accumulation, the expansion of consumption, enters into contradiction with another precondition, namely the realisation of profit. The conditions of realisation cannot be reconciled with the expansion of consumption, and since the former are decisive, the contradiction develops into a crisis' (FC, 241–2). However Hilferding does not show how this 'contradiction develops into a crisis', except in the special case of 'absolute overaccumulation' in which rising wages erode profits altogether.

In place of the orthodox underconsumptionism Hilferding developed a disproportionality theory of crisis. Hilferding's analysis focused on the role of trusts and cartels, and of credit and financial institutions, which had played such a central role in the revisionist controversy. For Hilferding the new stage of capitalism was defined as being under the domination of finance capital, which expressed the integration of bank and industrial capital under the domination of the banks. This development was determined primarily by the substantial increase in the importance of fixed capital, which tied up large amounts of capital for long periods. This reduced the mobility of capital, and so its flexibility in response to economic fluctuations and emerging disproportionalities, and this barrier to the equalisation of supply and demand was for Hilferding the source of crises.

'This enormous inflation of fixed capital means, however, that once capital has been invested, its transfer from one sphere to another becomes increasingly difficult ... The result is that the equalisation of the rate of profit is possible, increasingly, only through the influx of new capital into those spheres in which the rate of profit is above the average, whereas the withdrawal of capital from those branches which have a large amount of fixed capital is extremely difficult'. Moreover, since capacity can only be increased in large units, 'the rapid spurt in production may have an overcompensating effect on the rate of profit, which from having been above the average may now fall below the average'. Finally, 'not only does the large firm predominate, but these large, capital-intensive concerns tend to become more equally matched ... The competitive struggle is ... a struggle between equals, which can remain indecisive for a long time, imposing equal sacrifices on all parties', rather than restoring proportionality by driving out the weaker capitals (FC, 186, 188–9).

The growth of fixed capital was associated, particularly in Germany, with a growing role of the banks in industrial finance. Once the banks had become committed to financing industrial enterprises, they were compelled to protect their investments, which they sought to do by sponsoring the formation of trusts and cartels, which in turn increased the demands on the banks and stimulated the further centralisation of banking capital and its integration with industrial capital. The formation of trusts sets up further barriers to the equalisation of the rate of profit through the mobility of capital between branches of production.

In the course of the industrial cycle the output of extractive industry, which both has a large fixed capital and is heavily cartelised, lags behind that of manufactured goods, so that raw material prices tend to rise rapidly as the boom reaches its height, pushing up the rate of profit in extractive industry. In the depression the situation is reversed, with profits slumping in extractive industry and relatively higher in manufacturing. Thus the industrial cycle provides a powerful incentive to even out such profit differences by means of vertical integration, promoting the further integration of finance capital as a means of stabilising the rate of profit. Finally, the attempt of trusts to raise their rate of profit by restricting competition forces the unorganised capitalists to organise in their turn, to defend their own interests against their competitors.

The tendency of finance capital is towards the replacement of the market by the centralised control of the banks over production, but with the purpose of maximising profits, not of rationally adjusting production to social needs. While the unorganised capitalists find their profit rate pared to the bone, and so have little incentive to invest, the trusts restrict investment in order to maintain their own profits. The result is a surplus of capital, which cannot find outlets for profitable investment in the domestic economy. For Hilferding it was the consequent search for profitable outlets for surplus capital in overseas, and above all in colonial, investment that underlay imperialism, although he stressed that 'this is not in itself a consequence of cartelisation. It is a phenomenon that is inseparable from capitalist development. But cartelisation suddenly intensifies the contradiction and makes the export of capital an urgent matter' (FC, 234).

The source of disproportionalities for Hilferding was the existence of fixed capital. In response to the economic fluctuations to which this gave rise capitalists formed trusts and cartels, and banking and industrial capital were integrated in finance capital. However, far from stabilising the situation, as Bernstein had argued, these developments only increase instability and politicise competition. Thus Hilferding insisted that only comprehensive planning could overcome the tendency to crisis. 'Planned production and anarchic production are not quantitative opposites such that by tacking on more and more 'planning' conscious organisation will emerge out of anarchy. Such a transformation can only take place suddenly by subordinating the whole of production to conscious control.' (FC, 296) Although in principle the capitalists could achieve this with one giant cartel, Hilferding did not believe that such a possibility was politically realistic.

Competition and the investment cycle

Although Hilferding's analysis is presented within a Marxist framework, he departed fundamentally from the orthodox Marxist tradition, not only in abandoning the theory of underconsumption, but also in abandoning the orthodox Marxist account of the tendency to overproduction. For Engels and Kautsky the driving force of capitalist production was the need for capitalists constantly to invest in new methods of production in order to exploit the possibility of earning a surplus profit by introducing a more advanced method of production, and in order to meet the competitive threat of other capitalists doing the same thing. The incentive to develop the forces of production is determined by the opportunities of earning such surplus profits, which are related not to the size of the market, but to the advances which can be achieved in production. This is why the tendency of capitalist accumulation is to develop the forces of production without regard to the limits of the market.

Engels and Kautsky mistakenly identified this tendency to overproduction in each branch of production with a tendency to general overproduction in relation to the limited consumption power of the mass of the population, and Kautsky limited it to the elucidation of the secular tendencies of capitalist accumulation, attributing the cycle to the 'anarchy of the market'. What their analysis in fact provided was an explanation for the tendency to disproportionality that was inherent in the dynamics of capitalist production, as production in the more dynamic branches grows more rapidly than the market, while that in less dynamic branches lags behind.[16]

This analysis of the dynamics of capitalist accumulation is fundamentally different from that of bourgeois economics. For Engels capitalist production develops according to its own laws, which are determined by the dynamics of the development of the forces of production. It is only subsequently that capitalists submit their product to the judgement of the market, and in the event of overproduction the less efficient producers have to sell at a loss, which may force them eventually into liquidation. The equilibration of supply and demand through the equalisation of the rate of profit between branches of production is only a counter-tendency to the disequilibrating force

---
[16] In their more concrete writings they in fact used the theory in this way. Kautsky, for example, made much of the disproportionality between industry and agriculture on a world scale, which had nothing to do with underconsumption.

of inequalities of the rate of profit within a particular branch of production.

Bourgeois economic theories focus exclusively on the equilibrating tendencies of capitalist competition by assuming that every capitalist has the same technological opportunities available, and so each will choose the same technology in given conditions. This assumption of homogeneous production conditions implies that a uniform rate of profit is earned by all capitalists in a particular branch of production, so removing at a stroke the objective determinant of the tendency to overproduction inherent in the social form of capitalist production.[17] This assumption also implies that the distribution of new investment is determined exclusively by differences in the rate of profit *between* branches of production which arise because of disproportionalities between supply and demand. Far from generating disproportionalities, capitalist competition in the bourgeois model irons out emerging disproportionalities as capitalists invest in response to the signals of the market.

Hilferding's analysis of 'finance capital', based on the immobility introduced by the increasing role of fixed capital in capitalist production, could have been used to strengthen Engels's account of the tendency to disproportionality, because the greater is the role of fixed capital, the more we would expect investment decisions to be based on conditions of production and the less on temporary imbalances in the market. The result would be that the objective forces determining the disproportional growth of capitalist production would increasingly outweigh the equilibrating forces pressing for the restoration of proportionality. However Hilferding did not develop any such argument. He followed the bourgeois economists in abstracting from the social form of capitalist production, to concentrate only on the barriers to the equalisation of the rate of profit between branches of production erected by the immobility of capital.[18]

Hilferding removed the very source of capitalist dynamism with his assumption that 'large, capital-intensive concerns tend to become more equally matched ... The competitive struggle is ... a struggle between equals' (FC, 189), a tendency which is reinforced by carteli-

---

[17] This assumption equally removes the objective source of the dynamism of the capitalist mode of production, which then has to be attributed to the subjective motivation of the capitalist.

[18] This emphasis on the market as an allocative process, rather than as an expression of capitalist production relations, also marked Hilferding's defence of the Marxist theory of value against the critique of Böhm-Bawerk.

sation. Hilferding therefore focuses on the inequalities in the rate of profit *between* branches of production, which the bourgeois economist assumes are eliminated by competition, and his theory is then based on identifying the various barriers to the equalisation of the rate of profit. His underlying assumption is the assumption of bourgeois economics that if capital is mobile between branches of production any emerging disproportionalities between branches will be eliminated by movements of capital in response to inequalities in the rate of profit. The source of the instability of capitalist production is then identified in the barriers to the mobility of capital and equalisation of the rate of profit constituted by fixed capital, cartels, and the subordination of productive to banking capital. These barriers distort the price structure, and so introduce systematic disproportionalities into the relations between branches of production. While disproportionalities for Engels are the necessary result of capitalist competition, for Hilferding they are the result of barriers to competition.

Hilferding is quite clear that his theory of crisis is based not on the laws of capitalist production, but on an analysis of 'imperfect competition'. He insists that the *cause* of crises must lie in the failure of the mechanism by which 'the complicated relations of proportionality which must exist in production' are maintained. 'The disruption of these proportional relations must be explained in terms of a disruption in this specific regulatory mechanism of production, or in other words, in terms of a distortion of the price structure which prevents prices from giving a proper indication of the needs of production. Since such disruptions occur periodically, the distortions of the price structure must also be shown to be periodic' (FC, 257).

The disproportionalities that give rise to crises are not inherent in the capitalist mode of production as such, but in its developed stage of finance capital. These disproportionalities are not merely the accidental result of the 'anarchy of the market', since they arise as the systematic result of the distortions of the structure of profits introduced into the operation of the market by fixed capital and cartels. Thus Hilferding can still draw radical conclusions from his analysis, and assert that crises are the direct result of the system of production for profit. 'The possibility of crises is implicit in unregulated production, that is to say, in commodity production generally, but it only becomes a real possibility in a system of unregulated production which eliminates the direct relationship between production and consumption characterising other social formations, and interposes between production and con-

Hilferding and the Disproportionality Theory of Crisis

sumption the requirement that capital shall be valorised at a particular rate' (FC, 241).

The investment cycle and the crisis

Hilferding provided a powerful analysis of the investment cycle on the basis of his account of the barriers to the equalisation of the rate of profit presented by the dominance of fixed capital, the formation of cartels, and the integration of bank and industrial capital, and as such his work marked an enormous advance on the existing bourgeois theories of the business cycle, whose subsequent development was much influenced by Hilferding's work. However it was not at all clear what, if anything, was distinctively Marxist about the theoretical foundations of Hilferding's account. Although Hilferding formulates his theory of finance capital using the Marxist conceptual apparatus, crises for Hilferding do not derive from the laws of motion of the capitalist mode of production, but are only a phase of a business cycle which arises from market imperfections.

A crisis is marked by the appearance of general overproduction. Hilferding insists that this has nothing to do with underconsumption, but is a result of the fall in investment which follows a fall in the rate of profit. The question is then, how is the fall in the rate of profit to be explained?

Hilferding first appears to relate the fall in the rate of profit directly to an increase in the organic composition of capital, which underlies Marx's 'law of the tendency of the rate of profit to fall'. 'A crisis involves a slump in sales. In capitalist society this presupposes a cessation of new capital investment, which in turn presupposes a fall in the rate of profit. This decline in the rate of profit is entailed by the change in the organic composition of capital, which has taken place as a result of the investment of new capital. A crisis is simply the point at which the rate of profit begins to fall'. However Hilferding immediately observes that 'the crisis is preceded by a long period of prosperity, in which prices and profits are high' and asks 'how does this turn of fortune in the capitalist world occur?' (FC, 257–8).

It turns out that the connection with Marx's law is at best indirect. The association between the fall in the rate of profit and the organic composition of capital is explained by the fact that overproduction had previously developed to the greatest extent in those branches of production with a high organic composition of capital, which had enjoyed the highest rate of profit in the upswing of the cycle. The fall in the rate of profit is therefore a cyclical rather than a secular phenomenon, and Hilferding's account of the cycle, like that of Kautsky, is an orthodox, if sophisticated, version of the bourgeois theory of the trade cycle, in which a growing market in the upswing stimulates overinvestment, concentrated in branches of production with a high organic composition of capital, leading in turn to a crash when the results of overinvestment hit the market in the form of overproduction.

'The cycle begins with the renewal and growth of fixed capital, which is the main source of the incipient prosperity', stimulated by such factors as 'the opening of new markets, the establishment of new branches of production, the introduction of new technology, and the expansion of needs resulting from population growth'. The boom in demand and the shortening of the turnover time of capital raises the rate of profit as the result of 'improved conditions for the valorisation of capital. But the very conditions which at first make for prosperity contain within themselves potentialities which gradually worsen the conditions for valorisation'.

There are many reasons for this fall in the rate of profit. For example, new investment raises the organic composition of capital and lengthens the turnover time of capital, because of the larger amount of fixed capital. But other factors also lengthen the turnover time of capital, for example, the interruption of production by labour shortages and strikes, the breakdown of overworked machines, and the greater time taken to find more distant markets, all of which lead to a fall in the rate of profit. Pressure in the labour market leads to rising wages, which cuts into profits, while the rate of interest tends to rise, reducing the rate of entrepreneurial profit. The money accumulated in the banks is diverted into speculation, while growing trade requires a growth of 'circulation credit', which disrupts the process of production since 'a part of the productive capital intended for expanded reproduction remains unsaleable' (FC, 258–61).

There is, therefore, a wide range of factors which serve to reduce the rate of profit. 'A crisis begins at the moment when the tendencies toward a falling rate of profit ... prevail over the tendencies which have brought about increases in prices and profits as a result of rising demand.' This raises two questions 'First, how do these tendencies, which presage the end of prosperity, assert themselves in and through capitalist competition? Second, why does this occur in the form of a crisis, suddenly rather than gradually? The latter question is less

Hilferding and the Disproportionality Theory of Crisis

important, for it is the alternation of prosperity and depression which is crucial for the wave-like character of the business cycle, and the suddenness of the change is a secondary matter.' (FC, 261)

In answer to the first question Hilferding moves away from his analysis of a decline in the general rate of profit, to revert to the question of disproportionality and the analysis of the changing relationship between supply and demand through the investment cycle. The essential point is that a burst of investment increases demand without an equivalent increase in supply, and so boosts the rate of profit, until the new investment projects reach fruition, at which point the increased supply increases competition and profits tend to fall. The key is not the tendency for the rate of profit to fall, but changes in relative prices. 'If all prices rose equally there would be no change in the proportional relations ... and no disruption need occur'. But if prices do not change uniformly 'the changed prices structure may bring about changes in the proportional relations among the various branches of production ... And indeed, the existence of factors which prevent prices from rising uniformly can easily be shown' (FC, 261).

Hilferding notes that 'the greatest change in the organic composition of capital, which is responsible, in the last analysis, for the fall in the rate of profit, will occur where the use of machinery and of fixed capital in general is greatest' (FC, 261). But this increase in the organic composition of capital is associated with increased productivity, and so the opportunity for extra profit, so that capital flows into these branches of production until such time as an increase in supply leads to a fall in prices. Meanwhile the growing demand for the products of other sectors leads to rising prices and an influx of capital there too.

In the branches of production with a high organic composition of capital and a long turnover time the increase in production lags behind the increase in investment. 'Thus, while a higher organic composition of capital intensifies the causes which must bring about, in the long run, a fall in the rate of profit, these sectors are able, nevertheless ... to raise their prices more sharply than other branches of production', and so their prices and profits rise more steeply, and new capital is diverted into those branches of production. Moreover, because of the scale of production these industries tend to increase capacity 'on a large scale, in sudden spurts'. 'There is thus a tendency toward overinvestment and overaccumulation of capital in the sectors with the highest organic composition of capital'. A crisis then arises as 'the disproportion becomes apparent when the products of the first sector reach the market'. Production contracts, and prices fall, 'leaving the field to those which can achieve an average profit even at the lower prices. But the average profit is now at a different level. It no longer reflects the organic composition which existed at the start of the industrial cycle, but the changed, higher organic composition of capital' (FC, 262–4).

Although Hilferding links these aspects of disproportionality to the 'law of the tendency for the rate of profit to fall', the fall in the rate of profit has nothing to do with Marx's 'law', but is the result of cyclical overproduction in those branches of production with a high proportion of fixed capital and a long turnover time. Hilferding notes that 'crises are most severe in those branches of production which are technologically most advanced',[19] which he identifies as those with the largest fixed capital on the basis of the usual Marxist assumption of economies of scale. 'In general a crisis is most severe where the turnover of capital is most prolonged and technical improvements and innovations are most advanced, and hence, for the most part, where the organic composition is highest' (FC, 263). He later adds the inflexibility of agriculture and the extractive industries due to natural constraints.

Stabilisation and the necessity of crisis

Hilferding offers a very rich account of the cycle, in which it seems that underconsumption, the falling rate of profit, disproportionality, and the anarchy of production all have a part to play. But at the same time, Hilferding criticises each of these theories as, at best, one-sided. Underconsumption, overproduction, disproportionality and the fall in the rate of profit are not causes of the crisis, but are characteristic features of one phase or another of the investment cycle, simply examples of the general argument that 'disproportional relations arise in the course of the business cycle from disturbances in the price structure' (FC, 266). The business cycle does not express the laws of development of the capitalist mode of production, but is the self-reproducing expression of market imperfections. The explanation for this cycle is to be found in the rigidity introduced into the capitalist system by the existence of fixed capital, intensified by cartels, which

---

[19] He had earlier left aside the impact of technological revolutions in order to consider 'only the ordinary constant technical improvements' (FC, 261). Schumpeter brought technological revolutions to the heart of the theory.

distorts relative prices between branches of production and over time as a result of the immobility of capital. In the recovery phase of the cycle overinvestment occurs, concentrated in branches of production in which investment projects have a long gestation period. Once these projects reach completion the increase in supply increases competitive pressure, the rate of profit falls, investment is cut back and the system enters a crisis.

Hilferding's theory is certainly far more sophisticated than those of any of his contemporaries. It appears to establish that the necessity of crisis is inherent in the capitalist system, because the existence of fixed capital makes the emergence of disproportionalities inevitable. However, things are not quite what they seem. For Hilferding crisis is not inherent in the capitalist system, but in the investment cycle. Once the cycle gets underway, with over-investment taking place in the boom, the crisis becomes increasingly inevitable. However, if the over-investment could be avoided in the first place, then there would be no need for a crisis. Thus, Hilferding's whole theory of the cycle and the crisis hangs on his explanation for the capitalist tendency to over-investment. The problem is that Hilferding has abandoned the element of Engels's theory that would enable him to explain such over-investment as an objective feature of the capitalist mode of production. The result is that for Hilferding over-investment is a result of capitalist misjudgement. The deficiencies of the capitalist system have been reduced to the subjective irrationality of capitalists.

We saw earlier that for Engels, and for Kautsky in his secular theory, over-investment is the necessary result of capitalist competition based on different social and technological production conditions. In such circumstances competition compels the capitalist, on pain of extinction, to develop the forces of production without regard to the limits of the market, so that decisions to over-invest are perfectly rational. However, Hilferding does not explain over-investment on this basis, but on the basis of the miscalculation of capitalists. Capitalists in heavy industry over-invest because they base their investment decisions on the current rate of profit, which is inflated by the fact that demand is currently running ahead of supply as new capacity has not yet come into production.

Hilferding's account depends on this assumption that investment decisions are based on the current rate of profit. However any rational capitalist, when planning large scale investments with a long gestation period, must anticipate the future course of prices, and so would be expected to temper his momentary enthusiasm by anticipating both the fluctuation of prices in the course of the cycle and the secular fall in price as a result of the general fall in costs. The capitalist may misjudge the future, and be carried away by his optimism, but such misjudgement is by no means necessary, and the formation of a cartel should minimise the risk by restraining his enthusiasm. Thus Hilferding's model of the cycle depends on the assumption of irrational expectations on the part of the capitalists.[20]

This model of the trade cycle, based on successive waves of optimism and pessimism generated by irrational expectations, is almost as old as capitalism.[21] While capitalists undoubtedly do display irrational expectations, and Hilferding has made an important contribution to the theory of the investment cycle, his account does not by any means establish the necessity of crisis, primarily because crises can be avoided if the effect of irrational expectations can be neutralised by appropriate action on the part of the monetary authorities.

Overinvestment in fixed capital may be encouraged by the persistence of expectations of a relatively high rate of profit, but on the other hand it may be restrained by a high rate of interest. Bourgeois theories of the business cycle have traditionally argued that overinvestment in the upswing arises not because the rate of profit is artificially high, but because the rate of interest is too low. This raises the question of the role of money and credit in the cycle.

Hilferding recognises the central role of money and credit in the cycle, but insists that monetary movements reflect the real conditions of accumulation and do not determine them,[22] arguing that 'it is characteristic of almost all modern crisis theories that they explain business cycle phenomena in terms of changes in the interest rate, instead of explaining, conversely, the phenomena of the money market in terms of the conditions of production'. Hilferding argues that the rise in the

---

[20] This does not apply to Engels's model since the capitalist making new investments enjoys a permanent advantage, the losses being borne by those who lag behind.

[21] In Hilferding's day it was espoused by Alfred Marshall, from whom it descended to Keynes and to Maurice Dobb. In an early work Dobb presented a Marshallian theory of the cycle, based on psychological waves of optimism that fuel a boom, until profits are checked by rising costs or falling prices which result from disproportionalities. The thwarting of expectations then spreads a wave of pessimism which provokes a decline into depression (Dobb, 1925).

[22] The theoretical basis of Hilferding's analysis of money and credit is very shaky, resting on a version of the old and long discredited 'real bills doctrine', according to which the supply of money and credit instruments is constrained by the value of the commodities against which they were originally issued. Marx himself rejected the doctrine in the 1850s, although some Marxist economists still hold to it today.

Hilferding and the Disproportionality Theory of Crisis

rate of interest and the difficult of securing credit that precedes the crisis makes it appear that it is the scarcity of money that is choking the boom. But in reality 'the "scarcity" of money capital is only a symptom of the stagnation of the circulation process, as a result of overproduction having already begun' (FC, 285). Similarly the financial crisis may well 'precede the onset of a general commercial and industrial crisis. None the less, it is only a symptom, an omen, of the latter crisis, since the changes in the money market are indeed determined by the changes in production which lead to a crisis' (FC, 271). An easing of credit would relieve the immediate pressure, but only to encourage further overproduction and a more devastating crash in the future.

In the same way, at the bottom of the recession money capital lies idle in the banks and the rate of interest is low, but this cannot provide an incentive to renewed investment until a new price structure is established which permits 'a redistribution of capital among the various sectors of production' so that 'gradually the relations of proportionality are restored ... Prosperity can then get under way as soon as technical innovations or new markets generate increased demand, which in turn attracts new investment of productive capital' (FC, 298).

Hilferding's argument is largely correct, but it is beside the point. Once over-investment has taken place a crisis and depression are inevitable until the real disproportionalities had been removed. However, the crucial question is whether over-investment can be prevented by a rise in the rate of interest earlier in the upswing. Although Hilferding recognised that easing credit could sustain the boom but only to inflict a more severe crash, he did not consider the obvious corollary that an earlier restriction of credit would have avoided the crisis altogether. If this could be achieved, then the cycle could be eliminated and capitalism could enter a path of sustained growth. This question of the possibility of monetary regulation of the cycle became central to both Marxist and bourgeois debates during the 1920s.

Within bourgeois economics, until the publication of Keynes's *General Theory* in 1936, the presumption was that appropriate monetary policies could in principle regulate the cycle, and the central issue was to what extent such policies should be discretionary and to what extent they should be subordinate to the automatic mechanisms of the gold standard. The neo-Austrian economists, led by Hayek, insisted that the cycle was a monetary phenomenon, which arose because of the inflationary expansion of credit as banks, encouraged by politicians, issued money unbacked by gold. The strict imposition of the gold standard would ensure stability through the self-regulation of the market. However, most economists in the 1920s, including Keynes before *The General Theory* believed that discretionary monetary policies were appropriate to the regulation of the cycle, the main problem being the practical one of determining precisely what policy is appropriate.

In the matter of the regulation of the investment cycle it is largely inconsequential whether the cycle is a monetary or a real phenomenon. Even if the cause of the cycle was non-monetary, it could still be argued that appropriate monetary measures could ensure its stabilisation, and disproportionality theorists in the Soviet Union argued along just such lines. Pervushin argued against Bukharin in 1925 that credit restrictions in the late stages of the boom can prevent speculative overaccumulation, and so concluded that 'general overproduction and crises ... can only be explained on the basis of developments in the circulation of money, and of credit in particular' (quoted Day, 1981, 129). The Marxist Bazarov picked up this argument to see credit control as a form of indirect planning so that production would 'at all times and in all its components find itself under the control of real demand and thus would satisfy the latter in a *smooth manner* ... without crisis' (Day, 1981, 130). Lapinsky followed this line of argument to see the state, on the basis of the massive increase in state expenditure since the war, as 'the fundamental "regulating" organ' of capitalist society, which could control wages, prices and investments through the manipulation of money markets, although behind the state stands, in its turn, finance capital.[23]

Hilferding's theory was very popular among both Marxist and bourgeois economists in the 1920s, and there were many attempts to develop his theory of the investment cycle. However, while such a theory is intuitively very plausible, it faces a major empirical problem, which is that of showing that the periodicity of the cycle corresponds to the gestation period of the large investment projects that are supposed to determine its course. This is only part of the more general problem of relating crises, which always appear in the first instance as monetary phenomena, to their underlying causes in the conditions of the production and appropriation of surplus value. This problem has consistently been one of the strongest arguments in support of bourgeois theories of

---

[23] Day, 1981, 133–7. Hilferding increasingly came around to the view that the state could regulate capitalist accumulation, so that in the 1920s he came to believe that the priority was to democratise 'organised capitalism' rather than to transform it into socialism.

crisis, which have tended to see the cycle as a monetary phenomenon, and this monetary focus reasserted itself following the crash of 1929. Disproportionality theory has traditionally been dismissed by orthodox Marxists as inevitably reformist, in its implication that the defects of capitalism derive only from the anarchy of the market, and so can be remedied by improved co-ordination. However such a reformist politics by no means inevitably accompanies disproportionality theory. While appropriate monetary policies might be able to restrain over-investment if applied in the upswing, once overinvestment has taken place, monetary regulation can only restore stability through the devaluation of capital and destruction of productive capacity in a sustained depression. Thus disproportionality theorists in the 1930s argued against both Keynesians and Hayekians that only extensive state intervention to direct industrial restructuring could restore stability to the battered capitalist economies (c.f. Strachey, 1932).[24]

The more important political criticism of disproportionality theory, as it was developed by Hilferding, is that it identifies the deficiencies of capitalism at the level of the relations between capitalists, and not at the level of the class relation between capital and labour. It therefore tends to lead to corporatist conclusions, which can be reformist or revolutionary, but which are not specifically socialist. Although Hilferding was himself a staunch democrat, murdered by the Nazis, in the 1930s disproportionality theory came to be more closely identified with fascist corporatism, while the Communist movement was dominated by an underconsumptionism which, while theoretically crude, provided the focus for a politics which focussed on the hardship of the destitute working class rather than that of the bankrupt capitalists. The theoretical foundations of this underconsumption remained those developed by Rosa Luxemburg in her response to the revisionist critiques.

Rosa Luxemburg's Underconsumptionist Theory of Crisis

While Hilferding developed his disproportionality theory of crisis on the basis of Tugan's critique of underconsumptionism, Rosa Luxemburg rose to the revisionist challenge and attempted to set the theory of underconsumption on a rigorous foundation. Her book, *The Accumu-*

---

[24] Eaton (1951) was a later Marxist work which stressed, amongst other criticisms, that Keynesian remedies cannot deal with problems of disproportionality.

lation of Capital (AC), used Marx's reproduction schemes to assert the impossibility of capital accumulation in the absence of 'external' markets. The principal significance of Luxemburg's argument is that she shifted the emphasis of the orthodox theory of Engels and Kautsky towards a pure underconsumptionist theory. This underconsumptionism was used to explain the imperialist attempt to expand the market by destroying pre-capitalist production on a world scale, and at the same time to define the ultimate limits of capitalism, which determined its inevitable collapse once the conquest of the world was complete.

Luxemburg began her work by sharply distinguishing between the secular tendencies of capitalist accumulation and its cyclical form. She explained the cyclical form of accumulation as the accidental result of the anarchy of the market, but argued that 'the attempt to solve the problem of reproduction in terms of the periodical character of crises is fundamentally a device of vulgar economics' (AC, 36). The focus of her investigation, by contrast, was the secular tendency of accumulation, which she considered 'quite apart from the periodical cycles and crises' (AC, 35).[25]

The problem that Luxemburg raises is that of the source of the demand for the increasing product of capital corresponding to the increased surplus value that has been produced. This was not a problem for Tugan (or for Kautsky, Marx and Engels), who believed that capital accumulation has its own dynamic as competition compels capitalists to develop the forces of production without regard to the limits of the market, so that the additional demand, at least until markets are saturated and a crisis strikes, comes from other capitalists buying means of production and employing more workers. However Luxemburg argues that other capitalists will only employ more workers and demand more means of production if there is ultimately a market for the increased quantity of consumer goods which these means of production are destined to produce, so that investment presupposes an already existing increase in consumption.

Once Luxemburg has identified consumption rather than investment as the driving force of capitalist production, the problem becomes not so much that of explaining the breakdown of capitalism, but that of explaining how capitalism is possible at all. Demand cannot come from workers, because 'that implies a previous capitalist incentive to

---

[25] This is in accordance with the distinction that Luxemburg made between periodic crises, which had limited significance, and the terminal crisis that marked the breakdown of capitalism, which was the culmination of the secular tendencies of accumulation.

Rosa Luxemburg's Underconsumptionist Theory of Crisis 55

enlarge production; if new workers are set to work with new means of production, there must have been a new demand for the products which are to be turned out' (AC, 133). Luxemburg insists that third parties cannot fill the gap, since their income ultimately derives from wages or from surplus value. Nor can foreign trade produce the additional demand, since this simply shifts the problem from one country to another.

The only answer available to her is that capitalist accumulation is stimulated by sources of demand lying outside the capitalist system, and specifically from pre-capitalist modes of production, so that the very possibility of capitalism depends on its expansionist drive and its imperialist tendencies. This source of demand, however, is self-liquidating, as capitalist competition destroys the forms of production on which it is based. 'Capital cannot accumulate without the aid of non-capitalist organisations, nor, on the other hand, can it tolerate their continued existence side by side with itself' (AC, 416). The exhaustion of the pre-capitalist periphery leads to growing competition for the remaining markets, which marks the final phase of imperialism, which 'is the political expression of the accumulation of capital in its competitive struggle for what remains still open of the non-capitalist environment' (AC, 446), with the associated military expenditure, which, according to Luxemburg is financed by taxes on workers, and provides 'a pre-eminent means for the realisation of surplus value' (AC, 454).

Luxemburg's analysis has usually been criticised as being based on a crude misunderstanding of Marx's reproduction schemes. This is undoubtedly true, but it is beside the main point. Luxemburg accepts Tugan's use of the reproduction schemes to establish the *formal possibility* of capitalist reproduction, but she argues that the important issue is the dynamic question of the source of the *stimulus* to the expanded reproduction of capital. Thus Luxemburg criticises Bulgakov, Tugan and Lenin for their formalistic view of reproduction. Bulgakov 'believes that these mathematical *formulae* solve the problem of accumulation. No doubt we can easily imagine propositions such as he has copied from Marx, and *if there is expanding production*, these *formulae* will apply. Yet Bulgakov overlooks the principal problem: who exactly is to profit by an expansion such as that whose mechanism he examines?' (AC, 300)

The fallacy at the heart of Luxemburg's analysis is not her misunderstanding of the reproduction schemes, but her presumption that the spur to capitalist accumulation must come from an increased consumption demand, ignoring the fact that the driving force of capitalist production is not a growing demand, but the tendency to expand production without regard to the limits of the market, a tendency which is imposed on each individual capitalist by the pressure of competition, and which is driven by the constant revolutionising of the forces of production.[26]

Luxemburg's work was widely criticised for both the form of her argument and, even more, for the political conclusions that she drew from it, so that underconsumption theory came to be dissociated from Luxemburg's name. However Luxemburg had provided the only possible theoretical foundation for an underconsumptionist theory of crisis, in her insistence that only consumption can provide the ultimate spur to the expanded reproduction of capitalism, so that capitalism could only be sustained by external sources of demand.

Although underconsumption theory was much debated between the wars, and became the established orthodoxy in the 1930s, it made little theoretical advance. 'Varga's Law' defined Moscow's orthodoxy. According to Varga capital accumulation was associated with an absolute reduction in the number of productive workers employed, as workers were displaced by new technology and by the intensification of labour, so that the growth of production was associated not simply with a relative, but even with an absolute decline in consumption. In the West, Paul Sweezy's *Theory of Capitalist Development*, apart from providing a magisterial survey of the debate, sought to synthesize Luxemburg's underconsumptionism with an analysis of monopoly capitalism to provide a stagnationist theory according to which capitalism could be only be sustained by unproductive state and capitalist expenditure.

For Luxemburg imperialism and militarism provided the markets required to sustain capitalism, but in the 1920s the possibility that

[26] An alternative interpretation of Luxemburg's work has been proposed, which focuses not on the problem of demand, but on the problem of money (Marazzi, 1984). From this point of view the problem is not where does the demand come from, but where does the additional quantity of money required to realise that demand come from? Sweezy is dismissive of this aspect of Luxemburg's work, which he regards as 'a minor problem which is essentially irrelevant to her main thesis' (Sweezy, 1946, 204n.). Luxemburg also insisted that 'it is not the source of money that constitutes the problem of accumulation, but the source of the demand for the additional goods produced by the capitalised surplus value; not a technical hitch in the circulation of money but an economic problem pertaining to the reproduction of the total social capital' (AC, 147 c.f. 155, 159, 164–5, 300). Indeed she regards the formulation of the problem in terms of the question of 'the sources of money' as the basis of 'the flaw in Marx's analysis' (AC, 155), although Marx's purpose, as we shall see, was precisely to show that this is a non-problem.

rising wages and/or rising state expenditure might provide a renewed spur to accumulation was considered, raising the possibility that social democratic class collaboration might provide a basis for the stabilisation of capitalism, a possibility for which Keynes provided new theoretical foundations in the 1930s. There were obviously very close affinities between Keynesian and Luxemburgist underconsumptionism, the principal differences between Marxist and Keynesian underconsumptionist being not theoretical but political.

The dominant Marxist response to Keynes was to recognise that Keynesian reforms could in principle resolve the problem of underconsumption, but to argue that it was unrealistic to expect such reforms to be realisable under capitalism, since capitalists would resist attempts to expand consumption at the expense of profits, while no capitalist state could be expected to implement a Keynesian programme which put social need above profit (c.f. Sweezy, 1946). In the post-war period Keynesianism was adopted by the Western Communist Parties as the basis for a 'democratic road to socialism' through a political alliance between reformists and revolutionaries in which the balance of forces would shift in favour of the latter as, in the face of the inevitable crisis, capitalists resisted the attempt to bring the accumulation of capital under democratic social control.

Scepticism of the political practicality of Keynesian reformism persisted on the Left well into the 1950s, as the momentum of the postwar boom was sustained by the exceptional circumstances of reconstruction, re-armament and the development of new mass production industries.[27] However, as the boom persisted, underconsumptionist theories of secular stagnation and inevitable crisis appeared less and less convincing, while the claim that Keynesian reformism was in some way anti-capitalist appeared increasingly hollow. Underconsumptionism was now turned on its head, to explain the persistence of the boom as the result of Keynesian policies of public expenditure and fiscal regulation, the socialist character of the analyses lying in their identification of the class basis of such policies, with their emphasis on unproductive waste and military expenditure, rather than meeting basic human needs. Baran and Sweezy's *Monopoly Capitalism* (1966), and one version of the theory of the 'permanent arms economy' (Cliff, 1957) continued the underconsumptionist tradition, identifying the growth of 'unproductive expenditure' as the means by which capi-

---

[27] C.f. Dobb (1958) which is still anticipating the inevitable 1929.

tal had been able to avoid a crisis of overproduction without allowing the state to bring accumulation under democratic control.[28] Ernest Mandel's *Marxist Economic Theory* (1962), also remained firmly in the Keynesian mould, setting the Keynesian theory of the trade cycle on Marxist foundations as an integration of underconsumptionism and disproportionality theory. Aglietta's *Theory of Capitalist Regulation* (1979), has a similar theory for the regime of 'extensive accumulation', combined with a theory of disproportionality associated with the tendency for the rate of profit to fall for the regime of 'intensive accumulation' (Clarke, 1988a). Erik Olin Wright (1977) provided a similarly eclectic schema, with different theories appropriate to different historical periods. Thus Marxist underconsumptionism was gradually assimilated to a left Keynesianism, the differences between the two being primarily rhetorical rather than theoretical.

Crises Associated with the Falling Rate of Profit

The 1920s was dominated by the struggle between the followers of Hilferding and those of Luxemburg, with the underconsumptionists eventually emerging triumphant not on the basis of any analytical merits, but as a result of the triumph of Stalinism (Day). By the end of the 1930s Sweezy could dismiss disproportionality theory as a dead issue, 'a part of the history of socialist thought' whose 'intrinsic interest is not great' and which justly holds 'a position of secondary importance' (Sweezy, 1946, 161). For Sweezy the principal challenger to underconsumptionism was not disproportionality theory, but the law of the tendency for the rate of profit to fall, which had been linked to the tendency to crisis during the 1930s. The brief flourishing of this theory at that time can partly be explained as a response to the rise of Keynesian reformism and fascist corporatism, which claimed to resolve underconsumption and disproportionality crises on the basis of capital.

The law of the tendency for the rate of profit to fall had always been regarded in the orthodox Marxist tradition as a secular law that applied over the long run, and which had little or no significance for the theory of crisis. The tendency to crisis was linked to the growing

---

[28] An alternative formulation of the 'permanent arms economy' thesis saw military expenditure as a counter-tendency to the tendency for the rate of profit to fall by absorbing surplus capital unproductively (c.f. Kidron, 1970).

mass of profit, not to its falling rate, and the dismissal of the latter as a cause of crisis was linked to the observation that crises were generally preceded by a rise in the rate of profit, the fall in the rate of profit then being a result rather than a cause of the crash.[29]

The principal significance of a lower rate of profit was not in relation to the tendency to crisis, but in relation to the concentration and centralisation of capital. A low rate of profit put the greatest competitive pressure on the small and medium capitals which were identified as the source of the dynamism of capital accumulation, and so would intensify any underconsumptionist tendencies. Similarly small and medium capitals would be correspondingly more vulnerable in the crash if the rate of profit were lower. The tendency for the rate of profit to fall was seen as a factor which accelerated the concentration and centralisation of capital, and which might intensify the tendency to crises and ensure that successive crises are increasingly severe, but it was not in itself seen as a possible cause of crises.

Even if the rate of profit were to fall, there was not any obvious reason why a lower rate of profit should precipitate a crisis. The incentive to invest remains so long as the rate of profit remains positive.[30] On the other hand, the means available for investment are determined by the mass of profits and not by the rate. Even if the rate of profit has fallen each individual capitalist appropriates a larger mass of profit and so has the resources to finance both his consumption and his renewed investment.

We have noted above that Hilferding indicated that there was a contradiction between the 'expansion of consumption' and the 'realisation of profit', in the sense that an increase in wages would permit an increase in consumption, so overcoming underconsumption problems, but only at the cost of a fall in the rate of profit. However, this argument, as it is posed, is quite simply false: provided that wages have not risen so far as to exhaust the surplus altogether, the conditions for

---

[29] The revisionists, led by Tugan-Baranovsky, Croce, and Bortkiewicz had argued at the turn of the century that the rising organic composition of capital was associated with a rising rate of exploitation so that the tendency was, if anything, for the rate of profit to rise. Tugan noted that if the rate of profit did not rise, the new methods would not be introduced: 'the amount produced under the new technical conditions cannot on these assumptions decline, or there would be no economic sense in replacing hand production by machine labour' (*Studien*, 212, quote Howard and King, 1989, 188).

[30] All that is necessary is that the expected rate of profit on new investment should be positive — this might well be the case even if existing capitalists are all incurring losses so that the average rate of profit is negative.

the realisation of a profit are merely the conditions of proportionality for the realisation of the product as a whole. Provided that proportionality is maintained, the entire surplus can be raised however high or low may be the rate of profit. There is no contradiction involved here at all: underconsumption is not a result of an excessively high rate of profit, nor is a fall in the rate of profit the result of excessive consumption.[31]

Orthodox Marxists did not see the law of the falling rate of profit and the underconsumptionist theory of crisis as alternatives, but as complementary aspects of the same developmental tendencies, the former relating to the falling *rate* of profit, the latter deriving from the simultaneous rise in the *mass* of profit.[32]

The only case in which a fall in the rate of profit might precipitate a crisis would be that of what Marx called the 'absolute overaccumulation of capital', in which new investment was not able to earn a positive rate of profit at all (c.f. Hilferding, FC, 241–2). In the absence of other causes of a crisis this could only arise if wages had risen to such a level as to absorb the entire surplus value. This might happen if capital accumulation exhausted the reserve army of labour, the consequent fall in profits provoking a crisis.

Otto Bauer, in his critique of Luxemburg, developed an account of the business cycle along these lines, with the rate of accumulation being adjusted to the rate of growth of the labour force through the rise and fall of wages. 'The periodic alternation of prosperity, crisis, and depression is the empirical expression of the fact that the mechanism of the capitalist mode of production automatically generates overaccumulation and underaccumulation, with the accumulation of capital adjusting again and again to the growth of population' (O. Bauer, 'Die Akkumulation von Kapital', *Die Neue Zeit*, 31, 1913, 107, quoted Howard and King, 1989, 119). For Bauer this served as the basis for an explanation of international movements of capital and labour

---

[31] Ernest Mandel in his *Late Capitalism* (1972), puts forward a 'knife-edge' model of this kind, in which accumulation is threatened on two-sides: by realisation problems, if the rate of exploitation is too high, and profitability problems, if the rate of exploitation is too low. The tendency for the rate of profit to fall is then used as part of a neo-Schumpeterian long-wave theory, characteristic of a particular phase of the cycle. John Harrison (1978) proposes a similar dilemma.

[32] Wilson (1938) abandoned most of Marx's concepts, but provided a rigorous exposition of this interpretation, arguing that Marx had an eclectic theory of the trade cycle, but a long run theory in which the combination of a falling *rate* of profit with a rising *mass* of profit implied a tendency to underconsumption/underinvestment. Rosdolsky's *The Making of Marx's Capital* (1968/77) belongs strictly to the orthodox tradition in this respect.

in response to differences in wages and the rate of profit. Charasov, on the other hand, had proposed a theory of crisis in which the wage increases which eroded profit were not simply the result of market conditions, but the conscious result of working class struggle (quoted Grossmann, 1992, 50, c.f. Kühne, 1979, Vol II, 287).

This theory of 'overaccumulation with respect to labour power' was linked to the law of the falling tendency of the rate of profit by Erich Preiser in 1924. The normal Marxist expectation was that capital accumulation would not be curtailed by a shortage of labour power, because accumulation typically takes the form of the growing mechanisation of production, so that capitalism creates its own reserve army of labour. However, the extent to which accumulation takes this labour-saving form depends on the impact of mechanisation on the rate of profit.

If the increase in the organic composition of capital resulting from such mechanisation is not associated with a sufficient increase in the rate of exploitation, capitalists will continue to use the less mechanised but more profitable methods of production. However, providing that the rate of accumulation is greater than the rate of growth of the labour force, the expanded reproduction of capital will eventually face labour shortages, rising wages will erode profits, and this may provoke a crisis. Thus, in Preiser's formulation, the tendency for the rate of profit to fall does not manifest itself directly, but through the consequent overaccumulation with respect to labour power.

A similar formulation of the significance of the law of the tendency for the rate of profit to fall was proposed by John Strachey, for whom the falling rate of profit was not merely a tendency but an absolute law (Strachey, 1935, Part IV).[33] Strachey held to the orthodox view that 'it is the amount, and not the rate, of profit ... which matters'

---

[33] In an earlier work, *The Coming Struggle for Power* (1932), Strachey had drawn on Hayek's theory of over-investment and Keynes's *Treatise on Money* theory of under-investment, interpreting both as forms of disproportionality theory, exemplifying the anarchic consequences of the dissociation of savings from investment decisions in the face of the rising organic composition of capital, which he argued, is indeed 'at the root of the worst troubles of capitalism' (Strachey, 1932, 111n.). He criticised Hayek's monetary conservatism on the grounds that it would condemn capitalism to stagnation, amounting 'to saying that the way to have prevented crises in capitalism was to have prevented capitalism from ever arising' (ibid., 114n.). He criticised Keynes's belief that monetary policy could stabilise capitalism, by ensuring that the market rate of interest always coincided with the 'natural rate', on the grounds that the international movements of money capital made it impossible for nation states to pursue independent monetary policies, while the emergence of a world state is inconceivable. This kind of analysis tended to lead to corporatist rather than socialist conclusions, some socialist intellectuals of the early 1930s, such as Oswald Moseley, following the logic of the analysis and joining the fascist movement.

(ibid., 243). The impact of the fall in the rate of profit on the amount of profit is countered by rapid accumulation, the required pace being the more rapid the more the rate of profit falls. However, in rushing headlong from the threat of a fall in the mass of profit from one side, capital only confronts it on the other, as the exhaustion of the reserve army of labour leads to a fall in the mass of profit, and so precipitates a crisis.

Strachey was followed by Dobb, who argued in his *Political Economy and Capitalism* (1937) that 'it seems clear that Marx regarded this falling profit-rate tendency as an important underlying cause of periodic crises, as well as a factor shaping the long-term trend' (Dobb, 1940, 108). Although similar to Strachey, Dobb saw the fall in the rate of profit as the *result* of overaccumulation with respect to labour-power, whereas Strachey saw overaccumulation as the result of the attempt to stave off a fall in the mass of profit in the face of a predetermined fall in the rate. Moreover for Dobb this was one among a variety of possible forms of crisis, its realisation depending on contingent assumptions about the form of technological progress.

Neither Dobb nor Strachey explained why a rise in wages should provoke a crisis. A rise in wages is a normal part of the mechanism by which more backward capitalists are destroyed, to make space for the more advanced capitalists who replace them. If the rise in wages is particularly sudden, then it may erode the profits of the more advanced as well as the more backward capitalists, but such a rapid rise in wages is no more than a feature of the inflation that is an indication of the 'over-investment' identified by bourgeois economists as the cause of the crisis. A simple tightening of credit should restrain inflationary pressure, relieve the excessive pressure on the labour market, and avert the crisis. In short, if there is a crisis it is not because of the inherent and irremediable defects of capitalism, but because of the failure of the monetary authorities to restrain inflationary over-investment.

Neither Dobb nor Strachey spelt out their theory in any detail, and both soon moved away from the falling rate of profit theory of crisis, which was, moreover, in flagrant contradiction with 'Varga's Law' which became the Stalinist orthodoxy. The orthodox view of the theory of the falling rate of profit remained the dominant one until the 1970s. Thus Eaton (1951) dismissed the falling rate of profit as relating not to the cycle, but to the long-term trend, a view reiterated by Gillman in his *The Falling Rate of Profit* (1958), where he related the secular trend of the rate of profit to crisis theory in arguing that the importance of the theory was that it implied a deepening of successive crises.

The Reformulation of Marxist Crisis Theory in the 1970s

As the post-war boom approached its limits in the middle of the 1960s Keynesian orthodoxy, and the Marxist underconsumptionism which had become inextricably linked to it, began to unwind. Capitalism was unquestionable moving into a period of renewed crisis, which Keynesian measures proved unable to resolve. The crisis was marked in its first stages not by mass unemployment, but by a fall in the rate of profit and a decline in investment. The consequent decline in the rate of growth saw a rise in unemployment, associated not with deflation but with accelerating inflation. This 'stagflation' was a development which Keynesian underconsumptionism was unable to explain.

Every crisis is marked by a fall in the rate of profit. For underconsumptionists and disproportionality theorists alike the fall in profitability is a *result* of the crisis, as a lack of demand leads to falling prices and the failure to realise a profit. However, the fall in the rate of profit in the 1960s and 1970s was not associated with falling prices and appeared to have preceded the onset of crisis. By the early 1970s there was widespread agreement amongst Western Marxists that the fall in the rate of profit was the cause of the crisis and not its consequence.[34] However, heated theoretical debate centred on the causes of such a fall.

The central issue in this debate was whether the fall in the rate of profit which precipitated the crisis was the result of the erosion of profits by rising wages, either as the result of the growing militancy of the working class, or as a result of 'overaccumulation with respect to labour power', or whether it was an expression of Marx's 'law of the tendency for the rate of profit to fall', a result of the rising 'organic composition of capital' which was associated with the increasingly capital-intensive technology of production. The former explanations saw the crisis as a result of distributional changes, and were condemned by the proponents of the latter as 'neo-Ricardian'. The latter explanations saw the crisis as a result of changes in production technology, and were condemned by proponents of the former

---

[34] 'A falling-off of demand must stem from capital, and capital discontinues its demand only when the rate of profit falls. Thus logically, we can only deduce the overproduction of commodities from the fall in the rate of profit and not vice versa' (Cogoy, 1973, 64).

position as 'fundamentalist'. It is particularly striking that, although the proponents of each of these theories of crisis quoted extensively from Marx's works, neither of the theories could find any significant support from any earlier Marxist traditions.

Class struggle and capitalist crisis

The 'neo-Ricardian' view focussed on the distributional struggle between labour and capital, the source of the fall in the rate of profit being identified as rising wages. This approach related politically to the attempt to establish a continuity between the trade union militancy of the late 1960s and revolutionary politics.[35] The original formulation of this theory, in Glyn and Sutcliffe's *British Capitalism, Workers and the Profit Squeeze* (1972), emphasised the active role of working class militancy in forcing up wages and so provoking the crisis. However such a theory was widely condemned as non-Marxist, in focussing on distribution rather than production, and in being voluntaristic in its view of the class struggle.

In the absence of a mass socialist consciousness among the working class this analysis could easily be turned back on the working class, leading to reformist or even reactionary political conclusions, since crises are attributed not to the inherent contradictions of the capitalist mode of production, but to the demands of the working class. For the Trotskyite theory of 'transitional demands', with which this approach tended to be associated, the failure of capitalism to meet the material demands of the working class would stimulate the development of a socialist consciousness. However, the same theory could be (and was) used by the right-wing to argue that the failure of capitalism to meet the working class's aspirations was primarily the result of the 'mindless and irresponsible' militancy of a small minority of the working class, led astray by a politically motivated clique who dominate undemocratic trade unions. This implied that the solution to the crisis was not to overthrow capitalism, but to restrict wage increases and destroy the power of the organised working class in order to restore profitability, investment and prosperity for all.[36]

---

[35] The only Marxist precursor of this analysis that I have been able to discover is Charasov (1910). Boddy and Crotty developed a radical Keynesian version of the approach for the US (Boddy and Crotty, 1975).

[36] Many 'neo-Ricardians' of the early 1970s followed the logic of their theoretical position to become 'new realists' in the late 1970s, and even 'neo-liberals' in the 1980s.

The Reformulation of Marxist Crisis Theory in the 1970s 65

With the working class defeats of the late 1970s and early 1980s this approach lost its political foundations. It equally lost its theoretical plausibility as the offensive against organised labour was very effective in restoring the rate of profit through the 1980s, but did nothing to resolve the crisis tendencies of capitalist accumulation. By the late 1970s it was apparent that working class militancy was much more plausibly regarded as a defensive response to the crisis, and not as its cause. Workers had been militant in the late 1960s and early 1970s because the rate of growth of real wages fell as rising inflation eroded negotiated increases in money pay in the less successful capitalist economies.

Crisis and the law of the tendency for the rate of profit to fall

By contrast to the 'neo-Ricardians', the 'fundamentalists' insisted that the source of crises had to be located not in the 'subjective' conditions of the class struggle, but in the 'objective' tendencies of capitalist production, drawing on Marx's account of the law of the tendency for the rate of profit to fall.

In its pure form the falling rate of profit theory of crisis has tended to be associated politically with a sectarian millenarianism, the crisis being inscribed in the objective tendencies of accumulation regardless of the course of the class struggle, the task of the revolutionary sect being to prepare itself for the leadership role which will be thrust on it in the crisis. However, many contemporary Marxists rhetorically invoke the 'tendency for the rate of profit to fall' without associating it with any clear theory. In general the law has served not so much as the basis of a theory of crisis, as to indicate the absence of any such theory.

The law of the tendency for the rate of profit to fall derives from a simple mathematical relationship between the rate of profit, the rate of exploitation and the 'organic composition of capital'. If the total capital turned over in one year is composed of a constant component, C, which corresponds to the raw materials and means of production used, and V, which corresponds to the amount of capital laid out to buy labour power, the rate of profit is defined as the ratio of the surplus value produced in one year, S, to the total capital turned over, C + V. The rate of profit, $\frac{S}{(C+V)}$, can be expressed as $\frac{S/V}{(C/V+1)}$, where S/V is the rate of exploitation, and C/V is the ratio of constant to variable capital. It is then immediately obvious that the rate of profit varies directly with the rate of exploitation and inversely with the composition of capital. The historical tendency of capitalist production is to the progressive increase in the productivity of labour, so that each worker mobilises a growing mass of raw materials, and a progressive displacement of direct labour by machinery, so that each worker uses more fixed capital. In physical terms this means that there is clearly a tendency for the composition of capital to rise. The value expression of this composition may not rise so rapidly, because the machinery and the raw materials may become progressively cheaper compared to the cost of labour power, but it is not unreasonable to assume, as did Marx, that there is a constant tendency for the composition of capital to rise in value terms. With a given rate of exploitation, this would imply a constant tendency for the rate of profit to fall.

The tendency for the rate of profit to fall will be modified by factors which moderate the rise in the composition of capital. However, it will also be counteracted by the tendency for the rate of exploitation to rise which is inextricable linked to the tendency for the organic composition of capital to rise. The rising organic composition of capital and the rising rate of exploitation are complementary expressions of the increasing productivity of labour: with a given real wage increasing productivity immediately implies an increasing rate of exploitation. Whether the rate of profit falls, remains the same, or even rises, therefore depends on the relationship between the rate of increase in the composition of capital and the rate of increase in the rate of exploitation. There would seem to be no a priori theoretical reason to expect the rate of profit to fall rather than to rise (although it can be shown that its fall is 'ultimately' inevitable). This was the basis on which revisionists such as Tugan and Croce criticised the law at the end of the nineteenth century.

We have seen that the law of the tendency for the rate of profit to fall has never been attributed much significance by Marxists, and has very rarely been identified with the theory of crisis. Nevertheless a new orthodoxy became established during the 1970s according to which the falling rate of profit provided the only authentically Marxist theory of crisis, in contrast to the underconsumptionist theory which was a revisionist deviation introduced by the Marxists of the Second International. The source of this strange idea seems to be the inversion of Sweezy's argument in the *Theory of Capitalist Development*, which was the primary source for the regeneration of Marxian political economy in the 1960s. Sweezy presented the falling rate of profit theory of crisis as the logical alternative to the underconsumptionism that he himself espoused, although the only sources to which he referred were Dobb and Preiser who had, as noted above, offered a theory of the business cycle based on overaccumulation with respect to labour power.

The other source of the falling rate of profit theory of crisis was Paul Mattick's very influential *Marx and Keynes* (1969), which presented the falling rate of profit theory as the revolutionary alternative to Keynesian reformism. Mattick's argument derived from Grossmann's (1929) idiosyncratic 'shortage of surplus value' theory of overaccumulation, based on a bizarre representation of Marx's reproduction schemes. On the basis of a set of arbitrary arithmetical assumptions, that derived originally from Otto Bauer's critique of Luxemburg, Grossmann's model showed that capitalism would eventually collapse because the amount of investment required to maintain accumulation would be greater than the mass of surplus value appropriated by the capitalists. Grossmann was quite clear that this was not a falling rate of profit theory of crisis, insisting that the breakdown of capitalism cannot be derived from a fall in the rate of profit, so that 'an explanation is only possible when we relate the breakdown not to the rate of profit, but to its mass ... A falling rate of profit is thus only an index that reveals the relative fall in the mass of profit. The falling rate of profit is, moreover, only important for Marx in so far as it is identical with a relative decline in the mass of surplus value' (Grossmann, 1992, 103).

Mattick did not elucidate Grossmann's model, nor did he elaborate it rigorously. The strength of Mattick's work lay in its sharp rhetorical denunciation of Keynesian reformism on the basis of the contrast between underconsumptionism, which focuses on distribution and exchange, and the falling rate of profit, which focuses on the conditions of capitalist production. While the former type of crisis can be remedied by intervention at the level of distribution, the latter can only be remedied by the transformation of the social relations of production. Mattick's revolutionary rhetoric was then set on new theoretical foundations by David Yaffe and Mario Cogoy, who linked the tendency to crisis back directly to Marx's law of the falling tendency of the rate of profit, asserting that this is the only authentic Marxist theory of crisis (Yaffe, 1972; Cogoy, 1972, 1973).

The 'neo-Ricardians' responded to the 'fundamentalist' formulation of the law of the falling rate of profit with the standard criticisms of the law which date back to Croce and Tugan-Baranowsky. On the one hand, whether the rate of profit falls or rises depends simply on the relationship between the rate of increase of the organic composition of capital and the rate of increase of the rate of exploitation, and there is no special reason to expect the former to exceed the latter, so to expect the rate of profit to fall. On the other hand, if it is the case that an increase in the composition of capital would lead to a fall in the rate of profit, capitalists will not introduce the new method of production so that the rate of profit will not fall.

The 'fundamentalist' response to the first criticism was essentially to argue that the rate of profit must ultimately fall. While Tugan-Baranowsky was right in arguing that the impact of a rise in the organic composition of capital on the rate of profit could be offset by a corresponding rise in the rate of exploitation, the latter could not increase indefinitely. Moreover, a rise in the rate of exploitation implies the need for a further relative rise in demand for means of production, to compensate for the relative fall in demand for means of subsistence, and so demands a more rapid rise in the organic composition of capital. Thus mobilisation of the counter-tendencies to the tendency for the rate of profit to fall merely stimulates the more rapid rise in the organic composition of capital. At a certain point the rate of profit is bound to fall, provoking the inevitable crisis, but of course, as the neo-Ricardians noted, this point could be in the indefinite future.[37]

The second of Tugan's arguments was regarded as decisive by the neo-Ricardians. The capitalist's only purpose in introducing a new method of production is to increase the rate of profit that he can earn on his capital. If the new method would not increase his rate of profit, then he would continue to use the existing method of production and earn the old rate of profit. It might seem intuitively that the innovating capitalist would temporarily earn a higher rate of profit, which would then be reduced once the innovation is generalised.[38] However, if this

---

[37] Some falling rate of profit theorists, such as David Yaffe, interpreted the law as describing a permanent secular tendency. Others, such as Erik Olin Wright, 1977, saw it as a contingent possibility, characteristic of a particular stage of capitalist development.

[38] In his 1862 manuscript Marx noted that 'no capitalist voluntarily employs a new mode of production, even though it may be much more productive, and however high the ratio in which it increases the rate of surplus value, if it reduces the rate of profit' (CW33, 147). At first the innovator makes an extra profit by selling above his costs of production but below the value of the commodity, because 'his mode of production stands *above* the socially average level. Competition generalises this and subjects it to the general law. Then the fall in the rate of profit takes place, a law which is therefore completely independent of the will of the capitalist' (CW33, 147–8). This passage was incorporated by Engels as a 'supplementary remark' into Volume III of *Capital* (CIII, 259).

were the case the rate of profit could be increased by reverting to the old method of production. The generalisation of the innovation is a matter of redistributing the additional profit among the capitalists, and so it cannot reduce the rate of profit. This result was proved formally by Okishio (1961).

Although much was made of the 'Okishio theorem' in the 1970s, its significance is greatly exaggerated because it is a simple exercise in comparative statics, which makes no reference to disequilibrium or dynamics. The theorem does not prove that the rate of profit cannot fall, but at most that the proximate cause of a fall in the rate of profit must be something other than the increase in the composition of capital. Hilferding, in his discussion of the tendency for the rate of profit to fall, noted that in the first instance the increase in the organic composition of capital would be associated with an increase in the rate of profit, because investment in fixed capital has a long gestation period, the fall happening later as a result of the emergence of overproduction in the branches with a high organic composition of capital in the crisis. Strachey and Dobb saw the fall in the rate of profit as the proximate result of the increase in wages which resulted from overaccumulation with respect to labour power, which was itself a consequence of the barriers to the displacement of labour presented by the tendency for the rate of profit to fall.

Once the process of technical innovation is considered in the dynamic context the impact of innovation on the rate of profit is theoretically indeterminate, and there is no reason why the net impact might not be to lead to a fall in the rate of profit (c.f. John Weeks *Capital and Exploitation* (1981)). Anwar Shaikh has argued (1978), that a capitalist may rationally introduce a new method of production which cuts unit costs, even if it reduces the rate of profit, because it will enable him better to survive a competitive struggle.[39] It can further be shown, on this basis, that this strategy maximises the long-run rate of profit (Nakatani, 1980). A more satisfactory approach is that offered by Reuten (1991), who shows that if capitalists are using a range of

---

[39] The implication of Shaikh's argument is that a rational capitalist will maintain a range of technologies, to respond to changing circumstances. Thus, for example, the capitalist might combine plants with low unit costs, but a high organic composition of capital, which will remain profitable in the face of intense competition, with plants which have higher unit costs, but a lower organic composition, which can be moth-balled in the face of competition in a recession, and brought back on stream to raise the rate of profit in the boom. This implication clearly has a very direct application to the explanation of the uneven development of the forces of production in the course of accumulation.

technologies with different rates of profit, it is quite possible for an innovation to raise the rate of profit of the innovator at the expense of existing producers, so reducing the average rate of profit.

This whole debate is really a diversion from the central theoretical issue. It is clearly the case that there is no necessary tendency for the rate of profit to fall, and it is equally clearly the case that a fall in the rate of profit by one means or another is perfectly possible. However, the fundamental issue is not whether or not the rate of profit will fall, but why a fall in the rate of profit should lead to a crisis, rather than a smooth slowing down in the rate of accumulation.

Class Struggle and the Rate of Profit

The principal political weakness of the fundamentalist formulation of the law of the tendency for the rate of profit to fall was that it entirely detached the tendency to crisis from the development of the class struggle in presenting the law as the mechanical consequence of the increase in the organic composition of capital. This kind of criticism of fundamentalism led in two directions, each of which tried to integrate the analysis of the class struggle into the analysis of the tendency for the rate of profit to fall.

The first direction integrated the neo-Ricardian emphasis on the distributional struggle over wages with the fundamentalist analysis of the tendency for the rate of profit to fall by resurrecting the theory of overaccumulation with respect to labour power which had been proposed by Preiser, Strachey and Dobb, and presented by Sweezy as the most fruitful application of the theory of the falling rate of profit. The advantage of this theory is that it avoids both the voluntarism of the neo-Ricardian theory, which sees the fall in the rate of profit as the simple result of worker militancy, and the mechanistic economism of the fundamentalist theory, which neglects the role of class struggle in the determination of the rate of profit. The main source of this approach in contemporary Marxism has been the Japanese Uno School, and most particularly the work of Makoto Itoh (Itoh, 1980, 1988; Armstrong, Glyn and Harrison, 1984).

The Uno school does not link the theory of crisis directly to the tendency for the rate of profit to fall, but rests it on a model of monopoly capitalism based on monopolistic product markets and a competitive labour market, so that competition in the labour market replaces com-

Class Struggle and the Rate of Profit

petition in product markets as the spur to innovation. This leads to a model in which accumulation takes place with a fixed technology and a stable rate of profit until the pressure of rising wages squeezes profits, forcing a wave of labour-saving innovation and precipitating a crisis.[40] Itoh's development of the theory is a complex synthesis of neo-Ricardian, falling rate of profit, and disproportionality theories, each pertaining to a different phase of the cycle. The importance of Itoh's work is that, unlike almost all other falling rate of profit theorists, he does try to show how the fall in the rate of profit leads to a crisis. However, in doing so he effectively undermines his own theory, because in his account the cause of the crisis is not the fall in the rate of profit, but the failure of the fiscal and monetary authorities to check the inflationary over-expansion of the boom which leads to the erosion of profit, a failure which arises because his theory abstracts entirely from the role of the state.[41]

The second development shared the neo-Ricardian emphasis on the centrality of the class struggle, but shifted the focus from the struggle over distribution to the struggle over production.[42] This development was based on an interpretation of the law of the tendency for the rate of profit to fall which focused on Marx's analysis of the production of relative surplus value in Volume One of *Capital*, rather than his more mechanical presentation of the law of the tendency for the rate of profit to fall in Volume Three. The introduction of a new and more productive method of production will in the first instance have a depressing effect on the rate of profit by increasing the composition of capital. Of course this effect may be compensated by an increase in the rate of exploitation, but such an increase is not automatic and cannot be presumed. It can only be achieved by the capitalist as the outcome

---

[40] This idea that it is only through overaccumulation crises that the forces of production develop is a peculiar reversal of the orthodox Marxist view that it is the unfettered development of the productive forces which provokes crises.

[41] See my critique of Itoh and the Uno School (Clarke, 1989). Michel Aglietta's *Theory of Capitalist Regulation* and John Weeks's *Capital and Exploitation* also link the falling rate of profit to crisis via a theory of disproportionality and credit expansion.

[42] This approach was closely associated with the focus on the labour process stimulated by Harry Braverman's *Labour and Monopoly Capital* (1974) and by the Italian *autonomia* movement, and associated politically with an identification of growing shop-floor militancy as the focus of revolutionary politics. C.f. Bell, 1977. The focus on 'production' was a symbol of Marxist virility in the 1970s, carried to the most absurd lengths by the Althusserians. It rested on a metaphysical materialism according to which the immediate process of production was in some sense more 'real' than relations of distribution or exchange, which reflected a narrow conception of the class struggle which may have reflected the reality of the rank and file struggles of the 1960s, but which was already becoming out-dated by the mid-1970s.

of the struggle to intensify labour, extend the working day, and reduce the value of labour power. From this point of view the tendency for the rate of profit to fall is not an objective law, but an expression of the necessity of a constant class struggle in the sphere of production. The implication is that the source of crises is the resistance of the working class to the intensification of labour and the production of surplus value, which prevents the capitalist from appropriating sufficient profit.

While this approach avoids the mechanistic economism of the fundamentalist interpretation of the tendency for the rate of profit to fall, it shares the weakness of the neo-Ricardian theory in attributing the cause of the crisis to the resistance of the working class to capital, in this case the resistance to the restructuring of production. While this links the theory of crisis to the everyday reality of the class struggle, it does not necessarily lead to progressive conclusions. As in the case of the neo-Ricardian theory, if it is the resistance of the working class to the profitable introduction of advanced methods of production that leads to the crisis, the conclusion may be that capitalism should be overthrown, but it can equally be that such short-sighted resistance is detrimental to the interests of the working class, which are best served by class collaboration to meet the challenge of competition from other, especially foreign, capitalists and their workers. Both of these theories really only carried conviction for those in the mid-1970s who believed that capitalism was on the verge of a revolutionary crisis, in which socialism was on the immediate agenda. By the 1980s such a view had become unsustainable, and the theories associated with it could be seen to be inadequate.

Is There a Marxist Theory of Crisis?

Despite substantive differences, the approaches to the theory of crisis just considered all reflected the particular political and ideological conditions of the 1970s, and all came to a dead-end when those conditions changed in the early 1980s. On the one hand, the experience of defeat did not thrust the organised working class into the arms of the revolutionary left. On the other hand, the dramatic restoration of the rate of profit in the metropolitan centres of capitalism undermined revolutionary faith in the inevitability of crisis.

One response to this situation has been to abandon the theory of crisis altogether as misguided, 'essentialist', 'economistic' and 'dogmatic', in favour of an eclectic empiricism which finds particular causes for particular crises, plundering the various theories at will, or which sees different phases of accumulation as being marked by different kinds of crises, but which dissociates the 'political' struggle for socialism from the 'economic' development of capitalism. In abandoning the attempt to provide socialism with a foundation in the objective developmental tendencies of capitalism this response is closely associated today, as it was a century ago, with the return to an ethical conception of socialism, divorced from the material needs and aspirations of the working class which are expressed in the class struggle. Indeed for many the loss of socialist faith has led directly into a technologistic reformism, which acclaims the productive powers of new technology not as the harbinger of the crisis through which the working class would be forced to liberate itself from the capitalist yoke, but as a force which has made the class struggle irrelevant in offering liberation from the need to labour at all.

While such responses have an inherent ideological logic, there is something obscene about a socialism which turns its back on the deprivation, exploitation and oppression on a global scale which is as much a feature of capitalist accumulation today as it ever was. The inability of Marxists to develop an adequate theory of crisis by no means implies that the crisis tendencies have gone away. It may be the case that capitalism does not contain inherent crisis-tendencies, that the current dislocation of the capitalist system is merely the result of institutional and political failures, and that capitalism can be reformed on the basis of a humanitarian ethic. On the other hand, it is certainly the case that every attempt to reform capitalism on such a basis hitherto has failed, which would indicate that the attempt to discover necessary reasons for such a failure, rather than attribute it to contingent factors, is not dogmatism, but is the supreme responsibility of socialist, or even humanitarian, intellectuals.

Just as Marxists appear to be abandoning the idea that capitalism has inherent limits, the very same idea is becoming more widespread beyond the Marxist ghetto. The more far-sighted economists ask whether the recession of the early 1990s might not be different from previous recessions in having a structural character that prevents it from being rectified with any of the traditional policy instruments. On a much larger scale, there is an increasingly widespread belief that capitalism will founder not on its social or economic contradictions, but by destroying the global environment, and with it perhaps human life itself. The distinctiveness of the Marxist perspective is that it looks for the causes of crisis not in natural or quasi-natural economic, psychological or ecological limits, but in the social relations of the capitalist mode of production, and it looks for the resolution of crisis through the transformation of those social relations not from above but from within. It is ironic that a Marxist theory would seem to be most relevant and most necessary just at the point in history at which Marxism appears to be at its lowest theoretical ebb.

The failure of the theories of the 1970s to explain the crisis tendencies of capitalist accumulation should not lead us to abandon the attempt altogether, but to look for new foundations on which to build the theory. To develop such foundations it is necessary to return to first principles, to provide a basis on which to build a theory adequate to the crisis-ridden reality of global capitalism.

In this chapter I have briefly surveyed the development of Marxist theories of crisis over the past century. The most striking feature of this story is the extent to which such theories have progressively abandoned their distinctive Marxist foundations. An adequate theory of crisis must be a theory of the dynamics of the capitalist mode of production, which establishes the tendency to crisis as something inherent in those dynamics. The limits of capitalism have to be identified as something *internal* to capitalism. This is what is meant by saying that capitalist rests on a 'contradictory foundation' — we have to identify the forces that drive capitalism forward, but simultaneously drive it to its destruction.

Engels identified such a force in the tendency of capitalist competition to compel every capitalist to develop the forces of production without regard to the limits of the market, on the one hand, and the need for the capitalist to find a market for the final product in order to realise his expanded capital, on the other. This contradiction between the production of surplus value and the realisation of the surplus value through the sale of the use-values produced is the specific developed form of the fundamental contradiction of the capitalist mode of production between value and use-value, between the social relations and the forces of production. It therefore defines the tendency to crisis as inherent in the social relations of capitalist production, and a tendency that can only be overcome by going beyond the limits of capitalism.

Engels identified the consequence of this contradiction as being an inherent tendency to overproduction, as the development of production ran ahead of the growth of the market, which he saw as the basis of

Is There a Marxist Theory of Crisis? 75

the capitalist cycle of overaccumulation and crisis. Kautsky turned Engels's crisis theory into a theory of the secular tendency to underconsumption, replacing it by an explanation of crises in terms of the 'anarchy of the market'.

The revisionist critique of Marxism, most rigorously developed by Tugan-Baranovsky, undermined Kautsky's secular theory by showing that the barrier to the expansion of capitalist production lay not in underconsumption, but in disproportionality. The Marxist response to this critique was to move even further from Engels's formulation of the theory of crisis. Both Hilferding's and Luxemburg's theories removed the tendency to develop the forces of production without limit, which for Marx and Engels had been the driving force, the historical justification, and the ultimate limit of the capitalist mode of production, to replace it with the notion on which bourgeois economics was built, that it is the development of the market and the growth of consumption that is the driving force of capitalism. This led Hilferding to develop what was essentially an orthodox bourgeois theory of the business cycle, and Luxemburg a classically bourgeois theory of underconsumption (the former leading to Schumpeter and Hayek, the latter to Joan Robinson). Although both of these theories purported to show that the necessity of crisis was inherent in the social form of capitalist production, the growth of state intervention in the inter-war period progressively undermined the radicalism of both disproportionality and underconsumption theories of crisis.

The regeneration of Marxist crisis theory in the 1970s rejected both underconsumptionist and disproportionality theories to focus on the fall in the rate of profit that was supposedly the cause of the crisis although, as we have seen, no satisfactory explanation was provided of why a fall in the rate of profit should lead to a crisis. Although these theories appeared to reject the previous Marxist orthodoxies, this rejection was not as radical as it appeared. The basic critique of both underconsumptionist and disproportionality theories was that they focussed exclusively on relations of distribution and exchange, without any consideration of the determining role of capitalist relations of production, but this led to an equally one-sided emphasis on the barriers to the production of surplus value in the relation between capital and labour.

Although this single-minded focus on the capitalist class relation, in abstraction from the relations between particular capitals, sounded impeccably Marxist, it implied, explicitly or explicitly, the adoption of the general equilibrium framework of bourgeois economics. The adoption of a general equilibrium framework did not necessarily imply a belief that capitalism tended towards such equilibria, but rested on the insistence that the *necessity* of crisis had to be explained on the basis of the *production* of surplus value, in abstraction from the contingency of the 'anarchy of the market'. However the exclusive focus on the conditions of production makes it impossible to explain crises, because a crisis always takes the form of a *breakdown* in the circulation process of capital.

The weakness of the classical Marxist theories of crisis was not their one-sided concentration on the exchange relations between capitalists, as against an equally one-sided concentration on the production relation between capital and labour. It lay in their failure to analyse the relations between particular capitals within the context of an analysis of the reproduction process of capital as a whole, of which production, distribution and exchange are all necessary moments. This meant that they could provide very plausible accounts of the dynamics of crisis, without being able to provide any explanation of their foundations in the social relations of capitalist production. Contemporary theories fell into the opposite trap, of providing fundamentalist accounts of the social relations of production which could not account for crises.

It seems that the Marxist theory of crisis leads nowhere but to a series of dead ends. Yet the problem that Marx posed of explaining the crisis tendencies of capitalist accumulation remains to be solved. Marx did not provide a simple answer to this problem, but at least he presents the question in more productive ways than have his successors. Before we decide to wipe the slate completely clean, it is worth turning to the works of Marx himself.

3
Overproduction and Crisis in the Early Works

Engels's theory of crisis

The origins of the Marxist theory of crisis can be found in Engels's earliest economic work, the *Outlines of a Critique of Political Economy* (1843), which was the work which first brought Marx into contact with Engels, and which drew Marx to the study of political economy.

Engels's critique of political economy focused on the economic and moral evils to which competition gave rise. Competition was explained as the result of the private ownership of the means of production, and was in turn the foundation of both the class antagonism and the periodic crises on which Engels based his condemnation of capitalism.

Engels's theory of crisis is initially based on the 'anarchy of the market'. Producers are ignorant of the needs of buyers, which they only discover through the rise and fall of prices. The rise and fall of prices does not lead to the economists' smooth adjustment to equilibrium, but to the alternation of overproduction, stimulated by a rise in prices, and slump, provoked by their fall.[1] However, Engels also brings in another more fundamental factor underlying the tendency to crisis. Capitalism is marked by a constant tendency to overproduction driven by the pressure of competition, which ensures that the tendency to crisis is not accidental but systematic, crises being only the most dramatic manifestation of the secular tendency to overproduction, which is the source of both the dynamism of capitalism and of its historical limits.

With the development of capitalism, the centralisation of capital and the growth of monopoly mean that instability is generalised to all branches of production and extends to the world scale, so that the accumulation of capital takes on the cyclical form of boom and

---
[1] As we saw in the last chapter, this was the theory of the cycle proposed as the basis of the theory of crisis by Kautsky and Hilferding.

slump. Finally, Engels identifies the regular displacement of labour in the cyclical alternation of boom and slump as the essential mechanism through which the proletariat is formed as a revolutionary class. This is the basic model of crisis which recurs throughout the works of Marx and Engels, although Marx progressively refined its theoretical foundations.

Engels's critique of political economy was an attempt to show that private property is at the root of all the evils of the capitalist system. The basis of this demonstration was the conflict of economic interests to which private property gives rise in the sphere of competition. Thus Engels argued that 'the immediate consequence of private property is *trade*', which is immediately and necessarily antagonistic, based on 'diametrically opposed interests' and giving rise to 'mutual mistrust'. Values are established in the market, through the conflict between producers and consumers, a conflict which economists try to conceal by isolating value from exchange, reducing it either to production costs or to subjective utility, whereas the concept has no meaning in abstraction from the relation between the two in exchange. In the same way the economists conceal the conflict which underlies the distribution of the product. The economists' theory of rent claims that rent derives from differences in the productivity of the soil, whereas it is in fact determined by 'the relation between the productivity of the land, the natural side ... and the human side, competition'. Similarly the distribution of the product between profit, interest, rent and wages is not carried out according to some 'inherent standard; it is an entirely alien, and, with regard to them, fortuitous standard, that decides — competition, the cunning right of the stronger'. Thus the evil of private property is that it introduces fragmentation, setting capitalist against capitalist and worker against worker. 'In this discord ... is consummated the immorality of mankind's condition hitherto; and this consummation is competition' (CW3, 419, 421, 422, 429, 431, 432).

Private property not only establishes society on the basis of the antagonism of interest, it also determines a permanent imbalance between supply and demand. Engels's initial explanation for this imbalance, and for the crises to which it gives rise, is in terms of the instability of the adjustment process which follows from the ignorance of the economic actors. Supply

> is either too big or too small, never corresponding to demand; because in this unconscious condition of mankind no one knows

how big supply or demand is. If demand is greater than supply the price rises and, as a result, supply is to a certain degree stimulated. As soon as it comes on to the market, prices fall; and if it becomes greater than demand, then the fall in prices is so significant that demand is once again stimulated. So it goes on unendingly — a permanently unhealthy state of affairs — a constant alternation of over-stimulation and flagging which precludes all advance — a state of perpetual fluctuation without ever reaching its goal. This law with its constant adjustment, in which whatever is lost here is gained there, is regarded as something excellent by the economist. ... Yet it is obvious that this law is purely a law of nature and not a law of the mind. It is a law which produces revolution. The economist comes along with his lovely theory of demand and supply, proves to you that "one can never produce too much", and practice replies with trade crises, which reappear as regularly as the comets ... Of course these commercial upheavals confirm the law, confirm it exhaustively — but in a manner different from that which the economist would have us believe to be the case. What are we to think of a law which can only assert itself through periodic upheavals? It is certainly a natural law based on the unconsciousness of the participants. If the producers as such knew how much the consumers required, if they were to organise production, if they were to share it out amongst themselves, then the fluctuations of competition and its tendency to crisis would be impossible. Carry on production consciously as human beings — not as dispersed atoms without consciousness of your species — and you have overcome all these artificial and untenable antitheses. But as long as you continue to produce in the present unconscious, thoughtless manner, at the mercy of chance — for just so long trade crises will remain; and each successive crisis is bound to become more universal and therefore worse than the preceding one; is bound to impoverish a larger body of small capitalists, and to augment in increasing proportion the numbers of the class who live by labour alone, thus considerably enlarging the mass of labour to be employed (the major problem of our economists) and finally causing a social revolution such as has never been dreamt of in the philosophy of the economists. (CW3, 433–4)

Although Engels initially explains periodic crises simply in terms of the ignorance of the economic actors, it subsequently becomes clear that the imbalance of supply and demand is systematic, its source lying in the constant tendency to *overproduction*, which is the necessary result of competition.

> The struggle of capital against capital, of labour against labour, of land against land, drives production to a fever-pitch at which production turns all natural and rational relations upside-down. No capital can stand the competition of another if it is not brought to the highest pitch of activity ... No one at all who enters into the struggle of competition can weather it without the utmost exertion of his energy, without renouncing every truly human purpose. The consequence of this over-exertion on the one side is, inevitably, slackening on the other. (CW3, 427)

Engels does not explain *why* the rapid growth of production under the pressure of competition should lead to overproduction, but merely implies that those capitalists, workers or landowners who cannot withstand the pressure of competition find themselves redundant, because 'in the struggle the stronger wins' (CW3, 440), driving out the weaker. At first this redundancy exists alongside superabundance, but as capitalism develops this co-existence appears successively in the cyclical fluctuations of production.

> When the fluctuation of competition is small, when demand and supply, consumption and production, are almost equal, a stage must be reached in the development of production where there is so much superfluous productive power that the great mass of the population has nothing to live on, that the people starve from sheer abundance. For some considerable time England has found herself in this crazy position, in this living absurdity. When production is subject to greater fluctuations, as it is bound to be in consequence of such a situation, then the alternation of boom and crisis, overproduction and slump, set in. (CW3, 435–6)

Thus the ultimate expression of the contradictory character of the capitalist mode of production lies in this alternation of boom and crisis, and in the coexistence of poverty and superabundance, of over-work and unemployment (CW3, 436).

In his *Condition of the English Working Class* (1844–5) Engels equally links the crisis-tendencies of capitalism to competition (CW4, 508) and to the ignorance and uncertainty attached to the market, where co-ordination of supply and demand depends on 'luck', as 'everything is done blindly, as guess-work, more or less at the mercy of accident' (CW4, 382). However he also fills a gap in the analysis in linking the lack of co-ordination of supply and demand in individual markets to the overall cycle, the link being provided by the centralising tendencies of competition, the growing monopolisation of industry linking discrete cycles together into the regular five-yearly cycle. The resulting cyclical fluctuations in employment, and the regular augmentation of the 'reserve army' of labour by technological innovation (CW4, 384, 429), foster the growth of an organised working class, so that Engels refers to commercial crises as 'the mightiest levers for all independent development of the proletariat' (CW4, 580).

Marx's Early Development of Engels's Analysis

Engels's youthful *Outlines of a Critique of Political Economy* was both the beginning and the end of his original economic studies, but it provided only the starting point for Marx. Although Marx always paid homage to Engels's *Outlines*, in his own economic writings he went far beyond Engels's superficial analysis, and this led Marx to a rather different understanding of the character and significance of economic crises. Even though the differences are not immediately obvious, they have quite fundamental implications.

Marx's first economic writings, his *Comments* on James Mill's *Elements of Political Economy*, and the *Economic and Philosophical Manuscripts* of 1844, developed Engels's critique of capitalism, but set it on a quite different foundation. Marx picked up Engels's criticism of the economists' law of supply and demand as the starting point of his own critique of political economy. He begins his *Comments* on James Mill by noting that demand and supply are only in equilibrium 'sporadically, fortuitously', so 'it is just as much a *constant law* that they are not in equilibrium'. The real movement is one of fluctuation and disproportion, but 'this *real* movement, of which that law is only an abstract, fortuitous and one-sided factor, is made by recent political economy into something accidental and inessential' (CW3, 210). Marx does not stop here, but moves immediately beyond competition to look at money, in which 'the *human*, social act by which man's products mutually complement one another, is *estranged* from man and becomes the attribute of money, a *material thing* outside man', a decisive step that transforms the critique of political economy by attacking its theoretical foundations (CW3, 212).

Engels had established that private property was the foundation of the capitalist mode of production, and had argued that it was the root of all the evils of capitalism, but 'private property' remained an unexplored premise of Engels's analysis. In his writings of 1844 Marx explored this premise, and in so doing transformed Engels's analysis.

For Engels private property and exchange were inseparable, but property remained the foundation of exchange. Marx displaced the institution of private property from this fundamental role, arguing that private property is only the juridical expression of a more fundamental relation, the social relation of commodity production, in which production is subordinated not to the 'cunning right of the stronger', but to money, in which the social character of production confronted the producer as an external force. This led to a fundamentally different analysis of the social form of capitalist production to that proposed by Engels.[2]

Engels had focused on the conflict of interest between the owners of private property which was expressed in competition. However Marx did not see the exchange relation as expressing a superficial conflict of wills, but he saw it as a *mediated* relationship, in which exchange took the form of the purchase and sale of commodities for money. Behind this mediated exchange lies the subordination of social production to the alienated power of money. The *exchange* relation is merely the expression of the social relations of *commodity production*.

The relation between private property owners expressed in the exchange of commodities presupposes the existence of particular social relations of production, in which things are produced as commodities. The distinctive feature of commodity production is that things are not produced directly for social need, but are produced for sale, in order to acquire money. Things are produced not as use-values, but as values. The exchange relation is not a relationship between the owners of *private* property, since things have no value as *private* property. The plantation owner has no use for his bales of cotton, and the mill owner has no use for his rolls of cloth. If these things cannot be sold, they have no value, and may simply be destroyed or disposed of.

Things only acquire value when they are evaluated socially, in their exchange for money, through which they are related to all other

---

[2] This fundamental difference has escaped the attention of the commentators on Marx's and Engels's early works. For a fuller discussion see Clarke, 1991, Chapter 3.

commodities. Modern private property is a social quality of things, which they only acquire in consequence or in anticipation of their production and sale as commodities. 'The social relationship of private property to private property is already a relationship in which private property is estranged from itself. The form of existence for itself of this relationship, money, is therefore the alienation of private property, the abstraction from its *specific*, personal nature.' (CW3, 213)

Things only come to 'have value insofar as they *represent*' money, so that money is 'the lost, estranged *essence* of private property, private property which has become *alienated*, external to itself' (CW3, 212). The exchange relation is based not on the institution of private property, but on the social form of commodity production, in which production for social need takes the *alienated* form of the production of commodities, of which private property is merely the juridical expression. '*Private property* is thus the product, the result, the necessary consequence, of *alienated labour*, of the external relation of the worker to nature and to himself' (CW3, 279).

The exchange relation does not simply relate supply and demand, cost of production and utility, producer and consumer, as Engels had argued, but more fundamentally expresses the social relation between 'private' producers. It is only through the purchase and sale of commodities that private producers establish a social relationship between one another as participants in social production, so that the exchange relation relates not producer to consumer, but private to social labour. In exchange the product of private labour appears in the alienated form of the commodity, the price of the commodity being the form in which private labour is evaluated socially, and expressed as a sum of money. Thus commodity *production* is the foundation of both private property and commodity *exchange*.

The fundamental contradiction of the capitalist mode of production lies not in the conflict of wills expressed in competition, but in the social form of *alienated labour*, in which the social character of the producer's labour confronts the producer in the form of *money*, and in which production for social need only takes place in the alienated form of production for profit. 'What was the domination of person over person is now the general domination of the *thing* over the *person*, of the product over the producer. Just as the concept of the *equivalent*, the value, already implied the *alienation* of private property, so *money* is the sensuous, even objective existence of this *alienation*' (CW3, 221).

The exploitative character of the capitalist mode of production similarly lies not in the inequality of exchange, expressed in the 'cunning right of the stronger', but in the appropriation of labour without equivalent in production, based on the social form of wage labour in which the capitalist, as the owner of property, confronts the propertyless worker.

The implication of this analysis for the understanding of crises is that the roots of economic crises lie not in the accidental imbalance of supply and demand, but in the alienated confrontation of use-value and value, which appears in the confrontation of the commodity, as a use-value which is the concrete product of private labour, with money, as bodily form of that value which is the alienated form of social labour. This implication Marx began to develop in his works of the 1850s.

The Dynamics of Capitalist Production and the Tendency to Crisis

Engels declared himself Marx's unswerving disciple, but echoes of his earliest ideas appear in his own later work and in his popularisations of Marx. Whether the differences between Marx and Engels are a matter of substance, or merely a matter of emphasis, remains to be seen. However it is worth noting that Engels's focus on supply and demand implies a focus on the commercial crisis as the decisive moment of the crisis, and also implies that the displacement of competition by planning can eliminate the crisis tendencies of capitalism, and these are preoccupations that recur throughout Engels's work. Marx, on the other hand, was interested not so much in the relation between supply and demand as in the relation between the expenditure of productive labour as the basis of value and the realisation of that value in the form of money. This is reflected in Marx's detailed interest in banking and in financial crises, which was not shared by Engels. Moreover the implications of Marx's analysis are also much more radical, the elimination of crises requiring the abolition not merely of competition, but of the social form of capitalist production.

Marx did not follow up Engels's discussion of crises in his earliest works, since his main theoretical concern was to develop a methodological critique of the fundamental concepts of political economy, although he clearly took for granted the tendency to overproduction as a direct consequence of the growth of the forces of production (CW3,

258, 263, 310). It was only with Marx's first involvement with the emerging working class movement, in the Communist League which he joined in early 1847, that Marx turned his attention to more concrete economic developments. The first indication of this change of emphasis is to be found in *The Poverty of Philosophy*, written in the first half of 1847.

Marx's discussion of crises in *The Poverty of Philosophy* brings out the difference of emphasis between his and Engels's understanding of the capitalist mode of production. Marx explains 'overproduction and many other features of industrial anarchy' (CW6, 136) not simply as the result of competition, or the 'utmost exertion' of the capitalist's energy, but more fundamentally as the result of the 'evaluation of commodities by labour time', of which competition is only the superficial expression. In the capitalist mode of production every producer seeks to reduce the labour time necessary for production by developing the forces of production, and correspondingly increasing its scale. This leads to an increase in the quantity of commodities produced, and a fall in their price, as the more advanced producers displace those who have been less successful. Competition from more advanced producers depreciates the existing product, produced by older methods, breaking down the proportionality of production and consumption so that 'production is inevitably compelled to pass in continuous succession through the vicissitudes of prosperity, depression, crises, stagnation, renewed prosperity, and so on' (CW6, 137). Thus it is not just the anarchy of capitalist competition that gives rise to crises, but the conditions of capitalist production. Overproduction is the means by which backward producers are forced out of the market, and so is not just an accident of competition, but is its essential form in a capitalist society. Overproduction is the price that has to paid for the development of the forces of production within the capitalist mode of production. This implies that crises are not features of the *market* economy, but of the developed *capitalist* mode of production, whose driving force is the development of the forces of production.

In earlier times supply and demand had remained more or less in proportion to one another while 'it was demand that dominated supply, that preceded it. Production followed close on the heels of consumption. Large-scale industry, forced by the very instruments at its disposal to produce on an ever-increasing scale, can no longer wait for demand. Production precedes consumption, supply compels demand. In existing society, in industry based on individual exchange, anarchy of production, which is the source of so much misery, is at the same time the source of all progress' (CW6, 137).[3] In a letter to Annenkov (28.12.46) this argument is presented more fully, and the tendency to overproduction resulting from the transformation of the forces of production is related directly to the struggle between capitalist and workers over the production of surplus value. 'Until 1825 — the time of the first world crisis — one could say that the requirements of general consumption overtook production and that the development of machinery was the necessary consequence of market requirements'.[4] However in England, 'since 1825, the invention and the use of machinery has only been the result of the war between employers and workers', as employers have sought to displace their recalcitrant and increasingly militant skilled workers by machines.[5] British competition has in turn forced European and US capitalists to introduce the new methods of production in their turn, capitalists in the US also having the incentive of labour scarcity (CW38, 99). Thus the crisis tendencies of capitalist accumulation date from 1825, the point at which the driving force of capitalist accumulation becomes the development of the forces of production driven by the production of relative surplus value.

In *Wage Labour and Capital*, a series of lectures given in Brussels in December 1847 but only published in 1849, Marx develops in much more detail his explanation for the inherent tendency to overproduction.[6] The capitalist can only compete if he can sell more

---

[3] Marx stressed the priority of production over consumption in *The German Ideology*, noting that 'precisely those economists who took consumption as their starting point happened to be reactionary and ignored the revolutionary element in competition and large-scale industry' (CW5, 518–9).

[4] Engels had dated regular trade crisis back eighty years, to the 1760s (CW3, 433).

[5] This argument derived from Marx's reading of Andrew Ure. In the notes for his lectures on wages, written in December 1847, he similarly refers to the 'invention of machines in consequence of the combinations', and notes that 'every development of new productive forces is at the same time a weapon against the workers' (CW6, 420, 423). However, in the text of the lectures, which he published in April 1849 under the title *Wage Labour and Capital* (discussed below), he related the introduction of machinery to the concentration and centralisation of capital, which enabled capitalists to respond to growing competitive pressure by *bringing more powerful labour armies with more gigantic instruments of war into the industrial battlefield* (CW9, 222–3). These two different views of the dynamics of capital accumulation, the one relating it to the class struggle, the other to the inherent tendencies of capitalist accumulation, recur throughout Marx's work. Compare *Capital*, Volume One, Part IV.

[6] It seems that he had been discussing the matter with Engels, since Engels gave a lecture in London a few days earlier, in which he was reported to have proved 'that commercial crises are caused only by overproduction and that the stock exchanges are the main offices where proletarians are made' (CW6, 632), the text of which has not survived.

The Dynamics of Capitalist Production and the Tendency to Crisis 87

cheaply, and he can only sell more cheaply, without ruining himself, if he can produce more cheaply. 'But the productive power of labour is raised, above all, by *a greater division of labour*, by a universal introduction and continual improvement of *machinery*', and this, for Marx, is a function of the scale of production.

The capitalist who manages so to raise the productivity of labour must sell the increased product.

The more powerful and costly means of production that he has called into life *enable* him, indeed, to sell his commodities more cheaply, they *compel* him, however at the same time to sell more commodities, to conquer a much *larger* market for his commodities; consequently, our capitalist will sell his half yard of linen more cheaply than his competitors. ...He drives them from the field, he wrests from them at least part of their sales, by *underselling them*. ...However, the *privileged position* of our capitalist is not of long duration; other competing capitalists introduce the same machines ... on the same or on a larger scale, and this introduction will become so general that the price of linen is reduced not only *below its old*, but *below its new cost of production*. (CW9, 222-4)

This account of capitalist competition and the development of the forces of production is very different from that of the economist. For the economist, who presumes that every capitalist has perfect foresight, supply adjusts smoothly to the limits of demand as capitalists respond to present and anticipated changes in price. However, for Marx the process of competitive adjustment to technical change is by no means smooth. The capitalist does not increase production in response to the stimulus of the market, but is compelled to introduce new methods of production under the pressure of competition, as the condition for expanding the size of his capital, or even for maintaining it intact. The result of the introduction of these new methods of production is a reduction in costs, but also an increase in the quantity produced, both because of the increased scale of production, and because the innovating capitalist expects to be able to sell this increased product profitably, on the basis of his reduced costs of production. However, the increased production represents an *overproduction of commodities*, in relation to the earlier price and conditions of production, which can only be disposed of by reducing the price below the cost of production of the other capitalists, and so driving them from the market. In the face of this crisis of overproduction smaller capitalists may be driven from the field, but the larger competing capitalists by no means submit to their fate. They adopt the new methods of production in their turn, 'on the same or on a larger scale', leading to a further growth in production to the extent of an overproduction even in relation to the cost price appropriate to the new conditions of production.

This analysis of the dynamics of capitalist production distinguishes Marx's analysis of the capitalist mode of production most fundamentally from both classical political economy and modern economics, and its importance, which has been largely neglected even by 'Marxist economists', cannot be emphasised too strongly. The whole sophisticated edifice of bourgeois economics rests on the fragile foundation of its assumption that capitalist production tends to adjust itself to the limits of the market, the failure of such an adjustment being treated as a superficial imperfection, resulting from the subjective ignorance, uncertainty or misjudgement of individual capitalists. This is only an expression of its fundamental assumption, derived from Adam Smith that 'consumption is the sole end and purpose of all production', with profit as no more than the contingent reward for virtue which falls to the capitalist. Smith claimed that this maximum is 'so self-evident that it would be absurd to attempt to prove it' (Smith, 1910, Vol. 1, 385). despite the fact that it is transparently false and patently absurd, immediately contradicted by the very existence of capitalism.

The purpose of capitalist production is not consumption, but the appropriation of profit and the accumulation of capital. The means to the accumulation of capital is not the satisfaction of consumer need, the limit of which is only an unfortunate barrier that the capitalist has to overcome, but the development of the forces of production. The need to develop the forces of production is not merely an expression of the subjective motivation of the capitalist, but is imposed on the capitalist by the pressure of competition, which is no more and no less than the pressure of the immanent and self-reproducing tendency to overproduction, which compels every capitalist to expand production by developing the forces of production *without regard to the limits of the market*. The tendency to overproduction is not the result of ignorance or misjudgement of the limits of the market, since the innovating capitalist is able to dispose profitably of the whole of his expanded product, while the limits of the market only impose themselves on other capitalists *as a result* of the overproduction of commodities.

The tendency to overproduction and crisis is both the cause and

The Dynamics of Capitalist Production and the Tendency to Crisis 89

the consequence of the capitalists' revolutionising of the means of production. It is the form through which new methods of production displace the old. 'We see how in this way the mode of production and the means of production are continually transformed, revolutionised, how *the division of labour is necessarily followed by greater division of labour, the application of machinery by still greater application of machinery, work on a large scale by work on a still larger scale*' (CW9, 224). For the workers this means the deskilling of labour, growing competition in the labour market, falling wages and widespread redundancy as the capitalists '*compete with one another as to who can discharge most soldiers of industry*' (CW9, 226). Thus overproduction and crisis are inseparable, on the one hand, from the development of the forces of production, and, on the other hand, from the destruction of backward producers and the impoverishment and deskilling of the worker.

In these early works Marx, deepening and building on the foundations laid down by Engels, develops an extraordinarily acute and incisive account of the dynamics of overaccumulation and crisis as they affect a particular industry or branch of production. However, the generalisation of this analysis to the capitalist system as a whole is by no means as obvious as it might seem. If we look at one industry in isolation we may regard the market for its product as given, so that a rapid expansion of production in the wake of new investment will tend to lead to the overaccumulation of capital and the overproduction of commodities in relation to the limited market. However, when we move from the level of one industry to that of the system as a whole, the expansion of production in one branch of production creates a demand for the products of another, so if every branch of production were to grow together there would be no crisis.

There is no spontaneous tendency for production to develop proportionately in the various branches of production. But according to the economists competition achieves this result as production in each branch of production is adapted to the limits of the (growing) market, the more sluggish being stimulated, the more dynamic being restrained. To move from the dynamics of overaccumulation and crisis in one industry to that of the system as a whole therefore involves a much more complex exploration of the dynamics of adjustment, and particularly of the role of money in that adjustment, which was to preoccupy Marx in his more mature explorations of crisis.

In his early work, however, we find that Marx immediately generalises the analysis of one industry to the capitalist system as a whole, as production runs ahead of the growth of the market, giving his 'macroeconomic' theory of crisis a strong 'underconsumptionist' dimension, although this is merely stated rather than being explained. In *Wage Labour and Capital* Marx notes that the growth of capitalism is associated with increasingly severe periodic crises, in which workers' conditions become ever more insecure and their wages ever more fluctuating, and attributes the increasing severity of successive crises to the relative contraction of the world market, although without any explanation of this 'underconsumptionist' element of his analysis.[7] The growing accumulation of capital implies an

> increase in earthquakes, in which the trading world can only maintain itself by sacrificing a part of wealth, of products and even of productive forces to the god of the nether world — in a word, *crises* increase. They become more frequent and more violent, if only because, as the mass of production, and consequently the need for extended markets, grows, the world market becomes more and more contracted, fewer and fewer markets remain available for exploitation, since every preceding crisis has subjected to world trade a market hitherto unconquered or only superficially exploited. (CW9, 228)

The Theory of Crisis in the Communist Manifesto

The difference of emphasis in Marx's and Engels' understanding of the crisis tendencies of capitalist accumulation can be seen in the successive drafts of the *Communist Manifesto*, in which they summed up the programmatic implications of their analysis in the face of the revolutionary ferment of 1848, although it might be wrong to read too much into such differences, for the *Manifesto* is more rhetorical than analytical.

The first draft of *The Communist Manifesto*, written by Engels in June 1847, contained no reference to the significance of crises in the development of capitalism. By the time of the second draft, written in October 1847, the greatest crisis in the history of capitalism, which

---

[7] This is the theory of crisis picked up by Engels and Kautsky. In the manuscript 'Wages', which comprises the notes for these lectures, Marx notes that 'momentary overproduction becomes more and more necessary, the world market more and more extensive, and competition more universal' (CW6, 429), without any reference to a *contraction* of the world market.

would have world-wide economic and political repercussions, had broken, and Engels inserted a section on the significance of crises, which, he argued, 'entailed the greatest misery for the workers, general revolutionary ferment, and the greatest danger to the entire existing system'. In Engels's draft the tendency to crisis is related to 'competition and in general the carrying on of industrial production by individuals', and the new social order will accordingly remove the tendency to crisis inherent in competition by ensuring that all 'branches of production are run by society as a whole'. It is *because* 'private ownership cannot be separated from the individual running of industry and competition' that 'private ownership will also have to be abolished' (CW6, 347–8). However, in the final version, the tendency to crisis is not related to competition, but is related *immediately* to the narrowness of the 'conditions of bourgeois property' in relation to the constant revolutionising of the methods of production (CW6, 490).[8]

The final version of the *Communist Manifesto* acclaimed the revolutionary role of the bourgeoisie, whose power was based on its development of the means of production and exchange. The development of the forces of production enabled the bourgeoisie to sweep away all barriers to its development. 'The bourgeoisie cannot exist without constantly revolutionising the instruments of production, and thereby the relations of production, and with them the whole relations of society', thereby developing the world market, creating new wants, establishing 'universal inter-dependence of nations', in both material and intellectual life. 'It has agglomerated population, centralised means of production, and has concentrated property in a few hands. The necessary consequence was political centralisation' (CW6, 487–8).

However, the removal of the external barriers to its rule does not exhaust the revolutionary role of the bourgeoisie, as it confronts internal barriers which erupt in periodic crises.

> A similar movement is going on before our own eyes. Modern bourgeois society with its relations of production, of exchange, and of property, a society that has conjured up such gigantic means of production and exchange, is like a sorcerer, who is no longer able to control the powers of the nether world whom he has called up

---

[8] Although the final version does contain a reference to competition as the cause of crises in referring to 'the growing competition among the bourgeoisie, and the resulting commercial crises' (CW6, 492).

by his spells. For many a decade past the history of industry and commerce is but the history of the revolt of modern productive forces against the conditions of production, against the property relations that are the conditions for the existence of the bourgeoisie and of its rule. It is enough to mention the commercial crises that by their periodical return put on its trial, each time more threateningly, the existence of the entire bourgeois society. In these crises a great part not only of the existing products, but also of the previously created productive forces, are periodically destroyed. In these crises there breaks out an epidemic that, in all earlier epochs, would have seemed an absurdity — the epidemic of overproduction ... The productive forces at the disposal of society no longer tend to further the development of the conditions of bourgeois property; on the contrary, they have become too powerful for these conditions, by which they are fettered, and so soon as they overcome these fetters, they bring disorder into the whole of bourgeois society, endanger the existence of bourgeois property. The conditions of bourgeois society are too narrow to comprise the wealth created by them. And how does the bourgeoisie get over these crises? On the one hand by enforced destruction of a mass of productive forces; on the other, by the conquest of new markets, and by the more thorough exploitation of the old ones. That is to say, by paving the way for more extensive and more destructive crises, and by diminishing the means whereby crises are prevented. (CW6, 489–90)

The Early Theory of Overproduction and Crisis

We can now sum up the argument put forward by Marx and Engels, as it was developed in the 1840s, and expounded polemically in the *Communist Manifesto*. Marx and Engels insisted, above all, on the *systematic* and *periodic* character of capitalist crises. Any particular crisis might be precipitated by a singular event: a harvest failure, the disruption of trade by political change or by war, the collapse of fraudulent commercial or financial enterprises. This makes it appear as though crises are accidental phenomena, and indeed it is as such that the bourgeoisie interprets them, believing that modest reforms will remove the risk of such crises, and so permit the sustained expansion of capitalist prosperity. Thus, in Britain in the 1840s, liberal economists

The Early Theory of Overproduction and Crisis

argued that previous crises had been caused by the restrictions of the Corn Laws and the inadequate control of the currency. The 1844 Bank Act and the repeal of the Corn Laws were therefore proclaimed as measures which would forever banish the blight of general crisis. For Marx and Engels, on the other hand, crises were not accidental phenomena. They were the most superficial, but necessary, expression of the contradictory character of the capitalist mode of production.

The crisis-tendencies of the capitalist mode of production appear in the form of crises of overproduction. Overproduction is the result of the tendency to the unlimited development of the forces of production, imposed on each individual capitalist by the pressure of competition, which comes into conflict with the limited development of the world market, although there is no analysis of the latter limit, which is merely asserted.

The tendency to overproduction and crisis expresses the tendency for the productive forces to develop beyond the limits of bourgeois property relations, as overproduction leads to the collapse of prices and the elimination of profit, thereby removing the incentive to continue production. However the crisis is not an apocalyptic event, marking the final breakdown of the capitalist mode of production, but is a periodically recurring phase of the cyclical pattern which is the normal form of capitalist accumulation. Against the economists' presumption that the interaction of supply and demand underlies a constant tendency towards equilibrium, Marx and Engels insisted that it is only through periodic crises that the tendency to equilibrium is imposed.

The periodic crises of overproduction indicate the objective limits of the capitalist mode of production. Although there is a secular tendency to deepening crises, corresponding to the intensive and extensive development of the capitalist mode of production, these limits are not absolute. The destruction of existing products and previously created productive forces, the conquest of new markets, and the more thorough exploitation of old ones, removes the barriers to the further development of the forces of production, but only to pave the way for more extensive and more destructive crises. Nor do these limits define the inevitability of the demise of capitalism. The crisis-tendencies of capitalist accumulation define the 'weapon' with which the bourgeoisie will 'bring death to itself', but it is the proletariat which will 'wield those weapons' (CW6, 490).

The development of capitalist production develops the proletariat, reducing the worker to 'an appendage of the machine', driving wages down to the subsistence minimum, intensifying labour and extending the working day. The generalisation of capitalist production destroys artisanal petty production, while small capitalists cannot withstand the competition of the large, so that 'the lower strata of the middle class... sink gradually into the proletariat' (CW6, 491), leading to a progressive polarisation of society into two social classes.

'With the development of industry the proletariat not only increases in number; it becomes concentrated in greater masses, its strength grows, and it feels that strength more' (CW6, 492). Sectional and cultural divisions within the proletariat are broken down 'in proportion as machinery obliterates all distinctions of labour, and nearly everywhere reduces wages to the same low level', while commercial crises 'make the wages of the workers ever more fluctuating' and 'the unceasing improvement of machinery ... makes their livelihood more and more precarious' (CW6, 492). These are the conditions under which workers begin to form trades unions. This is not a continuous process, but one of advance and retreat, implicitly mirroring the economic cycle, with depressions weakening the union by increasing competition among the workers.[9] Despite competition between workers, the historical tendencies of capitalist accumulation ensure that the organisation of the workers takes on an ever-wider class character, which increasingly assumes a political form.

The analysis presented in *The Communist Manifesto* was not rigorously theorised, either in the *Manifesto* or in any of the other early works of Marx and Engels. The *Manifesto* offered a penetrating description of observable historical tendencies, but its prognosis was based not so much on an analysis of the historical laws of development of the capitalist mode of production as on an extrapolation of those tendencies. In this sense the *Manifesto* defined both a political and a scientific programme which remained to be accomplished. However, it is remarkable how much of the youthful analysis of Marx and Engels survived the elaboration of the underlying theoretical analysis, and continued to provide the guiding thread of Marxism until the death of Engels and beyond.

---

[9] Engels wrote to Bernstein (25.01.82): 'The fact that these crises are one of the most powerful levers in political upheavals has already been stated in the *Communist Manifesto* and is explained in the review section of the *Neue Rheinische Zeitung* up to and including 1848, but it is also explained that returning prosperity also breaks revolutions and lays the foundations for the victory of reaction.' (*Letters on Capital*, 209–10)

4

Production, Circulation and Global Crisis after 1848

The Politics and Theory of Crisis after the 1848 Revolutions

Inevitably the scientific and political aspects of the Marxist programme were intimately connected: the scientific priorities were dictated by the political priorities of the moment. The pressing theoretical issues which confronted Marxism at any stage in its historical development were those which were politically decisive. This relationship between political priorities and scientific tasks has been particularly marked in the development of the Marxist theory of crisis.

Marx's and Engels's concern with crisis in their early writings was political rather than theoretical. In their early writings the cycle was seen as decisive in underlying the growth of the proletariat as an independent political force. In the absence of any significant mass organisations of the working class Marx and Engels looked to the class struggles provoked by the disruption of economic crises as the primary source of the revolutionary mobilisation of the workers, while the financial pressures imposed by crises on the state reduced the latitude within which the bourgeoisie could respond. From the mid-1840s to the mid-1850s Marx and Engels expected the revolution in the very near future, as a result of the five-yearly cycle which they believed that they had identified.[1] In the *Condition of the English Working Class* (1844–5) Engels doubted that the people would endure more than one more crisis, implying that a crisis in 1847 would stimulate the further advance of the proletariat, and that the crisis of 1852 would be the final crisis of capitalism (CW4, 580–1).

In accordance with this diagnosis Marx and Engels threw themselves into the revolutionary movements of 1848 without any great

---

[1] In the *Principles of Communism*, second draft of the *Manifesto*, of 1847 Engels believed that period of the cycle was 5–7 years (CW6, 347. c.f. CW4, 384; CW11, 357).

expectation of a proletarian victory, but in the hope that the proletariat would emerge from the revolutionary uprisings as an independent political force. Despite their revolutionary enthusiasm they came to see the defeat suffered by the revolution as inevitable, as the return of prosperity eroded the vigour of the revolutionary forces, leaving only the political squabbles of 'the representatives of the individual factions of the Continental party of Order' (CW10, 135). As Marx wrote in *The Class Struggles in France* (1850): 'With this general prosperity ...there can be no talk of a real revolution. Such a revolution is only possible in the periods when *both these factors*, the *modern* productive *forces* and the *bourgeois forms of production*, come *in collision* with each other. ...*A new revolution is possible only in consequence of a new crisis. It is, however, just as certain as this crisis.*' (CW10, 135; c.f. CW39, 96.) As Marx noted in an article in the *New York Daily Tribune* in June 1853, since the beginning of the eighteenth century 'there has been no serious revolution in Europe which has not been preceded by a commercial and financial crisis' (CW12, 99), and this is all the more the case with the coming revolution. Without the trade cycle there would be political conflicts, but no class struggle, for it is only the rise and fall of wages that gives rise to continual conflicts between the masters and the men, their conflicts preventing the workers from 'becoming apathetic, thoughtless, more or less well-fed instruments of production ... a heart-broken, a weak-minded, a worn-out, unresisting mass' (CW12, 169).

After the defeat of the revolutions of 1848, in which the working class had for the first time asserted its independence, Marx and Engels looked forward to the next crisis with much greater expectations. Previous crises have been the condition for the advance of the industrial bourgeoisie over landed property and the finance bourgeoisie. The next will mark the beginning of the modern revolution (CW10, 264–5). As Engels argued in 'The Ten Hours' Question' (February 1850), the proletariat has served its apprenticeship, and capitalism has reached its limits. Although the struggle for the legal limitation of the working day was effectively lost the

> working classes, in this agitation, found a mighty means to get acquainted with each other, to come to a knowledge of their social position and interests, to organise themselves and to know their strength. ... The working classes will have learned by experience that *no lasting benefit whatever can be obtained for them by others,*

but that they must obtain it themselves by conquering, first of all, political power. ...The virtual repeal of the act of 1847 will force manufacturers into such a rush of overtrading that revulsions upon revulsions will follow, so that very soon all the expedients and resources of the present system will be exhausted and a *revolution*, made inevitable, which, uprooting society far deeper than 1793 and 1848 ever did, will speedily lead to the political and social ascendancy of the proletarians. ...the ascendancy of the manufacturing capitalists... is dependent upon the possibility of always extending production and, at the same time, reducing its cost. But this extended production has a certain limit: it cannot outdo the existing markets. If it does, a revulsion follows, with its consequent ruin, bankruptcy and misery. We have had many of these revolutions, happily overcome hitherto by the opening of new markets (China in 1842), or the better exploring of old ones, by reducing the cost of production (as by free trade in corn). But there is a limit to this, too. There are no new markets to be opened now ...It is evident that, with no chance of further extending markets, under a system which is obliged to extend production every day, there is *an end to mill-lord ascendancy.* And *what next?*; "Universal ruin and chaos", say the free-traders. *Social revolution and proletarian ascendancy, say we.* (CW10, 275–6; c.f. CW10, 299).[2]

The Historical Development of Capitalist Crises

Marx and Engels believed that they had established the inevitability of crisis as the necessary expression of the tendency to overproduction inherent in the capitalist mode of production. However, although their analysis was plausible, it was by no means rigorous. It was a long way from the inherent tendency to overproduction to the explanation of the concrete crises that arose in the course of capitalist development.

Although the successive crises between the mid–1820s and the early 1840s could plausibly be attributed to problems of overproduc-

---

[2] At the end of 1850 Marx and Engels were arguing that when the next crisis strikes in England 'for the first time the industrial and commercial crisis will coincide with a crisis in agriculture', but instead of arguing that this will unite the rural and industrial proletariat, they indicate that this will be the basis of sectional divisions as 'in all questions in which town and country, manufacturers and landowners are opposed to one another, both parties will be supported by two great armies; the manufacturers by the mass of industrial workers, the landowners by the mass of agricultural workers' (CW10, 503).

tion, liberal political economists explained these crises not as the expression of some fundamental contradiction inherent in the capitalist mode of production, but as the result of over-trading stimulated by the over-expansion of credit, on the one hand, and the restrictions on the world market imposed by the Corn Laws, on the other. The 1844 Bank Act supposedly restricted the ability of the banking system to over-expand credit, and the repeal of the Corn Laws had removed the barriers to the expansion of the market. While crises might occasionally recur, the political economists believed that future crises would only be the result of accidental factors and would have no systematic significance.

This diagnosis appeared at first sight to be confirmed by the development of the crisis of 1847–8. The crisis of 1847 in England was precipitated by poor harvests, which set off commercial and financial speculation. The Bank of England had resolved the crisis by suspending the 1844 Bank Act, which curbed speculation against the Bank, while increased interest rates eased the pressure on the financial system by attracting gold from the Continent. However, the drain of gold in turn spread the financial crisis to the Continent, playing its part in precipitating the revolutions of 1848, but also further relieving the pressure on England as gold flowed to London for safety, and the European recession left world markets open to English produce. The English recovery in turn stimulated a rapid recovery on the Continent, leading to a period of unprecedented prosperity.

Although the connection between economic crisis and political unrest was plain to see, there did not at first sight appear to be any particular connection between the supposed tendencies to overproduction and the actual course of the commercial and financial crises of 1847–8. Overproduction was a typically English phenomenon, where capitalism was most highly developed, but commercial and financial crises, with their political consequences, had struck more severely on the Continent. Moreover, the crises were soon overcome and capitalist expansion resumed.

It was clear that an understanding of crises, and the ability to predict the timing and course of the next crisis, demanded that Marx pay much closer attention to the relationship between production, commerce and finance than he had done hitherto.

Marx's first priority was to review the economic history of the previous ten years. 'Thereby what he had hitherto deduced, half *a priori*, from gappy material, became absolutely clear to him from the facts themselves, namely, that the world trade crisis of 1847 had been the true mother of the February and March Revolutions, and that the industrial prosperity, which had been returning gradually since the middle of 1848 and attained full bloom in 1849 and 1850, was the revitalising force of the newly strengthened European reaction.' (Engels, 1895 Introduction to *Class Struggles in France*, CW27, 507).

This work began with Marx's three 'Reviews' of the contemporary economic and political world situation, written with Engels and published in the *Neue Rheinische Zeitung* in the course of 1850.[3] In these works Marx developed his analysis of the mechanism through which overproduction in England, intensified by growing speculation as surplus capital sought profitable outlets, culminated in a commercial and financial crisis, which in turn precipitated a crisis in state finances in Europe and consequent revolutionary political upheavals (Bologna, n.d.; Ricciardi, 1987).

In the first of his Reviews Marx noted the growing political tensions on the Continent, and the impending crisis of state finances as the Continental states were forced into the expansion of the currency and increased borrowing, while the burden of taxation provoked growing civil discontent. In England recovery had been followed by a boom, with idle capital pouring into speculation. However, this boom cannot be expected to last long, with 'several of the largest markets, East India in particular, already glutted ... Soon the markets still left, particularly those of North and South America and Australia, will be similarly glutted, given the colossal forces of production which English industry added to those it already had ... and which are still being daily added to' (CW10, 264). Meanwhile the discovery of gold in California promises to move the centre of gravity of the world economy to the Pacific rim, to which Continental Europe must respond with a social and technical revolution if it is not to be reduced to 'the same industrial, commercial and political dependence to which Italy, Spain and Portugal are now reduced' (CW10, 266).

In the second Review Marx further developed his account of the impending English crisis, noting that prior to the crisis of 1845 'surplus capital' had 'found an outlet in railway speculation', but the extent of overproduction and over-speculation in railways had precluded a subsequent recovery, and cut off the railways as a possible

---
[3] Marx incorporated the relevant parts of the analysis of his *Reviews* into *The Class Struggles in France*, completed in November 1850.

outlet for surplus capital in the present boom, while depressed corn prices and the risk attached to state bonds prevent these too from being the objects of speculation. In the absence of alternative outlets surplus capital threw itself 'completely into industrial production and into speculation in colonial products and in the decisive raw materials of industry, cotton and wool'. The result was the unusually rapid growth of industrial production 'and with it the glutting of the markets, and hence the outbreak of the crisis was sufficiently hastened'. Marx saw signs of cutbacks in iron and cotton, and of problems in colonial trade, promising to superimpose an industrial crisis on the persistent agricultural crisis which resulted from the repeal of the Corn Laws. This crisis would have a revolutionary impact on the Continent, particularly in Germany, England's principal Continental trading partner (CW10, 339–40).[4]

By the autumn it was clear that the crisis had not come, and in his third Review Marx re-examined the situation in a wider perspective, looking more closely at the financial aspects of the crisis. The boom of the mid 1840s had culminated in the speculation 'which regularly occurs at times when overproduction is already in full swing. It provides channels by which this overproduction may temporarily be diverted, whilst by this very process hastening the onset of the crisis and magnifying its impact' (CW 10, 490). Speculation had focused first on the railways, but railway investment was already in difficulty by 1845, at which point speculation switched to corn. The speculative boom in corn collapsed in late 1847, hitting financial markets already weakened by the failures of railway investments, while cotton and iron were also in difficulties. Faced with a drain on its reserves the Bank of England raised the interest rate, curbed credit and called in its loans. At first it was commercial enterprises that were hit, but the tightening of credit soon hit the banks, financial collapse only being averted by the easing of credit made possible by the suspension of the Bank Act.

Meanwhile bankruptcies had spread to the Continent, while the easing of financial conditions in England increased the pressure on Continental banks as gold flowed into England from the Continent. The Revolution in France in February 1848, which soon spread throughout the Continent, intensified the panic flow of gold to England, easing the pressure in England but spreading the Continental panic.

---
[4] In a postscript, written in April, Marx recognised that spring had brought its usual temporary recovery, but argued that 'this only delays a little the development of the crisis' (CW10, 341).

The Historical Development of Capitalist Crises

In England recovery was rapid. New capital was added to 'existing capital which was lying dormant during the crisis' and, in the absence of other speculative outlets, was thrown into industry, particularly cotton. Despite the growth of speculative investment, Marx was now less confident that the crisis was at hand, noting that the opening of new markets, and the Great Exhibition planned for 1851, would provide new outlets for the product, and new sources of cheap cotton. The only sign of impending crisis now was the low rate of interest, which was an indication of a surplus of capital in search of speculative outlets. Meanwhile recovery and growing prosperity in England and America had rapidly transmitted themselves to the Continent, removing any threat of revolution. Although in France high taxation and the falling price of corn had plunged the peasantry, who form the mass of the population, into great depression, the experience of the past three years had proved 'that this class of the population is absolutely incapable of any revolutionary initiative' (CW10, 509). The renewal of the revolutionary impetus would have to await the outbreak of a new crisis in England, although this time the focus of over-speculation may well prove to be New York, stimulated by the boom in world shipping associated with the expansion of the world market.

The focus of the political crisis of 1848 was France. The repercussions of the English commercial and industrial crisis on France were so devastating because it brought the conflict between the industrial bourgeoisie and the finance aristocracy to a head. The French finance aristocracy had thrived on the expansion of public debt and public works, so that 'the July monarchy was nothing but a joint-stock company for the exploitation of France's natural wealth' (CW10, 50), against which was ranged the overwhelming majority of the population. However the fall of the bankocracy from political grace did not entail its loss of its social and economic power, for the limited development of capitalist production in France meant that many more depended for their livelihood on state debt, state employment and public works than depended on capitalist enterprise, while even the manufacturing capitalists depended on state protection, from both foreign competition and the threat of their own workers. Rather than allow the collapse of the Bank of France, and its replacement by a national bank, the Provisional government bolstered the Bank. Rather than declaring state bankruptcy to liquidate its debt, the government imposed an additional tax on the peasantry, paving the way to the counter-revolution which was essential if credit was to be restored, since credit 'rests on undisturbed and untroubled recognition of the existing economic class relations' (CW 10, 62).

Marx's close examination and re-examination of the course of the crisis of the late 1840s raised more questions than it answered. The theoretical model of the *Communist Manifesto* was all very well, but the more closely Marx looked into the development of a concrete crisis the more tenuous the links that he had mapped out between crisis and revolution appeared to be. Whatever else they might have been, the revolutions of 1848 were not the harbingers of the proletarian revolution. The crisis might have developed into a crisis of general overproduction, but it began as a result of over-investment in particular branches of production as surplus capital sought new outlets. The source of the crisis might well have been overproduction in England, but through the mechanisms of commercial and financial speculation the crisis was displaced, so that it appeared primarily in the form of a financial crisis in France. Correspondingly, the decisive struggles unleashed by the crisis were not the class struggles between the English operatives and their employers, but struggles between the industrial bourgeoisie, the financial and landed aristocracy and state dependents in France.

Money, Credit and Crisis in the Notebooks of 1851

These issues came to a head with the failure of the anticipated crisis to break in 1850, which led Marx to devote himself to more profound study of economic history and the theories of political economy, and particularly the study of the banking and financial system. Marx's 24 notebooks of the period between September 1850 and August 1853 consist almost exclusively of excerpts and summaries.[5] Neither his published notebooks, which do not extend beyond 1851, nor his journalistic writings, nor his extant correspondence give any indication that his own critique of political economy made much progress during this period.[6] In two letters to Engels in early 1851 (07.01.51 and

---

[5] Four additional notebooks, dated September 1853 to May 1854, contain extracts relating to the history of the Crimean War (Marx, *Fondements*, Vol. 2, 441).

[6] Extracts from notebooks IV (November-December 1850) and VIII (April 1851), dealing with Ricardo, were appended to the German and French editions of the *Grundrisse*, but did not appear in the English translation. The notebooks are being published in the current German edition of the Collected Works, which has so far reached the end of 1851. (MEGA IV, 7-8. CW 24, xxv and n.418, 703-4; CW28, xiii.)

03.02.51) Marx reported his criticisms of Ricardo's theories of rent and of money, but neither of these criticisms was original or profound, his criticisms of the quantity theory of money deriving essentially from Tooke and the Banking School. Nevertheless these notebooks do contain some indications of an important advance in Marx's theory of crisis, that laid the foundations for the analysis that he was to develop in his notebooks of 1857–63 (CW38, 258–63, 273–8).

The principal issue on which Marx did begin to develop his own ideas was that of the relation between the currency and crises, in order to show that a monetary crisis, in which it appears that the problem is a shortage of money, is only the superficial expression of a crisis of overproduction, a point that he had already made polemically in *The German Ideology*.[7]

Marx's manuscript 'Bullion. The Completed Money System' of February 1851 contains the first sketch of Marx's analysis of the money-form, as an expression of the social relations of commodity production, which harks back to his earliest '*Comments* on James Mill'. In this sketch Marx explicitly locates the source of crises in the money-form, of which the imbalance of demand and supply is but an expression, and links crises to the general phenomenon of 'disproportion'. 'Gold and silver in their capacity as money here appear as *mediator*. The act of exchange is separated into the mutually independent acts of purchase and sale. Demand and supply, the necessary consequence of money is, therefore, the *separation* of these two acts, which must, of course, eventually be equalised, but which at any given moment can be in *disharmony*, in *disproportion*. The foundation of crises, therefore, certainly lies in money.' (MEGA, IV, 8, 4, my translation. See also his exchange of letters with Engels of 03/02/51 and 25/2/51.)

In his 'Reflections', written in March 1851, Marx provides his first systematic account of the relationship between the tendency to overproduction and the financial and commercial crises in which the crisis of overproduction manifests itself. The starting point for Marx is the distinction, which was crucial in the debate between the Banking and Currency Schools, between the trade of capitalists with one another, on

---

[7] 'A crisis is in existence precisely when one ... *must* pay with money. And this again does not happen because of a shortage of money, as is imagined by the petty bourgeois who judges the crisis by his personal difficulties, but because the specific difference becomes fixed between money as the *universal* commodity ... and all the other *particular* commodities, which suddenly cease to be marketable property' (CW5, 396–7).

the one hand, and the trade between capitalists and consumers, on the other, a distinction which related directly to Marx's analysis of overproduction and crisis. In the trade between capitalists, commodities and money pass from hand to hand, without the commodities leaving the sphere of circulation. It is only in the trade between capitalists and consumers that the commodity leaves circulation and passes into the sphere of consumption. The distinction between these two kinds of trade was linked in the currency debates to Tooke's distinction between money as capital and money as means of circulation.

There was a tendency in the nineteenth century for different forms of money to perform the different roles, with credit money, including banknotes, circulating commodities between capitalists, and coin circulating commodities between capitalists and consumers (although this distinction was not clear cut, since it was only through their sale to the ultimate consumer that the commodity capital was finally realised in the form of money). The essential point is not the distinction between different kinds of money, but between the different functions which money performs, and it was primarily the failure to make this distinction that led to so much confusion in the currency debates.[8] The Currency School tended to reduce money to its function as means of circulation, focusing on the issue of the convertibility of the currency, while the Banking School tended to reduce money to its function as capital, focusing on the issue of bank credit. Marx was trying to get beyond this false opposition, to understand the interpenetration of circulation with the realisation of capital.[9]

The immediate producer realises his capital by selling commodities to the merchant capitalist, who buys the commodities on credit. Commodities and credit then pass from hand to hand in a series of exchanges, until eventually the commodity is sold to a consumer for cash, the final sale then permitting the repayment of the chain of credit. The question is, what is the relationship between the trade

---

[8] In his manuscripts of 1861–3 Marx criticised Tooke's distinction between 'capital' and 'currency', which Marx had himself borrowed earlier, on the grounds that 'he firstly confuses money and commodity with money and commodity as modes of existence of capital, with money and commodity capital, and secondly regards the particular money form in which the capital is circulated as a distinction between "capital" and "coin"' (CW33, 216). In Volume Two of *Capital* he stresses that the distinction is a functional distinction. 'The fact that the same money serves one purpose in the hands of the seller and another in the hands of the buyer is simply a phenomenon inherent in all purchases and sales of commodities' (CII, 515, c.f. 551–4).

[9] The difference broadly corresponds to that between Keynesians and monetarists today. See Clarke, 1988b, for a fuller discussion of these issues.

between dealers, and the ultimate sale of the commodity? For political economy, following Smith, overproduction was impossible because the trade between capitalists was necessarily limited by the consumer demand for the product. If the latter fell short of supply, wholesalers would cut back their orders and production would adjust to the limits of the market. However, Marx argued, 'all crises show in fact that the trade between dealers and dealers constantly exceeds the bounds set by the trade between dealers and consumers' (CW10, 584) — commerce tends constantly to expand beyond the limits of the market.

Marx does not provide a systematic account of this tendency here, but indicates a number of different reasons why commerce is unconstrained by consumer demand. First, the trade between dealers and dealers is not constrained by levels of demand in any one country, but by demand on a world scale. Second, 'the fact that the income of the working class decreases — not in one country, as Proudhon thinks, but on the world market — leads to an imbalance between production and consumption, and hence overproduction', although this is modified by the 'growing extravagance of the propertied classes' so that 'it would be wrong to put forward this proposition unconditionally'. Third, as the Banking School argued, 'the trade between dealers and dealers largely creates the trade between dealers and consumers'. An initial investment, however speculative it might be, creates new employment and stimulates wage rises, which in turn generate increased consumption. Similarly, the crisis always begins in the trade between dealers and dealers, and it is only subsequently, and in consequence of the crash, that consumption, and so the trade between dealers and consumers, falls (CW10, 585–6).[10] Fourth, Marx stressed that 'overproduction must not be attributed solely to disproportionate production, but to the relationship between the class of capitalists and that of workers' (CW10, 486), although he did not here show what was the connection between disproportionality, on the one hand, and the class relation between the capitalists and the workers, on the other.

The tendency to overproduction is not constrained within the limits of the market by the commercial activity of the dealers, since their

---

[10] Marx returns to this point in Volume Two of *Capital*, where he notes that the crisis breaks out with a demand for payment between capitalists, 'It has only to do with the *demand for payment*, with the absolute necessity of transforming commodities into money. At this point the crisis breaks out. It first becomes evident not in the general reduction of consumer demand, the demand for individual consumption, but rather in a decline in the number of exchanges of capital for capital, in the reproduction process of capital.' (CII, 156–7.)

activity has its own dynamic in its turn. This commercial activity can be sustained for as long as the banks are willing and able to finance it, and so a crisis appears when the banks begin to withdraw facilities. To understand the mechanisms of crisis Marx therefore turns to the matter of the currency.

In a period of crisis private individuals withdraw their money from the banks, forcing the banks to restrict credit, so that capitalists have to restrict their operations in turn, and 'the complaints about lack of money move from the commercial world into the world of the consumers' (CW10, 586). It appears in a crisis that the problem is one of the shortage of credit, which has forced the capitalists to curtail their operations, and the demand of reformers is therefore for an easing of credit and an expansion of the currency. But the real problem underlying the shortage of credit is not the shortage of currency, but overproduction reflected in the shortage of demand. The banks will no longer extend credit because the capital against which their credit is secured proves unrealisable, as the commodities in which the capital is embodied pile up unsold.

In the crisis commercial bills cannot be discounted and bank-notes cannot be redeemed for gold, but these are only symptoms of the crisis. The real difficulty in the crisis is not the convertibility of money, which can easily be solved (for example by suspending the Bank Act). 'The real difficulty is the *inconvertibility of commodities*, i.e. of the *actual capital*, into gold and banknotes' (CW10, 587).[11] The problem is not, therefore, the *particular* form of the monetary system, which has led to a shortage of money, but the monetary system itself, the mode of social production in which the object of production is not social need, but the appropriation of money.

This does not mean that one form of the monetary system is as good as any other, because the capitalist system requires sound money. 'The convertibility of bank-notes into gold is in the end necessary, because the convertibility of commodities into money is necessary, in other words because commodities have exchange value, and this requires a *special* equivalent distinct from the commodities, i.e. because in fact

---

[11] 'In crises, capital (as commodity) cannot be exchanged, not because there are *too few* means of circulation; it does not circulate because it is *not exchangeable*. The significance which cash acquires in times of crisis arises only from the fact that, while capital is not exchangeable for its value — and only for that reason does its value appear to confront it fixed in the form of money — it still has obligations to pay. Alongside the interrupted circulation, a *forced circulation* takes place' (CW28, 520).

the system of private exchange prevails' (CW10, 587). The currency reformers believe that they can solve the problem of the inconvertibility of capital by abandoning the convertibility of the currency, and try to modify the monetary system, 'as if the inconvertibility of capital were not already contained in the existence of any monetary system, indeed as if it were not contained even in the existence of products in the form of capital. Trying to alter this on the existing basis means depriving money of its monetary qualities, without conferring on capital the quality of always being exchangeable', so providing the worst of both worlds. Those who want to issue money freely, or who 'retain money but in such a way that it should no longer have the properties of money' are all fools (CW10, 588). It was with the development of this argument that Marx began the *Grundrisse* when he returned to his economic studies in 1857.

In March and April 1851 Marx returned to the study of Ricardo's work (MEGA IV.8, Notebooks VII and VIII). The importance of Ricardo is that he rejected any kind of underconsumptionism, vehemently denying the possibility of general overproduction on the grounds that 'overproduction' in one branch of production must correspond to 'underproduction' in another, an imbalance which would be rectified by the normal operation of the market. The confrontation with Ricardo, here as in his other work, forces Marx to clarify his own thought (and to anticipate the critique of the Marxist theory of crisis later put forward by Tugan).

In his notes on Ricardo Marx links together the tendency to the uneven development of the forces of production and the tendency to overproduction, the contradiction between the production of values and the production of use-values, the dynamism of capitalist production, and the necessity of crises in a passage which summarises past results and is an anticipation of work to come.

Marx recognises the force of Ricardo's critique of the underconsumptionist theory, and begins to bring his theoretical analysis into line with the results of his empirical investigations which had shown that it was the disproportional growth of production that lay behind the crisis. Marx particularly stresses the argument that it is the *uneven* development of the forces of production which stimulates the tendency to overproduction. If the forces of production advanced uniformly then the adoption of improved methods of production would lead to a growth in the size of the product, but not to any increase in the size of the capital, since prices would immediately adjust to the new level of costs, to yield the uniform general rate of profit (although the capital will subsequently expand as the fall in the value of labour power enables the capitalist to employ more labourers). The dynamism of the capitalist mode of production, and the associated tendency to overproduction, derives from the uneven development of the forces of production, which provides the more advanced capitalist with the opportunity of making a surplus profit until the new methods of production are generally adopted.

Bourgeois wealth and the goal of all capitalist production is *exchange value* and not use-value. There is no other way to increase this exchange-value — if one leaves aside mutual swindling — than to add to the products and to make more. To achieve this increase in production it is necessary to develop the productive forces.

But, in proportion to the growth of the productive power of a given amount of labour ... there is a fall in the exchange value of the products ... even without considering the depreciation [of fixed capital], which we must deal with later.

If the process was carried through uniformly, the value would never vary, so much so that every stimulus to bourgeois production would cease. It is only because it is produced unequally that one sees all the collisions arising, but at the same time bourgeois progress.

To produce more commodities is *never* the goal of bourgeois production. The goal of the latter is to produce more *values*. The *real* growth of the productive forces and of commodities therefore occurs despite it: all crises result from this contradiction in the *expansion of values* which is transformed, through its own movement, into an increase in production. Thus, bourgeois industry is constantly turned and overturned in this contradiction.

In becoming more productive, capital would not increase if all capitals became equally productive throughout the industry. The capital of the nation would remain the same, even though it would produce greater wealth in the Ricardian sense, i.e. more products, etc.

However, because the increase in the productive force of capital is always *unilateral*, it corresponds first to a growth of *values* (the improved machine would make its products at the same price as the average machine just as the worst land produces at the same price as the best, and as in the case of rent there is a creation of value). When in addition, the capitalist sets more labourers to work with the same capital ... in that way he also increases values. (MEGA IV.8, 364-5, my translation)

Marx also reiterates the connection between the disproportionality in the growth of production between the various branches of production and the growth of the world market. The crisis tendencies of accumulation work themselves out on a world scale, as capital turns to the world market in the attempt to find outlets for its surplus product: 'The disequilibrium between the market — the exchangers — and capital, the disproportionality of production within a particular country pushes commodities onto the world market, from one market to another. Once industry is modern, proportionate production — naturally within bourgeois limits — needs the sphere of the whole world if it wants to find an equivalent for its production, that is to say an active demand.' (MEGA IV.8, 417, my translation)

The remaining notebooks from this period remain unpublished, although there is no indication that they contain any original material. In their published writings and correspondence of 1852-3 Marx and Engels are still anticipating the final crisis lying just around the corner, but although there were episodes of commercial and financial distress, and clear signs of overproduction in one or another branch of production, the anticipated general crisis did not arrive.[12] The failure of the crisis to arrive on time did not dismay Marx and Engels. On the contrary, the longer the onset of the crisis was delayed by exceptional circumstances, such as free trade and the Crimean War, the more severe they expected it to be.

According to Marx and Engels the fact that the cycle had not entered the usual phase of commercial and financial speculation did not indicate a weakening of the crisis tendencies. On the contrary, the fact that surplus capital was continuing to be diverted into production and not financial and commercial speculation indicated that the crisis 'will take on a far more dangerous character than in 1847, when it was more commercial and monetary than industrial' (CW11, 361), but of its inevitability there remained no doubt.

In mid 1953 Marx wrote 'there must ever without any particular accident, in due time arrive a moment when the extension of the mar-

---
[12] They expected the crisis to break in 1852, on the basis of a five-yearly cycle (CW10, 502; Marx to Engels, 19.08.52, CW39, 162-3), then in 1853 (NYDT 01.11.52).

kets is unable to keep pace with the extension of British manufactures, and this disproportion must bring about a new crisis with the same certainty as it has done in the past' (CW12, 95–6), but by now references to the necessity or imminence of crisis were becoming few and far between.[13]

The Theory of Crisis in 1853

Although Marx and Engels had still not developed a completely coherent theory of crisis, the elements of such a theory can be gleaned from their writings of the period 1848–53. These can be drawn together in a number of points:

1) the crisis is one phase in the cycle which is the normal course of capitalist accumulation.

2) Marx and Engels always refer to crises as crises of *overproduction*, and such crises are always linked to the tendency for production to expand beyond the limits of the market (CW5, 518; CW10, 263, 338; CW11, 173–5; CW12, 95–9; CW13, 588; CW14, 23; CW19, 161; CW24, 412; CW25, 272).

The source of overproduction is the uneven development of the forces of production, which gives a competitive advantage to those capitalists who first introduce more advanced methods of production.

The dynamic force is the tendency for capitalism to develop the forces of production without limit, which arises as every capitalist is forced by the pressure of competition to reduce the labour time socially necessary for production, resulting in a larger product with a given size of capital, compounded by the ever-growing quantity of capital, which is constantly seeking new outlets for productive investment.

3) In his more general statements Marx still explains crises in underconsumptionist terms, the crisis arising because the growth of production runs ahead of the development of the market. However he was aware that it was not legitimate to generalise from the dynamic tendency of one branch of production to the tendencies of the system as a whole, because he recognised that the development of the forces of production simultaneously developed the market. His priority was, therefore, to understand more precisely the relationship between the

---

[13] I have only found one significant reference to crisis in works of the period 1854–5, which Marx relates to 'the fatal working of the English industrial system which leads to overproduction in Great Britain, and to over-speculation in all other countries' (CW13, 588).

tendency for capital to develop the forces of production without limit, on the one hand, and the concrete manifestation of crisis, on the other.

4) Theoretically this led Marx to consider the relationship between industrial capital, commercial capital and financial capital. It appears as though a crisis is precipitated by a financial and commercial crisis, which seems to arise as the consequence of speculation and 'overtrading'. However, Marx argues that over-trading is not the result of commercial and financial impetuosity, but of the tendency for production to run ahead of the expansion of the market. The source of crises therefore lies in the tendency to overproduction.

Speculation and over-trading are merely symptoms of overproduction, as surplus capital seeks profitable outlets. 'Speculation regularly occurs at times when overproduction is already in full swing. It provides channels by which the overproduction may temporarily be diverted, whilst by this very process hastening the onset of the crisis and magnifying its impact. The crisis itself first breaks out in the field of speculation and only seizes hold of production later. Not overproduction, but over-speculation, itself only a symptom of overproduction, therefore appears to the superficial view as the cause of the crisis' (CW10, 490).

5) Marx's examination of the relationship between overproduction, circulation and monetary crises leads him in his sketches of 1851 to consider the tendency to overproduction in relation to the tendency to disproportionality. From this perspective a crisis of overproduction is the result of the uneven development of capitalist production, which gives rise to disproportionalities between branches of production. The appearance of underconsumption is then the result of the collapse of production in the crisis.

Similarly, in Marx's empirical studies crises are not crises of general overproduction, but originate in overproduction in the particular branch of production in which the forces of production have developed most rapidly. More specifically, the dynamic force in the tendency to crisis is British manufacturing production in relation to the relatively slower growth of world markets. There is a suggestion that the overproduction of British manufactures is connected with the relative backwardness of agriculture on a world scale, as rising agricultural prices lead to falling demand for manufactures (CW12, 96–7).[14] However Marx has still to reconcile his concrete studies of the mechanism of

---

[14] This was an argument that Kautsky picked up as part of his theory of imperialism.

crisis with his theoretical account of the crisis tendencies of capitalist production.

6) This analysis implies that a crisis of overproduction will first be manifested in the sphere of commerce and finance, so that evidence of over-speculation is a clear index of the impending onset of a crisis of overproduction (CW10, 502). For this reason Marx and Engels were constantly attentive to evidence of over-speculation and over-trading, with Marx poring over the returns of the Bank of England and the Bank of France, while Engels, from Manchester, reported on evidence of commercial distress.

7) The further implication was that no measure of monetary reform, whether the 1844 Bank Act, or the Proudhonist and socialist proposals for free credit, could eliminate the crisis tendencies of capitalism. On the other hand, the failure of the expected crisis to arrive in 1853 made it clear that the relation between overproduction and over-speculation was not as simple as Marx and Engels had perhaps originally imagined, and it was this issue that provided the focus for Marx's economic studies of the 1850s.

8) The dynamic of crisis and revolution unfolds on a world scale, with its epicentre in England.

> Just as the period of crisis occurs later on the Continent than in England, so does that of prosperity. The original process always takes place in England; it is the demiurge of the bourgeois cosmos. ... While, therefore, the crises first produce revolutions on the Continent, the foundation for these is, nevertheless, always laid in England. Violent outbreaks must naturally occur rather in the extremities of the bourgeois body than in its heart, since the possibility of adjustment is greater here than there. On the other hand, the degree to which Continental revolutions react on England is at the same time the barometer which indicates how far these revolutions really call in question the bourgeois conditions of life, or how far they only hit their political formations (CW10, 509–10).

The Continent is the site of political revolutions, but the social revolution will occur in England.

Every local crisis has its own dynamics and its own particularity, but behind the contingent causes of such particular crises lies the more fundamental cause of the general state of the world market (CW11, 173–5). Each local crisis is therefore not significant in itself, but for its economic and political repercussions on a global scale and, most particularly, in England as the heart of the bourgeois world. Thus most of Marx's empirical researches in the 1850s concerned international trade, financial and monetary movements which constitute the links between the different parts of the world capitalist system. This explains the particular importance which Marx attached to France, which he regarded as playing a pivotal role in the transmission and generalisation of financial crises from the periphery to the centre. In the second half of the 1850s he studied the financial policy of the Bank of France in the unfolding of the crisis of the 1840s, and the international financial and commercial relations of France in the 1850s, as the basis on which to anticipate the pattern of the next great crisis.

Revolutionary Hopes and the Crisis of 1857

The long-awaited crisis did not arrive until November-December 1857, but Marx and Engels had been anticipating the crisis, noting the growing signs of speculation throughout Europe, since April 1856 (CW40, 32, 34–5). In June Marx wrote a series of three articles for the *New York Daily Tribune* on the *Crédit Mobilier*, which he and Engels regarded as no more than a vehicle for speculation, borrowing short to lend long, 'without any regard to the productive capacities of the country' while justifying its fraudulent activities with the rhetoric of Saint Simonian socialism (CW 15, 8–24). Marx returned to the *Crédit Mobilier* in September 1856, noting that its 'ruling principle ... is not to speculate in a given line, but to speculate in speculation, and to universalise swindling at the same rate that it centralises it' and describing it as 'that curious mixture of Imperial Socialism, St. Simonistic stock-jobbing and philosophical swindling' (CW15, 109–110).[15]

About the same day Marx wrote to Engels that he expected that the great monetary crisis would arrive by winter 1857 (26.09.56, CW40, 71). Engels, in his reply, agreed with Marx that the impending crisis would at last be the big one: 'This time there'll be a *dies irae* such as has never been seen before: the whole of Europe's industry in ruins, all markets over-stocked ..., all the propertied classes in the soup, complete bankruptcy of the bourgeoisie, war and profligacy to the nth degree.' (27?.09.56, CW40, 74)

---

[15] In fact the *Crédit Mobilier* survived the crisis of 1857–8, to fall in the crisis of 1867, being finally liquidated in 1871.

The following week Marx was publicly anticipating not only an economic crisis, but also a political crisis which would dwarf the revolutions of 1848. 'What the most far-sighted politicians now are sure of is an enlarged edition not only of the crisis of 1847 but also of the revolutions of 1848 ... In 1848 the movements which more immediately produced the Revolution were of a merely political character ... Now, on the contrary, a social revolution is generally understood, even before the political revolution is proclaimed; and a social revolution brought about by no underground plots of the secret societies among the working classes, but by the public contrivances of the Crédits Mobiliers of the ruling classes.' The impact of the monetary crisis reveals the delusory character of the proclamations of the 'official revolutionists' who 'know nothing of the economical life of peoples, of the real conditions of historical movement' (CW15, 113–5).

Despite the apparent recovery from the crisis, by November Engels's optimism was unbounded: 'Never again, perhaps, will the revolution find such a fine *tabula rasa* as now. All socialist dodges exhausted, the compulsory employment of labour anticipated and exploded 6 years since, no opportunity for new experiments or slogans. On the other hand, however, the difficulties will be starkly in evidence; the bull will have to be taken literally by the horns ... we longer have any reason to fear as swift an ebb as in 1848.' (Engels to Marx, 17.11.56, CW40, 83) Marx too expected the recovery to be only temporary, noting in the *New York Daily Tribune* that 'whatever may be the temporary cause of the monetary panic ... all the elements of commercial and industrial revulsion were ripe in Europe' (CW15, 122) so that 'it seems hardly possible that French commerce and industry should avoid a collapse, attended by political events more or less serious, and affecting to a most disastrous extent the stability of credit and of business, not only in Europe, but in America as well' (CW15, 135).

Throughout the summer of 1857 Marx continued to look to France, and particularly to the over-extended *Crédit Mobilier*, for the financial crisis which would herald the definitive crisis of capitalism (*New York Daily Tribune* articles of 12.05, 15.05, 02.06, 10.07, 08.09, CW15, 270–7, 289–92, 301–4, 357–60).

In late September and October Marx wrote a series of five articles on French financial policy, which have since been lost (CW 40, 181; n. 219, 606). On 20th October he wrote to Engels, noting the 'beautiful'

American crisis, and reporting on his work on French finances (CW40, 191–5), and on the 31st October he reported to Engels that as a result of the crisis the *New York Daily Tribune* had reduced his commission to one article per week, exclusively on the Indian war and the financial crisis (CW40, 197–8).

In the event this phase of the crisis had its greatest impact in England, leading to the immediate suspension of the Bank Act, an eventuality which Marx had predicted in an article written on 6th November (CW 15, 383), at the same time downplaying its significance in comparison with the impending industrial crash (c.f. CW40, 215). On November 13th Marx wrote to Engels expressing his delight at the crisis, despite his own financial distress, referring to another Tribune article 'The British Revulsion' in which he shows 'that the crisis ought by rights to have set in two years earlier. Moreover the delays are now explicable in such rational terms that even Hegel might, to his great satisfaction, have rediscovered the "concept" in the "empirical diversity of the world of finite interests"' (13.11.57, CW40, 199).

In fact Marx's article could hardly be said to *explain* the delays, merely asserting that arrivals of gold from Australia and the US had enabled the Bank occasionally to ease credit, 'while on the other hand ...it was shifted off through a series of temporary convulsions, and that, consequently, its final explosion, as to the intensity of symptoms as well as the extent of contagion, will exceed every crisis ever before witnessed' (CW15, 387).[16]

Engels replied two days later, joining Marx in seeing the American crash as ending the 'pre-crisis' period of French and German speculation, and bringing everything to a head. Engels documented the impact of the crisis throughout Europe (some of which documentation Marx used in his article on 'The Financial Crisis in Europe' for the *New York Daily Tribune*), anticipating its revolutionary impact after a long period of prosperity. Engels did not want the crisis to develop too fast, hoping for 'a period of chronic pressure ... to get the people's blood up', and to spread pressure around Europe as a whole. 'The long period of prosperity is bound to have made the masses damned lethargic', but Engels was optimistic: 'in 1848 we were saying: Now our time is coming, and so in a certain sense it was, but this time it is

---

[16] Marx added as a postscript to his letter that 'I am thinking of writing about the crisis for the benefit of the fatherland', which is the first reference in his correspondence to any resumption of independent work (13.11.57, CW40, 199). The reference to Hegel is also significant in this respect (c.f. CW40, 249).

coming properly; now it's a case of do or die' (CW40, 200–3).

In an article written on 27th November Marx stressed the systematic character of crises: 'the very recurrence of crises despite all the warnings of the past, in regular intervals, forbids the idea of seeking their final causes in the recklessness of single individuals ... speculation ... appears as the immediate forerunner of the crash ... [but] speculation itself was engendered in the previous phases of the period, and is therefore, itself a result and an accident, instead of the final cause and the substance'. The final cause and substance lies not in the money markets, but in the course of English trade, and is revealed by the fact that 'the industrial crisis now stands at the top and the monetary difficulty at the bottom'. The money market has been strengthened, but only by forcing up interest rates to the detriment of the manufacturers (CW15, 401–2).

Engels kept Marx informed of the development of the commercial and industrial crisis, which conformed closely to their predictions. On 11th December Engels wrote: 'Never before has overproduction been so general as during the present crisis ... That's what is so splendid, and is bound to have tremendous consequences. After all, so long as overproduction was confined to industry the thing was only half-way there, but as soon as agriculture is also affected, and in the tropics as well as the temperate zone, it will become spectacular.

'The outward and visible sign of overproduction is more or less always the expansion of credit, but this time it's especially *kite-flying*', which overexpands credit. The result is that 'everyone operated in excess of his resources, overtraded. Admittedly overtrading is not synonymous with overproduction, but it amounts to exactly the same thing', as the expansion of supply is not matched by growth of demand. 'This alone would be bound to precipitate the crisis, even if the money market, the weathercock of trade, were not already pointing in that direction. ... The present crisis provides an opportunity for a detailed study of how overproduction is generated by the expansion of credit and by overtrading' (CW40, 220–1).[17] The following week, however, Engels noted that the revolutionary consequences of the crisis were so far limited. 'Distress has also begun to set in among the proletariat. There are as yet few signs of revolution, for the long period of prosperity has been fearfully demoralising. The unemployed

---

[17] Note that Engels is here offering the political economists' explanation for the crisis, later picked up by Kautsky and Hilferding. For Marx the relationship is normally the other way around: overtrading is the symptom of overproduction, not its cause.

Revolutionary Hopes and the Crisis of 1857

on the streets continue to beg and to idle away their time' (17.12.57, CW40, 223).

At the end of December Marx turned his attention to France, spending Christmas Day writing a long letter to Engels and a leading article for the *New York Daily Tribune*. The problem was that Marx had been anticipating that France would be the centre of the financial crisis which, in the event, had largely passed France by. His explanation for this was primarily in terms of the favourable trade balance which France enjoyed with those countries hardest hit by the recession, a balance which supposedly meant that a crisis in trade with the latter could not precipitate a monetary crisis in France. Nevertheless Marx reiterated his expectation that when the French crisis comes, it will 'fall severely upon the stock market and endanger the supreme security of that market — the State itself' (CW15, 416). 'The whole rotten old structure is falling to pieces and the ludicrously rash surge hitherto manifested by the security market in England, etc., will likewise end in disaster.' (CW40, 231–2.)

Two weeks later Marx was pin-pointing the source of the contradiction faced by British capitalism, which he now envisaged as the basis not of a catastrophic crisis, but of secular decline.

> The really disquieting feature for England ... is this, that she is apparently at a loss to find at home a sufficient field of employment for her unwieldy capital; that she must consequently lend on an increasing scale, and similar, in this point, to Holland, Venice and Genoa, at the epoch of their decline, forge herself the weapons for her competitors. She is forced, by giving large credits, to foster speculation in other countries in order to find a field of employment for her surplus capital, and thus to hazard her acquired wealth in order to augment and conserve it. By being obliged to give large credits to foreign manufacturing countries, such as the continent of Europe, she forwards herself the means to her industrial rivals to compete with her for the raw produce, and thus is herself instrumental in enhancing the raw material of her own fabrics. The small margin of profit thus left to the British manufacturer, still reduced by the constant necessity ... constantly to undersell the rest of the world, is then compensated for by curtailing the wages of the labouring classes and creating home misery on a rapidly-enlarging scale. Such is the natural price paid by England for her commercial and industrial supremacy. (CW 15, 430)

On the same day Marx wrote to Engels, drawing comfort from the apparent recovery: 'The momentary lull in the crisis is, or so it seems to me, most advantageous to our interests — party interests, I mean' (07.01.58, CW40, 243). Six weeks later he was still optimistic: 'Taken all in all, the crisis has been burrowing away like the good old mole it is' (22.02.58, CW40, 274).

In February 1858 Marx returned to the economic crisis in France, now stressing the role of the government in inflating credit to sustain prices, despite industrial stagnation and high levels of unemployment. 'The government seems to imagine that by this exceedingly simple process of distributing bank notes wherever they are wanted, the catastrophe can be definitively warded off. Yet the real result of this contrivance had been, on the one hand, an aggravation of distress on the part of the consumers, whose diminished means have not been met by diminished prices; on the other hand, an enormous accumulation of commodities in the Customs entrepots which, when ultimately as they must be, they are forced onto the market, will collapse under their own weight.' (CW15, 461–2) Nevertheless, against Marx's expectations, the trick worked and the anticipated crisis did not come.

From March 1858 the topic of crises virtually disappears from Marx's and Engels's extant correspondence, only reappearing as a topic of relatively mild interest in the next crisis phase of 1866–8. By June 1858 Marx was noting that British exports had recovered, so that it appeared as though the crisis was over, although Marx insisted that the figures were misleading because of the extent of over-trading, particularly in Asia (CW15, 560–5).

By the autumn of 1858 it was clear that the crisis had passed, and a boom was underway again, fuelled particularly by exports to India, which, perhaps for the first time, raised doubts in Marx's mind as to the imminence of revolution. 'There is no denying that bourgeois society has for the second time experienced its 16th century, a 16th century which, I hope, will sound its death knell just as the first ushered it into the world. The proper task of bourgeois society is the creation of a world market, at least in outline, and of the production based on that market'. This task is now complete, but while capitalism may be approaching its limits in Europe, maybe there is more life in it in the rest of the world. 'For us, the difficult question is this: on the Continent revolution is imminent and will, moreover, instantly assume a socialist character. Will it not necessarily be crushed in this little corner of the earth, since the movement of bourgeois society is still in

Revolutionary Hopes and the Crisis of 1857

the ascendant over a far greater area?' (8.10.58, CW40, 346–7)

It is difficult to interpret Marx's writings on the political significance of the crisis of 1857. There is no doubt that in the wake of the revolutions of 1848 Marx and Engels had great hopes for the political impact of the next crisis, which they had expected in 1853, and Marx devoted himself to the detailed investigation of the concrete mechanisms of crisis in order to be able to anticipate their future course. Marx and Engels were certainly excited by the onset of the crisis of 1857, but despite their optimistic rhetoric, they didn't really seem to have much expectation that anything would come of it, they didn't throw themselves into political activity, and did not appear surprised when the crisis passed, leaving only minor dislocations in its wake.

Nevertheless the crisis, and its failure to develop according to the course anticipated by Marx, provided the stimulus for Marx to return to his economic studies, to look behind the symptoms of impending crisis, of over-speculation and over-trading, to find its roots in the capitalist mode of production itself. The starting point of Marx's investigations was again the central question of monetary circulation, which neither political economy nor the currency reformers had been able to understand.

5

Money, Capital and Crisis in the Grundrisse

Marx's intensive studies of political economy were carried out in three phases. Under the impetus of his meeting with Engels, he first engaged with political economy in the period 1844–7. Over the period of the 1848 revolutions he threw himself into political and polemical activity, returning to his economic studies in 1851–3 in order to understand the concrete mechanisms underlying the crisis of 1847–8. He then abandoned his studies in political economy some time in 1854, concentrating on journalistic work and political analysis of world events. He returned to his economic studies once more in the midst of the 1857 crisis, resuming the work he had left off three years before in the attempt to understand the relationship between financial crisis and the underlying contradictions of the capitalist mode of production. This time, however, his economic studies acquired their own momentum. In the notebooks since published as the *Grundrisse* Marx lay the foundations for the mature analysis which would culminate in *Capital*.

Marx first expressed a desire to return to his studies in a letter to Engels in April 1857, which would seem to indicate that he had at least been looking back over his notes: 'I haven't yet got round to it, but some time I must really investigate the relationship between the rate of exchange and bullion. The role played by money as such in determining the bank rate and the money market is something striking and quite antagonistic to all laws of political economy. Worthy of note are the 2 newly published volumes of Tooke's *History of Prices*. A pity the old man's head-on collision with the currency principle chaps should lead him to give such a one-sided turn to all his disquisitions.' (Marx to Engels, 23.04.57, CW40, 126; c.f. 24.02.57, CW40, 102)

Marx eventually got down to work in July 1857, when he began sketching some critical comments on Bastiat and Carey, from whom Bastiat derived most of his ideas. These comments begin in the form of a review of Bastiat, in which Bastiat and Carey are initially acknowledged as 'apparent exceptions' to the general stagnation of political economy since Ricardo and Sismondi, but half of the manuscript is devoted to a discussion of Carey (whose work Marx had excerpted extensively in June 1851 — MEGA IV.8, 672–81, 684–752), the second half consisting of an increasingly contemptuous discussion of Bastiat's chapter on Wages, which concludes *'It is impossible to pursue this nonsense any further'* (CW28, 6, 16). However this work seems to have stimulated Marx's appetite for his economic studies, and in late August 1857 he got down to work on a 'general introduction' to the manuscript known as the *Grundrisse*.

In his works of the early 1850s Marx had argued that the speculation and over-trading that appeared to be the cause of crises was only a superficial manifestation of the underlying tendency to overproduction inherent in the capitalist mode of production. The implication of this argument was that monetary and financial reforms could not eliminate the crisis tendencies of capitalist accumulation. However, Marx had not taken his analysis further than to make some programmatic statements to that effect. In the wake of the crisis of 1857 Marx sought to set this argument on more rigourous theoretical foundations.

There is no evidence that Marx resumed his economic investigations with the intention of achieving more than an element of self-clarification, which became more urgent in the face of the apparently deepening crisis. However, he very soon began to achieve results which pointed in the direction of a much more substantial study, which would set political economy on completely new foundations. These results particularly concerned the fundamental concept of value, as distinct from price, and surplus value, as distinct from profit, which Marx arrived at on the basis of his development of the analytical distinction between production and circulation which he had begun to explore in the early 1850s. As soon as he realised the implications of these results Marx resumed the plan to write a systematic critique of political economy that he had conceived in 1844, but soon abandoned. He would work on this critique intensively for the next ten years.

Marx began work on the main manuscript of the *Grundrisse* around the end of October 1857 and made rapid progress. On 16th January 1858 he wrote to Engels, announcing that 'I am, by the way, discovering some very nice arguments. E.g. I have completely demolished the theory of profit as hitherto propounded' (CW40, 249; c.f. Marx to Lassalle, 11.3.58, CW40, 286, where Marx notes that he has cleared up the matter of the conflict between Ricardo's exposition of profit and his definition of value.) By the 22nd February he was proposing that Lassalle arrange a publisher for a work comprising six books (Marx to Lassalle, 22.02.58, CW40, 270) and two additional small volumes. The planned books would cover: Capital, Landed Property, Wage Labour, The State, International Trade and the World Market. The two additional volumes would provide a short historical outline of the development of economic categories and relations yet a third. In the event, even the greatly expanded first book remained incomplete at Marx's death.

Production and Circulation

The fundamental problem which Marx addressed in the *Grundrisse* was that of the relationship between production and circulation, as the basis on which to explore the relationship between the underlying tendency to overproduction and the appearance of commercial and financial crises, developing the analysis sketched out in his 'Reflections' of 1851. In the *Grundrisse* Marx was concerned above all to get behind the superficial manifestations of capitalist accumulation, to uncover the most fundamental determinants of the contradictory course of accumulation by uncovering the contradictions inherent in the capitalist form of social production.

The method of analysis was to abstract from the everyday determinants of the activity of particular capitalists, to discover their presuppositions in the dynamics of the system of capitalist production as a whole. This led Marx to a focus on 'capital-in-general', as against the form in which capital appears as particular competing capitals, and to the analysis of the primacy of the production of surplus value over its circulation and distribution. The complexity of the task which Marx set himself was that of reconciling in a single theory the fundamental determinants of the capitalist system of production, based on the production and accumulation of surplus value, with its superficial manifestations in the sphere of competition between particular capitals.[1]

---

[1] Marx discussed his method of abstraction in a letter to Engels: 'Only by this procedure is it possible to discuss one relation without discussing all the rest'. The focus on value presupposes the 'transcendence of all undeveloped, pre-bourgeois modes of production which are not in every respect governed by exchange. Although an abstraction, it is an historical

Production and Circulation

This methodological concern led Marx from the consideration of monetary crises, with which the manuscript begins, to the consideration of the role of money in mediating the relationship between production and exchange, then back to the analysis of capital, and so, for the first time, to the theoretical consideration of the process of capitalist production, developing the outlines of the theory of surplus value which lay at the heart of all his subsequent work. The theory of surplus value then provided the basis on which Marx was able both to explain the foundations of capitalism as a system based on the exploitation of wage labour, and to begin to develop a deeper understanding of the tendency to crisis.

In the 'General Introduction' Marx outlined the theoretical and methodological principles of political economy, considering the question of the relationships between production, distribution, exchange and consumption in the most abstract terms, and concluding that 'they are all elements of a totality, differences within a unity', in which 'production is the dominant moment, both with regard to itself in the contradictory determination of production and with regard to the other moments. ... A definite [mode of] production thus determines a definite [mode of] consumption, distribution and exchange and *definite relations of these different moments to one another*' (CW28, 36).

Marx soon abandoned the introduction, partly because, as he noted in the Preface to the *Critique of Political Economy* (1859), 'it seems to me confusing to anticipate results which still have to be substantiated' (CW29, 261), a view also expressed early in the main manuscript, where Marx noted that the 'general question of the relationship of circulation to the other relations of production can be raised only at the conclusion' (CW28, 60–1). But it also seems likely that work on the Introduction was interrupted by the pressure of more mundane tasks.

The Notebook in which the Introduction is written is dated 23rd August 1857. At the same time as working on these notes Marx was collating voluminous notebooks on the course of the world crisis and was closely following the development of the Indian crisis, while he was also writing regular articles for the *New York Daily Tribune* and,

---

abstraction and hence feasible only when grounded on a specific economic development of society ...' (Marx to Engels, 02.04.58, CW40, 298, 301). Engels was not impressed. He replied that the work sounded very abstract, and he hoped that 'the abstract, dialectical tone of your synopsis will, of course, disappear in the development' (Engels to Marx, 09.04.58, CW40, 304).

with Engels, was writing a series of entries on military affairs for the *New American Cyclopaedia*. On average Marx wrote one article a week for the *New York Daily Tribune*, but in September and early October 1857 he wrote a total of 11, while his work on the Cyclopedia was at its heaviest during September and the first half of October 1857 (about twelve articles were written over this period), tailing off through November to nothing in the first quarter of 1858. With a total of 23 articles written in this six week period it seems unlikely that even Marx would have had much time or energy for any other work.[2]

By 20th October it seemed that the long-delayed crisis had at last broken out, perhaps persuading Marx of the urgency of addressing more concrete issues. As he wrote to Lassalle two months later, 'The present commercial crisis has impelled me to set to work seriously on my outlines of political economy, and also to prepare something on the present crisis' (CW40, 226.)

Marx probably began work on the main manuscript of the *Grundrisse* in late October or early November 1857.[3] Although the first mention of it in his correspondence is not until December, he had already made considerable progress by the end of November, the beginning of Notebook III being dated '29, 30 November and December' (CW28, 219 n. c). The need to maintain his journalistic output meant that Marx could work almost exclusively at night, to the serious detriment of his failing health.[4]

Money, Crisis and Currency Reform

The starting point of the main manuscript of the *Grundrisse* was Marx's renewed attack on the monetary reformers who believed that

---

[2] On 15th September Marx apologised to Engels for not having written, 'due firstly to a great deal of work and secondly to numerous time-consuming errands in which "inner compulsion" played no part whatever' (CW40, 168), and on 20th October apologised again for not writing due to spending a week showing a young visitor around and to 'much work' (CW40, 191).

[3] In view of the reference to Darimon's book in a letter to Engels earlier in the year (10.01.57, CW40, 90) it is possible that the first few pages of the manuscript were written earlier, as the editors of the English edition of the *Collected Works* suggest.

[4] Marx to Engels: 'I am working like mad all night and every night collating my economic studies so that I at least get the outlines clear before the *déluge*' (8.12.57, CW40, 217) ... 'working enormously, as a rule until 4 o'clock in the morning. ... 1. Elaborating the outlines of political economy. (For the benefit of the public it is absolutely essential to go into the matter au fond, as it is for my own, individually, to get rid of this nightmare.) 2. the present crisis - collecting lots of material'. (18.12.57, CW40, 224; c.f. Marx to Lassalle, 21.12.57, CW40, 226).

Money, Crisis and Currency Reform

the evils of capitalism could be overcome by altering the monetary system, without transforming the system of production based on private property, on the grounds that the evils of the capitalist system derived from the exploitation of the producers by the bankers. According to the monetary reformers the bankers abuse their monopolistic control of money to impose high interest rates by restricting credit, so misappropriating the legitimate profit of the producer, and precipitating commercial and financial crises, which they exacerbate by restricting credit just when it is most scarce.

This reformist framework of 'bourgeois socialism' was associated particularly with the name of Proudhon, whom Marx had mercilessly attacked in *The Poverty of Philosophy* (1846–7) and denounced in the *Communist Manifesto* for being 'desirous of redressing social grievances, in order to secure the continued existence of bourgeois society' (CW6, 513). Far from withering away, by the 1850s in France Proudhonian socialism was a more serious obstacle than it had been in the 1840s, promising to provide the Bonapartist regime with a reformist programme through which to acquire radical credentials and to maintain its petty bourgeois social base.

In the 1840s Proudhonian socialism had focused on distribution and the equalisation of property. By the 1850s the emphasis had shifted to circulation, and particularly to freeing production from the constraints imposed by the scarcity of credit, a scarcity which, the Proudhonians believed, was created by the continued attachment to metallic money which enabled the bankers to profit from their monopolistic control of the medium of exchange. The evil of the system of metallic money came to the fore in times of difficulty, when bankers took advantage of the shortage of cash to force up interest rates and provoke a crisis, just when trade and production needed a freeing of credit. Thus the Proudhonian socialists, like their English socialist and American populist counterparts, believed that a system of free credit, unconstrained by the limits of metallic convertibility, would eliminate both the capitalistic exploitation of the producers by the bankers, and the periodic crises to which the system of metallic money gave rise. The rhetoric of Proudhonism could also serve less radical purposes, being borrowed to cover the fraudulent speculation of the Crédit Mobilier, and the financial profligacy and inflationary expedients of the Bonapartist state.

The manuscript of the *Grundrisse* begins as a review of Darimon's book *De la réforme des banques*. This work was significant for Marx not just as a Proudhonian tract, but also because it had a preface by Girardin, a Bonapartist journalist, who 'betrays evident admiration for Isaac Pèreire [founder of the Crédit Mobilier]. Hence it enables one to get some idea of the kind of socialist coups d'etat Bonaparte thinks himself capable of resorting to, even at the eleventh hour.' (Marx to Engels, 10.01.57, CW40, 90).

Marx ridicules Darimon's ignorance, and focuses on his characteristically Proudhonian failure to understand the difference between the need for money as a form of capital and the need for money as means of circulation, which Marx had earlier explored in his 'Reflections' of 1851. In a crisis commodities remain unsold in the form of commodity capital because there is nothing against which they can be exchanged, not because there is no money to effect the exchange. The problem is not a shortage of money as the means of circulation which can facilitate the exchange of equivalents, but the shortage of the equivalents themselves. Trade can be inconvenienced, but it can never be disrupted by a mere shortage of money, since the supply of money as means of circulation fluctuates in accordance with the needs of trade, through changes in the velocity of its circulation.[5]

If the fundamental problem is an absence of equivalents against which the commodities can be exchanged, then no amount of money can compensate for this absence, for what is needed is not money, but capital, in the form of the equivalent commodities created by an increase in production. An attempt to overcome the crisis by the unrestrained issue of money will do nothing to remove the cause of the crisis, which in the specific case explored by Marx lies in the disproportionality of production, but will simply provoke inflation. On this basis Marx condemns Darimon's proposed recourse to the printing press as the panacea for the shortage of money which supposedly underlies commercial distress.

Marx's criticism of Darimon leads him immediately to 'the basic question'. 'The general question is: is it possible to revolutionise the existing relations of production and the corresponding relations of distribution by means of changes in the instrument of circulation — changes in the organisation of circulation?' (CW28, 60). Marx goes on to ask rhetorically 'whether it is not then necessarily a self-defeating

---

[5] Marx had earlier made this point in his discussion of the 1844 Bank Act, in which he argues that bank deposits have been displacing notes, so that the question of the currency issue has become largely irrelevant, the regulatory role of the Bank now being effected through the impact of its credit operations on the deposits of the joint-stock banks (CW16, 3–7).

effort to seek to overcome the essential conditions of a relationship by effecting a formal modification within it. The various forms of money may correspond better to social production at various stages of its development; one form may remove certain shortcomings with which the other cannot cope. But none of them, as long as they remain forms of money, and so long as money remains an essential relation of production, can resolve the contradictions inherent in the money relationship, they can all only express these contradictions in one form or another' (CW28, 61). The first task, then, is to identify these contradictions by investigating the determinations of money.

As we have seen, Marx had identified money as the focus of his critical attention in his earliest economic works, and had devoted most of his reading in political economy in the 1850s to the monetary debates. In his manuscript on Bullion of 1851 he had concluded that 'the foundation of crises, therefore, undoubtedly lies in money' (MEGA, IV, 8, 4), and in his 'Reflections' the following month he had concluded that the problem lay not in any particular monetary arrangements, but in the money system, the system of capitalist commodity production. However, in none of his earlier works had he got to the bottom of the relationship between production and circulation. It was this that he first attempted to do in the *Grundrisse*.

The Money Form and the Possibility of Crisis

Marx begins by summarising the results of his earlier researches. The 'contradictions inherent in the money relationship' derive not from the form or the existence of money, but from the social relations of production which money serves to mediate in its function as means of exchange. It is precisely because production is oriented to the production of exchange value, and not directly to social need, that there is no necessary relation established between the supply of the commodity and the demand for it. If there is not enough demand for the commodity, this appears as a shortage of money in the hands of prospective purchasers, but the problem is not the shortage of money, but the initial dislocation of supply and demand. Nevertheless, in a society in which the division of labour is mediated by the exchange of commodities, every producer 'becomes dependent on the exchange value of his commodity', so that 'the exchange relation establishes itself as a power external to and independent of the producers' (CW28, 83).

This external and independent power confronts the producers as the power of money, but 'money does not create this opposition and this contradiction; on the contrary; their development creates the apparently transcendental power of money'. The development of exchange means that the relationship between the commodity and money necessarily becomes an accidental relationship, since it is purely accidental that supply and demand should balance. 'As soon as money is an external thing alongside the commodity, the exchangeability of the commodity for money is immediately linked to external conditions, which may or may not be present. It is subject to external circumstances, ... therefore a matter of chance.' (CW28, 84–5)

If supply exceeds demand the commodity cannot be sold at a price corresponding to its value, but this is not the result of a shortage of money, but of the disproportionality of production which no amount of money can remedy. On the other hand, if we assume with the economists that supply and demand are already in balance, then it doesn't matter what serves as money. 'If the conditions under which the price of a commodity = its exchange value are assumed as fulfilled, i.e. balance of demand and supply, of production and consumption, in the final analysis proportionate production ... then the question of money becomes quite secondary, and especially the question whether blue or green tickets, metal or paper ones, are issued, or in what other form social book-keeping will be done' (CW28, 90).

This analysis of money brings us directly to the demonstration of the formal possibility of crises. The possible disproportionality of supply and demand, and so the failure of producers to be able to realise the value of their commodities, is already inherent in the separation of purchase and sale which marks the society based on the production of commodities, and herein lies the most abstract determinant of the *possibility* of crises. 'Hence, the quality of money as mediator, the separation of exchange into two acts, already contains the germ of crises, at least their possibility, which cannot be realised except where there exist the basic conditions of classically and fully developed circulation corresponding to its concept' (CW28, 133).[6]

The discussion of money does not solve the problem of crises, but it does establish the framework within which the problem can be addressed. The possibility of crisis is inherent in the subordination of

---

[6] 'the lack of congruence of C—M and M—C is the most abstract and superficial form in which the possibility of crises is expressed'(Marx to Engels, 02.04.58, CW40, 302).

the production of commodities to the circulation of money and capital, as Proudhon and his followers argued, but the latter is not an alien power superimposed on the 'freedom and equality' of the elementary exchange relationship, for money and capital are only different forms of exchange value, providing the motive for capitalist production and the driving force underlying the development of production and exchange. The alienated character of money and capital is no more than the developed form of the alienation already inherent in the social relations of commodity production. The separation of money and commodity is only an expression of the separation of purchase and sale, which is inherent in the elementary form of exchange. However, to get beyond the demonstration of the formal possibility of crises to the understanding of their necessity and of their concrete forms requires a closer analysis of the dynamics of capitalist production and reproduction, and this means going beyond money to develop an analysis of capital and, underlying capital, of the social form of capitalist production.

The Transition from Money to Capital

'Fully developed circulation' is not marked simply by the separation of purchase and sale, but also by the emergence of the specialised activity of trade, in which the purpose of the merchants is not to acquire commodities for use, but to make a profit (CW28, 86, 134–5). This adds another dimension to the consideration of money, for money is now no longer simply the means of exchange, but has become in the hands of the merchant 'an end-in-itself, which commodity trade and exchange merely serve to realise', so that money now 'possesses an independent existence outside circulation, and in this new determination *can* be withdrawn from it' (CW28, 137–8). However, while the possibility of withdrawal provides a more concrete determinant of the possibility of crisis, it does not yet explain why such a crisis should occur.

In this determination money 'has an independent existence outside circulation; it has stepped outside it. ... In this aspect its role as *capital* is already latent'. This independence is not absolute since 'devoid of all relation to circulation, money would not be money but a simple natural object, gold or silver. In this determination money is as much the premiss as the result of circulation. Its very independence is not a cessation of the relation to circulation, but a *negative* relation to it'. If money is withdrawn from circulation, circulation ceases, but this accumulated money can also be thrown back into circulation, in which case it realises its role as capital, and establishes a relation with wage labour (CW28, 151–2).

As capital money becomes an 'instrument of production', concerned 'with the creation of exchange values'. As such, money dissolves all earlier forms of communal production, but far from being destructive of capitalist social relations, money is the driving force of their development. 'It is inherent in the very nature of money itself that it can exist as a developed element of production only where *wage labour* exists, and hence far from dissolving the social order, it is indeed a condition for its development and a driving force for the development of all productive forces. ... As *material representative of general wealth*, as *individualised exchange value*, money must be the *immediate* object, aim and product of general labour, of the labour of all individuals. Labour must directly produce exchange value, i.e. money. It must therefore be *wage labour*. ... Hence *wage labour* on the one hand, and *capital* on the other, are only different forms of developed exchange value and of money as its incarnation' (CW28, 152, 156, 158).

The analysis of the relationship between money and circulation has led Marx directly to the problem of capital and, in particular, to that of the source of surplus value, which he addressed systematically for the first time in the *Grundrisse*.

Marx had been clear since 1844, on the basis of Ricardo's labour theory of value and Marx's own analysis of alienated labour, that the source of profit was the surplus labour of the worker, but he had never examined precisely how the capitalist managed to appropriate this surplus labour. In particular, Marx had never shown precisely how the exploitation of the worker could be reconciled with the freedom and equality of exchange, which provided the foundation for the illusions of Bastiat and Proudhon, for whom the source of exploitation was not to be found in the social relations of commodity production, but in the bankers' monopoly of money.

The key to resolving this paradox was the concept of labour power, which Marx introduced for the first time in the *Grundrisse*, in distinguishing between the *product of labour*, sold by the petty commodity producer, and the *capacity to labour*, sold by the wage labourer (CW28, 197). The source of profit is to be found in the time for which the worker is compelled to work, beyond that required to produce sufficient to reproduce her necessary means of subsistence. This surplus labour time is embodied in a mass of commodities, whose sale realises the capitalist's surplus value, of which profit, rent and interest are only component parts. With the development of the theory of surplus value Marx believed that he was now able to settle his accounts not only with Proudhon, but also with political economy as a whole.[7]

The Self-Expansion of Capital and Overproduction

The theory of surplus value has immediate implications for our understanding of the crisis tendencies of capitalist accumulation, for it immediately led Marx to identify the driving force of capitalism as the insatiable appetite of capital for surplus value. Ricardo identified the development of the productive forces as the distinguishing feature of the capitalist mode of production, but he did not relate this to the social form of capitalist production as the production of surplus value, and so was unable to understand the fundamental contradiction inherent in capitalist production (CW28, 277), between the tendency to develop the forces without limit, and the confinement of the development of the forces of production within the limits of profitability. It is the elucidation of this contradiction that provides the underlying theme for the rest of the *Grundrisse*, and whose development explains the crisis tendencies of capitalist accumulation.

In its drive to appropriate ever more surplus value capital tries to overcome all barriers to its self-expansion, and this leads it to expand production without limit, giving rise to the inherent tendency to the overproduction of commodities. This is not a contingent feature of capitalism, but derives from 'the exact development of the concept of capital' and 'the clear understanding of the basic premiss of the [capitalist] relationship' in order to 'reveal all the contradictions of bourgeois production, as well as the limits at which this relationship outgrows itself' (CW28, 256).

'Since capital represents the general form of wealth — money — it has a boundless and measureless urge to exceed its own limits. Every

---
[7] Marx wrote to Engels on 16th January 1858, while he was in the middle of this section of the manuscript, 'I have been overdoing very much my nocturnal labours ... I am, by the way, discovering some very nice arguments. E.g. I have completely demolished the theory of profit as hitherto propounded.' (CW40, 249)

boundary is and must be a barrier for it. Otherwise it would cease to be capital, money reproducing itself. If a particular boundary were not to be a barrier for it, but one to which it could confine itself without difficulty, capital would itself have declined from exchange value to use value, from the general form of wealth to a particular substance of it. Capital as such creates a particular surplus value, because it cannot create an infinite one at once; but it is the constant drive to create more of it. The quantitative border to surplus value appears to it only as a natural barrier, as a necessity, which it constantly tries to overcome and beyond which it constantly tries to go' (CW28, 259–60). This attempt to overcome all barriers, in the attempt to maximise the production of relative surplus value by reducing the necessary labour time to the minimum, appears as the tendency to develop the productive forces without limit.[8]

The capitalist appetite for surplus value can be met only by the constant development of the forces of production. Introducing new methods of production reduces the cost of production of the workers' means of subsistence, so reducing the value of labour power, and increasing the proportion of the working day whose product the capitalist can appropriate as a surplus value. Thus the drive for surplus value is a drive to develop the productive forces without limit, in order to reduce to a minimum the labour time necessary for the workers' subsistence.'As an infinite drive for enrichment, capital strives for an infinite enlargement of the productive forces of labour and calls them into being' (CW28, 266).

The production of a growing mass of commodities does not in itself provide a sufficient basis for the appropriation of a growing mass of surplus value, since the commodities have first to be turned into money as the embodiment of value, and to be turned into money they have to find a market. The need to realise the surplus value produced appears to the capitalist as the barrier of the limited extent of the market.

The capitalist process of production is at one and the same time a labour process, in which use values are produced, and a valorisation process, in which a sum of value is laid out in the form of money to be transformed into a greater sum of money. However, in the first instance the enlarged capital exists only as a mass of commodities, and so 'exists only in idea in the form of a certain sum of money,

---

[8] This is the first time that Marx used the concepts of necessary labour and relative surplus value.

The Self-Expansion of Capital and Overproduction 133

and which can be *realised* as such only in exchange'. In this sense 'the valorisation *process* of capital ... appears at the same time as its *devaluation process*, its demonetisation' (CW28, 328–9), since 'the product of the process in its immediate form is not *value*, but must first re-enter circulation to be realised as such. ... As *commodity* in general, capital now shares the fate of commodities in general; it becomes a matter of chance, whether or not it is exchanged for money, whether or not its *price* is realised' (CW28, 330–1).[9]

The barriers to the production of surplus value lie within the production process itself, and can, at least in principle, be overcome within that process, provided only that the capitalist has the requisite means of production and labour power to hand. However, when it comes to the realisation of the surplus value through the sale of the commodities produced, capital confronts an external barrier. 'Within the production process the valorisation appeared to be completely identical with the production of surplus labour ..., and thus without any *limits* other than those which are partly presupposed and partly posited within this process itself, but always posited within it as *barriers* to be overcome. But now barriers appear which lie *outside* the process.' (CW28, 331)

This leads us to the fundamental question of the relationship between the growth of production and the growth of the market, which is the key to the analysis of the tendency to overproduction. What is at issue is not just the availability of money to buy the product, as Proudhon and the currency reformers believed, but the existence of an effective demand for the growing product. Although Marx had asserted from his earliest works that there was a tendency to overproduction, he had analysed it only from the side of production, simply taking it for granted that capitalist production would exhaust the markets available to it. However the size of the market cannot simply be taken as given, since the growth of production itself expands the market. According to 'Say's Law of Markets', which was one of the fundamental laws of political economy, general overproduction is impossible because 'supply creates its own demand', as every sale leads to a corresponding purchase. If Marx is to establish a tendency to overproduction, he has to confront Say's Law.

---

[9] Marx notes that in general its price will not be realised, because the costs of production are constantly falling, so that 'a part of the existing capital is constantly devalued by the reduction of the costs of production at which it can be *reproduced*' (CW28, 329).

Production and Realisation

Marx begins his analysis with the problem facing the particular capitalist of realising the surplus value embodied in the increased product, in relation to an assumed constant level of demand on the part of all other capitalists and workers.

If the commodity is to be sold as an exchange value, it must constitute a use value, an object of consumption. 'The first barrier [it runs up against] is therefore *consumption* itself — the *demand for it*', and this demand must be effective demand, backed up by 'money to be given in exchange for the commodity demanded'. However, production has now increased, to the extent of the surplus value produced, while there has not yet been any increase in demand. This creates the second barrier to the valorisation of capital, 'since circulation was originally presupposed as a fixed magnitude, as having a given volume, while capital has produced a new value in the production process, it appears that there can in fact be no equivalent available for it' (CW28, 332).

Capitalist reproduction confronts a barrier since, 'if the process is to be renewed, the whole product must be converted into money'. The contradiction between the commodity as a value and the commodity as a use value, that appeared as a formal contradiction in the separation of purchase and sale which is characteristic of the exchange of commodities, has now become a substantial barrier which capital must overcome. 'These are the contradictions which cannot escape a simple, objective, impartial examination. How they are constantly transcended in production based on capital, yet constantly reproduced, and only forcibly transcended (although up to a point this transcendence appears merely as a smooth adjustment), is another question. For the moment, the important thing is to take note of the existence of these contradictions. ... All the contradictions of [simple commodity] circulation come to life again in a new form ... But this time the contradiction is no longer posited as *a purely formal difference*' (CW28, 333).

The money equivalent of the commodity cannot be conjured out of thin air (nor created by a banker). It can only exist if capitalist production has also taken place elsewhere, producing an equivalent surplus value embodied in commodities against which the first can be exchanged. Behind the need for a consumer of the increased production, therefore, lies the need for another capitalist producer whose activity will have promoted the increase in demand. The required equivalent may in the first place appear in the form of money, if this corresponds

Production and Realisation

to a real increase in the quantity of gold produced, although not if it is simply an addition to the sum of money in circulation, since what is required is 'money not as means of circulation but as money. ... The *surplus value* produced at one point requires the production of surplus value at *another* point, for which it may be exchanged. Initially the production of more gold and silver, more money, will suffice' (CW28, 334), in which case the enlarged capital will simply be held in the money form. More generally, however, what is required is an increase in production at other points in the system. Behind the growing market required to absorb the growing product, therefore, lies the systematic growth of capitalist production.

A condition of production based on capital is therefore *the production of a constantly expanding periphery of circulation*, whether the sphere is directly expanded, *or whether* more points within it *become points of production*. If circulation initially appeared as a given magnitude, it appears here as a moving one, expanding through production itself. In the light of this it already appears itself as a moment of production. (CW28, 334)

Although the existence of a market for the product is outside the control of a particular capitalist, we can now see that the market does not constitute an external barrier, since the market is simultaneously expanded by the growth of capitalist production, of which it is but an expression. The 'general concept of capital' embraces both production and circulation, since 'it is *this unity of production and valorisation*, not *immediately* but only as a *process* tied to certain conditions, and, as it appeared, *external* conditions.' (CW28, 334)

The tendency to expand the market develops alongside the tendency to expand production without limit, since it is capital which itself creates the world market in its own image. 'The tendency to create the *world market* is inherent directly in the concept of capital itself. Every limit appears as a barrier to be overcome. ... hence the tendency of capital (1) to continually enlarge the periphery of circulation; (2) to transform it at all points into production carried on by capital.'[10] The production of relative surplus value on the basis of increasing productivity, leads to 'firstly, quantitative increase in existing

---

[10] 'the world market is likewise both the presupposition of the totality and its bearer. Crises are then the general pointer to and beyond the presupposition, and the urge to adopt a new historical form' (CW28, 160).

consumption; secondly, the creation of new needs by the propagation of existing ones over a wider area; *thirdly*, production of *new* needs and discovery and creation of new use values', so developing the division of labour with the emergence of new branches of production (CW28, 334–5).

Just as production based on capital produces universal industry, i.e. surplus labour, value-creating labour, on the one hand, so does it on the other produce a system of universal exploitation of natural and human qualities, a system of universal utility, whose bearer is science itself as much as all the physical and spiritual qualities, and under these conditions nothing appears as something *higher-in-itself*, as an end in itself, outside this circle of social production and exchange. Thus it is only capital which creates bourgeois society and the universal appropriation of nature and of the social nexus itself by the members of society. Hence the great civilising influence of capital; hence its production of a stage of society compared to which all previous stages seem merely *local developments* of humanity and *idolatry of nature* (CW28, 336–7).

Marx's Theory of Crisis: One Theory or Three?

The discussion began by asserting the existence of a fundamental contradiction between the production and realisation of surplus value, which appears to the capitalist in the form of the barrier of the limited market for his product. However, Marx has also argued that capital regards all such limits as no more than barriers to be overcome. The conditions for the realisation of the surplus product are the conditions for the further extension of capitalist production, which is achieved by the intensive and extensive development of the capitalist mode of production: on the one hand, by the production of relative surplus value, and on the other by the development of the world market. We now seem to have discovered the ways in which capital is able to dissolve all barriers to its advance, its fundamental contradiction driving it forwards without limit.

However, the fact that capital can tear down the barriers that confront its advance, primarily through the development of the world market, does not mean that it necessarily does so. 'From the fact that capital posits every such limit as a barrier which it has *ideally* already

Marx's Theory of Crisis: One Theory or Three? 137

overcome, it does not at all follow that capital has *really* overcome it' (CW28, 337). Capital remains contradictory. Its dynamism may suspend the contradiction, but it can never resolve it. The point is neither that capitalism can develop without limit, nor that it faces fixed limits, but that it is a 'living contradiction'. It is therefore essential to see both sides of this contradiction. Ricardo, who looked only at the growth of capitalist production and ignored the barriers of circulation, could best see the positive side of capitalism, while Sismondi, who emphasised the barrier of consumption, was better able to grasp the negative side of production based on capital. Nevertheless, the two sides are inseparable one from the other.

So far Marx has specified the contradictory character of capitalist production only in the most abstract form. The question which now arises is whether this contradiction can be specified more concretely, in order perhaps to identify more specifically the determinants of the crisis tendencies of capitalist accumulation, or whether we have to regard the outbreak of crises as purely fortuitous, the result of contingent disruptions of accumulation which have no inner necessity.

It is at this point in the development of the argument that the interpretation of Marx's texts becomes extremely difficult. As we have seen, within the Marxist tradition three quite distinct theories of crisis have been proposed, based on rather different specifications of the underlying contradiction. These are the underconsumptionist theory, which dominated the Marxism of the Second International, disproportionality theories, which became popular in the early twentieth century, and theories which associate crises with the falling tendency of the rate of profit, which have come to dominate contemporary Marxism. In general these theories have been regarded as mutually exclusive, and have been the focus of the most bitter theoretical and political dispute. However, in the *Grundrisse*, as in Marx's later works, we apparently find all three theories co-existing, without Marx ever indicating that he regarded them as inconsistent one with another. Is this simply an indication of the undeveloped character of Marx's theorising, or of his undoubted confusion when he comes onto discussion of these matters, or of the successive stages of a developing argument co-existing with one another? Or do the different theories of crisis have some kind of unity? And if they have a unity, do they all have equal status, or do they enjoy some kind of a hierarchical relationship to one another? Or are the interpretations simply wrong so that, despite appearances, Marx has one consistent theory of crisis?

As we will see, there is an element of truth in all of these interpretations. There is no doubt that Marx's theorising is undeveloped, and that his discussion is often inconsistent and confused. There is certainly some development in his thought, with changing emphases in different texts. His theory of crisis undoubtedly contains elements of underconsumptionist, disproportionality and falling rate of profit theories, but it is not a confused or an eclectic combination of all three. There is a conceptual unity and coherence running through his discussions.

This coherence is most evident in the discussion of the *Grundrisse*, not least because this is the text in which Marx develops the conceptual foundations of his subsequent works, and because he wrote it in a single intensive burst, following through a single argument with relatively few distractions, while the discussion of the later works is more fragmented. I will try to bring out the coherence of Marx's theory in the discussion of the *Grundrisse* in the following sections, and in the next chapters follow the threads of the different theories through Marx's later works.

As in his earlier works, in the *Grundrisse* Marx usually specifies the abstract tendency to crisis in apparently underconsumptionist terms, relating the overproduction of commodities to the limited development of the market. However, as soon as he discusses the issue more concretely he formulates the problem in terms of the disproportionality of production, as we have already seen above, and this leads him to grapple at length with the problem of the relationship between disproportionality and general overproduction, a theme to which he returned again and again in his later manuscripts. Finally, it is in the *Grundrisse* that Marx turns his attention for the first time to the secular law of the tendency for the rate of profit to fall, which had been a long-standing preoccupation of classical political economy. The secular tendency for the rate of profit to fall does not provide an explanation for cyclical crises, but a lower general rate of profit makes crises more likely and more destructive.

Disproportionate Production and General Overproduction

Political economy recognised the possibility of disproportional production, particularly as the result of unforeseeable events such as harvest failure or the disruption of commerce by war, but the political economists believed that such disproportionalities would be smoothly

Disproportionate Production and General Overproduction

remedied through competition, as the rise in prices of commodities in short supply, and the fall in prices of those in excess, would induce capital to move from the latter branches of production to the former, in order to rectify the imbalance. On the other hand, political economy denied the possibility of general overproduction, on the basis of Say's Law. The problem from our point of view is whether general overproduction is possible as a phenomenon distinct from disproportionality, or whether the two are one and the same thing.

'The whole controversy as to whether *overproduction* is possible and necessary in production based on capital, is about whether the valorisation of capital in production directly posits its valorisation in circulation ... The attempts made from the orthodox economic standpoint to deny the fact of *general overproduction* at a given moment are indeed childish', simply relying on Say's law to assert the identity, and so the necessary correspondence, of supply and demand (CW28, 337–8).

However, Marx argues, the discussion of Say's law is very confused. The identity of supply and demand is established in terms of the identical value of the commodities which are supplied and those which are the objects of demand. But this identity is purely nominal, for the commodity can only be realised as a value 'through exchange for *money*; and as an object of exchange for money it depends upon its *use value*; and as use value, in turn, it depends upon ... the demand for it' (CW28, 338), which depends not on its value, but on the need for it, and supply of the commodity can by no means create the need for it. Every sale provides the seller with the money with which to make a subsequent purchase, but the seller is not thereby compelled to make that purchase, and if the specific commodities she needs are not available, she will be unable to make the purchase.

The economists argue that this is merely a matter of an imbalance of supply and demand, which is not a manifestation of overproduction, but only of the disproportionality of production, in which too many of some commodities are produced and too few of others, a disproportionality which will be rectified by the normal operation of the market. But, Marx argues, this is to ignore the role of money in mediating the reproduction of capital and the circulation of commodities. Ricardo simply presupposes the exchange of commodities at prices corresponding to their values, so that 'exchange itself can therefore be ignored altogether. The product — capital posited as product — is *in itself* exchange value, to which the act of exchange merely adds form, in Ricardo, formal form.' If the value equivalence is already presupposed, then proportionality is simply a matter of the concrete use values in which this value is embodied. 'In the form of *exchange*, all value etc., is purely *nominal*; it is real only in the form of the *ratio*. The entire exchange, in so far as it does not produce a greater *material variety*, is *nominal*' (CW28, 258).

The problem is not simply one of the inappropriate supply of use values, but of the inability to transform use values into value. 'What is forgotten here is the fact that producing capital demands not a particular use value but *value* for itself, i.e. money — money not in its role as means of circulation but as the general form of wealth, or as the form of the realisation of capital in one respect, and return to its original dormant state in the other' (CW28, 339). The problem is neither a matter of the inadequate production of value, nor is it a problem of the inappropriate production of use values. It is a manifestation of the fundamental contradiction between value and use value which is inherent in the capitalist form of social production, in which use values are produced only as the means towards the valorisation of capital. The capitalist is looking to buy commodities not as use values, but as the means of expanding his capital. If he is not able to anticipate employing means of production and labour power profitably, he will simply hold his capital in the form of money, so interrupting circulation, and potentially precipitating a crisis.

Once we recognise this contradiction we can see why disproportionality appears not just as an imbalance of production, but as an overproduction. Overproduction arises not in relation to need, but in relation to valorisation. This is why the overproduction of particular commodities appears not as a shortage of other commodities, but as a shortage of money. But then 'the assertion that too *little money* is being produced is tantamount to the assertion that production does not coincide with valorisation, hence is *overproduction* ... hence the illusion of the money-conjurers (also Proudhon, etc.) that there is a shortage of *means of circulation* because of the dearness of money, and that more money has to be created artificially' (CW28, 339).

There is no reason why disproportionality should *necessarily* lead to a crisis, for it is perfectly possible that the interaction of supply and demand might rectify the imbalance, as Ricardo expected. 'Since production is itself regulated by the costs of production, it regulates itself. And if a particular branch of production does not valorise itself, capital withdraws from it to a certain degree and moves into other branches in which it is necessary.' Against this Marx puts forward two arguments.

First, in a general crisis the problem is not that capital is more profitable in one or another branch of production, but that it appears to be unprofitable in all branches of production, so that 'in a general crisis of overproduction the contradiction is not between different types of productive capital, but between industrial and loan capital, between capital as it is directly involved in the production process and capital as it appears as money independently outside that process' (CW28, 340).

Second, the underlying tendency of capital accumulation is to break through all barriers, and so to break through the proportions, so that redistribution under the impact of supply and demand can only be a secondary counter-tendency. 'The very necessity of evening-up *presupposes* the imbalance, the disharmony and hence the contradiction, ...if it is the tendency of capital to distribute itself in the correct proportions, it is just as much its necessary tendency to drive beyond the correct proportion because it strives boundlessly for surplus labour, surplus productivity, surplus consumption, etc' (CW28, 340).[11]

Competition and Disproportionality

Disproportionality is not a mere accident. The tendency constantly to drive through the proportionate barriers is imposed on capital by competition. 'In *competition*, this immanent tendency of capital appears as a compulsion imposed upon it by *other* capital and driving it beyond the correct proportion with a constant *March, march!* As Mr *Wakefield* correctly sniffs out in his commentary on Smith, free competition has *never* been analysed *at all* by political economists, however much they may chatter about it, even though it is the basis of the entire bourgeois production based on capital.'

The economists only look at competition as the negation of monopoly, but they never consider its positive significance as the form in which the inherent tendencies of capitalist development are imposed on every individual capital as an external force. 'Conceptually, *compe-*

---

[11] This is an argument that Engels and Marx had each presented in their earliest economic writings, as we have seen. Marx repeated the point in *Capital*. The 'constant tendency to equilibrium, of the various spheres of production, is exercised only in the shape of a reaction against the constant upsetting of this equilibrium' (CI, 356).

tition is nothing but the *inner nature of capital*, its essential character, manifested and realised as the reciprocal action of many capitals upon each other; immanent tendency realised as external necessity.)(Capital exists and can only exist as many capitals; hence its own character appears as their reciprocal action on each other.)' 'A *universal capital*, not confronted by alien capitals with which it exchanges ... is ... an impossibility. The mutual repulsion of capitalists is already inherent in capital as realised exchange value' (CW28, 350).[12]

Competition, through the pressure of supply and demand, confines capitalist production within the limits of proportionality. But this is only because, through the pressure to develop the forces of production in order to reduce the labour time necessary to production, competition has driven capitalist production constantly beyond those limits. 'Capital is just as much the constant positing of, as it is the constant transcendence of proportionate production. The existing proportions must constantly be transcended through the creation of surplus values and the increase of productive forces. But to demand that production should be expanded *instantaneously, simultaneously* and in *the same proportions*, is to impose external demands on capital, which in no way correspond to anything arising from capital itself. In fact, the departure from the given proportion in one branch of production drives all the other branches out of that proportion, and at unequal rates' (CW28, 340–1). If one branch of production expands beyond the limits of the market, it spurs the development of complementary branches to overproduce in their turn, so that disproportionality is not confined to one branch of production, but is generalised.

In the inter-play of the tendency to disproportionality, and to the reimposition of proportionality by competition it appears that it is a matter of accident whether proportionality is in fact established or

---

[12] Marx repeats this fundamental point time and again in these manuscripts. The competition of capitals amongst each other is 'the real movement of capitals in which alone the laws of capital are realised. These laws are in fact nothing but the general relations of this movement, its result, on the one hand, its tendency on the other ' (CW33, 72). 'The competition of capitals is nothing more than the realisation of the immanent laws of capital, i.e. of capitalist production, in that each capital confronts the other as executor of these laws, the individual capitals bringing their inner nature to bear by the external compulsion which they exert on each other, according to their inner nature. But in competition the immanent laws of capital, of capitalist production, appear as the result of the mechanical impact of the capitals on each other; hence inverted and upside down. What is effect appears as cause, the converted form appears as the original one, etc. Vulgar political economy therefore explains everything it does not understand from competition, i.e. to state the phenomenon in its most superficial form counts for it as knowing the laws of the phenomenon' (CW33, 102).

not. 'So far, we have in the valorisation process only the indifference of the individual moments to each other, that they determine each other internally and search for each other externally, but that they may or may not find each other, balance each other, correspond to each other. The necessary inner connection of moments belonging together and their mutually indifferent, independent existence are already a foundation of contradictions.' (CW28, 340)

If we sum up the argument so far, we can say that Marx has established that there is a tendency inherent in the capitalist mode of production to develop the forces of production, under the pressure of competition, without regard to the limits of the market, as every capitalist seeks to increase his profits by introducing new methods of production on an increasing scale. The momentum of the development of production in any branch is not determined by the demand for the product, but by the opportunities for acquiring a surplus profit by advancing the productive forces. The result is that, although the growth of capitalist production at the same time develops the world market, the forces of production develop unevenly and without any reference to the requirements of proportionality, so that competition imposes a constant tendency to the disproportionate development of the various branches of production.

The interaction of supply and demand provides a counter-tendency to the disproportionate development of production, as the overproduction of particular commodities leads to a fall in their price. For political economy the unevenness in the rate of profit leads capital to flow smoothly into the underdeveloped from the overdeveloped branches of production. However, on the one hand the stimulus of profit is not determined by the relation between supply and demand, but by the uneven development of the forces of production, so the former can act only as a counter-tendency to the uneven development of the forces of production. On the other hand, this counter-tendency is only mobilised in the face of the overproduction of particular commodities. Since these commodities have already been produced, the market can only act as a countertendency through the devaluation of commodities and the destruction of productive capacity in the overextended branches of production. The losses incurred by these capitalists leads them to reduce their purchases in turn, so that overproduction is immediately generalised, and capitalists in all branches of production face the prospect of loss. The distinction made by classical political economy between particular and general overproduction is therefore entirely spurious.

Underconsumption and the Tendency to Crisis

Marx's discussion of the relationship between particular and general overproduction seems to have established that the basis of the tendency to crisis in the capitalist mode of production is the necessarily disproportional development of production that is inherent in the very nature of capitalist production and an expression of the most fundamental tendency of capitalist accumulation. However Marx does not stop at this point, but proceeds to formulate the contradiction between the tendency to develop the productive forces without limit and the need to confine production within the limits of profitability at a more general and abstract level. 'Of course, the point here is not yet to analyse overproduction in all its specific characteristics, but only the predisposition to it as it is posited in primitive form in the relation of capital itself' (CW28, 345). This general formulation has often been interpreted as a classically underconsumptionist formulation of the tendency to crisis, as a contradiction between the unlimited development of the productive forces and the limited consumption power of the mass of the population. The passage is difficult to interpret, and merits close attention.

Marx begins by stressing that the tendency to overproduction cannot be seen merely as the result of the accidental emergence of disproportionality, as what Kautsky called the 'anarchy of the market', but has to be seen as an essential feature of capitalist production.

> However, we have by no means finished yet. The contradiction between production and valorisation ... has to be grasped more intrinsically than merely as the mutually indifferent and apparently independent appearance of the individual moments of the process or, rather, of the totality of processes. To get closer to the point: *d'abord* there is a limit, not inherent to production generally, but to production founded on capital. This limit is two-fold, or rather it is the same limit considered from two different aspects. Here it is sufficient to demonstrate that capital contains a *particular* restriction on production — which contradicts its general tendency to drive beyond every barrier to production – to have uncovered the foundation of *overproduction*, the basic contradiction of developed capital. ... These inherent limits must coincide with the nature of capital, with the essential character of its very concept. (CW28, 342)

Overproduction arises because capital always seeks to go beyond

Underconsumption and the Tendency to Crisis

its inherent limits. Marx goes on to define these limits:

> These necessary limits are: (1) *necessary labour* as the limit on the exchange value of living labour capacity or on the wages of the industrial population. (2) *surplus value* as the limit on surplus labour time; and ... as the limit on the development of the productive forces; (3) what is the same, *transformation into money*, exchange value in general as the limit of production . ... It is: (4) again identical as the *restriction of the production of use values* by exchange value; or that real wealth has to assume a *specific* form distinct from itself ... if it is to become an object of production at all. (CW28, 342)

But 'it arises from the *general tendency of capital* (and this is what in simple circulation was manifest in the fact that money as a means of circulation appeared only fleetingly, devoid of independent necessity, and hence not as a limit and barrier) that it forgets and abstracts from' these limits as competition drives capital to ever greater exertions. *'Hinc* overproduction, i.e. a sudden *reminder* of all these necessary moments of production based on capital; hence general devaluation in consequence of forgetting them.' (CW28, 343)

The development of the productive forces means that each successive crisis will be worse than those that went before as there is an 'ever greater collapse *as capital.* Therefore clear that the higher the level in which capital has developed, the more it appears as a barrier to production' (CW28, 343).

It is on the basis of the first of Marx's four points that this argument is generally interpreted as an underconsumptionist one, the tendency to crisis expressing the fundamental contradiction inherent in the capitalist mode of production between the tendency to develop the productive forces without limit, and the tendency to restrict the consumption needs of the mass of the population to a minimum, leading to a crisis of realisation as supply runs ahead of the growth of consumer demand.[13] However, although such an interpretation seems perfectly plausible, the question is rather more complicated than it might appear at first sight, for Marx is clearly aware of the inadequacy of the underconsumptionist theory of crisis, and nowhere in the

---

[13] Rosdolsky interprets Marx's argument as being underconsumptionist here, noting that 'the larger the surplus labour, the smaller (relatively) the necessary labour; but also then, the smaller the possibility of the realisation of the surplus-product' (Rosdolsky, 1977, 326, c.f. Itoh, 1980, 96–8; Lallier, 1989, 100–1).

commentary that follows the passage in question does he explain crises in underconsumptionist terms.

It is trivially the case that the demand of the working class cannot make any contribution to the realisation of the surplus product. Marx recognises that the workers' demand corresponds only to the necessary labour, so that, quoting Malthus,' "the very existence of a profit upon any commodity pre-supposes a *demand exterior to that of the labourer who has produced it*" and hence the "*demand of the labourer himself can never be an adequate demand*" ' (CW28, 346). Without some other source of demand capitalist production would be not just crisis-ridden, but impossible.

Marx has already made this quite clear by starting from the problem of the realisation of the surplus product, which he argued was only resolvable through the all-round development of capitalist production. The surplus-product is then realised through its sale to other capitalists, as they capitalise their surplus value in order to expand production. The problem of realisation cannot therefore be reduced to that of the limited consumption of the working class, but has to be related to the possibility of the profitable investment of the growing mass of surplus value. The lower the necessary labour, the greater the amount of surplus value that must be realised, but the realisation of the surplus value produced depends on the demand of capitalists, never on that of workers.

These are the terms in which Marx had presented the problem earlier in the manuscript, in criticising Ricardo. The capitalist product is not an increased stock of commodities, but capital in the form of money. This sum of money has been withdrawn from circulation, is 'value made negatively independent in opposition to circulation' (CW28, 291), but 'the independent, illusory existence of money has been transcended; it exists now only to valorise itself, i.e. to become capital. ...*Money*, so far as it already exists *in itself* as capital, is thus merely a *draft on future* (new) labour ... a draft on the real possibility of general wealth — on labour capacity, and, more precisely, on *labour capacity coming into being* ... posits future labour as *wage labour*, as use value of capital. No *equivalent* exists for the newly created value; its possibility [exists] only in new labour' (CW28, 291–2).

The realisation of the increased product is only possible if it is bought by capitalists, as the means for the further expansion of surplus value. Indeed, this is true not only for the realisation of the surplus value produced, but for the realisation of the product as a whole, since

Underconsumption and the Tendency to Crisis

the consumption of the labourers derives from the expenditure of the capitalists who employ those labourers as the means to the further production of surplus value. When Marx refers to *'necessary labour* as the limit on the exchange value of living labour capacity or on the wages of the industrial population' he is not referring to the limited consumption power of the mass of the population, but to the fact that the workers will only be employed if their wages are limited to the necessary labour that allows for the possibility of producing surplus labour as the basis for the appropriation of surplus value.

The point of the argument at this stage is not that there is a single absolute limit to capital accumulation, but that there are limits inherent in the social form of capitalist production. Particular crises can arise from all manner of causes, but the ultimate cause of all crises lies in the tendency for capital constantly to expand the forces of production beyond the limits of profitability. The emphasis throughout Marx's discussion in this section is on profit, not the limited consumption of the working class, as the limit to capitalist production.

Marx develops the basic point already made by emphasising that although the capitalist relates to all other workers as consumers, it is only the wages of his own workers that he controls, and these he tries to reduce to a minimum. 'In relation to each capitalist the total mass of all workers except his own appears not as workers, but as consumers ... Each capitalist knows that he does not confront his own worker as a producer confronts a consumer, and so he wants to restrict his consumption ... as much as possible. But of course he wants the workers of *other* capitalists to be the greatest possible consumers of his commodity. Yet the relationship of *each* capitalist to *his* workers is the *general relationship* of *capital and labour*, the essential relation.' (CW28, 346) This is even more the case in the wake of a crisis, which is precisely when capitalists would like to see workers' demand receiving a boost, but is also when each is under pressure to cut the wages of his own workers, so intensifying the crisis. 'Capital itself then regards the *demand of the labourer*, i.e. the payment of wages on which this demand is based, not as gain but as loss, i.e. the *immanent relationship of capital and labour*, asserts itself' (CW28, 349).

This passage refers to the contradictory relationship between the capitalist and the working class, but Marx does not develop any underconsumptionist implications of this contradiction. Even in the one example discussed by Marx in which production has expanded beyond the limits of the demand of the workers, the crisis strikes when 'the demand *exterior to the demand of the labourer himself* disappears or shrinks, hence the collapse occurs.' Marx relates this example not to any underconsumptionist tendency, but to the '*competition of capitals,* their indifference to and independence of one another' which leads capitalists to overestimate the workers' demand so that production 'is driven beyond the right proportion' (CW28, 349). There is nothing special about the workers' demand. 'Exactly the same is true of the demand created by production itself for raw materials, semi-finished products ... etc.' (CW28, 349)

In summing up his discussion at the end of the passage Marx comes back to the contradiction between production and valorisation as defining the inherent limit of capital. Capital tends to expand the forces of production without limit, but at the same time the purpose of capitalist production is the appropriation and realisation of surplus value, which determines the inherent limit to capitalist production, which it nevertheless constantly seeks to overcome. Our interpretation of the earlier passage is confirmed by Marx's amplification of the point here. Necessary labour is a limit not as a limited source of demand, but as the source of surplus value, which can only be expended for the purpose of the production of surplus value.[14]

Marx goes on to specify two more specific limits to exchange, which capital treats merely as barriers to be overcome. The first limit is that capitalist production can only be reproduced if surplus labour is exchanged for surplus labour, which is, as we have already seen, the condition for the realisation of the surplus value produced.

The second limit arises because capital constantly tries to expand surplus labour by reducing necessary labour to a minimum, so that the amount of surplus value to be realised constantly grows (CW28, 350–351). However, this contradiction between the tendency to expand the production of surplus value and the tendency to restrict the demand of the workers is again not the basis of an underconsumptionist theory of crisis. Alongside the growing mass of profit, Marx also draws attention to the fall in its rate, as it becomes increasingly difficult to

---

[14] 'Capital posits necessary labour only *in so far as* and *to the extent to which* it is surplus labour, and is *realisable* as fn*surplus value*. It therefore posits surplus labour as a condition of necessary labour, and surplus value as the limit to objectified labour, to value in general. When it can no longer posit the former, it no longer posits the latter. ... By its very nature, therefore, capital sets a *limit* for labour and the creation of value, which stands in contradiction to its tendency to expand them boundlessly. And by both posing a limit *specific* to itself and on the other hand driving beyond *any* limit, it is the very embodiment of contradiction' (CW28, 350).

Underconsumption and the Tendency to Crisis 149

extract still more surplus value the more the productivity of labour increases. As capital expands, a proportionately greater increase in productivity is necessary to achieve a further increase in surplus value, and if this increase cannot be achieved then capital will be withdrawn from circulation — we here find the first suggestion of a 'falling rate of profit' theory of crisis: 'The more developed capital already is, the more surplus labour it has already created, the more tremendously it must develop productivity if it is to valorise itself. ...The smaller the fractional part already which represents necessary labour, the greater the *surplus labour*, the less can any increase in productivity perceptibly diminish necessary labour, for the denominator had grown enormously. The self-valorisation of capital becomes more difficult to the extent to which it is already valorised.'(CW28, 265–6).

He now links the two arguments together, noting that 'as we have seen, relative *surplus value* grows much less relative to the productive power ...*But the volume of products grows in similar proportion*' (CW28, 351), increasing the 'demands made on consumption' at the same time as making it more difficult to reduce the necessary labour time and keep down wages. As we will see, Marx develops this contradiction more fully in his discussions of the tendency for the rate of profit to fall. For now it is sufficient to note the essential point: capitalist development leads to a rise in the mass of surplus value to be realised, and in the quantity of commodities in which that surplus value is embodied, at the same time as it become progressively more difficult to increase the rate of surplus value, and so to prevent a fall in the general rate of profit.

Marx concludes this section by summing up again, in almost the same words as before, stressing that capitalist production is based on the production of surplus value, and this is the source of both the productivity and the limits of capitalism. On the one hand, capital tends to develop the forces of production without limit as the means of increasing the surplus value produced. On the other hand, the limits to the development of the forces of production are imposed by the need to realise an enlarged capital — to make a profit. It is this general contradiction, rather than any more specific formulation of it, that Marx regards as being fundamental (CW28, 351. Compare the later draft of the same argument in TSV2, 520, which reinforces the interpretation presented here).

Disproportionality and the Valorisation of Capital

Marx has now shown that there are limits inherent in the capitalist mode of production that underlie the predisposition to crisis. Overproduction is not simply a matter of the accidental imbalance of production that might be found in any mode of production, but is a specific feature of the barriers expressed in the contradiction between production and valorisation so that 'overproduction takes place in relation to valorisation, nothing else' (CW28, 352).

The limits inherent in the capitalist mode of production are not fixed limits, beyond which accumulation cannot go, for the specific characteristic of capitalism is constantly to drive beyond all such limits. The realisation of the surplus value produced is limited by the extent of the market, but every expansion of capitalist production at the same time expands these limits by expanding the market.

Marx links the predisposition to crisis to the contradiction between the tendency to maximise surplus value, on the one hand, and the need to realise that surplus value in the form of money, on the other. However, this is not the basis of an underconsumptionist theory of crisis, the limitations of which Marx fully appreciates.

Marx recognises that general overproduction arises as the generalisation of particular overproduction, so that if relations of proportionality between the various branches of production are maintained a crisis of general overproduction will not arise. Similarly in every hypothetical and historical example that Marx examines, crises arise not because of the inadequacy of consumption, but because of the disproportionality of production. Nevertheless Marx does not offer a simple disproportionality theory of crisis.

Marx is not satisfied to rest his theory on disproportionalities that might emerge through misjudgements or market 'imperfections'. First, because such accidental disproportionalities might perfectly well be rectified by Ricardo's competitive adjustment, rather than being liquidated through a general crisis. Second, and perhaps most important, because such disproportionality is a result of overproduction in relation to the use value requirements of expanded reproduction, and not specifically 'in relation to valorisation' (CW28, 352). It is for this reason that Marx wants to go deeper, and explain the tendency to crisis in terms of value relationships. This is why he reformulates the problem of proportionality not in terms of the proportional relations between branches of production, but in terms of the proportionality between necessary and surplus labour. Marx defines this as the specifically capitalist form of disproportionality, which underlies the predisposition to crises inherent in the capitalist mode of production.

The proportionality between necessary and surplus labour on the one hand defines the problem of realisation. There is a fundamental difference between the revenue of the capitalist and that of the worker. The worker has to spend her revenue immediately to purchase means of subsistence, but the capitalist will only spend his surplus value if there is a prospect of thereby increasing his capital. The tendency to increase the production of surplus value means that there must be a corresponding tendency to increase investment if the proportionality between necessary and surplus labour is not to break down. On the other hand, the driving force of such an increase in investment is the rate of profit, which is an alternative expression for the proportionality between necessary and surplus labour. Thus the problem of crisis comes back to the problem of the explanation of the fall in the rate of profit that precipitates the crisis by disrupting the relations of proportionality between the branches of production, primarily between those producing means of production and those producing means of subsistence. The problem is to locate the cause of the fall in the general rate of profit prior to, and in abstraction from, the competition between capitals in the crisis.

This brings Marx back to the specific dynamics of the capitalist mode of production, whose driving force, imposed on every capitalist by competition, is the development of the forces of production. Overproduction is the specific method by which new methods of production replace older methods, as overproduction leads to a fall in prices, a devaluation of capital, a consequent fall in profitability and bankruptcy of backward capitals. Disproportionality is therefore only an expression of the contradictory form of capitalist accumulation.

Marx's discussion of these issues arises out of a critique of Proudhon's underconsumptionist theory of crisis and an exploration of the role of changes in relative and absolute prices in the crisis. As in the previous sections, this passage is exploratory, as Marx follows the thread of his argument wherever it might lead, rather than expository, so that the discussion raises more questions than it resolves. However it leads to a crucial advance in Marx's consideration of the fundamental problem of the conditions for the realisation of the expanding surplus value, which he now formulates in terms of the first version of his 'reproduction schemes'.

The discussion begins with a consideration of the role of prices in determining or resolving the tendency to overproduction. We saw above that Ricardo believed that the rise and fall of relative prices would be sufficient to induce capital to flow between the various branches of production in order to restore proportionality. Marx argued, on the other hand, that the problem in a crisis was not one of the unprofitability of one or another branch of production, but of the collapse in the general rate of industrial profit, in relation to the returns on financial and monetary investments. This raises in turn the question of the level of profit and of the impact of changes in prices on the general rate of profit.

Marx begins the discussion by rejecting the crude underconsumptionism of Proudhon and his followers. Proudhon sees overproduction as the result of the existence of interest and profit, which capitalists can charge because of their monopoly over money, so that the worker cannot buy back the entire product. Free credit would, for Proudhon, remove the surcharge which the capitalist is able to impose, thereby allowing prices to fall, and removing the danger of overproduction. Marx rejects this argument. Overproduction is not a matter of the existence or level of profit, and so cannot be resolved by lowering prices. Indeed, as Marx notes elsewhere, it is precisely the relative rise in wages that indicates the imminence of the crisis, and the collapse of prices which is its most devastating result (CII, 486–7).

A general reduction of prices would simply leave everything where it originally stood, while the rise and fall of particular prices is simply a matter of the redistribution of surplus value within the capitalist class. Capitalist profit does not derive from overcharging the worker, but from surplus labour time, so that the problem of overproduction is not a matter of the unequal exchange between worker and capitalist. Proudhon's 'conclusion that *this is the cause* of overproduction is false at this level of abstraction' (CW28, 362).[15]

Proudhon's error is to confuse price and value, in seeing profit as an addition to price, rather than a part of the existing value, determined by the production of surplus value. Redistribution through changes in prices does not alter the general rate of profit, but merely redistributes profit among capitalists (Marx here refers approvingly to Ricardo, CW29, 135–6). This redistribution is the means by which a general

---

[15] Marx also reminds Proudhon that 'it is already evident from the previous argument that the volume of money as means of circulation has nothing to do with the difficulty of realising capital' (CW28, 362).

Disproportionality and the Valorisation of Capital   153

rate of profit is formed through competition between capitalists, but competition cannot reduce the general rate of profit. 'Competition cannot depress the general level itself, but only tends to create such a level. Further analysis [of this problem] belongs to the section on competition.' Workers may gain to a tiny degree, if the prices of the means of consumption fall, but in this case competition would soon lead to a compensating fall in the wage (CW28, 364, 365, 368).

The general fall of prices in a crisis is a quite different phenomenon from the rise and fall of relative prices through which capital is induced to flow from one branch of production to another. It is also quite different from the general reduction in prices envisaged by Proudhon as the means of averting the tendency to overproduction. In this case the general fall of prices has an impact on the rate of profit, but it is a *result* of the crisis, and so obviously cannot provide the explanation for the crisis, but must itself be explained.

In a crisis the general fall of prices does not simply redistribute profit between capitalists, but transforms the value relations between necessary and surplus labour. In a general crisis of overproduction prices fall so that there is a '*general devaluation* ... a destruction of capital', which appears on the other side as an appreciation of money. 'Thus in a crisis — with a general depreciation of prices — there also occurs up to a certain amount a *general devaluation* or *destruction of capital*. The devaluation can be *general*, absolute, and not just relative, as with a *depreciation*, because value does not, like price, merely express the relationship of one commodity to another, but the relationship between the price of the commodity to the labour objectified in it ... If these amounts are not equal, a *devaluation* occurs which is not compensated for by an appreciation on the other side, since the other side represents a fixed amount of objectified labour which cannot be altered by exchange. In general crises, this devaluation extends even to living labour capacity' (CW28, 375).

The crisis of general overproduction leads to a fall in the rate of industrial profit, so that capitalists withdraw their money from circulation, or throw it into speculative ventures, instead of investing it productively. This withdrawal of investment funds leads to a fall in the demand for commodities corresponding to the surplus value withdrawn from circulation, and so disrupts the normal proportional production relationships, which reacts back cumulatively through the system. Thus disproportionality is now the result of a fall in the general rate of profit, that disrupts the proportional relationships. As production and prices fall, capital is devalued and destroyed. The devaluation of capital and labour power in the crisis restores the rate of profit. However, we still have to explain the possibility of general overproduction and the fall in the rate of profit that precipitates the crisis. This brings us back to the development of the forces of production.

The general devaluation of capital in the crisis is only the other side of a general increase in productivity. 'According to what has been indicated above, the destruction of value and capital which occurs in a crisis coincides with — or means the same as — a *general growth of the productive forces*, which, however, does not take place through a real increase in the productivity of labour ... but through a diminution of the existing value of raw materials, machinery and labour capacity'. This devaluation of the existing capital through a fall in prices is the consequence of the increase in productivity achieved by more advanced capitals. This fall in prices undermines the profitability of existing capitals, and thereby may provoke a crisis. 'Likewise, on the other hand, a sudden general growth of the productive forces would devalue all *existing values* ... and therefore destroy existing capital just as it would destroy existing labour capacity. The other aspect of the crisis resolves itself into a real fall in production, in living labour, in order to restore the correct proportion of necessary to surplus labour, on which, in the last analysis, everything rests' (CW28, 375).[16]

How does a general increase in the productive forces lead to a fall in the general rate of profit? It is clear that if there is a large increase in productivity in a *particular* branch of production the extra profits available might stimulate a substantial overproduction, and the consequent devaluation and destruction of existing capitals in that branch of production. But if a general increase in productivity led to a *general* increase in production, distributed proportionately across all branches of production, there would not necessarily be any change

---

[16] Marx does not develop the implications of this argument about the restorative power of the crisis further at this stage. In his article on 'Manufactures and Commerce', written in September 1859, Marx notes that it is a 'law of production' that 'if, by overproduction and over-speculation, a crisis has been brought about, still the productive powers of the nation and the faculty of absorption on the market of the world, have, in the mean time, so much expanded, that they will only temporarily recede from the highest point reached, and that after some oscillations spreading over some years, the scale of production which marked the highest point of prosperity in one period of the commercial cycle, becomes the starting point of the subsequent period' (CW16, 493).

Disproportionality and the Valorisation of Capital

in prices, in which case there would be no devaluation.[17] The result would merely be that newer capitals would earn a higher rate of profit than older capitals. So how does a general increase in productivity lead to a fall in the general rate of profit?

Marx notes that competition can reduce the rate of profit in a particular branch of production, but the general rate of profit can only fall if the rate of surplus value falls, or if there is an increase in the organic composition of capital. 'Consequently, the *general rate of profit* can fall in one or another branch of business, because competition, etc., forces the capitalist to sell below *value* ... But the general rate [of profit] cannot fall in this way; it can fall only because of a *relative* fall in the ratio of surplus labour to necessary labour [and constant capital]. And this, as we have seen earlier, occurs if the ratio [of constant to variable capital] is already very large ... In that case the general rate of profit may fall, even though absolute surplus labour rises' (CW28, 363). However, Marx does not pursue the implied association between the tendency for the rate of profit to fall and crises at this stage, but turns instead to the role of competition in equalising the rate of profit as surplus value is redistributed among the capitalists. This leads in turn to the relations between the various branches of production, and back to the problem of disproportionality between the various branches of production.

The problem of overproduction does not derive from the excessive level of prices, as Proudhon believed, but from the need to sell the surplus product. We have seen that the capitalist cannot sell the surplus product to the workers, however much prices might be manipulated. In value terms, the problem arises from the need to realise the commodity capital corresponding to the surplus value produced. But so far we have asked nothing about the character of the concrete use values in which that surplus value is embodied, or about the conditions under which such realisation might or might not be possible.

To explore this problem further Marx develops a simple model with five branches of production, two producing raw materials, one produc-

---

[17] Whether or not there would be a change in the general level of prices as a result of a general increase in production is essentially a monetary question. One interpretation of Luxemburg's argument is that the growth of production, without a corresponding growth in the quantity of money, will lead to such a fall in prices (Marazzi, 1984). Marx's view was that the money supply and/or velocity of circulation would adjust to the increased demand for money, so that there would be no impact on prices. Once we move beyond a pure commodity money, and allow monetary authorities discretion, this becomes an issue of monetary policy rather than of the laws of motion of the capitalist system.

ing machinery, one producing for workers' consumption and one for the consumption of capitalists. This model confirms the results of Marx's more abstract discussion of disproportionality by showing that the whole product can be realised, in the anticipation of a renewed and expanded investment, as capitalists exchange commodities corresponding to the surplus value produced amongst themselves. 'The valorisation consists in each capitalist exchanging his own product for a fractional part of the products of the other four, and this in such a way that a part of the surplus product is destined for the consumption of the capitalist, and a part is converted into surplus capital with which to set new labour in motion. The valorisation consists in the *real possibility* of greater valorisation — the production of new and larger values' (CW28, 371).[18]

This reproduction scheme also confirms the earlier conclusion that a problem of general overproduction arises not because there is too little consumption, but because of the disproportionality of production, which is then generalised as capitalists in one branch of production are not able to valorise their capital through the sale of the product. If there happens to be overproduction of capitalists' or workers' means of consumption '*general overproduction* would occur, not because relatively *too little* ... [would have been consumed], but because too much of *both* would have been produced — too much *not for consumption*, but too much to maintain the *correct ratio between consumption and valorisation; too much for valorisation*' (CW28, 372).

At a given point in the development of the forces of production the proportions in which various commodities are required are given, but the producers act independently of one another and have no knowledge of these proportions. '*Exchange* in and for itself gives these conceptually distinct moments a being indifferent to one another. They exist independently of one another; their inner necessity becomes *manifest* in crises, which makes short shrift of the semblance of their mutual indifference'. The development of the productive forces alters the proportions between the branches of production, freeing capital and living labour to be employed in expanding production, but these may 'both remain unused, because they are not present in the proportions required by production on the basis of the newly developed productive

---

[18] This is the first sketch of Marx's 'reproduction schemes', which he expanded in his 1863 manuscript, and developed systematically in Part III of Volume II of *Capital*. Here he introduces the schemes initially in considering the distribution of surplus value in the form of profit.

Disproportionality and the Valorisation of Capital

forces' (CW28, 372–3).

Marx's reproduction schemes provide a more rigourous demonstration of the relationship between disproportionality and general overproduction. However, Marx does not take the discussion of overproduction and disproportionality any further at this stage, and at this point he loses patience with the argument. The problem is that he wants to analyse capital at a high level of abstraction, concentrating on the value relations which constitute the essence of capital. This means abstracting from the reality of exchange and competition, and the complications introduced by the rise and fall of prices. But at the same time, exchange is a part of the general concept of capital, so that capital cannot be looked at in abstraction from exchange. 'The movement in which this really takes place can only be considered when we consider *real* capital, i.e., competition, etc. ...On the other hand, *without* exchange, the production of capital as such would not exist' (CW28, 376).[19] So Marx at this point breaks off his examination of the problems of realisation, and assumes that they have been resolved. 'At the point which we have now reached, where capital is only being considered in general, the real difficulties of this third process exist only as *possibilities*, and are therefore likewise transcended as *possibilities*. Hence the product is now posited as having been transformed back into money' (CW28, 376).

The problem of abstraction is particularly important with regard to the analysis of disproportionality. In his earlier discussion Marx had established that disproportionality was a necessary feature of capitalist production, and not merely a contingent result of the anarchy of the market, on the basis of the tendency for capitalist production to develop without regard to the limits of the market. However, there is a methodological problem with this argument. It is clear that the tendency to overproduction can provoke a crisis by disrupting the proportional relations between branches of production, the collapse of one branch of production then being generalised into a a general crisis.

---

[19] Marx frequently comments in the *Grundrisse* on the problem of where to put the 'relationship between production and consumption' , 'under capital and profit etc., or also under accumulation and competition of capitals' (CW28, 217). Similarly the problem of the devaluation of capital by a fall in the cost of production, just considered, 'belongs to the doctrine of concentration and competition of capitals' (CW28, 330). 'As yet we cannot go on to the relationship of demand, supply, prices for they presuppose capital in their characteristic development. In so far as demand and supply are abstract categories, not yet expressing any particular economic relationships, they should perhaps be considered along with simple circulation or production?' (CW28, 334).

However, such disproportionality only arises when we consider the use value aspect of capitalist production and the relations between particular capitals, and so cannot be specified in the most abstract terms of value relations and capital-in-general on which the argument of the *Grundrisse* is based. Marx has still not explained the necessity of general overproduction inherent in the essence of capital, as opposed to the generalisation of overproduction arising in particular branches of production.

In the reproduction schemes Marx formulates the problem of disproportionality in terms of the disproportionality between necessary and surplus labour. This leads Marx in turn to identify disproportionality not in terms of particular use values, but in terms of the component parts of capital. The 'reproduction scheme' therefore divides the branches of production into those producing means of consumption and those producing means of production in order to show the connection between the proportionality of production and the expanded reproduction of capital. If the expanded reproduction of capital is disrupted, for example by a fall in the rate of profit, this will immediately lead to a disproportionality in the branches of production in relation to the (reduced) requirements of reproduction, and so to a general crisis. But the reproduction schemes do not answer the question, how is general overproduction, which leads directly to a general fall in the rate of profit, possible?

The Tendency for the Rate of Profit to Fall

Marx devotes a large proportion of the manuscript of the *Grundrisse* to the examination of the relationship between surplus value and profit, which necessitates a detailed consideration of the relationship between fixed and circulating capital, and between the production time and the circulation time, in order to establish the magnitude of the capital to which the surplus value must be related in order to transform it into the rate of profit. At the end of this long discussion he comes back to a question that he had examined briefly earlier, that of the tendency for the organic composition of capital to rise, and the corresponding possibility of a fall in the rate of profit, despite the continued rise in the mass of profit. 'The general laws we have so far developed can be briefly summarised thus: ...*assuming* the same surplus value ... the *rate of profit* depends on the ratio between the part of capital exchanged for living labour and the part of it existing in the form of raw material and means of production. So, as the portion exchanged for living labour declines, there is a corresponding decline in the rate of profit.' (CW29, 130–1)

The tendency for the composition of capital to rise

In view of the controversy surrounding the 'law of the tendency for the rate of profit to fall' it is worth considering a little more closely the terms in which Marx introduces it into his discussion. The starting point of the law is the observation that the proportion of capital employed in purchasing labour power progressively falls with the development of capitalist production, as an increasing proportion is tied up in the growing mass of raw material and means of production set in motion by labour. It is the latter that is expressed in the concept of the 'rising organic composition of capital'.

The rising organic composition of capital is a consequence of the growing productivity of labour, as each labourer uses more machinery, and processes a greater quantity of raw material. However, growing productivity also reduces the value of both labour power and means of production, so that changes in the value relation will not necessarily mirror changes in the technical relation. If the value of labour power does not fall significantly, while the value of means of production falls more rapidly than their mass increases, it would be quite possible for the value composition of capital to fall. However, to cut a long story short, Marx generally assumes without further consideration that the tendency is unequivocally for the composition of capital to rise, although he was certainly aware from the beginning that the devaluation of constant capital countered this tendency (CW28, 309).

In Volume One of *Capital* Marx spelled out the distinction between the 'technical' composition of capital, which expressed the physical relationship between means of production and living labour power, and the value-composition, which expressed the value relationship between constant and variable capital, and then defined his central concept, the organic-composition of capital, as 'the value-composition, in so far as it is determined by its technical composition and mirrors the changes of the latter' (CI, 612).

Many of Marx's critics have regarded the concept of the 'organic composition of capital' as a gratuitous device introduced to preserve the assumption of a rising composition of capital by ignoring the changes in value relations which might negate that assumption, and so undermine the law of the tendency for the rate of profit to fall. Ben Fine has argued that the distinction is between the immediate impact of a technical change, in abstraction from changes in value, and the longer term impact, when values have also changed (Fine and Harris, 1990, 59–60). This argument does not adequately respond to the criticisms of Marx's formulation of the law of the tendency for the rate of profit to fall. Although the concept of the rising organic composition of capital is associated with the law of the tendency for the rate of profit to fall, this was not the context in which Marx originally introduced it or generally applied it.

The composition of capital and the formation of a relative surplus population

The concept of the composition of capital first appears explicitly in Marx's notes for his lectures on 'Wages' in December 1847, over ten years before he applied it to the explanation for the tendency for the rate of profit to fall. In these lectures Marx uses the concept to show, against the Malthusians, that over-population is not the result of the natural growth of population in relation to the limited production of the means of subsistence, but is the specific result of the accumulation of capital, as workers are displaced from production. 'It is, therefore, a general law which necessarily arises from the nature of the relation between capital and labour that in the course of the growth of the productive forces the part of productive capital which is transformed into machinery and raw material, i.e., capital as such, increases in disproportion to the part which is intended for wages.' The competition between the workers, therefore, 'becomes more and more violent ... This law, which arises simply from the relation of the workers to capital, and which turns even the condition most favourable to him, the rapid growth of productive capital, into an unfavourable one, the bourgeois have changed from a social law into a law of nature by saying that by a law of nature the population grows more rapidly than the means of employment or the means of subsistence' (CW6, 432).

The concept of the 'organic' composition of capital is appropriate in this context, because what is at issue is the division of an existing capital between investment in labour power and investment in means of production. A technical change leads to a change in the division between the component parts of the capital, but in the first instance this division is based on existing values.

The immediate implication of the rising organic composition of capital is that the accumulation of capital is necessarily associated with growing 'technological unemployment', the creation of a 'relative surplus population'. A diminishing proportion of capital is laid out as variable capital, and so, given the value of labour power and the absolute size of the capital, a diminishing number of workers is employed.

This argument was already well-established in political economy, and its validity was recognised by Ricardo in his notorious addition of the chapter 'On Machinery' to the third edition of his *Principles*, in which he recognised that the immediate result of the introduction of machinery would be the creation of unemployment, as a result of the increased proportion of capital laid out as fixed capital and consequent fall in the amount available to employ labourers. Ricardo was confident that in the longer term employment would be restored as increased profits increased the rate of capital accumulation, although he did not explore the relationship between the rate of accumulation and the composition of capital.[20]

Marx's distinction between the organic and value compositions of capital corresponds to Ricardo's approach to the question, which similarly dealt with the change in technical relations before noting the significance of changes in value, although Ricardo did not develop the argument. Marx's innovation in relation to Ricardo's argument was to replace Ricardo's formulation in terms of the relation between fixed and circulating capital by his own, more adequate, formulation in terms of constant and variable capital.

The impact on employment of a rising organic composition of capital is countered both by the tendency for the value of labour power to fall, so that a given amount of capital employs more workers (CW28, 328), and by the growing absolute size of the capital, which may lead to an absolute growth in employment. The interaction of these factors is complex, and Marx explored them at great length in the successive drafts of *Capital*. Nevertheless, whatever may be the overall outcome, Marx generally presumes that the immediate impact of an increase in the composition of capital as the result of technical advance is the displacement of labour.

---

[20] Note that the implication of this argument is that changes in the *mass* of profit are critical for the immediate impact of capital accumulation on the level of employment, while changes in the *rate* of profit are critical for the re-absorption of the unemployed.

The composition of capital and the tendency for the rate of profit to fall

The concept of the organic composition of capital was first connected with the rate of profit in the *Grundrisse*, in the context of Marx's exploration of the distinction between the rate of surplus value and the rate of profit. The rate of surplus value is defined as the relationship between surplus value and the variable capital laid out in the purchase of labour power, but the rate of profit is defined as the relationship between surplus value and the total capital. It is immediately apparent that differences in the rate of profit do not necessarily reflect differences in the rate of surplus value, so that 'the rate of profit of capital therefore by no means expresses the rate at which living labour increases objectified labour' (CW28, 297).

Marx goes through some tortuous arithmetical examples, in which he assumes that the size of the capital and the rate of profit are unchanged, so that different compositions of capital are associated with different rates of surplus value, and then asks 'can its surplus value not increase, though relative to total capital it declines, i.e. the so-called rate of profit declines?' (CW28, 306), before concluding that it is perfectly possible for this to happen. This enables him to identify the source of Ricardo's false conclusion, that the decline in the rate of profit is the result of the rise in wages as agricultural productivity falls, a conclusion which is based on Ricardo's failure to distinguish between the rate of surplus value and the rate of profit. However Marx does not immediately develop his critique of Ricardo's theory of profit, but returns to the implications of a changing composition of capital for the theory of population.[21]

The accumulation of capital involves the expansion of surplus value by expanding the working population. But at the same time, a rising organic composition of capital implies that capital employs proportionately fewer labourers. The result is that the growing supply of workers is provided by those laid off as a result of growing productivity. 'It is therefore the tendency of capital to create as much labour as possible, just as it is its tendency to reduce necessary labour to a minimum. It is therefore as much the tendency of capital to enlarge the working

---

[21] In his later discussion he links the law of population directly to the law of the tendency for the rate of profit to fall. 'The same law is expressed simply ... as the relation of the growth of the population, notably of the working part of it, to the capital already presupposed' (CW29, 135).

population, as well as constantly to make a part of that population surplus ... Hence the correctness of the theory of surplus population and surplus capital' (CW28, 326).

Marx returned to his critique of Ricardo's explanation for the tendency for the rate of profit to fall later in the manuscript. Marx introduces the discussion by explicitly *assuming* a given rate of surplus value (CW29, 131), in which case the tendency for the rate of profit to fall immediately follows from the postulated tendency for the organic composition of capital to rise.[22]

Marx was certainly aware that an increase in the rate of surplus value would counteract the impact of a rising organic composition of capital on the rate of profit. As we have just seen, Marx's initial hypothesis was based on the co-existence of a falling rate of profit and a rising rate of surplus value, which was decisive in the critique of Ricardo, for whom the rate of profit could fall only as a result of a fall in the rate of surplus value. In the present discussion he immediately considers the moderating impact of a rise in the rate of surplus value. The rate at which the rate of profit falls, in relation to the growth in the size of the capital, depends on whether the gross profit continues to rise, remains stationary, or falls (CW29, 133).

Marx also recognises that an increase in the rate of surplus value is not a contingent counter-tendency, but is inseparable from the rise in the organic composition of capital, since both are complementary results of increasing productivity. In summing up the discussion of the law Marx notes that the 'growth of the productive power of labour is synonymous with' both the growth of relative surplus value and the rise in the composition of capital, with the result that 'the rate of profit is thus inversely related to the growth of relative surplus value' (CW29, 147). However, nowhere in the discussion in the *Grundrisse* does Marx even consider the possibility that the rate of surplus value might rise sufficiently to offset the rise in the organic composition of capital, so that the rate of profit might rise.

---

[22] Marx immediately recognises that the rate of profit will not fall if the organic composition of capital does not change, but he dismisses this possibility, since it would assume that methods of production are not changing and that productivity is not growing, which 'contradicts the law of development of capital and especially that of the development of fixed capital' (CW29, 132), and so can only occur where the capitalist mode of production is not yet established.

The tendency for the tate of profit to fall and the tendency to crisis

The discussion of the tendency for the rate of profit to fall completes the discussion of the reproduction process of capital. From this point of view the law is another expression of the familiar characterisation of the contradictory character of capital, which depends on the exploitation of living labour, but at the same time tries to reduce it to a minimum. 'By striving to reduce labour time to a minimum, while, on the other hand, positing labour time as the sole measure and the source of wealth, capital itself is a contradiction-in-process' (CW29, 91). The culmination of this contradiction arises when capitalist production reaches its fullest development and 'the development of the productive forces, brought about by capital itself in its historical development, at a certain point abolishes the self-valorisation of capital, rather than posits it. Beyond a certain point, the development of the productive forces becomes a barrier to capital, and consequently the relation of capital becomes a barrier to the development of the productive forces ' (CW29, 133).[23]

Marx immediately links this fall in the rate of profit to the eruption of crises, without giving any indication of precisely how the fall in the rate of profit might precipitate a crisis. Nevertheless Marx presents an apocalyptic vision of the fate of capitalism as the result of the fall in the rate of profit. At this point the system of wage labour becomes a fetter on the development of social wealth, and is cast off, as the result of the development of the contradictions of the capitalist form of production itself. The growing discordance between the development of production and the existing relations of production is expressed in 'acute contradictions, crises, convulsions. The violent destruction of capital as the condition for its self-preservation, and not because of external circumstances, is the most striking form in which it is advised to be gone and to give room to a higher state of social production ... '

---

[23] Earlier Marx had pointed to the ultimate self-negation of capital in similar terms, but without reference to the rate of profit. As the rate of surplus value rises, and the amount of necessary labour time falls, the impact of increasing productivity on the rate of surplus value becomes proportionately less, to the point at which it becomes insignificant. 'The increase in productivity could become a matter of indifference to capital; its valorisation itself could cease to matter, because its proportions have become minimal; and it would have ceased to be capital', although he immediately qualified the point by noting that 'all these propositions correct in this degree of abstraction only for the relation at this particular stage of the analysis. Further relations will come in later which modify them significantly'(CW28, 265–6). In a later passage he links this development to the application of science, concluding that 'capital works to dissolve itself as the form which dominates production' (CW29, 86).

The Tendency for the Rate of Profit to Fall

(CW29, 134). Capital will try to restore the rate of profit by

> reducing the allotment made to necessary labour and by still more expanding the quantity of surplus labour with regard to the whole labour employed. Hence the highest development of productive power together with the greatest expansion of existing wealth will coincide with depreciation of capital, degradation of the labourer, and a most straightened exhaustion of his vital powers. These contradictions lead to explosions, cataclysms, crises, in which by momentaneous suspension of labour and annihilation of a great portion of capital the latter is violently reduced to the point where it can go on fully employing its productive powers without committing suicide. Yet, these regularly recurring catastrophes lead to their repetition on a higher scale, and finally to its violent overthrow. (CW29, 135)

Various factors intervene to counteract the tendency for the rate of profit to fall. 'In the developed movement of capital, this process is slowed down by moments other than crises; e.g. the continuous depreciation of a part of the existing capital; the conversion of a large part of capital into fixed capital which does not serve as an agent of direct production; the unproductive dissipation of a large part of capital, etc.' (CW29, 135). It can also be checked by the reduction or elimination of existing deductions, such as taxes or rent, by the development of new branches of production in which the organic composition of capital is lower, or by the emergence of monopolies. However Marx does not develop the implications of the law further, noting in relation to this, and to the law of population, that 'this point is to be developed in more detail only in the examination of accumulation'.[24] Moreover, in concluding the discussion he seems to be aware that he has perhaps got a little carried away, adding that 'at this stage we must not be diverted from our subject by the conclusions following from the laws stated above or by any speculations on that matter' (CW29, 148).

It is difficult to know how much significance to attach to Marx's discussion of the law of the tendency for the rate of profit to fall, here as in his later work. Marx repeatedly notes the importance of the law.

---

[24] The short first draft of the section on accumulation, which became the famous Part VII of Volume I of *Capital*, was only written at the end of Marx's 1861–3 manuscript, and focused on the law of population, with no reference to the law of the tendency for the rate of profit to fall.

'In every respect, this is the most important law of modern political economy, and the most essential one for comprehending the most complex relationships. It is the most important law from the historical viewpoint. Hitherto, despite its simplicity, it has never been grasped and still less has it been consciously formulated'(CW29, 133).[25] This would seem to imply that the law lies at the core of his analysis of capitalism, and yet, despite his apocalyptic tone, he deals very cursorily with it here. Although he develops the analysis more fully in his 1861–3 manuscript, and in that of 1864–5 which Engels used as the basis of Volume III of *Capital*, it does not appear at all in any of the works which Marx published in his own lifetime. In Volume One of *Capital*, as we shall see, the organic composition of capital plays a central role, but in relation to the law of population, not that of the tendency for the rate of profit to fall.[26]

It remains to be seen what significance is to be attached to the law of the tendency for the rate of profit to fall in the understanding of the crisis tendencies of capitalist accumulation. At the present stage in the development of Marx's analysis, the law of the falling tendency of the rate of profit has a purely formal significance: it is possible that general overproduction, as distinct from the disproportionality between different branches of production, could be explained by a fall in the general rate of profit, so that the tendency to crisis would be inherent in the very concept of capital. However Marx has, as yet, made no attempt to demonstrate the possibility, either by rigourously establishing the law of the tendency for the rate of profit to fall, or by following through the mechanism by which such a fall precipitates as crisis of general overproduction.

It is important to note, before concluding, that the linking of crises to the tendency for the rate of profit to fall does not contradict the earlier analysis of deepening crisis tendencies, which was related to

---

[25] Marx describes the law as 'the most important law in political economy' in his 1861–3 manuscripts (CW33, 104). In Volume III of *Capital*, written in 1864–5, he characterised the law as being 'of great importance to capitalist production' (CIII, 209), and in a letter to Engels of 30th April 1868 he described it as 'one of the greatest triumphs over the pons asinorum of all previous economics' (*Letters on Capital*, 137).

[26] Note that Marx always characterised his work as a *critique* of political economy, so the assertion that 'this is the most important law of political economy' does not necessarily bear the interpretation usually put on it, that Marx regarded it as the most important law for his own theory. The assertion that 'it is the most important law from the historical viewpoint', is also not as significant as might appear, for what Marx means is that it is most important in defining the ultimate historical limits of capitalism, which is not to imply that it is of such great contemporary significance.

The Dynamics of Capitalism and the Tendency to Crisis

the problem of realising a growing mass of surplus value embodied in an even more rapidly growing mass of commodities, since the fall in the *rate* of profit is perfectly consistent with a growing *mass* of surplus value, and even more so with a growing mass of commodities produced. The rate of profit falls because the organic composition of capital rises more rapidly than does the rate of surplus value. Similarly, the association of the law of the tendency for the rate of profit to fall with crises does not undermine the analysis of disproportionality, since the crisis arises because the fall in the rate of profit, by curtailing the expanded reproduction of capital, disrupts relations of proportionality. The underconsumption, disproportionality and falling rate of profit theories of crisis are not inconsistent with one another, but are part of a coherent scheme. However, the precise relationship between these parts still has to be clarified and evaluated.

The Dynamics of Capitalism and the Tendency to Crisis

Marx abandoned the manuscript of the *Grundrisse* shortly after this point. Before moving on to the development of his analysis in the later works, it is worth summing up the progress that he had made in the *Grundrisse*.

The *Grundrisse* is very much a working draft, which provides an invaluable insight into the development of Marx's fundamental theoretical ideas. The work began with the specific problem of explaining the form and determinants of the periodic crises that beset the capitalist system, and in particular with the critique of Proudhonian socialism. However, this critique immediately led Marx behind the money form to explore the social form of capitalist production as a whole, and so to discover the origins of profit in the surplus value appropriated by the capitalist.[27] The emphasis on the social form of capitalist pro-

---

[27] It is in this methodological respect that Marx's return to Hegel was quite fundamental. 'What was of great use to me as regards *method* of treatment was Hegel's *Logic* at which I had taken another look by mere accident ... If ever the time comes when such work is again possible, I should very much like to write 2 or 3 sheets making accessible to the common reader the *rational* aspect of the method which Hegel not only discovered, but also mystified' (Marx to Engels, 16.01.58, CW40, 249). However it would be quite wrong to see the *Grundrisse* as an *application* of Hegel's *Logic*, as Uchida, 1988, tends to do. As Marx noted in criticism of Lassalle, 'it is one thing for a critique to take a science to the point at which it admits of a dialectical presentation, and quite another to apply an abstract, ready-made system of logic to vague presentiments of just such a system' (Marx to Engels, 01.02.58, CW40, 261). Hegel's dialectic is also important in providing a critique of the subjective idealism of political

duction was fundamental, for it enabled Marx to get beyond both the Ricardian socialists, for whom the origin of profit lay in the immediate appropriation of surplus labour, and the Proudhonians, for whom the origin of profit lay in circulation.

The exploration of the social form of capitalist production led Marx directly to the elucidation of the concept of labour power, the commodity purchased by the capitalist, as distinct from the labour expended in production, and the concepts of constant and variable capital, which enabled him to distinguish between surplus value and profit. This led him in turn to develop the concept of relative surplus value, and so to identify the central dynamic of capitalist accumulation in the tendency, imposed on every individual capitalist by the pressure of competition, to develop the forces of production without limit. This tendency comes into conflict with the limited social basis of the capitalist mode of production, which confines the development of the forces of production within the limits of profitability. This fundamental contradiction then provides the guiding thread of the analysis of the dynamics of capitalist development in the *Grundrisse*.

The contradiction between the tendency to develop the forces of production without limit, and the need to confine that development within the limits of profitability, immediately appears as the limit of the market, which confronts each individual capitalist in the form of competition from other capitalists. Capitalists try to overcome this barrier by intensifying labour, extending the working day, extending the market and developing the forces of production. But these attempts to overcome the fundamental barrier only serve to reproduce it at a higher level. The increase in the productivity of labour results in an ever growing quantity of commodities to be sold. The growing rate of surplus value implies that a growing proportion of the social product has to find a market through its sale to other capitalists, as the commodity equivalent of their expanded capital. The expansion of the world market brings ever more remote regions into the orbit of the capitalist mode of production, and subject to its laws.

The possibility of crisis is inherent in the commodity form, already present in the separation of purchase and sale, and the separation of money as independent form of existence of value. The realisation of

---

economy, which attributes the defects of capitalism to the subjective deformation of capitalist rationality. Although Marx sometimes takes his flirtation with Hegel to the point of offering an objective idealist (essentialist) account of the self-development of the concept of capital, he regularly corrects and draws back from such a formulation.

The Dynamics of Capitalism and the Tendency to Crisis

this possibility depends on the withdrawal of money from circulation, which will leave a corresponding quantity of commodities unsold. Within simple commodity production there is no reason to withdraw that money from circulation, so there is no reason why the possibility of crisis should be realised, other than through accidental disturbances. It was because classical political economy regarded capitalism as no more than the generalisation of simple commodity production that it could not understand capitalist crises.

The problem of crises arises in capitalism because the capitalist's purpose in laying out money is not need but the production and appropriation of surplus value. The capitalist withdraws money from circulation in the form of money capital, and will only throw this money back into circulation if he anticipates realising a profit by so doing. Any disruption of the conditions for the profitable accumulation of capital will therefore lead to the withdrawal of money from circulation, thereby precipitating a crisis by removing the money equivalent of the surplus value already produced, which is embodied in the commodities destined to serve as the means for the expanded reproduction of capital. The problem gets progressively more difficult as capitalism develops because there is a growing mass of surplus value to be realised, embodied in an even more rapidly growing mass of commodities, making capital accumulation increasingly vulnerable to disruption as the mass of capital seeking new outlets grows.

The realisation of a growing surplus value depends on the all-round development of capitalist production, but the more surplus value grows, the more is reproduction dependent on its continued valorisation. At the same time, as the rate of surplus value increases the necessary labour time becomes a progressively diminishing proportion of the working day, and it becomes progressively more difficult to reduce the necessary labour time and increase the rate of surplus value further. This difficulty is expressed in the tendency for the rate of profit to fall.

The disruption of the conditions for the production and appropriation of surplus value is not a sufficient condition for the immediate onset of crisis. While productive capitalists may be withdrawing money from circulation as conditions deteriorate at the height of the boom, commodity and money capitalists are indulging in increasingly frenzied speculation, buying up commodities and investing in new ventures even when there is no prospect of these commodities finding a market. The crisis breaks out when these speculative investments collapse. In this way speculation sustains and intensifies the boom, but at the cost of precipitating an even more destructive collapse. These movements of money and commercial capital make it appear as though the dynamic of the cycle lies in the fluctuating moods of bankers and traders, reinforced or constrained by the credit policies of the banks and government. However the origins of the crisis, and the source of the limits to capital accumulation, lie in the sphere of production.

Whenever Marx looks concretely at crises, either in his historical studies or his hypothetical examples, we find that they arise with the emergence of disproportionality between branches of production, with a crisis in one branch of production being generalised through the commercial and credit system, so that a crisis of disproportionality becomes a general crisis of overproduction. The disproportional development of production is not simply a result of the 'anarchy of the market', but is inherent in the social form of capitalist production as the production of relative surplus value through the constant development of the forces of production, which dictates that capitalists expand the forces of production without regard to the limits of the market. However Marx is reluctant unequivocally to endorse a disproportionality theory of crisis, referring back to the more abstract and general disproportionality between necessary and surplus labour, and between the restricted consumption of the workers and the growing surplus produced, which leads back to consideration of underconsumption and the tendency for the rate of profit to fall.

In his early works Marx, following Engels, explained crises in terms of the tendency for production to run ahead of the growth of the market, which becomes an increasing barrier as capital penetrates every nook and cranny of the world, the theory which Engels later passed on to Kautsky. There are still suggestions of such a barrier in the *Grundrisse*, but now Marx puts more emphasis on the intensive development of capitalism. It is not the limited extent of the market which is the barrier to the realisation of an expanded capital. The problem of realisation is that of selling the growing mass of commodities corresponding to the growing surplus value produced, and this can only be sold to other capitalists, laying out their capital in the expectation of a profitable return. The problem of realisation is therefore the problem of identifying the limits to the production and appropriation of surplus value.

For classical political economy the barrier to the indefinite expansion of capitalist production lay in the tendency for the rate of profit to fall. For Adam Smith the rate of profit tended to fall as a growing

The Dynamics of Capitalism and the Tendency to Crisis

mass of capital confronts a limited range of outlets, so that competition between capitalists forces down the rate of profit. For Ricardo competition could redistribute profit between capitalists, but it could not reduce the rate of profit. He therefore explained the tendency for the rate of profit to fall in terms of the tendency for rent to rise as the pressure of demand for bread to feed the growing population made it necessary to bring ever less fertile land into production.

Marx followed Ricardo in denying that the secular fall in the rate of profit could be a result of competition between capitalists, but he argued that within capitalism any tendency for rent to rise is equally a matter of the redistribution of surplus value within the capitalist class. For Marx the rate of profit falls not because of technological limits on the opportunities for profitable investment, nor because of the parsimony of nature, but because of the tendency inherent in capitalist accumulation for the organic composition of capital to rise. With a given rate of surplus value, an increase in the composition of capital will lead to a fall in the rate of profit.

Although Marx certainly links the tendency for the rate of profit to fall to the ultimate limits of capitalism, it is not at all clear what is the connection between the tendency for the rate of profit to fall and crises. If the rate of profit is relatively low the capitalist system may well be more vulnerable to crisis, and when they come the crises might be more acute, but Marx does not establish a direct link between the tendency for the rate of profit to fall and the necessity of crisis, primarily because the tendency for the rate of profit to fall is formulated only at the most abstract level of the internal relations of capital-in-general, while the tendency to crisis is only realised in the concrete relationships between particular capitals expressed in the sphere of competition.

It is important to stress that Marx was well aware that a mere *fall* in the rate of profit is not sufficient to provoke a crisis — it is still worth re-investing capital, rather than leaving it to lie idle, even if the rate of profit has fallen, as long as the rate of profit is still positive. Thus the relationship between a fall in the rate of profit and the tendency to crisis is not direct. In particular, at least implicitly, it is linked to the emergence of disproportionalities. On the one hand, a change in the composition of capital associated with the introduction of new methods of production in itself changes the proportional relations between the branches of production, with a relative increase in the demand for means of production and a relative fall in the demand for means of subsistence. This disproportionality, which Ricardo considered in his chapter 'On Machinery', arises regardless of the impact of the composition of capital on the rate of profit. On the other hand, a fall in the rate of profit will itself introduce disproportionalities as capital is diverted into speculative channels, inflating the demand for particular commodities, and then, with the collapse, as speculative and investment demand is withdrawn.

We will return to the significance of the tendency for the rate of profit to fall later, but for now it is worth recalling three points which Marx draws out of his discussion of the historical tendencies of capitalist accumulation, to which he perhaps attaches more significance than to any mechanical notion of a tendency for the rate of profit to fall. First, Marx does not simply characterise the tendency for the rate of profit to fall as an inevitable secular tendency. He discusses the tendency in terms of the problem confronting capital that the greater the rate of surplus value, the greater the increase in productivity that is needed to have a significant impact on the rate of profit. This increase in productivity is not determined by technology alone, but by the outcome of the class struggle over the production of surplus value. Thus the capitalist seeks to overcome the tendency for the rate of profit to fall by all the means at his disposal, intensifying labour, extending the working day, forcing down wages, economising on constant capital and accelerating the turnover of capital. From this point of view the conclusion is not that there is a mechanical tendency for the rate of profit to fall, but an historical tendency for the class struggle over the production of surplus value to intensify as capitalism develops (c.f. CIII, 227; CW33, 111; TSV3, 365). Second, the greater the mass of surplus value, the greater the mass of commodities to be realised through their sale to other capitalists, and so the more vulnerable is capitalism to crisis. Thus Marx links the law of the falling tendency of the rate of profit to the tendency for the quantity of profit, and the mass of commodities within which that is embodied, to rise. Third, the rising organic composition of capital and the growing mass of surplus value is associated with the concentration and centralisation of capital, the growing relative surplus population, the pauperisation of ever wider strata of the population, and the growing polarisation of society into two classes — the 'absolute general law of capitalist accumulation' that was to play the central role in volume I of *Capital*.

The Methodology of the Grundrisse and the Theory of Crisis

Although the *Grundrisse* marks an enormous theoretical advance on Marx's earlier works, it does not solve the problem with which it began, that of explaining the necessity of crisis.

The problem that Marx faces in explaining the necessity of crisis is to some extent determined by his own methodology, which is based at this stage of his work on a radical analytical separation of production and circulation. He insists that the problem of crisis is not a problem that arises in the sphere of circulation — it is not a problem in a world of simple commodity production, but only in a world based on capitalist production, in which the production of things is subordinated to the production and appropriation of profit. However, he also recognises that the problem does not arise in the sphere of production either. The condition for the production of surplus value is simply that labour should be sufficiently productive that the value of commodities produced should exceed the value of those required for the labourer's subsistence. The historical dynamic of, and historical justification for, the capitalist mode of production is the tendency to develop the forces of production without limit. Far from presenting barriers to the production of surplus value, the development of capitalist production sweeps away all such barriers.[28] The problem of crisis therefore arises *between* production and circulation.

Similarly the tendency to crisis arises *between* value and use value. Commodities do not lie unsold because they are not needed, but because they cannot be bought, and they cannot be bought because they cannot be profitably employed: they are redundant not as use values but as values. On the other hand, if we look only on the side of value relations it is difficult to see why there would ever be a crisis: so long as the rate of surplus value, and so the rate of profit, is positive, then any additional capital can be profitably employed, even if the rate of profit should fall. A mere fall in the rate of profit will only lead to the withdrawal of capital from circulation if there are more profitable opportunities elsewhere, for example in lending at interest. But in this event the problem is not the fall in the rate of profit, but the failure of the rate of interest to fall commensurately as a result of the restriction

---

[28] The resistance of the working class to its subordination in production is a quite different matter. It is obvious that a crisis would be provoked if workers refused to work beyond the labour time necessary for their own reproduction.

of credit by the monetary authorities. It was precisely to destroy this explanation of crisis that Marx began work on the *Grundrisse* in the first place.

The conclusion that Marx repeatedly moves towards in the *Grundrisse* is that the tendency to crisis arises somewhere *between* production and circulation, and *between* use value and value. However he does not follow up his insights because as soon as he moves beyond consideration of the production of surplus value he postpones further discussion until the consideration of circulation.

The failure to develop a systematic analysis of crisis in the *Grundrisse* is also connected with the methodological problem of the relationship between the abstract and the concrete. Crises are an expression of the most fundamental contradiction of the capitalist mode of production, but they are also the most superficial and dramatic expression of that contradiction. This must have come home to Marx very forcefully by the time he was writing the *Grundrisse*. In the early 1850s he and Engels had been expecting the next crisis to follow the pattern of the last, with a financial and commercial crisis leading to the collapse of production and the intensification of class struggle, perhaps culminating in the anticipated revolution. By 1858 it was clear that the timing, origins and course of development of each crisis was distinctive, determined by a range of concrete and contingent factors. Marx could perhaps establish that there is a tendency to crisis inherent in the capitalist mode of production. He could perhaps also establish that the combination of a growing mass of surplus value, a rising organic composition of capital, and a falling rate of profit meant that there was a growing potential for crisis. But the problem was to link these abstract determinants of the crisis to the actual onset of a real crisis, which seems to be determined by specific, and maybe contingent, historical factors.

The immediate cause of a crisis may be the disproportionality between branches of production, and its generalisation a matter of the breakdown of chains of credit. The significance of disproportionalities is that they lie at the boundary of production and circulation, value and use value. However the theoretical problem is to explain why such disproportionalities are necessary, and not just contingent misjudgements. This links up with the problem of the relationship between disproportionality and general overproduction, that Marx discusses at such length in the *Grundrisse* without ever reaching a clear conclusion. It also links up with his suggestion, again undeveloped, that there is

The Methodology of the Grundrisse and the Theory of Crisis 175

a difference between the disproportionalities between branches of production, which may be contingent, and the disproportionality between necessary and surplus labour, which is not. The former disproportionality can, in principle, be resolved by the adjustment of proportions in response to changes in relative prices, while the latter cannot (which is what Keynes realised, rather more superficially, seventy five years later).

Finally, there is the question of the significance of the theory of crisis in the overall structure of the argument developed in the *Grundrisse*. The text begins, and more or less ends, with consideration of crisis. But in between the analysis establishes a continuity between the crisis tendencies and the everyday dynamics of capitalism, which had not existed in Marx's earlier works. In this sense Marx establishes that capitalism is in permanent crisis: the dynamic of capital accumulation is precisely the result of the attempt constantly to stave off a crisis, driven by the permanent contradiction underlying the capitalist mode of production. This identification of the contradictory foundation of capitalist accumulation and crisis is the basis on which the emphasis of Marx's theoretical attention moves away from crisis, which has very little part to play in his later works, just as politically Marx moved away from the apocalyptic vision of the revolution as a political event precipitated by a crisis, to the vision of the revolution as the culmination of a longer struggle to build a working class movement.

Although Marx had extended the foundations of his analysis of the tendency to overproduction and crisis in the *Grundrisse* this analysis was by no means complete, primarily because Marx was trying to keep the analysis at a high level of abstraction, while the concrete mechanisms of crisis necessarily require consideration of the processes of competition and competitive adjustment, and, above all, of the intervention of money and credit. Although Marx had begun his analysis with the latter question, in seeking to destroy once and for all the Proudhonian illusions that monetary reform could dispel the crisis tendencies of capitalism, he soon came to focus his attention on the process of production and the immediate relation between production and circulation, without returning to the mediating role of money and credit in the reproduction of capital, and in particular their possible roles in ameliorating or intensifying the crisis tendencies of capitalist accumulation. We need to see how much further he was able to take his analysis in his more mature works of the 1860s.

6
Underconsumption, Disproportionality and Overproduction

In the *Grundrisse* Marx developed a systematic critique of political economy on a rigorous and coherent theoretical basis, which thereafter shaped and was shaped by Marx's political activities. Starting from the problem of crisis Marx dug down to the foundations of the capitalist mode of production, creating the basis on which to build up his own analysis of the contradictory dynamics of capitalism. Although Marx continued to address the problem of crises, from the late 1850s crises played a much less important role in his theoretical work and in his political prognoses.[1]

Having at last secured a publisher for his 'Economics' through Lassalle at the end of March 1858, Marx broke off work on the *Grundrisse* and began to work on the next draft of *The Critique of Political Economy* by preparing an analytical contents of the *Grundrisse* manuscripts. Marx had originally intended to complete *The Critique of Political Economy* by May 1858, but the work took far longer than he had anticipated, partly because of renewed bouts of ill-health, and by June he had still not even begun. He began a first draft in the autumn of 1858, but was not happy with it, and started again. It soon became clear that the work would be much larger than Marx had

---

[1] Through the 1860s and early 1870s Marx looked to war rather than economic crisis as the precipitant of the political development of the working class. By the middle 1870s, however, Marx and Engels had come to see war, like crises, as events which divided and demoralised the working class. Engels wrote to Sorge that the old international was now dead, as national rivalries and differences emerged after the fall of the Paris Commune (04.08.74). Marx clearly regarded a further war as a barrier to the progress of the working class. 'A new war is inevitable *au peu plus tôt, au peu plus tard*, and before its conclusion there are hardly likely to be any violent popular movements anywhere.' (Marx to Kugelman 18.05.74, CW45, 18) 'General European conditions are such as to increasingly wage a *general European war*. We shall have to pass through it before there can be any thought of decisive overt activity on the part of the European working class.' (Marx to Sorge, 12-17.09.74, CW45, 30)

envisaged, and the manuscript delivered in January 1859, published as *The Critique of Political Economy* in June of that year, comprised only the first two chapters of the complete work.[2]

Marx returned to his work on the manuscript in August 1861, but over the next two years it continued to expand, and remained unpublished in Marx's lifetime, although the extended critical survey of the earlier economic literature, which formed over half the manuscript, was published by Karl Kautsky after Marx's death as *Theories of Surplus Value*.[3]

The published portion of *The Critique of Political Economy* ultimately formed the basis of the first two chapters of Volume One of *Capital*. The unpublished portions of the manuscript comprised the first draft of most of the rest of Volume One, dealing with the transformation of money into capital, the labour process and the valorisation process, and the production of absolute and relative surplus value, and also included elements later incorporated by Engels into Volumes II and III of *Capital*. These manuscripts offer a development and systematisation of the analysis first worked out in the *Grundrisse*.

Marx re-drafted the manuscript in 1864–5, before completing the final version of the first part, which was published as Volume One of *Capital* in 1867, revising this text again for subsequent French and German editions. The bulk of the text published by Engels as Volume Three of *Capital* was drawn from these notebooks of 1864–5. Marx returned to the manuscript in two bursts in 1870 and 1878, which work formed the basis of Volume Two of *Capital* which was eventually completed by Engels.

When looked at chronologically it is noticeable that the problem of crisis plays a progressively diminishing role in these works. There is a fairly extensive discussion in the *Theories of Surplus Value*, which is taken up again in connection with the law of the tendency for the rate of profit to fall in the manuscript of 1864–5, which Engels

---

[2] Marx was still preoccupied with the demolition of Proudhonian socialism. Having sent in the manuscript of the *Critique of Political Economy* Marx wrote to Weydemeyer: 'In these two chapters the Proudhonist socialism now fashionable in France — which wants to retain private production *while organising* the exchange of private products, to have *commodities* but not *money* — is demolished to its very foundations.' (01.02.59, CW40, 377)(c.f. Marx to Engels: '1. that it extirpates Proudhonism root and branch, 2. that the *specifically* social, by no means *absolute*, character of bourgeois production is analysed straight away in its simplest form, that of the commodity' (22.07.59, CW40 ,473.

[3] The full manuscript has now been published in the latest edition of the German Collected Works (MEGA II.3.1 – II.3.6), and comprises volumes 30–34 of the English edition of the *Collected Works*.

incorporated into Volume Three of *Capital*, but thereafter we find no significant theoretical discussion of crisis in Marx's work, the topic only being picked up again by Engels in his *Anti-Dühring*. On the other hand, the problem of the secular tendency and ultimate limits of the capitalist mode of production plays an increasingly important role in Marx's theoretical writings. In the manuscripts of 1861–5 Marx's analysis of the secular tendencies of accumulation is dominated by his analysis of the law of the tendency for the rate of profit to fall. However, in Volume One of *Capital* there is no mention of this law, and it is replaced by the 'absolute general law of capitalist accumulation', which refers to the secular tendency to the relative pauperisation of the mass of the population and to the progressive polarisation of class relations that had played the central role in the analysis of the *Communist Manifesto*, and remained the foundation of Marxist orthodoxy.

The analysis of crisis in the manuscripts of the first half of the 1860s is fragmentary. The discussion is difficult to interpret because the problem of crisis is only taken up as it arises in the course of Marx's critical comments on political economy, its fuller development being repeatedly postponed to the consideration of competition and credit. Throughout these manuscripts Marx is concerned to discover the 'inner nature' of capital, and so the most general determinants of the tendency to crisis, and not its superficial manifestations which develop in the relations between particular capitals in the sphere of exchange. Nevertheless the problem remains of connecting the inner tendencies of capitalist production with their superficial manifestations, to show that the latter are indeed expressions of the former. The central issue throughout these manuscripts remains that of the relationship between 'underconsumptionist', 'disproportionality' and 'falling rate of profit' theories of crisis.

The manuscripts of 1861–5 build on the insights gained in the *Grundrisse*, recapitulating and developing the arguments in that text. The foundation of Marx's mature analysis, developed in the *Grundrisse*, systematically elaborated in the *Critique of Political Economy*, and summarised in the first part of Volume One of *Capital*, is the contradiction between value and use value, which is inherent in the commodity form of the product. This fundamental contradiction appears in a developed form in the separation of purchase and sale and which is expressed in the contradictory relationship between commodities and money. At this level of abstraction the possibility of crisis is already inherent in the social form of commodity production. 'The division of exchange into purchase and sale ... contains the general possibility of commercial crises, essentially because the contradiction of commodity and money is the most abstract and general form of all contradictions inherent in the bourgeois mode of labour. Although circulation of money can occur therefore without crises, crises cannot occur without circulation of money' (CW29, 332).

Although crises appear as monetary crises, the latter are only the superficial manifestation of the more fundamental contradictions of commodity production. The monetary crisis expresses the underlying contradiction between value and use value in its most general form because money is ultimately the only 'adequate form of exchange value ... The fact that money is the sole incarnation of wealth manifests itself in the actual devaluation and worthlessness of all physical wealth ... This particular phase of world market crises is known as monetary crisis.' (CW29, 378) Ever since 1825 commercial crises have been not singular phenomena, but 'big storms on the world market, in which the antagonism of all elements in the bourgeois process of production explodes'. The economists look to the circulation of the currency to explain crises, since the latter are associated with the rise and fall of prices, or the appreciation and depreciation of the currency. But the monetary crisis is only the superficial expression of a deeper seated crisis, the sphere of currency is only 'the most superficial and abstract sphere of this process' (CW29, 412).

The *Critique of Political Economy* does not get beyond the abstract analysis of the commodity and money, and at this level there is not much more to be said about crises than to identify their general possibility and their most abstract form. In the *Grundrisse* Marx had identified the foundation of the tendency to crisis in the contradiction inherent in the subordination of the production of things to the production and appropriation of surplus value. This implied that the development of the theoretical understanding of crisis has to wait on the development of the theory of surplus value which preoccupied Marx through the first half of the 1860s.

Marx's discussion of crisis in the manuscripts of 1861–5 arises in three different contexts, each of which picks up themes first developed in the *Grundrisse*, and develops them through the critique of political economy. The theory of crisis is in many respects a pivotal point of this critique, since it was a focus of debate within political economy itself, in which Say and Ricardo insisted that general overproduction was impossible, against Malthus and Sismondi who proposed an underconsumptionist theory of crisis. Marx engaged with both sides in this debate in the attempt to develop a critique of their common theoretical foundation. This led Marx to look for a theoretical basis on which to develop his own analysis of the ultimate limits of the capitalist mode of production in the secular tendency for the rate of profit to fall. In the rest of this chapter I will look at the theory of crisis in the context of Marx's critique of political economy, before turning to the question of the falling rate of profit in the next chapter.[4]

Underconsumption Theories: Malthus and Sismondi

Marx discusses the underconsumption theories of Malthus and Sismondi relatively briefly in two separate passages, but in terms which can give the impression that he is unequivocally endorsing those theories. Marx certainly endorses Malthus's and Sismondi's emphasis on the crisis tendencies of capitalist accumulation, against Ricardo's assumption of smooth equilibration, and he agrees with them that the barrier to sustained capitalist accumulation appears in the problem of disposing of the ever-growing surplus product. However, nowhere does Marx endorse their underconsumptionist explanation for this problem, because he is absolutely insistent in his rejection of the underlying premise that they share with Ricardo and derive from Adam Smith, that 'consumption is the sole end and purpose of all production'. For Marx the driving force of production is not consumption, but the production and appropriation of a surplus value. The barriers to accumulation are not to be found in any contradiction between production and consumption, but in the contradiction inherent in the production and realisation of surplus value.

Marx first raises the issue of underconsumption in the course of a discussion of the problem of productive and unproductive labour in the manuscript published as the first volume of *Theories of Surplus Value*. For Adam Smith, and after him for Ricardo, unproductive labour was a pure drain on the surplus, reducing the resources available for investment in the development of the productive forces. For Malthus,

---

[4] Needless to say, modern economics remains on the same theoretical foundations as did the political economy that Marx was criticising, so that his critique is as valid today as it was when he wrote. I will not draw attention to the obvious parallels, but leave it to the interested reader to do so for herself.

Underconsumption Theories: Malthus and Sismondi

by contrast, the growth of unproductive labour played an essential role in averting the tendency to crises. Malthus justified the existence of a parasitic landowning class that consumes without producing on the grounds that unproductive consumption is necessary to absorb the growing surplus, and so avoid the problem of overproduction. Marx was contemptuous of Malthus's apologetic defence of the landed class, but appeared to be much more sympathetic to his underconsumptionist theory of crisis.

The basis of Malthus's conception is the view that regards '*consumption* as a necessary spur to production' (TSV1, 272), a view which, of course, Marx dismissively rejects. But what lies behind Malthus's theory is the fact that 'the labourer's consumption on the average is only equal to his costs of production, it is not equal to his output. He therefore produces the whole surplus for others and so this whole part of his *production* is *production for others*. Moreover, the industrial capitalist who drives the labourer to this *overproduction* ... appropriates the surplus-product for himself. But as personified capital he produces for the sake of production, he wants to accumulate wealth for the sake of the accumulation of wealth ... If the labourer's overproduction is *production for others*, the production of the normal capitalist ... is *production for the sake of production*' (TSV1, 273–4).

Although capitalists certainly enjoy their wealth, 'the industrial capitalist becomes more or less unable to fulfil his function as soon as he personifies the enjoyment of wealth, as soon as he wants the accumulation of pleasures instead of the pleasure of accumulation.

'He is therefore also a producer of *overproduction, production for others*. Over against this overproduction on one side must be placed overconsumption on the other, production for the sake of production must be confronted by consumption for the sake of consumption.' (TSV1, 274)

Marx then links this approach to his familiar characterisation of the capitalist separation-in-unity of production and consumption, which is the developed form of the separation of purchase and sale inherent in the system of commodity production. 'Production and consumption are *in their nature* inseparable. From this it follows that since in the system of capitalist production they are in fact separated, their unity is restored through their opposition.' (TSV1, 274)

Marx does not at this point indicate any criticism of Malthus's theory, so that his observations, taken in isolation, could be read as an endorsement of Malthus's underconsumptionism, and indeed have been so read by many commentators. However, in earlier sections of the manuscript Marx had already made it quite clear that there was not in principle a problem of the realisation of the growing surplus value, since surplus value was expended not for consumption, but to expand the existing capital.

In his discussion of Smith's failure to understand the reproduction of constant capital, which arose because Smith resolved the whole product into wages, rent and profit, Marx noted that the profit of the capitalist is 'in part a consumption fund for the capitalist, and in part is transformed into additional capital' (TSV1, 106). Similarly, Marx insisted with Ricardo, and against Malthus, that there is no need for unproductive consumption to absorb any increase in surplus value, because additional 'productive consumption' is created as profit is converted into additional capital, employing additional labour and means of production.[5] 'On the one hand it is the tendency of capital to reduce to a dwindling minimum the labour-time necessary for the production of commodities, and therefore also the number of the productive population *in relation to* the amount of the product. On the other hand, however, it has the opposite tendency to accumulate, to transform profit into capital, to appropriate the greatest possible quantity of the labour of others. It strives to reduce the norm of necessary labour, but to employ the greatest possible quantity of productive labour at the given norm. ... The constant retransformation of profit into capital always restores the same cycle on a wider basis.' (TSV1, 221-2) The implication is that if there is a problem of realisation, it is not the result of the production of a surplus, but of an interruption to that production.[6]

Marx returns to Malthus and Sismondi in the later part of the manuscript, published as Volume Three of *Theories of Surplus Value*, which deals primarily with Malthus's and Ricardo's successors, and in which Marx again appears to endorse the underconsumptionist theory of crisis. Marx opens the discussion by treating Malthus with his

---

[5] Although the initial displacement of labour by machinery certainly creates a 'shock (to which perhaps the section of the population which is directly affected cannot offer any resistance)' (TSV1, 222), and 'machinery always creates a relative surplus population, a reserve army of workers, which greatly increases the power of capital' (TSV2, 554).

[6] The discussion of Malthus and Sismondi is incomplete for the familiar reason that the question of realisation can only be discussed in connection with competition. As Marx notes later in the manuscript, 'I exclude Sismondi from my historical survey here because a critique of his views belongs to a part of my work dealing with the real movement of capital (competition and credit) which I can only tackle after I have finished this book' (TSV2, 53).

usual contempt, although he acknowledges that Malthus recognised that there is a problem with the realisation of surplus value, which Ricardo simply ignored because he 'always presupposes the finished product which is divided between the capitalist and the worker without considering exchange, the intermediate process which leads to this division' (TSV3, 16). However it is not Malthus whom Marx counterposes to Ricardo, but Sismondi. Ricardo and Sismondi between them captured both the positive and the negative sides of the capitalism, without being able to see that the two were inseparably linked, expressing the contradictory foundations of the capitalist mode of production.

Consideration of Sismondi enables Marx to reiterate the view with which he had concluded the discussion of Ricardo a few pages earlier in his notebook, and to which he assimilates Sismondi. The only fault with Sismondi, at this stage in Marx's argument, is that Sismondi clearly saw the contradictions inherent in capitalism, but could not see their foundations in the capitalist mode of production, and so could not see the way beyond them:

> Sismondi is profoundly conscious of the contradictions in capitalist production; he is aware that, on the one hand, its forms — its production relations — stimulate unrestrained development of the productive forces and of wealth; and that, on the other, these relations are conditional. ... He is particularly aware of the fundamental contradiction: on the one hand, unrestricted development of the productive forces and increase of wealth which, at the same time consists of commodities and must be turned into cash; on the other hand, the system is based on the fact that the mass of the producers is restricted to the necessaries. Hence, according to Sismondi, crises are not accidental, as Ricardo maintains, but essential outbreaks — occurring on a large scale and at definite periods — of the immanent contradictions. He wavers constantly: should the State curb the productive forces to make them adequate to the production relations, or should the production relations be made adequate to the productive forces. He often retreats into the past ... or he seeks to exorcise the contradictions by a different adjustment of revenue in relation to capital, or of distribution in relation to production, not realising that the relations of distribution are only the relations of production seen from a different aspect. He forcefully *criticises* the contradictions of bourgeois production but

does not *understand* them, and consequently does not understand the process whereby they can be resolved. (TSV3, 55-6)[7]

Sismondi only confirms Marx's own diagnosis of the fundamental contradiction underlying the tendency to crisis. 'The fact that bourgeois production is compelled by its own immanent laws, on the one hand, to develop the productive forces as if production did not take place on a narrow restricted social foundation, while, on the other hand, it can develop these forces only within these narrow limits, is the deepest and most hidden cause of crises, of the crying contradictions within which bourgeois production is carried on and which, even at a cursory glance, reveal it as only a transitional, historical form.' (TSV3, 84)

These passages appear to provide an unequivocal endorsement of the underconsumptionist theories of crisis proposed by Sismondi and Malthus, despite the fact that Marx had repeatedly made it clear that he was well aware of the limitations of such a theory. Marx firmly rejects Malthus's starting point, the view that regards '*consumption* as a necessary spur to production' (TSV1, 272). The purpose of capitalism is production for the sake of production — the production not of things but of profit, not of use values but of values. The conditions for the realisation of this surplus value therefore have nothing to do with the consumption either of the workers or of the capitalists, but rather have to do with the conditions for the sustained accumulation of capital. Provided that capital continues to confront profitable opportunities for renewed investment, such investment will provide the growing demand for the products of capital, corresponding to the additional surplus value produced, as capitalists purchase additional labour power and means of production.

This apparent contradiction appears starkly in the contrast between two brief passages from Marx's later notebooks, which Engels incorporated into Volume Two of *Capital*, each of which follows a more

---

[7] Compare the similar argument in the *Grundrisse*: Ricardo 'considers the barriers which production encounters in this direction as accidental, as barriers which are simply overcome ... *Sismondi*, by contrast, emphasises not only the encountering of the barrier but its creation by capital itself, which thus gets itself into contradictions, contradictions in which he glimpses the impending breakdown of capital. He therefore wants to impose barriers on production from outside, by means of custom, laws, etc., which, as merely external and artificial constraints, would necessarily be demolished by capital. On the other hand, Ricardo and his entire school have never comprehended the real *modern crises* in which this contradiction of capital discharges itself in violent thunderstorms, which more and more threaten capital itself as the basis of society and production'. (CW28, 338)

concrete reference to crises. The two passages appear directly to contradict one another. The first passage derives from a notebook of 1870 and is a 'note for further elaboration', which is widely quoted as an endorsement of an underconsumptionist theory of crisis.

> Contradiction in the capitalist mode of production. The workers are important for the market as buyers of commodities. But as sellers of their commodity — labour-power — capitalist society has the tendency to restrict them to their minimum price. Further contradiction: the periods in which capitalist production exerts all its forces regularly show themselves to be periods of overproduction; because the limit to the application of the productive powers is not simply the production of value, but also its realisation. However the sale of commodities, the realisation of commodity capital, and thus of surplus value as well, is restricted not by the consumer needs of society in general, but by the consumer needs of a society in which the great majority are always poor and must always remain poor. This however belongs rather to the next Part. (CII, 391n.)[8]

The second passage derives from a notebook of 1878 and presents an unequivocal critique of underconsumptionist theories, which Engels in a footnote directs at the 'prospective supporters of Rodbertus's theory of crises', and follows an account of the rise in wages and the growth of consumption in the boom, when 'the working class (in which the entire reserve army of labour has now been enroled) also takes a temporary share in the consumption of luxury articles that are otherwise for the most part "necessary" only for the capitalists.' Marx continues:

> It is a pure tautology to say that crises are provoked by a lack of effective demand or effective consumption ... The fact that commodities are unsaleable means no more than that no effective buyers have been found for them ... If the attempt is made to give this tautology the semblance of greater profundity, by the statement that the working class receives too small a portion of its own product, and that the evil would be remedied if it received a bigger share, i.e. if its wages rose, we need only note that crises are always prepared by a period in which wages generally rise, and the working

---

[8] The 'next part' referred to is the section of the manuscript dealing with the reproduction process, in which there is no hint of an underconsumptionist theory.

class actually does receive a greater share in the part of the annual product destined for consumption. From the standpoint of these advocates of sound and 'simple' (!) common sense, such periods should rather avert the crisis. It thus appears that capitalist production involves certain conditions independent of people's good or bad intentions, which permit the relative prosperity of the working class only temporarily, and moreover always as a harbinger of crisis.' (CII, 486–7)

These apparently flagrant contradictions cannot be put down to the maturing of Marx's thought, since they appear side by side in the same manuscripts. So how do we reconcile Marx's apparently unequivocal endorsement of Malthus's and Sismondi's underconsumptionist theories of crisis, with his equally unequivocal critique of their primitive theoretical conceptions? What is that Marx is endorsing in Malthus and Sismondi, and where does he depart from them?

The issue is the same as that which we have already addressed in the discussion of the *Grundrisse*. What Marx endorses in Malthus, and particularly in Sismondi, is the understanding of the inherent tendency to overproduction, in the sense of the production of a growing surplus value, embodied in a growing mass of commodities, which has to be sold if capitalist accumulation is to be sustained. However, the identification of a tendency to overproduction is by no means the same thing as the advocacy of an underconsumptionist theory of crisis.[9] Marx indicates quite clearly that working class consumption can never be adequate to the realisation of one iota of the surplus value. However great or small the surplus product might be, it can only be realised through its sale to other capitalists. Sismondi may have identified the fundamental contradiction at the heart of the capitalist mode of production, but to understand the crisis tendencies of capitalist accumulation it is necessary to explore the development of this contradiction by locating the barriers to the expanded reproduction of capital.

There is a tendency to overproduction, but this tendency is related to the limited opportunities for the reconversion of surplus value into capital. But if the tendency of the capitalist mode of production is to develop the forces of production without limit, it is not clear why

---

[9] Nothing could be more misleading in this respect than Sweezy's casual assertion that overproduction and underconsumption are 'opposite sides of the same coin' (Sweezy 1946, 183).

accumulation should not continue indefinitely. Malthus and Sismondi do not solve the problem raised by Ricardo of the possibility of general overproduction, and it is this issue that Marx addresses in the most substantial discussion of crises in the manuscripts of the 1860s.

Overproduction and Crisis: Say and Ricardo

The most substantial discussion of the theory of crisis in any of Marx's works is found in the manuscripts published as Volume Two of *Theories of Surplus Value*, in the context of Marx's critique of Ricardo's analysis of accumulation and of Ricardo's denial of the possibility of general overproduction. This long passage builds on the parallel discussion in the *Grundrisse*, as Marx tries to establish the relationship between the overproduction of particular commodities, which arises from the disproportional development of the branches of production, and the general overproduction which appears in a crisis.

The production of surplus value and the possibility of crisis

Marx begins by stating the problem, raising the question of the conditions under which the sustained accumulation of capital is possible. These are '*the very same as those for its original production or reproduction in general*' (TSV2, 483).[10] The capitalist has appropriated a sum of money, equivalent to his original capital increased by the amount of surplus value produced, which he wants to spend on expanding production. To do this the capitalist must find additional labour power and means of production available on the market, which 'presupposes the production of a *surplus-product*' (TSV2, 484). The necessary means of production are more likely to be available the more highly developed is capitalist production. 'It seems therefore, that for accumulation to take place, continuous *surplus production* in all spheres is necessary' (TSV2, 485). And if such production is taking place, and sufficient labour is available, then the sustained accumulation of capital would appear to face no further difficulties.

There seems to be no barrier inherent in the conditions of capitalist production to the sustained expansion of capitalist production. The

---

[10] Marx does not here 'consider the case in which it is impossible to sell the mass of commodities produced, crises etc. This belongs into the section on competition' (TSV2, 484. c.f. TSV2, 468).

growth of production is determined not by any stimulus of growing consumption, but is inherent in capital itself. This immediately implies that capitalist accumulation is not limited by consumption needs, since 'in capitalist production what matters is not the immediate use value but the exchange value and, in particular, the expansion of surplus value. This is the driving motive of capitalist production, and it is a pretty conception that — in order to drive away the contradictions of capitalist production — abstracts from its very basis and depicts it as a production aimed at the direct satisfaction of the consumption of the producers.' Production on an expanding scale 'forms an inherent basis for the phenomena which appear during crises' (TSV2, 495), but in relation not to consumption but to the possibilities of the renewed production of surplus value.

Marx stresses that crises can arise in many different ways, but here he is not concerned with the 'real conditions within which the actual process of production takes place ... We do not examine the competition of capitals, nor the credit system, nor the actual composition of society'. He is concerned here with the possibility of crisis, inherent in the general nature of capital, not the actual mechanisms of crisis. 'Just as the examination of money — both insofar as it represents a form altogether different from the natural form of commodities, and also in its form as means of payment — has shown that it contained the possibility of crises; the examination of the general nature of capital, even without going into the actual relations which all constitute prerequisites for the real process of production, reveals this still more clearly' (TSV2, 492–3).

The condition for the renewed production of surplus value is not the prior existence of an appropriate level of consumption, but the availability of labour power and means of production in the appropriate proportions. This would seem to imply that the basis of crises must be the accidental emergence of disproportionalities, since the relations of proportionality are by no means guaranteed.

> The criterion of this expansion of production is *capital* itself, the existing level of the conditions of production and the unlimited desire of the capitalists to enrich themselves and enlarge their capital, but by no means *consumption*, which from the outset is inhibited, since the majority of the population, the working people, can only expand their consumption within very narrow limits, whereas the demand for labour, although it grows *absolutely*, decreases *rela-*

tively, to the same extent as capitalism develops. Moreover, all equalisations are *accidental* and although the proportion of capital employed in individual spheres is equalised by a continuous process, the continuity of this process itself equally presupposes the constant disproportion which it has continuously, often violently, to even out. (TSV2, 492)

As in the *Grundrisse*, the examples Marx gives of the concrete ways in which the reproduction of capital might be disrupted are all examples in which disproportionalities lead to price changes which erode profitability in one branch of production. Such disproportionalities may come about because of an especially poor or especially good harvest, because of the disruption of trade, because of an acceleration in the rate of accumulation, because of overproduction in a particular branch of production, or because of the development of the forces of production, which devalues existing capital and the existing mass of commodities. If either the market price of the product falls below its cost-price, or a shortage of means of production pushes up their cost, the reproduction of capital will be curtailed.

Disproportionality leads to a general crisis as money is withdrawn from circulation in the face of the threat of a loss. The threat of loss means that accumulation 'stagnates even more. Surplus value amassed in the form of money (gold or notes) could only be transformed into capital at a loss. It therefore lies idle as a hoard in the banks, or in the form of credit money, which in essence makes no difference at all' (TSV2, 494). This is very likely to occur 'since the circulation process of capital ...extends over a fairly long period'. During this period changes in the market and in the productivity of labour can lead to considerable changes in value, so that 'great catastrophes must occur and elements of crisis must have gathered and develop' (TSV2, 495).

The crisis does not mark the end of the capitalist mode of production, but only one phase of a cycle in which the crisis is the means of capital's rejuvenation. Marx distinguishes between the destruction of real capital and the devaluation of capital, the latter preparing the way for recovery. In the former case, overproduction is extinguished as means of production and labour power are destroyed as both values and use values. In the latter we mean the 'depreciation of *values* which prevents them from later renewing their reproduction process as capital on the same scale. This is the ruinous effect of the fall in the prices of commodities.' The devaluation of capital imposes huge losses on existing capitalists. However it does not destroy the means of production, but restores the profitability of their employment by reducing their value. 'It does not cause the destruction of any use values. What one loses the other gains. ... A large part of the nominal capital of the society, i.e., of the *exchange value* of the existing capital, is once for all destroyed, although this very destruction, since it does not affect the use value, may very much expedite the new reproduction. This is also the period at which moneyed interest enriches itself at the cost of industrial interest.' (TSV2, 496) The distinction between the destruction of use values and the devaluation of capital makes it clear once again that the problem is not a problem of overproduction in relation to social need, but of overproduction in relation to the restricted conditions of capitalist production, of production for profit, since a fall in price rekindles the need for the product.

The crisis seems to be something purely accidental, the result of the 'anarchy of the market', and not clearly inherent in the capitalist mode of production. Political economy was perfectly ready to admit the possibility of such accidental crises, although it expected the market to rectify disproportionalities smoothly as capital flowed between branches of production in response to differences in the rate of profit. Clearly Marx needs to look more closely at the relation between disproportionalities and general overproduction, and at the relation between money, exchange and capitalist production, more closely.

Disproportionality and general overproduction

To address these issues Marx picks up his discussion from the *Grundrisse* of the problem of the relationship between disproportionately and the emergence of general overproduction, which political economy denied on the basis of Say's law of markets. Marx's essential point is that once we recognise that the production and exchange of commodities is mediated by the circulation of money, and subordinated to the production and appropriation of surplus value in the form of money, the distinction between particular and general overproduction disappears.

Marx asserts once more that the problem of crises is a specifically capitalist problem, which political economy ignores in asserting that the purpose of production is consumption, so that nobody sells except in order to buy, from which Ricardo, following Say, concluded that general overproduction is impossible since every sale generates an equivalent purchase. The purpose of capitalist production is not consumption, as political economy constantly asserts, but the appropriation of money. For Say and Ricardo one does not sell if one does not wish to make a subsequent purchase. However, Marx insists,

> A man who has produced does not have the choice of selling or not selling. He must *sell*. In the crisis there arises the very situation in which he cannot sell ... or must even sell at a positive loss. ... Ricardo even forgets that a person may *sell* in order to *pay*, and that these forced sales play a very significant role in the crises. The capitalist's immediate object in selling, is to turn his commodity, or rather his commodity capital, back into *money capital*, and thereby to *realise* his profit. Consumption — revenue — is by no means the guiding motive in this process ... Everyone *sells* first of all in order to sell, that is to say, in order to transform commodities into money. ... The crisis is precisely the phase of disturbance and interruption of the process of reproduction. And this disturbance cannot be explained by the fact that it does not occur in those times where there is no crisis. ... The immediate purpose of capitalist production is not "the possession of other goods" [Ricardo], but the appropriation of value, of money, of abstract wealth. (TSV2, 503; c.f. *Grundrisse*, CW28, 339)

The argument that only particular commodities, and not all commodities, can be overproduced is ridiculous. The interdependence of the various branches of production means that if *one* cannot be sold, then the circulation of *all* commodities is disrupted, so that the possibility of the overproduction of a *particular* commodity immediately implies the possibility of *general* overproduction. '[The proposition] *the* commodity must be converted into money only means that: *all* commodities must do so. And just as the difficulty of undergoing this metamorphosis exists for an individual commodity, so it can exist for all commodities. The general nature of the metamorphosis of commodities — which includes the separation of purchase and sale just as it does their unity — instead of excluding the *possibility* of a general glut, on the contrary, contains the possibility of the general glut.' (TSV2, 504)

A general glut arises when capitalists transform their commodities into money, but then withdraw their money from circulation, when 'the motive to turn the commodity into money, to realise its exchange value, prevails over the motive to transform the commodity again into use value' (TSV2, 505). It is no escape to argue that all commodities could be sold if their prices fell, because the fall in prices is what precipitates the crisis. 'The excess of commodities is always relative; in other words it is an excess at particular prices. The prices at which the commodities are then absorbed are ruinous for the producer or merchant.' Similarly, it may well be the case that the crisis of overproduction first affects a particular commodity, but it may soon become generalised. 'For a crisis (and therefore also for overproduction) to be general, it suffices for it to affect the principal commercial goods.' (TSV2, 505)

Despite the periodic recurrence of crises, in which overproduction extends to all branches of production, the economists deny the possibility of general overproduction, explaining crises as the result of an 'overabundance of capital', which was usually explained as the result of the speculative expansion of credit which had been permitted by the over-indulgence of the bankers.[11] However, Marx insists, the overabundance of capital is exactly the same thing as the overproduction of commodities. The only sign that capital is 'overabundant' comes when capitalists are unable to sell the commodities that they have produced, so the overabundant capital is no more than an accumulation of commodities which cannot be sold. The 'over-production of capital' simply means the 'over-production of value destined to produce surplus value ... over-production of commodities destined for reproduction — that is, *reproduction on too large a scale*, which is the same as over-production pure and simple' (TSV2, 533).[12]

The tendency to crisis and the critique of political economy

The economists' denial of the possibility of general overproduction takes us to the heart of Marx's critique of political economy. 'In the crises of the world market, the contradictions and antagonisms of bourgeois production are strikingly revealed', but the economists simply deny that they exist, 'insisting, in the face of their regular and periodic recurrence, that if production were carried on according to

---
[11] Ricardo is partially exonerated by Marx since the crises that he saw could be given accidental explanations, but this denial was no longer possible after 1825, since when crises have clearly recurred periodically.

[12] The overproduction of capital and the overproduction of commodities 'express *the same antinomy*, only in a different form' (CW33, 114).

the textbooks, crises would never occur. Thus the apologetics consist in the falsification of the simplest economic relations, and particularly in clinging to the concept of unity in the face of contradiction'. These contradictions appear in the contradiction between production and realisation, between the production of commodities as things, and their sale as values. It is true that production and circulation represent the unity of two phases of a single process of reproduction, but these two phases are independent of one another. 'It is just the *crisis* in which they assert their unity ... There would be no crisis without this inner unity of factors that are apparently indifferent to one another' (TSV2, 500).[13]

Marx links Ricardo's failure to understand the possibility of crisis inherent in the contradictory form of the commodity to his most fundamental theoretical misunderstanding, which lies in his failure to understand the contradictory forms of money and value, reducing exchange to the most primitive form of barter. 'In order to prove that capitalist production cannot lead to general crises, all its conditions and distinct forms, all its principles and specific features - in short *capitalist production* itself — are denied' (TSV2, 501). Thus Marx links the phenomenon of crises directly to his critique of the conceptual foundations of political economy, which he first outlined in the *Economic and Philosophical Manuscripts* and developed in the *Grundrisse*, which in its mature form runs through the whole of *Capital*.

Ricardo is 'the economist of production' who regards exchange as the purely formal link between successive phases of production, so ignoring all barriers that confront the need to realise the commodity in the form of money, and to reconvert that money into the material elements of capital as the basis for renewed accumulation. Ricardo reduces the act of exchange to an act of barter, so that money and exchange 'appear only as a purely formal element in his political economy ... He nowhere investigates the form of the mediation' (CW28, 252), the '*specific economic forms of exchange* themselves play *economically* no role at all in his political economy' (CW28, 256). This

---

[13] 'The apologetic phrases used to deny crises are important in so far as they always prove the opposite of what they are meant to prove. In order to deny crises, they assert unity where there is conflict and contradiction. They are therefore important in so far as one can say they prove that there would be no crises if the contradictions which they have erased in their imagination did not exist in fact. But in reality crises exist because these contradictions exist. ... The desire to convince oneself of the non-existence of contradictions, is at the same time the expression of the pious wish that the contradictions, which are really present, *should not* exist.' (TSV2, 519)

is why he loses sight of overproduction because exchange is purely nominal (CW28, 258), and money functions only as the means of exchange. However, money is not only the medium of exchange, 'but at the same time the medium by which the exchange of product with product is divided into two acts, which are independent of each other, and separate from each other in time and space', this separation being expressed in the separation of money from the act of exchange, as the independent form of value, which can serve equally as store of value and as means of payment.

Similarly, Ricardo is only concerned with determining the magnitude of value, and pays no attention to the social form within which social labour is represented in the alienated form of value. He looks only at the '*quantitative determination* of exchange value, namely that it is equal to a definite quantity of labour-time, forgetting on the other hand the *qualitative* characteristic that individual labour must present itself as *abstract, general social* labour only through its alienation' (TSV2, 504; c.f. TSV3, 131–9).

In abstracting altogether from the limits of the commodity form Ricardo is actually asserting the opposite of what he means to say, 'namely, that production takes place without regard to the existing limits of consumption, but is limited only by capital itself. And this is indeed characteristic of this mode of production' (TSV2, 520). The theoretical limitation of Ricardo's political economy is related directly to the ideological presupposition that means that in the last analysis even Ricardo's economics has an apologetic character.

> The limits to production are set by the profit of the capitalist and in no way by the needs of the producers. But over-production of products and over-production of *commodities* are two entirely different things. If Ricardo thinks that the *commodity* form makes no difference to the product, and furthermore, that *commodity circulation* differs only formally from barter, that in this context the exchange value is only a fleeting form of the exchange of things, and that money is therefore merely a formal means of circulation — then this in fact is in line with his presupposition that the bourgeois mode of production is the absolute mode of production, hence it is a mode of production without any definite specific characteristics, its distinctive traits are merely formal. He cannot therefore admit that the bourgeois mode of production contains within itself a barrier to the free development of the productive forces, a barrier which

comes to the surface in crises and, in particular, in *over-production* — the basic phenomenon in crises.' (TSV2, 527–8)[14]

To understand the possibility of crises we therefore have to return to the contradictory foundations of the capitalist mode of production, which lie in the subordination of the production of use values to the production and appropriation of a surplus value.

The contradictions of capital and the possibility of crisis

As we have seen on a number of occasions, as soon as we examine the *form* of capitalist production we find that the possibility of a crisis of general over-production is already inherent in the very first moment of the separation of purchase and sale, behind which lies the separation of production and circulation as moments of the process of capitalist reproduction. The tendency to crisis lies in the *relation between* production and circulation that political economy ignores. 'The *possibility* of crisis, which became apparent in the *simple metamorphosis* of the commodity, is once more demonstrated, and further developed, by the disjunction between the (direct) process of production and the process of circulation. As soon as these processes do not merge smoothly into one another but become independent of one another, the crisis is there.' (TSV2, 507)

The crisis itself arises when the commodity capital which emerges from the process of production cannot be transformed into money. This happens because elsewhere somebody is holding money, which they do not immediately transform into commodities, so it is the existence of money which makes crises possible, and this is precisely what the

---

[14] 'Ricardo championed bourgeois production insofar as it [signified] the most unrestricted development of the productive forces' (TSV3, 52) but Ricardo 'transforms bourgeois production into mere production of use value ... He regards the specific form of bourgeois wealth as something merely formal which does not affect its content. He therefore also denies the contradictions of bourgeois production which break out in crises. Hence his quite false conception of money. Hence, in considering the production process of capital, he ignores completely the circulation process, insofar as it includes the metamorphosis of commodities, the necessity of the transformation of capital into money. ... Ricardo regards bourgeois, or more precisely, capitalist production as the *absolute form* of production, whose specific forms of production relations can therefore never enter into contradiction with, or enfetter, the aim of production. ... In actual fact, what he admires most about bourgeois production is that its definite forms — compared with previous forms of production — provide scope for the boundless development of productive forces. When they cease to do this, or when contradictions appear within which they do this, he denies the contradictions, or rather, expresses the contradiction in another form by representing *wealth as such* — the mass of use values in itself — without regard to the producers, as the *ultima Thule*.' (TSV3, 54–5; c.f. CI, 80, n. 2)

economists deny in reducing the act of exchange to an act of barter, in which money plays only a formal role. 'Crisis results from the impossibility to sell. The difficulty of transforming the *commodity* — the particular product of individual labour — into its opposite, money, i.e. abstract general social labour, lies in the fact that *money* is not the particular product of individual labour' (TSV2, 509), but provides the means of buying any particular product at any time, so the person who has money doesn't have to spend it. In barter no such crisis could arise, all that could happen would be that an exchange would not take place, but money makes crises possible by making possible the separation of purchase and sale.

The separation of the moments of production and circulation establishes the possibility of crisis, which is not a pathological phenomenon appearing on the surface of capitalist society, but the normal and regular means by which prices and production are adjusted in order to make possible the renewed reproduction of capital. 'We have said that this *form* contains the *possibility of crisis*, that is to say, the possibility that elements which are correlated, which are inseparable, are separated and consequently are forcibly reunited, their coherence is violently asserted against their mutual independence. *Crisis* is nothing but the forcible assertion of the unity of phases of the production process which have become independent of each other' (TSV2, 509).[15]

The commodity form, based on the separation of purchase and sale, and the money form, in which this separation is developed as value acquires a bodily form independent of the act of exchange, explain the possibility of crisis, and define the form in which a crisis must necessarily appear. However, they still tell us nothing about how any particular crisis might occur, nor do they contain within themselves the explanation for the *necessity* of crisis, for they existed long before the emergence of modern crises, which are associated not only with the commodity and money forms, but with the capitalist form of production.

The general, abstract possibility of crisis denotes no more than the *most abstract form* of crisis, without content, without a compelling motivating factor. Sale and purchase may fall apart. They

---

[15] 'The circulation process as a whole or the reproduction process of capital as a whole is the unity of its production phase and its circulation phase, so that it comprises both these processes or phases. Therein lies a further developed possibility or abstract form of crisis. ... Crisis is the forcible establishment of unity between elements that have become independent and the enforced separation from one another of elements which are essentially one.' (TSV2, 513)

thus represent potential *crisis* and their coincidence always remains a critical factor for the commodity. The transition from one to the other may, however, proceed smoothly. The *most abstract form of crisis* (and therefore the formal possibility of crisis) is thus the *metamorphosis of the commodity* itself; the contradiction of exchange value and use value, and furthermore of money and commodity, comprised within the unity of the commodity, exists in metamorphosis only as an involved movement. The factors which turn this possibility of crisis into [an actual] crisis are not contained in this form itself; it only implies that *the framework* for a crisis exists. (TSV2, 509)[16]

It is not enough to recognise the existence of crises, or even to refer to the separation between purchase and sale as containing the possibility of crises, as does John Stuart Mill, because this still leaves actual crises accidental and unexplained. 'These factors which explain the possibility of crises, by no means explain their actual occurrence. They do not explain *why* the phases of the process come into such conflict that their inner unity can only assert itself through a crisis, through a violent process. This *separation* appears in the crisis; it is the elementary form of the crisis. To *explain* the crisis on the basis of this, its elementary form, is to explain the existence of the crisis by describing its most abstract form, that is to say, to explain the crisis by the crisis' (TSV2, 502).

'This shows how insipid the economists are who, when they are no longer able to explain away the phenomenon of overproduction and crises, are content to say that these forms contain the possibility of *crises*, that it is therefore *accidental* whether or not crises occur, and consequently their occurrence is itself merely a *matter of chance*.' (TSV2, 512)

If we are to explain crises we have to develop the analysis progressively from the more abstract determinants of crises to their concrete

---

[16] 'Crisis, therefore, cannot exist without manifesting itself at the same time in its simple form, as the contradiction between sale and purchase and the contradiction of money as a means of payment. But these are merely *forms*, general possibilities of crisis, and hence also forms, abstract forms, of actual crisis. In them, the nature of crisis appears in its simplest forms, and, in so far as this form is itself the simplest content of crisis, in its simplest content. But the content is not yet *substantiated*. Simple circulation of money and even the circulation of money as a means of payment — and both come into being long *before* capitalist production, while there are no crises — are possible and actually take place without crises. These forms alone, therefore, do not explain why their crucial aspect becomes prominent and why the potential contradiction contained in them becomes a real contradiction.' (TSV2, 512)

manifestation. From this point of view the explanation of crises is the most difficult task which Marx's theory faces, for crises are the most concrete manifestation of the most abstract contradictions inherent in capitalist production. 'The world trade crises must be regarded as the real concentration and forcible adjustment of all the contradictions of bourgeois economy. The individual factors, which are condensed in these crises, must therefore emerge and must be described in each sphere of the bourgeois economy and the further we advance in our examination of the latter, the more aspects of this conflict must be traced on the one hand, and on the other hand it must be shown that its more abstract forms are recurring and are contained in the more concrete forms.' (TSV2, 510)

Money, credit and the possibility of crisis

The abstract form of crisis tells us the form within which a crisis must necessarily occur, as the breakdown of the relation between production and circulation expressed in the breakdown of the unity of purchase and sale. To move towards the more concrete analysis Marx needs to show that the abstract forms of the crisis 'receive a content, a basis on which to manifest themselves' in the reproduction process of capital (TSV2, 510).

In the immediate relationship between purchase and sale money plays the transitory role of means of exchange. However, on this basis money can acquire a second function, 'the function of money as a means of payment, in which money has two different functions and figures in two different phases, divided from each other in time'. The development of credit money, based on the role of money as means of payment, makes it possible to dissociate purchase from sale, but also increases the likelihood that the interdependent network of purchases and sales will break down.

The reproduction process of capital involves a large number of separated and interdependent purchases and sales between capitalists, with demand being determined by the requirements of expanded reproduction, but supply by the imperatives of the production of surplus value. Sales and purchases of intermediate products generate chains of credit, whose repayment depends on the sale of the final product. If that sale breaks down, then a whole chain of payments are not made. 'here — in capitalist production — we can already see the connection between the mutual claims and obligations, the sales and purchases, through which the possibility can develop into actuality ' (TSV2, 511–2).

With the development of money as the means of payment we have now uncovered two inter-related aspects of the crisis. 'The general *possibility* of crisis is given in the process of *metamorphosis of capital* itself, and in two ways: in so far as money functions as *means of circulation,* [the possibility of crisis lies in] the separation *of purchase and sale;* and in so far as money functions as *means of payment,* it has two different aspects, it acts as *measure of value* and *as realisation of value.* These two aspects [may] become separated. (TSV2, 513–4) If the commodity is devalued in the interval between them a whole series of transactions cannot be settled so that '*inability to pay* occurs not only at one, but at many points, hence a *crisis* arises' (TSV2, 514).

We now have a more concrete picture of the development of crises, with credit establishing the interconnection of a whole series of transactions extending over a period of time, and this enables us to understand why there is no distinction between a crisis of overproduction of a particular commodity and a crisis of general overproduction. It also enables us to see how a crisis of overproduction appears in the form of a money crisis. Once the capitalist is trading on credit, he must sell the commodity in time to redeem his debt. 'The crisis occurs not only because the commodity is unsaleable, but because it is not saleable within a *particular period of time* and the crisis arises and derives its character not only from the *unsaleability* of the commodity, but from the *non-fulfilment of a whole series of payments* which depend on the sale of this particular commodity within this particular period of time. This is the *characteristic form of money crises.*' (TSV2, 514) Once credit has developed, a money crisis 'follows as a matter of course' in the wake of a trade crisis.

The introduction of money as the means of payment has not got us any nearer to an explanation of crises, we are still only at the level of 'the *formal possibilities* of crisis' (TSV2, 514). If sales are satisfactorily achieved, then all the debts can be repaid and there can be no crisis.[17] This means that, while we have a more developed understanding of the *mechanism* of crises, introduction of money as means of payment takes us no nearer to their *explanation,* because a money crisis presupposes a crisis in the purchase and sale of commodities.

---

[17] Marx excludes consideration of fraud here, and postpones consideration of the question of *'excess credit'* (TSV2, 515).

The breakdown in the function of money as the means of payment can only be the result of the breakdown of circulation, and we have still not explained why circulation should break down. 'Crises are possible without credit, without money functioning as a means of payment. But the second form is not possible *without the first* — that is to say, without the separation of purchase and sale. ...In investigating why the general *possibility of crisis* turns into a *real* crisis, in investigating the *conditions* of crisis, it is therefore quite superfluous to concern oneself with the *forms* of crisis which arise out of the development of money as *means of payment*. This is precisely why economists like to suggest that this *obvious* form is the *cause* of crises.' (TSV2, 514–5)

Capitalist production and the possibility of crisis

So far Marx has been examining the tendency to crisis in relation to the contradictions inherent in the social form of commodity production, and the function of money as means of payment, with no particular reference to the specifically capitalist character of production.

Consideration of the capitalist character of production at first sight adds nothing to the analysis. If we look specifically at the role of circulation in the reproduction of capital we simply find the basic contradictions of the commodity and money forms reproduced. 'The contradictions inherent in the circulation of commodities, which are further developed in the circulation of money — and thus, also, the possibilities of crisis — reproduce themselves, automatically, in capital, since developed circulation of commodities and of money, in fact, only takes place on the basis of capital.'(TSV2, 512)

If we turn back from circulation to the process of capitalist production we still cannot find anything which could explain the tendency to crisis. Once the capitalist has the elements of production to hand, he merely has to set them to work, so that the production of surplus value is entirely in his hands, facing no external barrier. The fact that surplus value is being produced has implications when we come on to consider the question of realisation, but this question does not arise in connection with its production.[18] 'The mere (direct) *production process* of capital in itself, cannot add anything new in this context.

---

[18] Of course there are technical and social barriers to the production of surplus value, most particularly the resistance of the workers, but the only limits are 'those which are partly presupposed and partly posited within this process itself, but always posited within it as *barriers* to be overcome' (*Grundrisse*, CW28, 331).

In order to exist at all, its conditions are presupposed. The first section dealing with capital — the *direct* process of production — does not contribute any new element of crisis. Although it *does* contain such an element, because the production process implies appropriation and hence production of surplus value. But this cannot be shown when dealing with the production process itself, for the latter is not concerned with *realisation* either of the reproduced value or of the surplus value' (TSV2, 513).

If the tendency to crisis cannot be explained in terms of the characteristics of the circulation of commodities and money, nor in terms of the characteristics of capitalist production, it can only be explained in terms of the specifically capitalist character of the inter-relation between production and circulation, that is to say in the purchase and sale of commodities as the products of capital, as a part of the reproduction process of capital as a whole. 'This can only emerge in the circulation process, which is in itself also a *process of reproduction*. (TSV2, 513)

Capitalist Reproduction, Disproportionality and Crisis

To get beyond the abstract form of the crisis we have to look more concretely at the reproduction process of capital, but Marx cannot do this fully until he has considered the interaction of particular capitals within the movement of capital-in-general, in the analysis of competition and credit (which he never got around to writing). 'But now the further development of the potential crisis has to be traced — the real crisis can only be deduced from the real movement of capitalist production, competition and credit — in so far as crisis arises out of the special aspects of capital which are peculiar to it as capital, and not merely comprised in its existence as commodity and money.' (TSV2, 512–3). 'The actual movement starts from the existing capital — i.e. the actual movement denotes developed capitalist production, which starts from and presupposes its own basis. The process of reproduction and the predisposition to crisis which is further developed in it, are therefore only partially described under this heading and require further elaboration in the chapter on "*Capital and Profit*".' (TSV2, 513)

At the same time, Marx still wants to locate the source of crises in the reproduction process of capital as a whole, that is to say in the relationship between the production of commodities as use values and their purchase and sale as the means for the production and appropriation of surplus value, and not only in the accidental interactions of particular capitals. This brings us back once again to the problem of the proportionality of production, to which Marx returns in a series of notes which he appended later, in which he tries to disentangle those causes of crises inherent in the general nature of capital from those which arise only in the interaction of particular capitals as a result of the 'anarchy of the market'.

Marx notes once again the distinction between the formal possibility of crisis and the cause of the crisis. 'The *general possibility* of crisis is the formal *metamorphosis* of capital itself, the separation, in time and space, of purchase and sale. But this is never the *cause* of the crisis. For it is nothing but the *most general form of crisis*, i.e. the crisis itself in *its most generalised expression*. But it cannot be said that the *abstract form of crisis* is the *cause of crisis*. If one asks what its cause is, one wants to know why *its abstract form*, the form of its possibility, turns from possibility into *actuality*.' (TSV2, 515)

Marx insists that we are looking for a cause of crises which is independent of the accidental fluctuations of prices. 'The *general conditions* of crises, insofar as they are independent of *price fluctuations* (whether these are linked with the credit system or not) as distinct from fluctuations in value, must be explicable from the general conditions of capitalist production.' Where crises arise from changes in prices which do not coincide with changes in values these 'cannot be investigated during the examination of capital in general, in which the prices of commodities are assumed to be *identical* with the *values* of commodities' (TSV2, 515). This is not a matter of methodological dogmatism, but of Marx's determination to show that crises are inherent in the capitalist mode of production, and so will arise even if commodities are sold at prices corresponding to their values. This means that the source of crises must be found in changes in value relations, that is to say in changes in the conditions of production.

Marx considers the case of a crisis which arises from a change in value, the example being a rise in the value of cotton following a fall in the harvest.[19] The reduction in the quantity of cotton produced

---

[19] This is not a particularly helpful example. On the one hand, it is debatable whether a harvest failure should be considered to lead to a rise in value, rather than of price. On the other hand, political economy was quite ready to admit that such natural calamities could precipitate a crisis.

disrupts the '*proportions* in which money has to be reconverted into the *various component parts of capital* in order to continue production on the former scale' (TSV2, 515). The increased cost and reduced quantity of cotton means that less labour can be employed, so that workers are laid off and capital lies idle. The increased cost of raw materials and the reduced scale of production leads to a fall in the rate of profit, so that the capitalist is unable to meet the fixed charges of interest and rent, and a crisis arises. Meanwhile the price of the cotton goods rises, disrupting the proportions in other branches of production, and diverting demand from other commodities, so that the crisis is generalised.

Marx recognises that exactly the same process could be set in motion not by the natural circumstances of a bad harvest, but by the '*disproportionate* conversion of additional capital into its various elements', for example if too much was invested in machinery in a particular branch of production, increasing the demand for the raw material, whose supply was sufficient for the old level of production, but insufficient for the increased scale (TSV2, 516), although in this case there is no change in the conditions of production, so that logically we are dealing with a change in price which does not correspond to a change in value.

This, and the other examples that Marx considers here, are all cases of the disruptive effects of disproportionalities in production, in which a crisis is generalised as the result of over-production in a particular branch of production. These examples show that 'partial crises can thus arise from *disproportionate production*'.[20] If overproduction occurs in a few leading branches of production the partial crisis might be generalised, so that the crisis of overproduction extends even to those producers who 'had not over-produced in their own spheres' (TSV2, 523). On this basis 'it can be understood how overproduction in these few, but leading articles, calls forth a more or less general (*relative*) over-production on the whole market'(TSV2, 523). But Marx reiterates that 'this can only be dealt with in connection with the competition of capitals' (TSV2, 521), whereas what he is still trying to establish is the conditions for *general* overproduction inherent in the concept of capital-in-general.

---

[20] 'In world market crises, all the contradictions of bourgeois production erupt collectively; in particular crises (*particular* in their content and in extent) the eruptions are only sporadical, isolated and one-sided.' (TSV2, 534).

There are two problems with the explanation of the *necessity* of crises on the basis of disproportionality. The first is to explain why over-production should arise in the leading branches of production in the first place. We can understand how a crisis in the leading branches of production can be generalised, but 'it is by no means clear how over-production of these articles can arise' (TSV2, 523). So long as the growth of production in the leading branches is maintained 'a general growth in revenue, and therefore in their own consumption, seems assured' (TSV2, 524), so they seem to be locked into a virtuous circle of growth.

The second problem is that of explaining why disproportionality should necessarily lead to a crisis. The emergence of disproportionalities is countered by the process of capitalist competition, which 'has the effect of distributing the total mass of social labour-time *among the various spheres of production* according to the social need' (TSV2, 209–10) as 'the rise or fall of market value which is caused by this disproportion, results in the withdrawal of capital from one branch of production to another' (TSV2, 521). The result is that 'competition constantly regulates this distribution, just as it equally constantly disorganises it' (TSV1, 225).

Partial or localised crises provide the normal form of equilibration through capitalist competition. 'This equalisation itself however already implies as a precondition the opposite of equalisation and may therefore comprise *crisis*; the crisis itself may be a form of equalisation. Ricardo etc. admit this form of crisis'. (TSV2, 521) It is in crises that the social character of capitalist production reasserts itself against the apparent independence of the producers. 'It is *crises* that put an end to this apparent *independence* of the various elements of which the production process continually consists and which it continually reproduces' (TSV3, 518).[21]

Towards the end of the passage Marx poses the rhetorical question 'how is it possible to achieve the necessary balance and interdependence of the various spheres of production, their dimensions and the proportions between them, except through the constant neutralisation of a constant disharmony?' (TSV2, 529). However, although Marx provides a penetrating critique of the economists' picture of com-

---

[21] 'the contradictions existing in bourgeois production ... are reconciled by a process of adjustment which, at the same time, however, manifests itself as crises, violent fusion of disconnected factors operating independently of one another and yet correlated' (TSV3, 120; c.f. *Grundrisse*, CW28, 340–1).

petition as a smooth transition to a stable equilibrium, the fact that competition can restore proportionality implies that disproportionality does not *necessarily* lead to general crises.

At the same time, Marx recognises that general overproduction is always associated with disproportionality. 'In times of general overproduction, the over-production in some spheres is always only the *result*, the *consequence*, of over-production in the leading articles of commerce; [it is] always only *relative*, i.e. over-production because over-production exists in other spheres.)' (TSV2, 529).

Universal over-production is impossible, in the absence of disproportionalities, because '*universal* over-production is proportional production'. If all the relations of proportionality held, there 'would not be over-production but only a greater than usual development of the productive forces in all spheres of production' (TSV2, 530). Marx rejects the ridiculous conclusion of the economists, that the problem is not over-production in the leading branches of production, but underproduction in the backward branches, before reaching the important conclusion that uneven development is not a contingent accidental feature of the capitalist mode of production, but is essential to it. 'Since, however, capitalist production cannot allow itself free rein only in certain spheres, under certain conditions, there could be no capitalist production at all if it had to develop *simultaneously* and *evenly* in all spheres' (TSV2, 532).

The argument that the disproportionate development of production is inherent in the tendency for capital to develop the productive forces without limit would seem at last to provide the key to the problem, since it establishes the necessity of crisis at the heart of the social form of capitalist production. However, Marx does not take the argument any further, assimilating such disproportionality back to the many contingent factors which can cause crises. 'The circulation of capital contains within itself the *possibilities* of interruptions', including barriers to the reconversion of money into the elements of production which arise, for example, when raw materials rise in price, together with 'a large number of other factors, conditions, possibilities of crises, which can only be examined when considering the concrete conditions, particularly the competition of capitals and credit' (TSV2, 533).

Marx concludes the passage by returning to the problem of general overproduction and the limits of the market, without advancing the argument any further. General overproduction implies that the growth of the market lags behind the growth of production. Marx recognises that this is no explanation, but simply describes the phenomenon of the crisis more concretely. However, having discussed the problem of over-production in some detail in terms of the interconnectedness of production and consumption, Marx then goes on to dissociate them, asserting their independence of one another. 'The admission that the market must expand if there is to be no over-production, is therefore also an admission that there can be over-production. For it is then possible — since market and production are two independent factors — that the expansion of one does *not* correspond with the expansion of the other' (TSV2, 525).

The only explanation for this failure of the market to expand sufficiently rapidly to meet the needs of production is provided at the end of the passage, where Marx reiterates the underconsumptionist implications of the fundamental contradiction of capitalist accumulation. '*Over-production* is specifically conditioned by the general law of the production of capital: to produce to the limit set by the productive forces, that is to say, to exploit the maximum amount of labour with the given amount of capital, without any consideration for the actual limits of the market or the needs backed by the ability to pay; and this is carried out through continuous expansion of reproduction and accumulation, and therefore constant reconversion of revenue into capital, while on the other hand, the mass of the producers remain tied to the average level of needs, and must remain tied to it according to the nature of capitalist production' (TSV2, 534–5). But Marx has already established that if capitalism depended on the consumption needs of the working class, it would be not merely crisis-prone but its very existence would be impossible. The problem remains, therefore, of connecting the fundamental contradictions of capital with the concrete manifestations of those contradictions in the form of crises.

The insistence that there is a necessary tendency to crisis inherent in the capitalist mode of production is not simply a dogmatic requirement of Marx's own theory, but is a problem presented by the historical course of capitalist accumulation itself. Commercial and financial crises have occurred since the first appearance of commerce and commodity production, but with the generalisation of the capitalist mode of production crises have become a regularly recurring feature of capitalist accumulation. The economists can come up with contingent explanations for each individual crisis, but they cannot explain why capitalist accumulation has a cyclical character in which capital accumulation can only be sustained through the destruction of means of production, the redundancy of labour, and the devaluation of capital in periodic crises. The attempt to establish the necessity of crisis is not a matter of stubborn dogmatism, but of the need to explain an obvious fact.

The condition for general overproduction is that money acquired through the sale of commodities should be withdrawn from circulation, leaving a corresponding amount of commodity capital unsold. The only reason for the capitalist withdrawing money from circulation is the absence of opportunities to re-invest that money profitably. We can therefore re-formulate the problem of crisis as the problem of explaining the fall in the rate of profit that precipitates the crisis. The question therefore arises of whether the 'law of the tendency for the rate of profit to fall' provides an alternative foundation for a theory of crisis. We have already seen that in the *Grundrisse* Marx linked the tendency for the rate of profit to fall to the recurrence of crisis and the ultimate demise of the capitalist system, but he did not integrate the law of the tendency for the rate of profit to fall into the theory of crisis.

The great attraction of the law of the tendency for the rate of profit to fall is that it can be derived at the most abstract level of the analysis. 'Here, therefore, we once again stand on firm ground, where, without entering into the competition of the many capitals, we can derive the general law directly from the general nature of capital as so far developed. This law, and it is the most important law of political economy, is that the *rate of profit has a tendency to fall with the progress of capitalist production*' (CW33, 104).

7
The Falling Rate of Profit and the Tendency to Crisis

Marx's discussion of the falling rate of profit is to be found in various parts of the manuscript written during 1862, some of which was included in the second and third volumes of TSV, but the most systematic treatment is to be found in the previously unpublished part of the 1861–3 manuscript, which was the basis of the draft of 1864–5 that Engels incorporated into Volume Three of *Capital*. The recent publication of this intervening manuscript does not solve all the problems of interpretation, but it makes it easier to follow the development of Marx's thought.

Marx considered the law of the tendency for the rate of profit to fall as only one aspect of the secular tendencies of capitalist accumulation, as one expression of the more fundamental contradictions underlying the capitalist mode of production. To consider the law in isolation, or in relation to the tendency to crisis, as the vast majority of commentaries do, is to look at it out of this wider theoretical context, and so to distort Marx's discussion in which the law is part of a much broader and more complex analysis of the secular tendencies of capitalist accumulation to a rising rate of exploitation, on the one hand, and a rising organic composition of capital, on the other.

Much of Marx's discussion of the falling rate of profit represents an attempt to work out the relationship between these different tendencies as Marx considers the factors that might ameliorate or counteract the rise in the organic composition of capital. The complexity of the interactions involved means that Marx frequently gets lost in this attempt, and short-circuits the discussion to reach unwarranted conclusions. The issues could have been addressed much more simply and rigorously through an algebraic formulation, but the disadvantage of such a formulation for Marx is that it provides a purely formal representation of substantive processes, and so does not distinguish the formally possible from the substantively probable. The relationships are not purely mechanical, since capitalists do not simply accept the consequences of an increase in the organic composition of capital for the rate of profit, but make every effort to counteract its negative impact by increasing the rate of exploitation, accelerating the turnover of capital, etc.[1]

In this chapter I will try to set Marx's discussion of the law of the tendency for the rate of profit to fall in its context within his work as a whole, and on that basis draw out its implications for the theory of crisis. In the first section I will set the discussion in the context of Marx's critique of political economy, of which it was an important part. I will then discuss the 'technical' question of whether Marx believed that there was an inevitable tendency for the rate of profit to fall, before proceeding to a discussion of the relationship between the secular tendencies of capitalist accumulation and the rate of profit, concluding with a discussion of the relationship between the tendency for the rate of profit to fall and the tendency to crisis. The discussion is necessarily somewhat inconclusive, because Marx's own notes are inconclusive, often following up themes and raising questions which were never subsequently developed in Marx's own work.

The critique of political economy and the falling rate of profit

Marx did not invent the law of the tendency of the rate of profit to fall, which was one of the fundamental laws of political economy. What Marx did was to provide a new explanation for what was generally regarded as an unquestionable empirical fact which demanded scientific explanation. Adam Smith had explained the fall in the rate of profit as the result of increasing competition between capitalists for scarce investment outlets. David Ricardo had denied that competition could reduce the rate of profit, explaining the fall in the rate of profit as a result of the rise in wages which followed from the diminishing fertility of the soil with the growing population. Marx criticised both Smith's and Ricardo's explanations, accounting for the tendency as

---
[1] Marx devoted a large part of his time in 1875 to 'mathematical investigations', as a result of which he reformulated the relationship between the rate of surplus value and the rate of profit mathematically. Engels used these notes in preparing Chapter Three of Volume III of *Capital*, but he did not use them in relation to the law of the tendency of the rate of profit to fall.

the outcome of the interaction of the countervailing tendencies for the organic composition of capital and the rate of exploitation to rise.

Marx had initially used the concept of the rising organic composition of capital in order to assert the tendency to the displacement of labour in the course of capital accumulation, counterposing his concept of 'relative surplus population' to Malthus's law of population in order to show that unemployment was the specific result of capitalist accumulation. He had used the idea of a tendency to an increasing rate of exploitation as the basis of his most abstract and apparently 'underconsumptionist' formulation of the problem of crises, as the growing mass of surplus value is embodied in a growing mass of commodities which have to be sold by capitalists to one another as the basis for renewed capital accumulation. In the *Grundrisse* he then combined the two concepts to demonstrate, against Ricardo, that a falling rate of profit was quite consistent with a rising rate of exploitation. Although he did not there connect the tendency of the rate of profit to fall directly to the theory of crisis, he did conclude his discussion with an apocalyptic vision of the collapse of capitalism, as the fall of the rate of profit withdrew the stimulus to accumulation.

Marx returned to the issue of the falling tendency of the rate of profit in his 1861–3 manuscripts, where it first arises in the course of Marx's detailed consideration of the theory of rent. The main purpose of this section is to show the error of Ricardo's theory of rent, on which Ricardo based his explanation of the tendency for the rate of profit to fall. Here, as elsewhere, Marx takes it for granted that there is a tendency for the rate of profit to fall.[2] The problem is to explain this tendency (TSV2, 438). Marx presents his explanation in opposition to those of Adam Smith and David Ricardo.

Adam Smith had argued that the fall in the rate of profit was the result of a secular tendency to the overproduction of capital in relation to the limited opportunities for investment, so that increased competition between the capitalists reduced prices, and so reduced the rate of profit. Marx argues that Ricardo was correct to deny that the tendency for the rate of profit to fall could be the result of growing

---

[2] This despite the fact that Marx notes that during the period 1797–1813 both agricultural prices and the rate of profit rose, which he regards as a disproof of Ricardo's theory. Marx explains this rise in the rate of profit by the increase in the rate of exploitation, associated with the lengthening of the working day and the fall in prices of manufactured goods entering workers' consumption, and by the inflationary redistribution of revenue from rent to profit (TSV2, 460).

competition between capitals: 'Competition can level out profits in the different spheres of production ... but it cannot lower the general rate of profit' (TSV2, 438).[3]

Marx had criticised Smith's argument in similar terms in the *Grundrisse*. 'Competition can permanently depress ... the average rate of profit only if, and only to the extent that, a general and permanent fall in the rate of profit operating as a law is conceivable also *prior to and regardless of competition*' (CW29, 136). Marx had also rejected Wakefield's approach, which derives from that of Smith in showing 'a preoccupation with *the difficulty for capital to realise a growing volume of profit, which amounts to a denial of the immanent tendency of the rate of profit to fall*. And the necessity for capital to seek a constantly expanding field of employment is itself a consequence.' (CW29, 138) Finally, he had dismissed the attempt of Bastiat and Carey to explain the fall in the rate of profit as the result of rising wages (although this does not, of course, imply that a rise in wages will not reduce the rate of profit).

Ricardo's own account of the tendency for the rate of profit to fall was in error. Because he did not distinguish between profit and surplus value, Ricardo believed that the fall in the rate of profit could only be the result of a fall in the rate of surplus value, which is explained by the increase in the value of labour power that results from the decline in the productivity of agriculture. However Marx argues that the rate of profit tends to fall even when the rate of surplus value rises.

Against Ricardo, Marx asserts that the rate of profit can fall, 'although the rate of surplus value remains the same or rises, because the proportion of variable capital to constant capital decreases with the development of the productive power of labour. The rate of profit thus falls, not because labour becomes less productive, but because it becomes more productive. Not because the worker is less exploited, but because he is more exploited. ... for capitalist production is inseparable from falling value of labour' (TSV2, 439; c.f. TSV2, 90; TSV3, 302).[4]

---

[3] Later in the manuscript Marx notes that competition can reduce the rate of industrial profit in all branches of production by lowering prices, so that rent and interest gain at the expense of industrial profit, but he argues that this can only be a temporary effect, and one which concerns only the distribution of surplus value, and so its consideration is not appropriate at this level of abstraction (CW33, 92).

[4] The rising organic composition 'is only another *expression for the increased productivity of labour*' (TSV2, 596). 'The growth of the productive power of labour is synonymous with (a) the growth of relative surplus value or the relative surplus labour time which the worker

In these discussions Marx very clearly distinguishes the secular decline of the rate of profit that is in question here from the cyclical fall in the rate of profit in a crisis. While Ricardo was right to criticise Smith's belief that the falling rate of profit was a result of increasing competition, he was quite wrong in linking this argument to the denial of the possibility of a fall in the rate of profit as the result of a crisis of overproduction, which Marx here links to the inadequacy of demand from both workers and capitalists. Ricardo sought 'to refute Adam Smith by arguing that *overproduction* in one country is impossible. ... He overlooks that the output level is by no means arbitrarily chosen, but the more capitalist production develops the more it is forced to produce on a scale which has nothing to do with the immediate demand but depends on a constant expansion of the world market. He has recourse to Say's trite assumption that the capitalist produces not for the sake of profit, surplus value, but produces use value directly for consumption — his own consumption. He overlooks the fact that the commodity has to be converted into money. The demand of the workers does not suffice ... The demand of the capitalists among themselves is equally insufficient.' (TSV2, 468)

The fall in the rate of profit that results from a general crisis of overproduction is not a permanent condition, which could explain a secular decline in the rate of profit, but on the other hand the secular decline in the rate of profit cannot explain the transitory crises that disrupt accumulation. 'When Adam Smith explains the fall in the rate of profit from an over-abundance of capital, an accumulation of capital, he is speaking of a *permanent* effect and this is wrong. As against this, the transitory over-abundance of capital, over-production and crises are something different. Permanent crises do not exist' (TSV2, 497n.).

'Over-production does not call forth a *constant* fall in profit, but *periodic* over-production recurs constantly. It is followed by periods of under-production etc. Over-production arises precisely from the fact that the mass of the people can never consume more than the average quantity of necessaries, that their consumption therefore does not grow correspondingly with the productivity of labour.' Thus we find Marx

---

gives to capital; (b) the diminution of the labour time necessary for the reproduction of the labour capacity; (c) the decrease of the part of capital exchanged in general for living labour relative to those parts of it which participate in the production process as objectified labour and preposited value.' (CW29, 147)

proposing a combination of the theory of the falling rate of profit as a theory of the secular tendency of capitalist accumulation with what appears to be an unambiguously underconsumptionist theory of crisis, but he does not pursue the analysis here, for the usual reason: 'the whole of this section belongs with the *competition of capitals*' (TSV2, 468).

Is there a tendency for the rate of profit to fall?

There have been three principal criticisms of Marx's law of the tendency of the rate of profit to fall. First, the increase in productivity that leads to a growth in the mass of constant capital mobilised by the labourer also leads to a decline in its value, which will counteract and may even neutralise the former tendency so that we cannot assume that the composition of capital in value terms will necessarily rise. Second, Marx largely ignores the fact that the rise in the rate of exploitation may perfectly well be sufficient to counteract any increase in the composition of capital, so that the rate of profit might well rise. Third, Marx ignores the fact that the capitalist will only introduce a new method of production if it provides an increased rate of profit, so that faced with the prospect of such a fall capitalists will continue to use the old method of production and earn the old rate of profit, at least until such time as a shortage of labour leads to a fall in the rate of profit as a result of rising wages, at which point labour-saving methods might become profitable.

These criticisms undoubtedly undermine any attempt to propose the law as a mechanical law of capitalist development or of capitalist crisis, and certainly indicate points of confusion in Marx's own discussion. However, Marx was not trying to develop such a mechanical law, but to locate the tendency for the rate of profit to fall within the wider context of the tendencies of capitalist development. It was this, rather than his neglect of the issues or his algebraic ineptitude, that was the source of the confusion in Marx's discussion.[5]

It is important to stress that Marx, like his contemporaries, took it for granted that there was a tendency for the rate of profit to fall,

---

[5] The bulk of the discussion of the law in the manuscripts of the 1860s concerns this problem of the relationship between the rate and mass of surplus value, the organic composition of capital, and the rate of profit. The discussion makes extensive use of arithmetical examples, which often do not bear the weight that Marx tries to place on them.

and that the task of political economy was to explain this tendency. Indeed Marx regarded the analytical problem not as that of explaining why the rate of profit falls, but of explaining why it does not fall as rapidly as one might expect, given the enormous growth in the productivity of labour. The difficulty is 'to explain why this fall is not greater and more rapid. There must be some counteracting influences at work, which cross and annul the effect of the general law, and which give it merely the characteristic of a tendency' (CIII, 227; c.f. CW33, 111; TSV3, 365), as capitalists try, by all the means at their disposal, to find ways of sustaining their profitability. The result is that 'the same influences which produce a tendency in the general rate of profit to fall, also call forth counter-effects, which hamper, retard and partly paralyse this fall. The latter do not do away with the law, but impair its effect. Otherwise, it would not be the fall of the general rate of profit, but rather its relative slowness, that would be incomprehensible. Thus, the law acts only as a tendency. And it is only under certain circumstances and only after long periods that its effects become strikingly pronounced' (CIII, 233). Marx was clearly aware that the devaluation of constant capital would ameliorate the rise in the composition of capital, that the rate of exploitation would rise, and that the tendency for the rate of profit to fall is not unequivocal, but he nevertheless assumed that an increasing composition of capital would outweigh any influence of an increasing rate of exploitation, and so took it for granted that the secular tendency was for the rate of profit to fall.

The tendency for the composition of capital to rise

For Marx the tendency for the 'technical' composition of capital to rise was a direct result of the increasing productivity of labour in two respects. First, with increasing productivity each worker processes an increased volume of raw material. Second, for Marx the increase in productivity was associated with a growth in the scale of production associated with the application of ever more massive machines which provided growing economies of scale.

The increasing productivity of labour also has an effect on the value relationships between the component parts of capital. On the one hand, as the workers' means of subsistence become cheaper, the value of labour power falls, and so the variable capital falls as a proportion of the capital as a whole, reinforcing the technical determinants of an

… *Is there a tendency for the rate of profit to fall?* 215

increasing composition of capital. On the other hand, the 'elements of constant capital' also become progressively cheaper as productivity rises, providing a counteracting force, with the net effect depending on the relative rates of growth of productivity in the production of means of subsistence and means of production.[6]

Marx was always well aware that the increasing productivity of labour will reduce the value of raw materials and machinery (CW28, 309). This cheapening of the elements of constant capital, which Marx considers as one of the counteracting influences in volume III of *Capital*,[7] reduces the tendency for the organic composition of capital to rise, and this is one reason why the decline in the rate of profit 'is far smaller than it is said to be' (TSV3, 365). Nevertheless, Marx assumes that this is not sufficient to reverse the tendency for the organic composition of capital to rise. Marx asserts that 'it is an incontrovertible fact that, as capitalist production develops, the portion of capital invested in machinery and raw materials grows, and the portion laid out in wages declines' (TSV3, 364).

Marx makes the point even more strongly a few pages later: 'It is therefore self-evident or a tautological proposition that the increasing productivity of labour caused by machinery corresponds to increased value of the machinery relative to the amount of labour employed' (TSV3, 366–7). But earlier in the 1862 manuscript Marx had already qualified this 'tautological proposition'. Marx notes that, apart from Ricardo's rise in the value of labour power, 'the rate of profit cannot *fall* unless ... there is a rise in the *value of constant capital in relation to variable.*' Far from being tautologically true, Marx notes that 'the latter would appear to be restricted to cases where the productive power of labour does not rise *equally* and *simultaneously* in all the branches of production which contribute to produce the commodity' (CW33, 33-34), the point being that if 'productivity grows simultaneously and *in the same measure* in those branches of industry which produce constant capital and those which use it up' (CW33, 33), then the organic composition of capital will not change.[8] On the following

---

[6] Marx also considers further complications raised by changes in the turnover time of capital — a reduction in the stock of means of production, for example arising from improvements in transport, will reduce the composition of capital.

[7] Marx considers the cheapening of the elements of constant capital and the depreciation of existing capital as counteracting influences in which 'the same influences which tend to make the rate of profit fall, also moderate the effects of this tendency', in the sense that both increase the physical quantity of capital while reducing its value (CIII, 231, c.f. 233).

[8] Marx's example oversimplifies the issue, but the general point is clearly recognised. Marx

page Marx notes that the rate of profit 'rises, falls or remains the same' (CW33, 35), although this is not related to his discussion of the law of the tendency for the rate of profit to fall.

The rate of exploitation and the rate of profit

Just as Marx was well aware that changes in value relations moderated the tendency for the composition of capital to rise, so he was equally well aware that an increase in the rate of exploitation tended to moderate the tendency for the rate of profit to fall. Indeed the whole point of Marx's original discussion of the law was to show, against Ricardo, that a fall in the rate of profit was quite compatible with an increase in the rate of exploitation, and so with an increase in the mass of profit.

The point is obvious, but it merits some attention since many commentators have argued that Marx neglected it. This is because in the version published in Volume Three of *Capital* Marx derives the law on the initial assumption that 'the rate of surplus value, or the intensity of exploitation of labour by capital, remain the same' (CIII, 208). This assumption has been the basis of the most widespread criticism of Marx's formulation of the law.

The assumption was clearly introduced by Marx as a methodological device, since he was well aware that it would not hold in reality, but in the discussion published in *Capital* Marx did not systematically explore the consequences of relaxing the assumption, although he was by no means consistent in maintaining it (CIII, 209, 210, 221-2, 234, 242, 243).[9]

Marx also failed to consider an increase in relative surplus value among the 'counteracting influences' to the tendency for the rate of profit to fall in Volume Three of *Capital*, except when this arises from 'mere improvement in methods ... without altering the magnitude of the invested capital' (CIII, 228). The most important counteracting tendencies which Marx considers are those mobilised by the capitalist in the desperate attempt to stave off a fall in the rate of profit — the lengthening of the working day, the employment of the labour of women and children, and the intensification and super-exploitation of

---

repeats the point, but only as an exceptional case, in volume III of *Capital*, when he notes that the organic composition will rise 'outside of a few cases (for example, if the productiveness of labour uniformly cheapens all elements of the constant, and the variable, capital)'.

[9] Marx also notes that 'the factors that check the fall of the rate of profit ... always hasten its fall in the last analysis' (CIII, 228), because by raising the rate of profit they accelerate the pace of accumulation, so that in the long run a fall in the rate of profit is inevitable.

Is there a tendency for the rate of profit to fall?

labour, all of which increase the production of surplus value not by increasing the productivity of labour, but by reducing the paid portion of the working day at the expense of the living and working conditions of the labourer. In addition, Marx notes that a growing relative surplus population means that there is a growing abundance of cheap labour, which can be employed in branches of production which cannot so easily be mechanised, and in which the organic composition of capital is correspondingly relatively low.[10]

We have to remember that volume III of *Capital* was compiled from Marx's notes of the third draft of this discussion made in 1864–5, in which Marx would have taken points elucidated in earlier drafts for granted. An increase in the rate of exploitation associated with an increase in relative surplus value is not a 'counteracting influence', but an inseparable part of the tendency. Marx shows that he is aware of the importance of this factor when, at the very end of the chapter on the 'counteracting influences', he refers to the increase in the rate of exploitation which inevitably accompanies an increase in the organic composition of capital as a point to be recalled, 'to avoid misunderstandings', stressing against Ricardo that 'the tendency for the rate of profit to fall is bound up with a tendency for the rate of labour exploitation to rise. Nothing is more absurd, for this reason, than to explain the fall in the rate of profit by the rise in the rate of wages, although this may be the case by way of an exception ... The rate of profit does not fall because labour becomes less productive. Both the rise in the rate of surplus value and the fall in the rate of profit are but specific forms through which growing productivity of labour is expressed under capitalism' (CIII, 234).

This comment is by no means an afterthought, but a reference back to earlier notes. In the *Grundrisse* Marx described these two effects of the increasing productivity of labour as 'synonymous' (CW29, 147). Similarly in the 1862 manuscript we find that Marx is quite clear that the two factors, the rate of surplus value and the organic composition of capital, tend to move in opposite directions, with contrary influences on the rate of profit.

---

[10] Foreign trade can also have an impact on the rate of profit by reducing the value of the elements of constant and variable capital, and because of the higher rates of profit earned in colonial trade, as a result of the competitive advantage of the more advanced producer, and because of the super-exploitation of colonial workers. On the other hand, some of the branches of production with the highest organic composition of capital, such as railways, operate as 'stock capital', paying only the average rate of interest, so allowing capital in other branches of production to earn higher rates of profit.

The general rate of profit can only fall: 1) if the absolute magnitude of surplus value falls. The latter has, inversely, a tendency to rise in the course of capitalist production, for its growth is identical with the development of the productive power of labour, which is developed by capitalist production; 2) because the ratio of variable capital to constant capital falls. ...But the law of development of capitalist production ...consists precisely in the continuous decline of variable capital ...in *relation* to the constant component of capital. (CW33, 106)

The development of productive power has a double manifestation: in the increase of surplus labour, i.e. the curtailment of the necessary labour time; and in the reduction of the component of capital which is exchanged with living labour relative to the total amount of capital. ...Both movements not only go [hand in hand] but condition each other. They are only different forms and phenomena in which the same law is expressed. But they work in opposite directions in so far as the rate of profit comes into consideration. (CW33, 109)

Marx does not conclude that the rise or fall of the rate of profit will depend on the relationship between the change in the rate of surplus value and the change in the composition of capital because he has set himself the task of explaining a fall in the rate of profit that he, along with all his contemporaries, regarded as an established fact. The task, therefore, is to explain why the increase in the rate of surplus value is not sufficient to counteract the increase in the composition of capital.

Part of the explanation is that there are various factors tending to limit the increase in the rate of exploitation. 'If one considers the development of productive power and the relatively not so pronounced fall in the rate of profit, the exploitation of labour must have increased very much, and what is remarkable is not the fall in the rate of profit but that it has not fallen to a greater degree. This can be explained partly by circumstances to be considered in dealing with competition between capitals, partly by the general circumstance that so far the immense increase of productive power in some branches has been paralysed or restricted by its much slower development in other branches' (CW33, 111).[11]

---

[11] The reference to competition here is a reference to the destructive impact of crises, not to Smith's idea, dismissed by Marx, that competition can reduce the general rate of profit.

The result of the uneven development of capitalism is that 'the value of labour-power does not fall in the same degree as the productivity of labour or of capital increases'. This is not because of the diminishing fertility of the soil, as Ricardo claimed, but because 'it is in the nature of capitalist production that it develops industry more rapidly than agriculture', primarily because capitalist social relations of production are developed more slowly in agriculture (TSV3, 300–1). This uneven development of production is 'one of the main reasons why the rate of surplus value ... does not grow in the same proportion as the variable capital declines in its proportion to the total capital' (CW33, 131). Marx also notes that in other branches the product does not enter into the workers' means of subsistence, so that the increase in productivity has no impact on the value of labour power. More generally it is the case 'that the development of the productive power of labour reduces the value of labour, the necessary labour, only in certain capital investment spheres, and that, even in these spheres, it does not develop uniformly'.

The increase in the rate of exploitation is also limited by the ability of the workers to achieve increases in real wages, thereby checking the fall in the value of labour power, 'for example, the workers themselves, although they cannot prevent reductions in (real) wages, will not permit them to be reduced to the absolute minimum; on the contrary, they achieve a certain quantitative participation in the general growth of wealth' (TSV3, 312).[12]

For these various reasons Marx concludes that any increase in the rate of exploitation will be insufficient to outweigh the impact of a rising composition of capital on the rate of profit, simply noting that 'the rate of surplus value does not rise in the same proportion as the variable capital falls in comparison with the total amount of capital. Hence a diminution in the relative magnitude of the surplus value. Hence *a decline in the rate of profit. A constant tendency towards a decline in the same*' (CW33, 148).

---

[12] Marx distinguishes this effect, which concerns the value of labour power, from the temporary rise and fall of wages as a result of changes in the balance of supply and demand. The latter 'has as little to do with the general law of the rise or fall in the profit rate as the rise or fall in the market prices of commodities has to do with the determination of value in general. This has to be analysed in the chapter on the real movement of wages' (TSV3, 312). In Volume I of *Capital* Marx links the rise in wages to the intensification of labour (CI, 635), so that workers pay the price of their 'participation in the general growth of wealth'.

The Falling Rate of Profit and Relative Surplus Population

Marx's formulation of the law of the tendency of the rate of profit to fall, which he never prepared for publication, is unsatisfactory. He was clearly aware of the complex range of factors which had to be taken into account, recognising those factors which counter-act such a tendency, but like all his contemporaries he regarded the law as an 'incontrovertible fact' that needed to be explained. However, more important than the question of the degree of rigour with which Marx established the law, which was certainly a great advance on any of his contemporaries, is the question of the significance that Marx attached to the law. It will be remembered that in the *Grundrisse* the significance of the law was summed up in an apocalyptic vision of the end of capitalism.

The fall in the rate of profit is only one of the consequences derived from the interaction of a rising organic composition of capital and an increasing rate of exploitation which are the inseparable consequences of the increasing productivity of labour. In all his discussions Marx is concerned to assess the relationship between conflicting tendencies, not to derive mechanical laws. For example, the increasing rate of exploitation means that the mass of surplus value increases, and consequently, as Marx had argued in the *Grundrisse*, the problem of realisation becomes more acute, while a fall in the rate of profit reduces the stimulus to accumulation. Malthus and Sismondi had stressed the former limit to capitalist accumulation, Smith and Ricardo the latter. In his critique of political economy Marx is concerned to relate the two together, to show that there is a tendency at the same time for the mass of profit to increase and the rate of profit to fall, increasing both the risk and severity of crisis.

The discussion of the falling tendency of the rate of profit is only part of a broader discussion of the historical tendencies of capitalist accumulation running through Marx's work, in which the tendency to crisis occupies no more than a few pages. The issue to which Marx devotes much the largest part of his attention is that which follows most directly from the rising organic composition of capital, the fact that a given mass of capital will employ proportionately fewer workers. The issue is made more complicated, however, by the need to consider not only the immediate impact of technical change on employment, but also the consequent changes associated with both the rise in the mass of surplus value and the fall in the rate of profit, which were noted but not analysed by Ricardo. In both the 1862 and the 1864–5 manuscripts Marx discusses the impact of accumulation on employment at great length, but in terms that confuse this issue with that of the impact of the composition of capital on the rate of profit.

In both of these texts Marx argues that the rise in the rate of surplus value is counteracted by a fall in the (relative) number of workers employed, so that the mass of surplus value does not rise as rapidly as its rate. This discussion links up with Marx's later development of the 'absolute general law' of capitalist accumulation in raising the issue of the creation of unemployment as a result of capital accumulation. However in relation to the tendency for the rate of profit to fall the discussion is very confused, primarily because Marx does not seem to notice in these discussions that the tendency to employ relatively fewer workers (with a given value of labour power) is only another way of expressing the tendency for the composition of capital to rise, with a given rate of exploitation.[13]

Marx notes that although the rate of exploitation increases, the rise in the composition of capital means that the number of workers employed by a given mass of capital will fall, so that the mass of surplus value appropriated will fall relative to the capital employed. 'It is already strikingly apparent ... that it is ... the tendency towards a fall in profit — or a *relative* decline in the amount of surplus value hand in hand with the growth in the rate of surplus value — which must predominate, as is also confirmed by experience.' (CW33 110) Marx goes through this argument by working through a number of arithmetical examples, including one in which the number of workers increases (CW33, 113), but he starts going around in circles trying to sort it out, noting that the number of workers will be reduced, '*relatively* anyway' (CW33, 123), before concluding that 'a *fall* in the amount of surplus value ... must necessarily come about with the development of machinery [...] it is [shown] here that capitalist production enters into contradiction with the development of the productive forces and is by no means their absolute [...] and final form' (CW33, 125).

Marx discusses the same point in the 1864–5 manuscript, but whereas in the earlier manuscript Marx tended to assume that the number of labourers employed would fall, either relatively or absolutely, so that the mass of surplus value might also fall, in the later

---

[13] Marx had clarified his argument by the time that he wrote Volume One of *Capital*, where the issue of relative surplus population is discussed clearly and concisely.

discussion Marx stresses that the fall in the rate of profit is necessarily associated with a rise in the mass of surplus value, and of the absolute number of workers employed.[14] He notes that the number of labourers employed, and so the mass of surplus value produced, '*can* ... increase ... in spite of the progressive drop in the rate of profit. And this not only *can* be so. Aside from temporary fluctuations it *must* be so, on the basis of capitalist production' (CIII, 213), because the process of capitalist production is simultaneously a process of accumulation.[15] 'Hence, the same laws produce for the social capital a growing absolute mass of profit, and a falling rate of profit' (CIII, 214), a conclusion which Marx elaborates at some length as he lays great stress on the 'seeming contradiction' (CIII, 217) between the fall in the rate of profit and the rise in its mass.[16]

Marx stresses that however much the mass of surplus value might grow, the mass of capital will grow faster, so that the rate of profit will still tend to fall, although repetition does not strengthen the argument. Marx simply assumes that the mass of surplus value will rise more slowly than the size of the aggregate capital because of the *relative* fall in the number of labourers employed, noting that 'since the aggregate mass of living labour operating the means of production decreases in relation to the value of these means of production, it follows that the unpaid labour and the portion of value in which it is expressed must decline as compared to the value of the advanced capital' (CIII, 211). He refers to this tendency simultaneously to maximise the amount of surplus value produced, while minimising the amount of labour

---

[14] In the *Grundrisse* Marx had already stressed that an example in which the number of workers actually fell was 'improbable and cannot count as a general example in political economy' because an increase in the composition of capital presupposes 'a [growing] division of labour in the whole [of society], therefore an increase in the number of workers at least in absolute terms, even though not relatively to the volume of capital employed' (CW28, 307).

[15] 'it is but a requirement of the capitalist mode of production that the number of wage-workers should increase absolutely, in spite of its relative decrease' (CIII, 258).

[16] Although Marx does note that 'a development of productive power which reduced the absolute number of workers ... would bring about revolution, because it would demonetise the majority of the population. Here there appears once again the limit of bourgeois production, and the fact becomes obvious that it is not the absolute form for the development of productive power, that it rather enters into collision with the latter at a certain point. In part this collision appears constantly, with the crises, etc., which occur when now one now another component of the working class becomes superfluous in its old mode of employment. Its limit is the surplus time of the workers; it is *not concerned* with the absolute surplus time gained by society. *The development of productive power* is therefore only important in so far as it increases the surplus labour time of the workers, not in so far as it reduces labour time for material production in general. It is therefore embedded in a contradiction.' (CW33, 142. This passage was incorporated into Capital III as a supplementary note, CIII, 258.)

The Falling Rate of Profit and Relative Surplus Population

employed by a given capital as 'the real secret of the tendency for the rate of profit to fall' (CIII, 228). It is 'the same development of the productiveness of social labour' that leads to a fall in the rate of profit and at the same time 'aside from temporary fluctuations' to an increase in the total employed labour-power and the absolute mass of profit. Thus it is a 'double-edged law of a decrease in the *rate* of profit and a simultaneous increase in the absolute *mass* of profit arising from the same causes' (CIII, 215).

Against the Malthusian argument that unemployment arises because of the falling productivity of (agricultural) labour, so that a growing population cannot be supported, Marx argues that unemployment is the result of the growing productivity of labour, so that 'the possibility of a relative surplus of labouring people develops proportionately to the advances made by capitalist production not because the productiveness of social labour *decreases*, but because it *increases*' (CIII, 218). Marx keeps on stressing this implication, that 'the same development of the social productiveness of labour expresses itself with the progress of capitalist production on the one hand in a tendency of the rate of profit to fall progressively and, on the other, in a progressive growth of the absolute mass of the appropriated surplus value, or profit; so that on the whole a relative decrease of variable capital and profit is accompanied by an absolute increase of both. This two-fold effect, as we have seen, can express itself only in a growth of the total capital at a pace more rapid than that at which the rate of profit falls' (CIII, 218). Therefore 'on a capitalist foundation, the increasing productiveness of labour necessarily and permanently creates a seeming over-population of labouring people' (CIII 219.)

This discussion of the impact of accumulation on the number of labourers employed and the rate of surplus value is an extremely cumbersome and confusing way of analysing the law of the tendency for the rate of profit to fall, not least for Marx himself. However the reason for discussing the issues in this way is that Marx is not particularly concerned to develop such a law for its own sake. The fundamental issue is the historical tendencies of capitalist accumulation, of which the tendency for the rate of profit to fall is only one aspect to be considered within a wider framework. Although the starting point of Marx's discussion is his critique of the classical law of the tendency for the rate of profit to fall, it is quite misleading to confine his discussion within that framework. As we will see, the culmination of Marx's discussion of the historical tendencies of capitalist accumulation is not a mechanical economic law, but the 'absolute general law of capitalist accumulation' which is presented in Volume One of *Capital*. One side of this law is the formation of a 'relative surplus population'. The other is the concentration and centralisation of capital, which is similarly connected to the tendency for the rate of profit to fall.

The Concentration of Capital, the Rate of Profit and Crisis

In the 1862 manuscript the primary significance of the law of the tendency of the rate of profit to fall is identified as the concentration of capital in the hands of a diminishing number of people to which it leads as a result of the increasing scale of production and the intensification of competition that it provokes. This links back to Marx's characterisation of the tendency of capitalist development to polarise class relations which lay at the heart of the *Communist Manifesto*. Marx notes that the fall in the rate of profit 'implies, at the same time, the concentration of capital in large amounts at a small number of places' (CW33, 108), and concludes that

> Capital shows itself more and more as a *social power*, ... but an *alienated social power which has become independent*, and confronts society as a thing — and through this thing as a power of the individual capitalist. On the other hand, constantly increasing masses [of people] are thereby deprived of the conditions of production and find them set over against them. The contradiction between the *general social power* which capital is formed into, and the *private power of the individual capitalist* over these social conditions of production becomes ever more glaring, and implies the dissolution of this relation, since it implies at the same time the development of the material conditions of production into general, therefore communal social conditions of production. (CW33, 144)

> Apart from the terror which the law of the declining rate of profit inspires in the economists, its most important corollary is the presupposition of a constantly increasing concentration of capitals, that is, a constantly increasing decapitalisation of the smaller capitalists. This, on the whole, is the result of all laws of capitalist production. (TSV3, 447)

Similarly in the 1864–5 manuscript incorporated into Volume III of *Capital* Marx argues that the accumulation of capital hastens the fall

The Concentration of Capital, the Rate of Profit and Crisis

in the rate of profit by raising the scale of production, while the fall in the rate of profit hastens the concentration and centralisation of capital with the expropriation of smaller capitalists and petty producers, so hastening the polarisation of society. 'The causes which concentrate masses of labourers under the command of individual capitalists, are the very same that swell the mass of the invested fixed capital, and auxiliary and raw materials, in mounting proportion as compared to the mass of employed living labour' (CIII, 215). Marx repeats the argument at the end of the chapter, noting that the concentration and centralisation of capital 'would soon bring about the collapse of capitalist production if it were not for counteracting tendencies, which have a continuous decentralizing effect alongside the centripetal one' (CIII, 241).

In the 1862 manuscript Marx notes that the law of the falling tendency of the rate of profit 'has caused a great deal of anxiety to bourgeois political economy.' (CW33, 105) because it threatens the 'day of judgement', although 'others have brought forward grounds of consolation'. However, Marx does not at any point in this manuscript argue that a fall in the rate of profit is the direct cause of the crisis. The argument is simply that capitalism is, for a number of reasons, more vulnerable to crisis when the rate of profit is relatively low. The connection between a fall in the rate of profit and crisis is closely linked to the tendency to the concentration and centralisation of capital, and it is the latter that is more directly linked to the tendency to crisis.

For Marx an increase in productivity is inevitably linked to an increase in the scale of production, which means that larger capitals are needed. Larger capitals also have advantages in securing access to credit and other resources, and larger capitals accumulate more rapidly because less surplus value has to be deducted for the capitalist's consumption. The smaller capitals then find themselves unable to compete, and enter into speculative adventures whose collapse provokes the crisis. Marx links this tendency to the tendency for the rate of profit to fall, but the argument does not require a fall in the general rate of profit, merely that there are backward capitalists unable to compete. 'Once it has reached a certain level, this rising concentration in turn brings about a new fall in the rate of profit. The mass of the lesser, fragmented capitals are therefore ready to take risks. *Hinc* crisis. The so-called plethora of capital refers only to the plethora of capital for which the fall in the rate of profit is not counterbalanced by its size. (See Fullarton)' (CW33, 112).

These crises, provoked by speculation, are then the means by which the rate of profit is restored. 'But apart from theory there is also the practice, the crises from superabundance of capital or, what comes to the same, the mad adventures capital enters upon in consequence of the lowering of [the] rate of profit. Hence crises — see Fullarton — acknowledged as a necessary violent means for the cure of the plethora of capital, and the restoration of a sound rate of profit' (CW33, 105).[17]

The fall in the rate of profit and the concentration of capital are also linked together with the tendency to crisis in the 1864–5 manuscript. 'The rate of self-expansion of the total capital, or the rate of profit, being the goad of capitalist production ... its fall checks the formation of new independent capitals and thus appears as a threat to the development of the capitalist production process. It breeds over-production, speculation, crises and surplus-capital alongside surplus-population ... capitalist production meets in the development of its productive forces a barrier which has nothing to do with the production of wealth as such; and this peculiar barrier testifies to the merely historical, transitory character of the capitalist mode of production; testifies that for the production of wealth it is not an absolute mode, moreover, that at a certain stage, it rather conflicts with its further development.' (CIII, 237)

The significance of the fall in the rate of profit in this explanation is not that it is the cause of the crises, which arise from speculation provoked by the concentration of capital, but that it makes such crises more likely. Similarly, Marx links the severity of these crises not to the fall in the rate of profit, but to the growing mass of surplus value which has to be realised, leading to a crisis of overproduction arising as production runs ahead of the limited consumption power of the mass of the population. 'This production on a large scale ... presupposes an immense production, and therefore consumption, of use values, hence

---

[17] Fullarton did not refer to smaller capitals, but to a surplus of capital, augmented by remittances from the colonies, in relation to the opportunities for profitable investment, which led to a fall in the rate of interest and an abundance of credit, and so promoted a speculative boom. The destruction of capital in the crisis 'relieves the moneymarket for a season of the load which had oppressed it, abates competition, and restores the marketrate of interest to the level from which it had declined'. Fullarton concludes that 'one would almost be tempted to suspect, that a periodical destruction of capital has become a necessary condition of the existence of any marketrate of interest at all' so that 'these awful visitations ... may be nothing more than the natural and necessary corrective of an overgrown and bloated opulence, the *vis mediatrix* by which our social system, as at present constituted, is enabled to relieve itself from time to time of everrecurring *plethora* which menaces its existence, and to regain a sound and wholesome state' (excerpted by Marx, MEGA, IV.7, 50).

always leads to periodic overproduction, which is periodically solved by expanded markets. Not because of a lack of demand, but a lack of paying demand. For the same process presupposes a proletariat on an ever-increasing scale, therefore significantly and progressively restricts any demand which goes beyond the necessary means of subsistence, while it at the same time requires a constant extension of the sphere of demand. Malthus was correct to say that the *demand of the* worker *can never suffice for the capitalist*' (CW33, 114).

Marx seems to ignore the demand of the capitalist with this apparent endorsement of Malthusian underconsumptionism, although he notes that 'foreign trade, luxury production, the state's extravagance ... — the massive expenditure on fixed capital, etc. — hinder this process' (CW33, 113–4). However, Marx immediately goes on to stress the limitation of the Malthusian conception, according to which consumption is the driving force and limit of capitalist production, to stress the role of the rate of profit as the primary stimulus to capitalist production, and so the fall in the rate of profit as decisive in removing the stimulus of capitalist production.

> *The development of the productive force of social labour is the* historic task and justification of capital. It is exactly by doing this that it unconsciously creates the material conditions for a higher mode of production. What makes Ricardo uneasy here is that profit — the stimulus of capitalist production and the condition for accumulation, as also the driving force for accumulation — is endangered by the law of development of production itself. And the quantitative relation is everything here. There is in reality a deeper basis for this, which Ricardo only suspects. What is demonstrated here, in a *purely economic* manner, from the standpoint of capitalist production itself, is its barrier — its *relativity*, the fact that it is not an *absolute*, but only an historical *mode of production*, corresponding to the material conditions of production of a certain restricted development period. (CW33, 114; c.f. CIII, 237)

Internal Contradictions of the Law

The links between the falling tendency of the rate of profit and the tendency to crisis in the 1862 manuscript are all inserted as asides, and none of the points are developed theoretically. The analysis of the relationship is developed at greater length in the 1864–5 manuscript, incorporated into Volume Three of *Capital*, where the tendency to crisis is discussed in the context of the 'internal contradictions' of the law of the tendency for the rate of profit to fall.

In this chapter, which is clearly a development of the 1862 manuscript, the tendency to crisis is not seen as a mechanical result of the tendency for the rate of profit to fall, but is related to the fundamental contradiction between the 'tendency towards the absolute development of the productive forces, regardless of the value and surplus value it contains, and regardless of the social conditions under which capitalist production takes place' and the aim 'to preserve the value of the existing capital and promote its self-expansion to the highest limit' (CIII, 244). As we have already seen, this contradiction appears not only in the tendency for the rate of profit to fall, but also in the tendency to the concentration of capital and the polarisation of class relations, in the tendency to the production of an ever-growing mass of surplus value, and in the tendency to the formation of a relative surplus population, each of which is independent of, though related to, the tendency for the rate of profit to fall. Here Marx again discusses the tendency to crisis in relation to these various tendencies, and not simply in relation to a fall in the rate of profit. It is important to keep these inter-relationships in mind, otherwise the chapter simply appears to be internally contradictory, offering a succession of theories of crisis.

The mass of profit, the rate of profit and the tendency to crisis

The first section of the chapter is usually read as an endorsement of an underconsumptionist theory of crisis. Marx reiterates the point made in the *Grundrisse*, that the capitalist mode of production presents no inherent barriers to the *production* of surplus value. 'Given the necessary means of production, i.e., a sufficient accumulation of capital, the creation of surplus value is only limited by the labouring population if the rate of surplus value ... is given; and no other limit but the intensity of exploitation if the labouring population is given' (CIII, 238). The problem comes when the capitalist tries to sell the increased mass of commodities.

> The creation of this surplus value makes up the direct process of production, which, as we have said, has no other limits but those mentioned above. As soon as all the surplus-labour it was possible

Internal Contradictions of the Law 229

> to squeeze out has been embodied in commodities, surplus value has been produced. But this production of surplus value completes but the first act of the capitalist process of production — the direct production process. Capital has absorbed so and so much unpaid labour. With the development of the process, which expresses itself in a drop in the rate of profit, the mass of surplus value thus produced swells to immense dimensions. Now comes the second act of the process. The entire mass of commodities, i.e., the total product, must be sold ... If this is not done, or is done only in part, or only at prices below the prices of production, the labourer has been indeed exploited, but his exploitation is not realized as such for the capitalist. (CIII, 239)

Marx immediately specifies the reason why the realisation of surplus value appears as a barrier to the capitalist, referring both to disproportionality and to the limited consumer power of society. 'The conditions of direct exploitation, and those of realizing it, are not identical. They diverge not only in space and time, but also logically. The first are only limited by the productive power of society, the latter by the proportional relation of the various branches of production and the consumer power of society' (CIII, 239).

What is in question here is not the absolute consumption power of society, but the dynamic *relationship* between production and consumption. The source of the crisis tendency lies not in limited consumption, but in the contradictory dynamics of the capitalist mode of production, expressed in the constant tendency to overproduction. The greater the mass of surplus value to be realised, the more frantically must capital seek new markets, and the more vulnerable is accumulation to disruption when it confronts the limit of profitability.

Every capitalist is forced by the pressure of competition to develop the productive forces without limit, and therefore is equally compelled to seek to expand the market by all means. But the more extensive is the market, the less can it be controlled, and so the more vulnerable is it to disruption as proportional relationships break down, while the larger is the mass of surplus value to be realised, the more likely is its realisation to confront barriers.

> The consumer power of society ... is not determined either by the absolute productive power, or by the absolute consumer power, but by the consumer power based on antagonistic conditions of

distribution, which reduce the consumption of the bulk of society to a minimum varying within more or less narrow limits. It is furthermore restricted by the tendency to accumulate, the drive to expand capital and produce surplus value on an extended scale. This is law for capitalist production, imposed by incessant revolutions in the methods of production themselves, by the depreciation of existing capital always bound up with them, by the general competitive struggle and the need to improve production and expand its scale merely as a means of self-preservation and under penalty of ruin. The market must, therefore, be continually extended, so that its interrelations and the conditions regulating them assume more and more the form of a natural law working independently of the producer, and become ever more uncontrollable. This internal contradiction seeks to resolve itself through expansion of the outlying field of production. But the more productiveness develops, the more it finds itself at variance with the narrow basis on which the conditions of consumption rest. It is no contradiction at all on this self-contradictory basis that there should be an excess of capital simultaneously with a growing surplus of population. For while a combination of these two would, indeed, increase the mass of produced surplus value, it would at the same time intensify the contradiction between the conditions under which this surplus value is produced and those under which it is realised. (CIII, 239–240)

Marx does not specify the relationship between the tendency for the rate of profit to fall and the tendency to crisis inherent in the growth in the mass of profit delineated here. On the one hand, the tendency for the rate of profit to fall might alleviate the tendency to overproduction, because the fall in the rate of profit leads to a fall in the rate of accumulation (CIII, 236, 243), so that the market equally has to be expanded at a relatively lower *rate*, even if the mass of surplus value, and the mass of commodities in which it is embodied, grows ever larger. On the other hand, the fall in the rate of profit removes the stimulus to accumulation, so that the withdrawal of capital from circulation might provoke a crisis. However, at this point Marx notes that the pace of accumulation is not determined by the rate of profit 'but in proportion to the impetus it already possesses' (CIII, 240), noting that capital accumulates only slowly in the early stages of capitalist development, even though the rate of profit is high.

At the equivalent point in the discussion in the 1862 manuscript Marx equally related the 'rate of accumulation' to the mass of profit, and not to its rate (CW33, 113), referring to Richard Jones, whom he quotes in a passage incorporated as a supplementary remark in CIII:

> in spite of the falling rate of profit the inducements and faculties to accumulate are augmented; first, on account of the growing relative over-population; second, because the growing productivity of labour is accompanied by an increase in the mass of use values represented by the same exchange value, hence in the material elements of capital; third, because the branches of production become more varied; fourth, due to the development of the credit system, the stock companies, etc., and the resultant case of converting money into capital without becoming an industrial capitalist; fifth, because the wants and the greed for wealth increase; and, sixth, because the mass of investments in fixed capital grows, etc. (CIII 260–1)

It is clear that there is no unambiguous relationship between the general rate of profit and the tendency to crisis. In particular, in these passages Marx downplays the significance of the general rate of profit as the spur to accumulation, which would imply that a fall in the rate of profit does not in itself constitute a barrier to accumulation. The issue is further complicated when we consider the relationship between the general rate of profit and the rate of profit achieved by particular capitals because, as we have seen, the smaller capitals face a fall in their rate of profit as a result of the growing scale of production, regardless of the course of the general rate of profit, and it is their speculative adventures that precipitate the crisis. Although a fall in the general rate of profit might make the position of such capitals even more precarious, there are other factors that could precipitate a crisis, such as overproduction in a particular branch of production, or an increase in the dispersion of profit rates as a result of the concentration of capital, both of which Marx considers under the heading of the internal contradictions of the law of the tendency of the rate of profit to fall, but which are independent of any such tendency. There is no inconsistency here, it is simply that a fall in the rate of profit is only one of the factors associated with the development of the forces of production, each of which contributes to the crisis tendencies of capitalist accumulation.

The rate of profit, crisis and the depreciation of capital

The second section of the chapter on the internal contradictions of the law focuses on the depreciation of capital as a consequence of the tendency to over-production, itself an expression of the fundamental 'conflict between expansion of production and production of surplus value'. The depreciation of capital resolves the crisis by serving as the mechanism through which the rate of profit is restored, by reducing the value of the capital to which the mass of surplus value is related. However, this is the case whether the fall in the rate of profit is the cause or the consequence of the crisis.

In general, crises derive from a number of 'contradictory tendencies and phenomena', which the crisis temporarily resolves. 'From time to time the conflict of antagonistic agencies finds vent in crises. The crises are always but momentary and forcible solutions of the existing contradictions. They are violent eruptions which for a time restore the disturbed equilibrium' (CIII, 244). But what precisely are these contradictions?

Marx begins by itemising a number of contradictions inherent in the accumulation of capital. While the growth in capital tends to increase employment, it simultaneously reduces employment as it minimises living labour. While rising productivity tends to reduce the rate of profit, it simultaneously depreciates the existing capital, 'which checks the fall and gives an accelerating motion to the accumulation of capital values' (CIII, 244). While productivity (and so the rate of exploitation) rises, so does the organic composition of capital.

These particular contradictions all express a more fundamental contradiction, which Marx first characterises as the contradiction between the growing mass of labour employed and surplus value produced, on the one hand, and the growing value of capital, on the other (CIII, 243), before specifying it as the familiar contradiction between the tendency to develop the productive forces without limit, and the need to confine production within the limits of profitability. 'The contradiction, to put it in a very general way, consists in that the capitalist mode of production involves a tendency towards absolute development of the productive forces, and regardless of the social conditions under which capitalist production takes place; while, on the other hand, its aim is to preserve the value of the existing capital and promote its self-expansion to the highest limit' (CIII, 244).

A crisis arises because the growth of capitalist production has run

Internal Contradictions of the Law

ahead of the opportunities for the profitable realisation of an expanded capital, the contradiction appearing at first as a fall in the rate of profit. The crisis resolves this contradiction by destroying existing forces of production, devaluing a part of the existing capital, and so restoring the rate of profit. 'The specific feature about it is that it uses the existing value of capital as a means of increasing this value to the utmost. The methods by which it accomplishes this include the fall of the rate of profit, depreciation of existing capital, and development of the productive forces of labour at the expense of already created productive forces' (CIII, 244).

The depreciation of capital is then a means by which the rate of profit is restored through periodic crises. 'The periodical depreciation of existing capital — one of the means immanent in capitalist production to check the fall of the rate of profit and hasten accumulation of capital value through formation of new capital — disturbs the given conditions, within which the process of circulation and reproduction of capital takes place, and is therefore accompanied by sudden stoppages and crises in the production process' (CIII, 244).

In his discussion of the depreciation of capital Marx elucidates the mechanism through which the rate of profit is restored in a crisis. However this mechanism applies whatever may be the cause of the crisis, and when we look more closely at the analysis of this section we find that the fall in the rate of profit in this instance is a consequence of a crisis of overproduction. The crisis restores profitability and so serves as a 'counteracting influence' on the secular tendency of the rate of profit to fall, but the cause of the crisis lies elsewhere.

To clarify the issues at stake we need to look a little more closely at the depreciation of capital. The general tendency to the depreciation of capital is a feature of overproduction, which appears most dramatically in a crisis. The depreciation of capital 'always goes hand in hand with' increasing productivity, as falling costs of production devalue existing means of production and commodities (CIII, 243). More advanced capitalists introduce new methods which lead to an increase in production and a corresponding fall in price. Those producing using the old methods of production now face a loss, which has to be absorbed through the depreciation of their existing capital.

The depreciation of fixed capital is a permanent feature of the capitalist mode of production, regardless of the course of the general rate of profit, and irrespective of the existence of general crises. Such a depreciation of capital is allowed for in the calculations of capitalists, who amortise their investment in accordance with an estimate of its 'moral' depreciation, not of its physical durability. However, it may cause a general crisis if, for example, its depreciation is more rapid than had been expected, inflicting losses on particular capitalists which then precipitate a chain of bankruptcies.

In the first instance, the crisis will lead to a fall in the rate of profit, as the production of surplus value falls, but the liquidation of surplus productive capacity, and the devaluation of capital through bankruptcy, will eventually restore the rate of profit. In this case the depreciation of capital as a result of the development of the productive forces is a *cause* of the crisis, whose immediate *result* is a fall in the rate of profit, which in turn leads to the further depreciation of capital as an *effect* of the crisis, through which the rate of profit is restored. On the other hand, capital will equally be depreciated if there is a general crisis which originates from some other cause, for example a fall in the rate of profit, in which case the fall in the rate of profit is the *cause* of the crisis, and the depreciation of capital an *effect* of the crisis.

The essential point is that, whatever its particular cause, the crisis is ultimately one or another expression of the contradiction between the tendency to develop the forces of production without limit, and the subordination of production to the valorisation of capital, while the effect of the crisis is always to restore the rate of profit through the devaluation of capital and the destruction of productive capacity. This explains how Marx can hold a number of apparently quite different theories of crisis at one and the same time, and is crucial to understanding the discussion in Volume III of *Capital*, where Marx moves from one to another.

Marx concludes that the devaluation of capital through crises only temporarily removes the barriers to accumulation, since they are removed only to be re-created.

> Capitalist production seeks continually to overcome these immanent barriers, but overcomes them only by means which again place these barriers in its way and on a more formidable scale. The *real barrier* of capitalist production is *capital itself*. It is that capital and its self-expansion appear as the starting and the closing point, the motive and the purpose of production; that production is only production for *capital* and not vice versa, the means of production are not mere means for a constant expansion of the living process of the *society* of producers. ...The means — unconditional

development of the productive forces of society — comes continually into conflict with the limited purpose, the self-expansion of the existing capital. The capitalist mode of production is, for this reason, a historical means of developing the material forces of production and creating an appropriate world-market and is, at the same time, a continual conflict between this its historical task and its own corresponding relations of social production. (CIII, 245).

The falling rate of profit and the absolute overaccumulation of capital

Marx introduces the next section of the chapter on the 'internal contradictions of the law' by returning to the relationship between the falling rate of profit and the tendency to the concentration and centralisation of capital which he had already discussed in the 1862 manuscript. As in the earlier discussion, the fall in the rate of profit is significant primarily for the smaller capitals who are the source of innovation, but who are increasingly unable to compete as they do not have the advantage of economies of scale and are not able to sustain accumulation because they do not have the funds to expand the scale of production. The destruction of the smaller capitals at the same time throws the workers they had employed onto the scrap heap, since the larger capitals employ proportionately fewer workers. The rise in the organic composition of capital is therefore linked to structural changes in the capitalist mode of production rather than to the secular trend in the rate of profit.

At a certain high point this increasing concentration in its turn causes a new fall in the rate of profit. The mass of small dispersed capitals is thereby driven along the adventurous road of speculation, credit frauds, stock swindles, and crises. The so-called plethora of capital always applies essentially to a plethora of the capital for which the fall in the rate of profit is not compensated through the mass of profit — this is always true of newly developing fresh offshoots of capital — or to a plethora which places capitals incapable of action on their own at the disposal of the managers of large enterprises in the form of credit. This plethora of capital arises from the same causes as those which call forth relative overpopulation, and is, therefore, a phenomenon supplementing the latter, although they stand at opposite poles — unemployed capital at one pole, and unemployed worker population at the other. (CIII, 246; c.f. CW33, 105, 112 and the note on Fullarton above)

A mere fall in the rate of profit is not a sufficient condition for the overaccumulation of capital, for investment remains profitable so long as capital can continue to earn a positive rate of profit. The condition for the 'absolute' overaccumulation of capital is that an addition to capital leads to a fall not only in the rate, but even in the mass of profit (c.f. *Grundrisse*, CW29, 140, where Marx comments on Ricardo's discussion of this possibility in the *Principles*), but this implies that wages have risen to absorb the entire surplus product (CIII, 246-7) as the reserve army of labour is absorbed, and wages rise to the point at which profit is extinguished.[18]

The erosion of profits by an increase in wages is quite distinct from the tendency of the rate of profit to fall. Thus Marx frequently condemned attempts to explain the fall in the rate of profit as the result of a rise in wages. In the 1861-3 manuscript Marx noted that the temporary rise and fall of wages as a result of changes in the balance of supply and demand 'has as little to do with the general law of the rise or fall in the profit rate as the rise or fall in the market prices of commodities has to do with the determination of value in general' (TSV3, 312). And a few pages earlier in *Capital* he notes that the fall in the rate of profit is related to a rise in the rate of exploitation so that: 'Nothing is more absurd, for this reason, than to explain the fall in the rate of profit by the rise in the rate of wages, although this may be the case by way of an exception' (CIII, 234). However, the case of the absolute overaccumulation of capital does indicate a relationship between the tendency for the rate of profit to fall and the rise in wages. If the introduction of new methods of production were to lead to a fall in the rate of profit, capitalists would persist with using the existing methods, in which case accumulation might proceed until the reserve army of labour is exhausted and accumulation is checked by a rise in wages. The rise in wages is therefore a part of the mechanism of the crisis, even if it is not its ultimate cause, and it is this mechanism that Marx goes on to explore.

---

[18] This passage has been picked up by the advocates of the 'over-accumulation with respect to labour-power' theory of crisis as an indication that Marx saw this as the most fundamental source of crisis. However this is to misread the significance of this passage, in which Marx considers the abstract possibility of the 'absolute' overaccumulation of capital as a very specific phenomenon, a hypothetical condition based on the assumption of 'extreme conditions' (CIII, 250).

Overaccumulation and crisis

If the overaccumulation of capital affected all capitals equally there would be a uniform fall in the rate of profit and a slowing down of accumulation, but not necessarily a crisis. However, in practice the uneven development of capital means that all capitals are not affected equally. The newly formed capital might have the prospect of good profits, but would be unable to find labourers to employ, until rising wages press the older capitals into unprofitability so that they are forced to lay-off workers, risking a crisis. Thus it is not necessary that the reserve army of labour should be exhausted, but only that wages should rise sufficiently to lead to 'a fall in the intensity of exploitation below a certain point. ...It is no contradiction that this over-production of capital is accompanied by more or less considerable relative over-population ... an over-population of labourers not employed by the surplus-capital owing to the low degree of exploitation at which alone they could be employed, or at least owing to the low rate of profit which they would yield at the given degree of exploitation.'(CIII, 250–1)

The absolute overaccumulation of capital can only be overcome through a restructuring of capital. This does not take place smoothly but only through a crisis which is only resolved through the devaluation of capital, the destruction of productive capacity, and the redundancy of labour to bring the supply of capital back into line with the supply of labour-power. This adjustment will only be achieved through a competitive struggle: 'this actual depreciation of the old capital could not occur without a struggle'. Although it appears to particular capitals that the rate of profit falls as a result of this competitive struggle, in fact 'the rate of profit would not fall under the effect of competition due to over-production of capital. It would rather be the reverse; it would be the competitive struggle which would begin because the fallen rate of profit and over-production of capital originate from the same conditions' (CIII, 247), 'a fall in the rate of profit calls forth a competitive struggle among capitalists, not vice versa' (CIII, 251).

We have moved on from the specific discussion of the crisis associated with the tendency for the rate of profit to fall, or the absolute overaccumulation of capital, to a discussion of the mechanics of capitalist restructuring through overaccumulation and crisis, which is Marx's counter to the economists' picture of the smooth achievement of a competitive equilibrium. Overaccumulation and crisis is here not so much the exceptional event, the end of history, as the everyday experience of capitalism, in which capitalists do not *choose* to adjust in response to the incentives of the market, in full knowledge of the consequences of their actions, but in which capitalists are compelled to adjust by competitive pressure, which they experience as pressure on their realised profit.

Faced with a fall in the rate of profit existing capitalists would keep their additional capital idle to prevent depreciation of their existing capital, or even use it at a loss to shift idleness onto their competitors, while new capital seeks to drive out old. In either case 'a portion of the old capital has to lie unused under all circumstances ... The competitive struggle would decide what part of it would be particularly affected' (CIII, 248). Eventually 'the equilibrium would be restored under all circumstances through the withdrawal or even the destruction of more or less capital. This would extend partly to the material substance of capital ... The main damage ... would occur in respect to the *values* of capitals' (CIII, 248–9). This comes about through the depreciation of promissory notes and instruments of credit, while gold lies idle, and

> part of the commodities on the market can complete their process of circulation and reproduction only through an immense contraction of their prices, hence through a depreciation of the capital which they represent. The elements of fixed capital are depreciated to a greater or lesser degree in just the same way. It must be added that definite, presupposed, price relations govern the process of reproduction, so that the latter is halted and thrown into confusion by a general drop in prices. This confusion and stagnation paralyses the function of money as a medium of payment, whose development is geared to the development of capital and is based on those presupposed price relations. The chain of payment obligations due at specific dates is broken in a hundred places. The confusion is augmented by the attendant collapse of the credit system, which develops simultaneously with capital, and leads to violent and acute crises, to sudden and forcible depreciation, to the actual stagnation and disruption of the process of production, and thus to a real falling off in reproduction. (CIII, 249)

The development of the crisis prepares the way for a restoration of accumulation. In the course of the crisis the competitive struggle forces capitalists to introduce new machinery, which lowers the value of

Internal Contradictions of the Law

commodities, increases the rate of surplus value, and creates a surplus population, while less efficient producers are destroyed. The growth in the surplus population leads wages to fall, while the depreciation of constant capital raises the rate of profit. 'The ensuing stagnation of production would have prepared — within capitalistic limits — a subsequent expansion of production. And thus the cycle would run its course anew.' (CIII, 250)

The crisis provides a mechanism by which the older and smaller capitals are driven out, and so by which the historical tendency to the concentration and centralisation of capital makes itself felt. 'Compensation of a fall in the rate of profit by a rise in the mass of profit applies only to the big, firmly placed capitalists. The new additional capital operating independently does not enjoy any such compensating conditions. It must still win them, and so it is that a fall in the rate of profit calls forth a competitive struggle among capitalists, not vice versa.' (CIII, 251) This competitive struggle is initially the result of the additions to productive capacity as capitalists introduce new methods of production. The growing demand for labour power means that 'the competitive struggle is accompanied by a temporary rise in wages and a resultant temporary fall of the rate of profit', while the growing mass of commodities thrown onto the market leads to a fall in their price, which equally leads to a fall in the rate of profit (CIII, 251).

The crisis appears as an intensification of the competitive struggle in which the weaker or more exposed capitals fail. Behind the intensification of competition Marx has identified the fall in the rate of profit that is the immediate result of the rise in wages and the fall in prices. However the crisis is no more the result of the rise in wages than it is of the competitive struggle which that rise has unleashed. The rise in wages is a result of the overaccumulation of capital, which is in its turn promoted by the competitive struggle between capitalists, and intensified by the concentration and uneven development of capital. This raises once again the problem of general overproduction, the necessity of a fall in the rate of profit being explained by the fact that 'a rift must continually ensue between the limited dimensions of consumption under capitalism and a production which forever tends to exceed this immanent barrier' (CIII, 251).

Marx does not explore the matter any further, and the section concludes with some general comments, which recapitulate but add nothing to earlier discussion of overproduction, disproportionality and the falling rate of profit.

To say that there is no general overproduction, but rather a disproportion within the various branches of production, is no more than to say that under capitalist production the proportionality of the individual branches of production springs as a continual process from disproportionality, because the cohesion of the aggregate production imposes itself as a blind law upon the agents of production. ...If it is said that overproduction is only relative, this is quite correct; but the entire capitalist mode of production is only a relative one ...If it is finally said that the capitalists have only to exchange and consume their commodities among themselves, then the entire nature of the capitalist mode of production is lost sight of; and also forgotten is the fact that it is a matter of expanding the value of the capital, not consuming it. ...The contradiction of the capitalist mode of production ...lies precisely in its tendency towards an absolute development of the productive forces, which continually come into conflict with the specific *conditions* of production in which capital moves, and alone can move. (CIII, 251–252)

The limitations of the capitalist mode of production come to the surface: 1) In that the development of the productivity of labour creates out of the falling rate of profit a law which at a certain point comes into antagonistic conflict with this development and must be overcome constantly through crises. 2) In that the expansion or contraction of production are determined by ...a definite rate of profit, rather than the relation of production to social requirements ...It is for this reason that the capitalist mode of production meets with barriers at a certain expanded stage of production. (CIII, 253)

What is the significance of FROP?

We have considered Marx's discussion of crises associated with the falling rate of profit at some length, because it has been this theory of crisis that has dominated contemporary Marxist theorising. It is now time to draw together the threads of this discussion to ask what is the significance of the law of the tendency of the rate of profit to fall? On the whole, our conclusions reinforce those already drawn from Marx's first examination of the law in the *Grundrisse*. The law of the tendency of the rate of profit to fall is located within a wider discussion of the secular tendencies of capital accumulation, as a factor that intensifies the cyclical form of overaccumulation and crisis through which the secular tendencies of accumulation work themselves out.

The first and most fundamental conclusion is that Marx did not see the 'law of the tendency for the rate of profit to fall' as an objective economic law that mechanically determines the fate of the capitalist mode of production. Ricardo was justifiably worried about 'the bare possibility' of a decline in the rate of profit, but Marx criticises Ricardo not only for his specific theory of the fall in the rate of profit, but also because Ricardo is preoccupied with the tendential fall in the rate of profit as a mechanical law — for Ricardo 'the quantitative proportion means everything'. Marx makes it clear that for him the law is only an expression of something more fundamental. 'There is, indeed, something deeper behind it, of which he is only vaguely aware. It comes to the surface here in a purely economical way — i.e. from the bourgeois point of view, within the limitations of capitalist understanding, from the standpoint of capitalist production itself — that it has its barrier, that it is relative, that it is not an absolute, but only a historical mode of production corresponding to a definite limited epoch in the development of the material requirements of production.' (CIII, 254)

For Marx the law of the tendency for the rate of profit to fall is but an expression of the fundamental tendency and limit of capitalist accumulation implicit in the role of the rate of profit. 'The rate of profit is the motive power of capitalist production. ... Development of the productive forces of social labour is the historical task and justification of capital. This is just the way in which it unconsciously creates the material requirements of a higher mode of production' (CIII, 254).

Nowhere does Marx simply argue that a rise in the organic composition of capital leads to a fall in the rate of profit and so to a crisis. Marx looks at the relationship between the organic composition of capital and the rate of profit dynamically. A rise in the organic composition of capital has to be compensated by an increase in the rate of surplus value if the capitalist is to avoid facing a fall in the rate of profit.

This challenge confronts each individual capitalist, as well as the capitalist system as a whole. Big capitals are able to respond to this challenge more effectively because they enjoy the advantages of economies of scale, they have more resources at their disposal, they have better access to credit, and they can establish monopoly positions. Smaller capitalists do not have these advantages, and it is they who confront the fall in the rate of profit in the form of intensified competitive pressure. Small capitals respond to this pressure both by introducing new methods of production, laying off workers and intensifying the pressure of overproduction, and/or by engaging in swindles and speculative ventures which stave off their individual crisis, at the risk of provoking a crisis of the system as a whole.

'If the rate of profit falls, there follows, on the one hand, an exertion of capital in order that the individual capitalists, through improved methods, etc., may depress the value of their individual commodity below the social average value and thereby realise an extra profit at the prevailing market price. On the other hand, there appears swindling and a general promotion of swindling by recourse to frenzied ventures with new methods of production ... all for the sake of securing a shred of extra profit.' (CIII, 254)

The attempt to maintain the rate of profit in the face of the increase in the organic composition of capital and the growing scale of production leads to an intensification of the competitive struggle, leading in turn to the further concentration and centralisation of capital and the further development of the forces of production and expansion of productive capacity, which further intensifies competitive pressure in a cumulative spiral. Some of those capitalists unable to compete will divert their capital into speculative channels, while others will face bankruptcy, leading to the destruction of productive capacity and the devaluation of capital, which may be absorbed, but may also precipitate a crisis as it reverberates through the credit system.

This dynamic of overaccumulation and crisis is the specific mechanism through which new methods of production are introduced and generalised within the capitalist system. The historical tendency of this dynamic is towards the concentration and centralisation of capital, which may reduce the tendency to overaccumulation and crisis by reducing competition, but at the cost of removing the source of capitalist dynamism. The alternative to regular crises is secular stagnation. 'As soon as formation of capital were to fall into the hands of a few established big capitals, for which the mass of profit compensates for the falling rate of profit, the vital flame of production would be altogether extinguished. It would die out.' (CIII, 254)

Although Marx provides an extensive discussion of crises in his chapter on the 'internal contradictions' of the law of the tendency for the rate of profit to fall, we have seen that in practice he moves between a number of different explanations of crises, all of which derive from different aspects of the fundamental tendencies of capitalist accumulation, and all of which express in one way or another the fundamental contradiction between use-value and value, production for need and production for profit. The tendency for the rate of profit to fall is not identified as a privileged cause of crises, but plays the role of a factor which makes crises more likely, primarily because it leads to an intensification of the competitive struggle between capitalists.

The rise in the organic composition of capital plays a much more important role than does any fall in the rate of profit in this discussion, as in the earlier texts. The importance of a rising organic composition of capital is twofold. On the one hand, it underlies the tendency to the concentration and centralisation of capital, which increases the competitive pressure on smaller capitals, which reduces the spur to innovation, and which paves the way to a new form of society through its socialisation of the forces of production. On the other hand, it underlies the tendency to the production of a 'relative surplus population'.

It is the consequences of these two tendencies, rather than of the tendency for the rate of profit to fall, that Marx comes back to at the end of his examination of the internal contradictions of the law. On the one hand, he relates crises to the restructuring of production, noting that 'periodical crises ... arise from the circumstance that now this and now that portion of the labouring population becomes redundant under its old mode of employment' (CIII, 258). On the other hand, the growing accumulation of capital implies growing concentration. 'The contradiction between the general social power into which capital develops, on the one hand, and the private power of the individual capitalists over these social conditions of production, on the other, becomes ever more irreconcilable, and yet contains the solution of the problem, because it implies at the same time the transformation of the conditions of production into general, common, social conditions. This transformation stems from the development of the productive forces under capitalist production' (CIII, 259).

It was these aspects of the analysis, and not the law of the tendency for the rate of profit to fall, that Marx developed in his characterisation of the historical tendencies of capitalist accumulation in Volume One of *Capital*. From the point of view of the interpretation of the development of Marx's ideas it is important to note not only that the published version of Volume One of *Capital* was written after the manuscripts on which Volume Three was based, but also that the section on the historical tendencies was a late addition to the plan for Volume One, which had otherwise been relatively stable over a period of years.

The section on accumulation did not appear in any of the early plans of *Capital*. In all of the early plans, and in the 1861–3 manuscript, Marx looks at the production of surplus value, and then moves on immediately to circulation and the distribution of surplus value in the forms of rent and profit, which includes consideration of the law of the tendency for the rate of profit to fall. As we have seen, Marx's discussion of that law is mixed up with his discussion of the historical tendencies of capitalist accumulation and the creation of a relative surplus population, the two being linked as aspects of the tendency for the organic composition of capital to rise. It is only near the end of the 1861–3 manuscript that Marx disentangles the two by including a short section on accumulation which discusses the latter independently of the falling tendency of the rate of profit, but this section is sketchy and disjointed.

The first plan of *Capital* in which the section on the accumulation of capital appears is the plan made at the very end of the 1861–3 manuscript (CW33, 347), which refers to the 'reconversion of surplus value into capital' as part of a chapter leading in to primitive accumulation and the theory of colonisation, but there is no indication of what this section would contain, and in this plan the work still concludes with the chapter 'Results of the Production Process', which Marx drafted in full as a part of the 1864–5 revision. It was only in the published version of Volume One of *Capital* that the chapter on the historical tendencies of capitalist accumulation replaced that on the results of the immediate process of production as the culmination of the analysis in what was the only major substantive change between the 1861–3 draft and the final version of Volume One.

Marx does not discuss this late change in the plan of *Capital* in any of his extant correspondence. We might surmise that there are two reasons for the change. First, he had intended to publish what are now the three volumes of *Capital* simultaneously, and it was only in the autumn of 1866 that he realised that this was impractical and that he would have to publish Volume One independently. The original concluding chapter of Volume One, the 'Results of the Immediate Process of Production', summarised the theoretical argument of Volume One, leading in to the circulation of capital which was the subject-matter of Volume Two. The replacement both gave Volume One a coherence and completeness which it would otherwise have lacked, and provided a conclusion which was of immediate political significance, in relating the historical development of capitalist accumulation to the development of class relations and class struggle, and to the ultimate limits of capitalism.

This last point draws our attention to the second possible reason for the change, which is Marx's increasingly active involvement in working class politics in the mid-1860s, a politics which was no longer that of small communist sects, but of a developing international working class movement based on the trade unions. Although Marx always gave priority to his theoretical over his political work, changing political conditions cannot but have been reflected in changing theoretical emphases. Thus the theory of crises plays a rapidly diminishing role in Marx's work after 1862, to be replaced by an emphasis on the secular tendencies of capitalist accumulation, just as the conception of revolution as the culmination of struggles unleashed by economic crisis is replaced by a conception of revolution as the outcome of an extended period of class development. The theoretical reflection of this return to a more active involvement in working class politics would seem to be a return to the emphasis on the secular development of capitalist class relations that had characterised Marx's writings of 1848. Perhaps the best indication of the importance that Marx attached to the law of the tendency of the rate of profit to fall is that he did not mention it in any of the works published in his lifetime, nor did he give it any further consideration in the twenty years of his life that followed the writing of the manuscript on which Volume Three of *Capital* is based.

8
Crises and the General Law of Capitalist Accumulation

The Theory of Crisis in Capital

By mid 1863 Marx had established the outlines of the analysis that would form the core of his *Capital*. The manuscripts of 1861–3 provide the first draft of the bulk of Volume One of *Capital*, and, in a more fragmentary form, much of the analysis that would be developed in Volumes Two and Three. Marx continued working intermittently on the manuscript of *Capital*, amidst bouts of ill-health and increased political activity with the formation of the First International in the autumn of 1864. However, none of the drafts made after 1863 have been published. Volumes Two and Three of *Capital* were put together after Marx's death by Engels, with the bulk of the materials for Volume Three deriving from Marx's manuscripts of 1864–5, and Volume Two from later manuscripts, written in 1870 and in 1877–8. The final manuscript of Volume One of *Capital* was written between 1865 and 1867, but Marx continued to revise it for subsequent editions, rewriting the first section on value for the second German edition of 1872, and making substantial further revisions for the French edition, published in instalments between 1872 and 1875.

The most remarkable feature of Volume One of *Capital* is the extent to which the analysis presented in the *Communist Manifesto* in 1848 has been preserved through twenty years of theoretical development.[1] This is testimony to Marx's penetrating insight into the fundamental tendencies of capitalist historical development in his early work, rather than an indication of any dogmatic adherence to established positions, for nobody can read Marx's manuscripts without being aware of his willingness to follow an argument through to its logical con-

---

[1] It might be more accurate to say that is has re-surfaced since, as we saw in the last chapter, the discussion of the historical tendencies of capitalist accumulation with which Marx concludes Volume One of *Capital* plays a very limited role in the manuscripts of 1857-63.

Politics and the Theory of Crisis 247

clusion, wherever it may lead. In Volume One of *Capital* Marx at last succeeded in providing the rigourous theoretical foundations for the intuition of his youth, relating the politically most decisive features of capitalist development to the fundamental characteristics of the capitalist mode of production.

The theory of crisis plays little role in the analysis of Volume One of *Capital*, and figures only in the margins of the subsequent two volumes. One reason for this is Marx's desire to found his analysis on the 'inner tendencies' of capital, and not on its superficial manifestations. For this reason Marx explicitly developed his analysis of the capitalist mode of production in Volume One of *Capital* at the level of 'capital-in-general' and with a focus on the production process of capital, abstracting from the competition between capitals, and the circulation and reproduction of capital, whose consideration Marx had repeatedly asserted is necessary to the analysis of crisis. As Marx notes in his consideration of money,

> The antithesis, use-value and value; the contradictions that private labour is bound to manifest itself as direct social labour, that a particularised concrete kind of labour has to pass for abstract human labour; the contradiction between the personification of objects and the representation of persons by things; all these antitheses and contradictions, which are immanent in commodities, assert themselves, and develop their modes of motion, in the antithetical phases of the metamorphosis of the commodity. These modes therefore imply the possibility of, and no more than the possibility, of crises. The conversion of this mere possibility into a reality is the result of a long series of relations, that, from our present standpoint of simple circulation, have as yet no existence. (CI, 114)

Politics and the Theory of Crisis

There is a political as well as a theoretical reason for the relative neglect of crisis in Volume One of *Capital*, and this connects with the changing focus of Marx's theoretical and political work in the 1860s. It had been the political importance that Marx attributed to economic crises that had led him back to his theoretical studies at the end of the 1850s, as he sought to counter the 'petit bourgeois' socialism of Proudhon, which claimed to provide a reformist solution to the contradictions of capitalism.

We have seen that through the 1850s Marx looked to the onset of the crisis as the precipitant of an upsurge of working class militancy, which would provide the driving force of the coming revolution. This expectation was based on little more than wishful thinking, for nowhere in their works did Marx or Engels spell out precisely how they saw such a development taking place, and they certainly had little faith in the ability of any of the revolutionary groupings with which they were loosely associated to provide a political focus for such a revolutionary upsurge. They hailed the crisis of 1857 as the herald of the revolution, but when it passed without significant political incident they didn't express any surprise, nor feel any need for a re-evaluation of their position. Although the rapid recovery from crisis prevented the expected revolutionary upsurge from happening, it also swept Proudhon and his followers from the political stage.

While Marx had been attentive to every hint of a crisis in the 1850s, in the 1860s he paid much less attention to everyday economic developments, and regarded the onset of crisis much more prosaically. In a letter to Engels in November 1864 Marx commented that although crises had lost in intensity, they had perhaps gained in frequency (CW42, 19), but this was only an aside in a letter which had much more important news to impart, that of Marx's involvement in the founding of the First International, which brought Marx for the first time into close contact with the trade union movement, giving some political substance to the prognostication of *The Communist Manifesto* which had anticipated that the basis of the revolution lay in the political development of the trade union movement.

From this point on Marx's political activity and revolutionary hopes were focused not on the expectation of a catastrophic revolutionary crisis, but on the slow development and progressive politicisation of an organised movement of the working class.[2] From this point of view the secular tendencies of capitalist accumulation have a much more fundamental importance than does its cyclical form, which merely accelerates the secular developmental tendencies, and it is with these secular tendencies that Volume One of *Capital* is primarily concerned. Economic crises play an important political role, but this role is not

---

[2] There is no significant discussion of economic crises, or of their political significance, in any of the documents Marx prepared for the First International, including his Inaugural Address or in his 1865 lectures, later published as 'Wages, Price and Profit'.

that of the revolutionary cataclysm, but of the impact of economic insecurity and intensified exploitation on the development of the working class movement. From this point of view a 'partial crisis', which affects only one branch of production, is at least as significant for the growth of the working class movement as the more dramatic general crises which periodically reverberate through the financial system.

It is notable that Marx and Engels showed only a mild interest in the next impending crisis during 1866–7, and when the crisis broke it passed almost without comment, their main satisfaction being that the form and timing of the crisis confirmed Marx's theoretical analysis. As Engels wrote to Marx in December 1868, 'here we have the finest crisis, and this time *pure* (though only relative) overproduction' (11.12.68. The crisis was only one of relative overproduction because cotton prices were still high).

The Theory of Crisis in the First Volume of Capital

Volume One of *Capital* develops Marx's analysis of the secular tendencies of capitalist accumulation on the basis of his systematic development of the theory of value and surplus value, and contains no theoretical discussion of crises, beyond brief reference to the possibility of crisis inherent in the contradiction between value and use-value, quoted above, which is amplified in an equally brief reference to the development of this contradiction in the function of money as means of payment summarising the discussion in *Theories of Surplus Value*. Marx notes that 'the function of money as the means of payment implies a contradiction without a terminus medius ... This contradiction comes to a head in those phases of industrial and commercial crises which are known as monetary crises. Such a crisis occurs only where the ever-lengthening chain of payments, and an artificial system of settling them, has been fully developed. ... In a crisis, the antithesis between commodities and their value-form, money, becomes heightened into an absolute contradiction.' (CI, 137–8).[3]

The analysis of the secular tendencies of capitalist accumulation is rooted in the expansionary tendency of capitalist production. Once

---

[3] In a note Marx distinguishes the monetary crisis referred to here, which is a phase of every crisis, from the kind of monetary crisis 'which may be produced by itself as an independent phenomenon in such a way as to react only indirectly on industry and commerce. The pivot of these crises is to be found in moneyed capital, and the sphere of direct action is therefore the sphere of that capital, viz., banking, the stock exchange and finance.' (CI, 138n.)

the general conditions of modern capitalist production are established through the industrialisation of the production of machinery, the growth of capitalist production 'finds no hindrance except in the supply of raw materials and in the disposal of the produce', which barriers are overcome through the conquest of the world market, which simultaneously provides sources of raw materials and markets for the product of capitalist industry. 'By ruining handicraft production in other countries, machinery forcibly converts them into fields for the supply of its raw material.'(CI, 450–1)

The removal of these barriers, and the huge profits appropriated as the result of the application of machinery in new branches of production, give free rein to the tendency to overproduction, leading to the alternation of boom and slump in the industrial cycle and underlying the intense capitalist competition which, as we have seen, drives capitalists both to introduce new methods of production and, as the pressure of competition increases, to force down wages.

> The enormous power, inherent in the factory system, of expanding by jumps, and the dependence of that system on the markets of the world, necessarily beget feverish production, followed by overfilling of the markets, whereupon contraction of the markets brings on crippling of production. The life of modern industry becomes a series of periods of moderate activity, prosperity, over-production, crisis and stagnation. ... Except in the periods of prosperity, there rages between the capitalists the most furious combat for the share of each in the markets. This share is directly proportional to the cheapness of the product. Besides the rivalry that this struggle begets in the application of improved machinery for replacing labour-power, and of new methods of production, there also comes a time in every industrial cycle, when a forcible reduction of wages beneath the value of labour-power, is attempted for the purpose of cheapening commodities. (CI, 453)

Marx repeatedly draws attention to the impact of industrial crises on the condition of the working class, as increased competition leads capitalists to attempt to force down wages and illegally to extend the working day, provoking increasingly organised working class resistance, and to lay-off workers, exacerbating the problem of pauperism (e.g. CI, 241–2, 284, 434n., 453, 653). However, the most important role of crises is in relation to the secular tendencies of accumulation, which Marx and Engels had already characterised in *The Communist*

Manifesto as the tendency to the concentration and centralisation of capital and the relative pauperisation of the mass of the population.

The General Law of Capitalist Accumulation

Marx sums up the historical tendencies of capitalist development in his 'general law of capitalist accumulation', which is the culmination of the analysis of Volume One of *Capital*, and which is for Marx politically the most important consequence of the contradictory form of capitalist production. It is in relation to the general law that Marx situates the principal significance of industrial crises.

The *'absolute general law of capitalist accumulation'* defines the necessary polarisation of capitalist society between the growing power and wealth of capital, on the one hand, and the growing misery of the mass of the population, expressed in the growth of the 'relative surplus population' which constitutes the reserve army of labour and the pauperised layer of the working class, on the other.[4]

The political significance of the general law does not lie, as many commentators imagine, in any belief on Marx's part that pauperism breeds revolution, for Marx was quite clear that pauperism bred degradation and demoralisation. The political significance of the law lies in its *generality*, the fact that every worker is subject to the same law, since every worker is, from the point of view of capital, merely a part of the common mass of disposable labour power, facing competition from other workers, and the constant threat of expulsion into the reserve army. The general law is thus the basis of a common experience of the working class, and so the foundation on which workers can unite as a class.

> The action of supply and demand on this basis completes the despotism of capital. As soon, therefore, as the labourers learn the secret, how it comes to pass that in the same measure as they work more, as they produce more wealth for others, and as the productive power of their labour increases, so in the same measure even their function as a means of the self-expansion of capital becomes more and more precarious for them; as soon as they discover that the degree of intensity of the competition among

---

[4] Marx immediately notes that 'like all other laws it is modified in its working by many circumstances, the analysis of which does not concern us here' (CI, 644).

themselves depends wholly on the pressure of the relative surplus-population; as soon as, by Trades' Unions etc., they try to organise a regular cooperation between employed and unemployed in order to destroy or to weaken the ruinous effects of this natural law of capitalistic production on their class, so soon capital and its sycophant, Political Economy, cry out at the infringement of the "eternal" and so to say "sacred" law of supply and demand. (CI, 640)

Marx introduces his discussion of the general law by defining the value, technical and organic compositions of capital, the *organic composition* being the fundamental concept, which is defined as 'the value-composition, in so far as it is determined by its technical composition and mirrors the changes of the latter' (CI, 612). The introduction of the concept of the organic composition of capital at this point allows Marx to analyse the relationship between the accumulation of capital and the demand for labour power by considering separately the impact of the absolute growth of capital and that of changes in its composition on the demand for labour-power. In this way he can develop the 'absolute general law' much more clearly, concisely and systematically than he had done in any of his earlier discussions, where it was mixed up with the discussion of the tendency for the rate of profit to fall, which now disappears from the discussion altogether.

Labour shortage, wages and crisis

With a constant 'organic composition of capital', which would be the case if the technical conditions of production do not change, the demand for labour-power would grow *pari passu* with the accumulation of capital. If capital accumulates more rapidly than the supply of labour power grows, with a constant organic composition of capital, then eventually wages must rise. 'A lamentation on this score was heard in England during the whole of the fifteenth, and the first half of the eighteenth centuries' (CI, 613). Marx argues that such a rise in wages has no significance for our understanding of the capitalist mode of production, it means only that 'the length and weight of the golden chain the wage-worker has already forged for himself, allow of a relaxation of the tension of it' (CI, 618), for the worker must always perform a certain portion of unpaid labour.

Marx makes it quite clear that such an increase in wages is not a cause of crisis, for the pace of accumulation can adjust smoothly to such a rise. He argues that the diminution in the rate of exploitation 'can never reach the point at which it would threaten the system itself' (CI, 619), because at a certain point 'accumulation slackens in consequence of the rise in the price of labour, because the stimulus of gain is blunted. The rate of accumulation lessens; but with its lessening, the primary cause of that lessening vanishes, *i.e.*, the disproportion between capital and exploitable labour-power. The mechanism of the process of capitalist production removes the very obstacles that it temporarily creates. The price of labour falls again to a level corresponding with the needs of the self-expansion of capital.' (CI, 619)

It appears that it is wages which are regulating the accumulation of capital, accumulation slowing down as wages rise, and accelerating as they fall, leading economists to explain the cycle in terms of the relative scarcity and abundance of labour. But Marx argues that this is not the case, because the supply of labour power is not an independent variable, but is itself determined by the absorption and expulsion of labour in the course of accumulation. The relationship between the supply and demand for labour is not an external relation between capital and the supply of labour-power. It is 'only the relation between the unpaid and the paid labour of the same labouring population' — if so much unpaid labour is extracted that the demand for labour-power runs ahead of its supply, the rise of wages brings it back into line as labour is displaced by the displacement of outdated by more advanced means of production. 'The rise of wages is therefore confined within limits that not only leave intact the foundations of the capitalistic system, but also secure its reproduction on a progressive scale.' (CI, 320). The result is that 'it is these absolute movements of the accumulation of capital which are reflected as relative movements of the mass of exploitable labour-power, and therefore seem produced by the latter's own independent movement. To put it mathematically: the rate of accumulation is the independent, not the dependent, variable; the rate of wages, the dependent, not the independent variable' (CI, 620).[5]

It is important to stress this point, since some commentators have interpreted these passages, in the light of the tentative discussion of the 'absolute overaccumulation of capital' in Volume Three of *Capital*, as the outline of a theory of crisis based on overaccumulation with

---

[5] 'Taking them as a whole, the general movements of wages are exclusively regulated by the expansion and contraction of the industrial reserve army, and these again correspond to the periodic changes of the industrial cycle' (CI, 637).

respect to the supply of labour power. As in the discussion in Volume Three of *Capital*, Marx insists that it is not the rise and fall of wages which is the primary determinant of the pattern of accumulation, because the rise and fall of wages is only a mechanism through which capitalists are compelled to develop the forces of production. While Marx certainly sees rising wages as playing a role in the development of the crisis, he is dismissive of the attempt to *explain* the cycle in terms of the supply of labour. The point is not that such overaccumulation does not happen, but that it is only a mediating link in the process of accumulation and crisis, as one of the forms of competitive pressure through which backward capitalists are displaced as profits are squeezed.[6]

While the currency school sees the cycle as the result of fluctuations in the quantity of money, the economists repeat such 'ignorance and complete misunderstanding of facts ... by saying that there are now too few, now too many wage-labourers' (CI, 620), 'but in fact it is capitalistic accumulation itself that constantly produces ... a relatively redundant population of labourers' (CI, 630). While the exhaustion of the reserve army of labour may trigger a crisis, overaccumulation with respect to labour power cannot be seen as a fundamental tendency of capitalist accumulation. Indeed the tendency is quite the contrary, expressed in the 'absolute general law of capitalist accumulation', according to which 'the labouring population always increases more rapidly than the conditions under which capital can employ this increase for its own self-expansion' (CI, 645).

Crises and the historical tendency of capitalist accumulation

In the course of accumulation the technical composition of capital rises as each worker uses more raw materials and sets in motion a greater mass of means of production. The value of these elements of constant capital falls as their scale increases, so the organic composition of

---

[6] In a description of the cycle in Volume Two of *Capital* Marx refers to the rise of wages as the reserve army of labour is absorbed in advance of a crisis, without indicating this as a cause of the crisis. During the boom rapid accumulation draws 'great numbers of the latent relative surplus population, and even workers already employed, into the new lines of business. ... A part of the reserve army of workers whose pressure keeps wages down is absorbed. Wages generally rise, even in the formerly well employed sections of the labour market. This lasts until, with the inevitable crash, the reserve army of workers is again released and wages are pressed down once more to their minimum and below it' (CII, 391). Marx immediately follows this passage with a note referring to the contradiction between the expansionary tendency of capitalist production and the limited consumption power of the mass of the population.

capital does not rise to anything like the same extent as the technical composition. Nevertheless, Marx assumes that it does continue to rise. At the same time, Marx recognises that the total amount of capital is also increasing, so that the relative decline in the number of workers employed does not necessarily imply an absolute decline in their number (CI, 623).

The increasing organic composition of capital is also associated with the growing scale of capitalist production, and so with the concentration of capital into ever larger units of production. Larger capitals have the competitive advantage not only technologically, but also in, for example, their access to credit, so that the tendency to the *concentration* of capital is reinforced by the tendency to the *centralisation* of its ownership. 'The smaller capitals, therefore, crowd into spheres of production which Modern Industry has only sporadically or incompletely got hold of. Here competition rages in direct proportion to the number, and in inverse proportion to the magnitudes, of the antagonistic capitals. It always ends with the ruin of many small capitalists, whose capitals partly vanish into the hands of their conquerors, partly vanish. Apart from this, with capitalist production an altogether new force comes into play — the credit system, which ... soon becomes a new and terrible weapon in the battle of competition and is finally transformed into an enormous social mechanism for the centralisation of capitals.' (CI, 626) The centralisation of capital in turn speeds up the socialisation of production and the rise in the organic composition of capital.

New methods of production are generally introduced by additions to capital, so that at first the increase in the organic composition of capital only affects the rate of growth of new employment opportunities, but once the old capital is renewed its impact extends to all workers. 'But in time the old capital also reaches the moment of renewal from top to toe, when it sheds its skin and is reborn like the others in a perfected technical form'. So 'additional capital formed in the course of accumulation attracts fewer and fewer labourers in proportion to its magnitude. On the other hand, the old capital periodically reproduced with change of composition, repels more and more of the labourers formerly employed by it.' (CI, 628)

The organic composition increases, 'and at an accelerated rate' with the centralisation of capital and technological changes. 'The intermediate pauses are shortened, in which accumulation works as simple extension of production, on a given technical basis' (CI, 629). At this point in the French edition Marx notes that the higher is the organic composition of capital, the more rapidly must accumulation proceed to maintain employment, 'but this more rapid progress itself becomes the source of new technical changes which further reduce the relative demand for labour' (MEGA, II.7, 552, my translation), and Marx goes on to consider circumstances under which the accumulation of capital can prove more favourable to the workers, but argues that such circumstances are increasingly exceptional. For example, Marx notes that the growth of the productivity of labour in the more advanced branches of production stimulates other branches of industry, which can lead to a considerable growth of employment if handicraft production still prevails in these branches. Nevertheless 'all these industries in turn pass through the technical transformation which adapts them to the modern mode of production' (MEGA II.7, 552).

Marx also recognises that 'there are intervals in which ... accumulation appears more as a movement of quantitative extension on the newly acquired technical basis', and so in which employment grows in proportion to capital. These are the circumstances under which a rise in wages becomes possible. As we saw above, a few pages earlier Marx indicated that the rate of accumulation would smoothly adjust to the rise in wages, but in the French edition he implicitly links it to crises. However, although the rise in wages might be the trigger that sets off the crisis, it is not the cause of the crisis. The crisis may be precipitated by the rise in wages because it is just at this point of overaccumulation that the system is most vulnerable to disruption. The crisis itself forces the capitalists to economise on labour and to transform their methods of production, creating the conditions for renewed accumulation.

> But, at the same time as the number of workers attracted to capital reaches its maximum, the products become so superabundant that the smallest obstacle to their sale can make the social mechanism appear to halt; the repulsion of labour by capital happens suddenly, on the largest scale and in the most violent manner; the disorder itself imposes on capitalists supreme efforts to economise on labour. Gradually accumulated improvements of detail are so to speak concentrated under this great pressure; they are incorporated in technical changes which revolutionise the composition of capital in all the branches surrounding the great spheres of production. It was in this way that the American Civil War pressed

The General Law of Capitalist Accumulation

the mill-owners to populate their workshops with more powerful machines and depopulate them of workers. Finally, the duration of these intervals in which accumulation is more favourable to the demand for labour progressively shortens. (MEGA II.7, 553) [7]

With the growing scale of capitalist production 'there is also an extension of the scale on which greater attraction of labourers by capital is accompanied by their greater repulsion; the rapidity of the change in the organic composition of capital, and in its technical form increases, and an increasing number of spheres of production becomes involved in this change, now simultaneously, now alternately. The labouring population therefore produces, along with the accumulation of capital produced by it, the means by which itself is made relatively superfluous, is turned into a relative surplus population; and it does this to an always increasing extent.' (CI, 631) [8]

This *industrial reserve army* becomes 'the lever of capitalistic accumulation, nay, a condition of existence of the capitalistic mode of production'. This is because the 'power of sudden expansion of capital grows ... not merely because the elasticity of the capital already functioning increases, not merely because the absolute wealth of the society expands, of which capital only forms an elastic part, not merely because credit, under every special stimulus, at once places an unusual part of this wealth at the disposal of production in the form of additional capital; it grows, also, because the technical conditions of the process of production themselves – machinery, means of transport, etc. — now admit of the rapidest transformation of masses of surplus-product into additional means of production.' As a result of the rapid growth of old and new branches of production 'there must be the possibility of throwing great masses of men suddenly on the decisive

---

[7] In Volume Three of *Capital* Marx sees the economy of labour as a direct result of the rise in wages, without the intervention of a crisis. 'A momentary excess of surplus-capital over the working population it has commandeered, would ..., by applying methods which yield relative surplus-value ... produce a far more rapid, artificial, relative over-population ... It therefore follows of itself from the nature of the capitalist process of accumulation, which is but one facet of the capitalist production process, that the increased mass of means of production that is to be converted into capital always finds a correspondingly increased, even excessive, exploitable worker population' (CIII, 214).

[8] The numbers employed are also reduced by intensification of labour, while they may be increased by employing a 'greater number of inferior labour-powers by displacement of higher'. Thus: 'The overwork of the employed part of the working-class swells the ranks of the reserve, whilst conversely the greater pressure that the latter by its competition exerts on the former, forces these to submit to over-work and to subjugation under the dictates of capital.' (CI, 635–6)

points without injury to the scale of production in other spheres. Overpopulation supplies these masses. The course characteristic of modern industry, viz., a decennial cycle ... depends on the constant formation, the greater or less absorption, and the re-formation of the industrial reserve army or surplus population' (CI, 632–3).

If there were no reserve army of labour, created by the expulsion of living labour with the increase in the organic composition of capital, then there would be no cycles, but only because the dynamism of capitalism would be extinguished. The cyclical course of accumulation is spelt out more fully in the French edition, which explicitly refers to the 'rejuvenating' role of crises as a normal part of the course of capitalist accumulation.

> If this system endows social capital with a power of sudden expansion, with a marvellous elasticity, it is because, spurred on by favourable opportunities, credit floods new capitals, whose owners, impatient to enlarge them, are permanently on the look-out for the favourable moment, into the production of extraordinary quantities of the growing social wealth; it is, on the other hand, that the technical resources of large scale industry permit both the sudden conversion of an enormous expansion of products into additional means of production, and to transport commodities more rapidly from one corner of the world to another. If the low price of these commodities at first opens up new outlets, and enlarges old ones, their superabundance little by little comes to constrict the general market to the point at which they are abruptly rejected. In this way commercial vicissitudes come to combine with the alternating movements of social capital which, in the course of its accumulation, now undergoes revolutions in its composition, now grows on the already acquired technical basis. All the influences work to provoke sudden expansions and contractions in the scale of production.
>
> The expansion of production in jerky movements is the first cause of its subsequent contraction; the latter it is true, provokes in its turn the former, but would the exorbitant expansion of production, which forms the point of departure, be possible without a reserve army at the disposal of capital? (MEGA II.7, 556)

The inherent tendency of the capitalist mode of production is to develop the forces of production without limit, a tendency that is imposed on every individual capitalist by the pressure of competition. The rapid

The General Law of Capitalist Accumulation

accumulation of capital is made possible by the availability of labour power and means of production, by the expansion of the world market, and by the development of the credit system. At a certain point one or another of these factors proves inadequate to maintaining the pace of accumulation, and competition between capitalists for markets and/or resources intensifies as profits come under pressure. Competitive failures may then rebound through the system to provoke a general crisis. The cause of the crisis appears to lie in the particular factor which triggered the crisis, which may be a shortage of labour power or raw materials, or the limitations of the market, or a tightening of credit, but which of these emerges as the immediate barrier to accumulation is a subsidiary issue to the fundamental determinant of the tendency to crisis, which is the tendency to the overaccumulation of capital in relation to the opportunities available to it.

Overaccumulation is inherent in the social form of capitalist production. In the wake of a crisis it appears that overaccumulation has been stimulated by the excessive expansion of credit that has made it possible, while the crisis appears to have been provoked by the contraction of credit required to bring accumulation back within the limits of profitability. However, while the expansion and contraction of credit makes the cyclical form of accumulation possible, it is an effect rather than a cause of the cycle. 'The superficiality of Political Economy shows itself in the fact that it looks upon the expansion and contraction of credit, which is a mere symptom of the periodic changes of the industrial cycle, as their cause.' (CI, 633)

Once the cycle begins, it is regularly repeated. 'Effects, in their turn, become causes, and the varying accidents of the whole process, which always reproduces its own conditions, take on the form of periodicity' (CI, 633). The French edition continues 'But it is only in the epoch in which mechanical industry, having grown deep roots, exerts a preponderant influence over the whole of national production; in which, thanks to this, foreign trade begins to prevail over internal trade, in which the universal market successively annexes vast territories in the New World, in Asia and in Australia; in which, finally, the industrial nations joining the fray have become sufficiently numerous, it is only from this epoch that the rejuvenating cycles date, cycles whose successive phases last for years and which always lead to a general crisis, the end of one cycle and the starting point of another.' (MEGA II.7, 557)

The Necessity of Crisis and the Periodicity of the Cycle

At first sight the theory of crisis appears only in the margins of Volume One of *Capital*, with the most extensive discussion appearing only in the French edition. However, the importance of this discussion is that it is the first time since the *Communist Manifesto* that Marx discusses crises in the context of his own analysis of the historical tendencies of capitalist accumulation, rather than in the context of his critique of political economy. For political economy crises were exceptional events, divorced from the normal course of accumulation, to be explained in terms of special circumstances. In developing an analysis of crisis through his critique of political economy Marx was to some extent forced to discuss the theory on political economy's own ground. But at the same time, as we have seen, Marx's critique always sought to relate the tendency to crisis back to the most fundamental tendencies of capitalist accumulation, in order to reconcile the apparently contingent causes of each individual crisis with their underlying necessity by showing that crises are only the most dramatic manifestation of the underlying contradictions of the capitalist system, and this is precisely the context in which they appear in Volume One of *Capital*.

The secular tendency of capitalist accumulation is to the development of the productivity of social labour through the development of the forces of production. This secular tendency is expressed in the rising organic composition of capital that expresses both the growth in productivity and the growth in scale of capitalist production. The historical tendency of capitalist accumulation is therefore a tendency to the concentration and centralisation of capital, to the development of the world market, and to the creation of a relative surplus population. The result is the generalisation of capitalist production on a world scale and the polarisation of class relations. But the course of capital accumulation is by no means smooth, but proceeds only through the mechanism of overaccumulation and crisis, in which precapitalist forms of production are displaced, backward capitals are bankrupted, outdated means of production destroyed, and the reserve army of labour replenished.

This analysis certainly reconciles the necessity of crisis with the contingency of explanation of any particular crisis. However, one fundamental feature of crises remains unexplained, which is their periodic character. We can understand that a period of overaccumulation necessarily culminates in a crisis, which prepares the way for a new burst of overaccumulation, but why should this alternation of boom and bust have an apparently regular periodicity? This brings us to two issues that Marx never discussed systematically in his work, but which are treated most fully in Volumes Two and Three of *Capital*, which are the role of credit and of fixed capital in the cycle.

Political economy explained the periodicity of the business cycle as a consequence of the periodicity of the credit cycle in which an over-expansion of credit is necessarily followed by its contraction. Marx was at great pains to recognise the important role of credit in the cycle, while at the same time seeking to show that this role was only an expression of the more fundamental contradictions of the capitalist mode of production. Against this account, Marx tentatively identified the replacement cycle of fixed capital as the basis of the periodicity of the business cycle. However, such a theory is at variance with the spirit of Marx's analysis, and is really a non-solution to a non-problem: it is by no means the case that the business cycle has a quasi-natural periodicity, so there is really nothing to explain.

Fixed Capital and the Periodicity of the Cycle

Marx considers the role of fixed capital in the cycle in Volume II of *Capital*, which was compiled by Engels from manuscripts most of which date from 1870 and 1877–8, and which is concerned with the relationship between production and circulation in the reproduction process of capital as a whole.

In the first part of Volume II Marx looks at the role of circulation within the reproduction process, in order to show that money and commodities are as much forms of capital within the reproduction process as are the labour power and means of production employed in production itself. At this stage in the analysis circulation is important not because it is the sphere in which commodity capital is realised in the form of money, since Marx still assumes that this realisation is unproblematic. Its importance is that circulation involves various costs, such as storage, transport and book-keeping, which constitute deductions from the surplus-value produced, and that it takes a certain amount of time, in which capital is locked up unproductively. The latter consideration leads Marx into the examination of the turnover of capital in the second part of Volume II.

The importance of the turnover of capital is quite straightforward.

The more rapidly a particular capital can complete its cycle of reproduction, the larger the scale of production that can be supported, and the greater the amount of surplus value that can be appropriated in a given time with a given capital. A capital which can complete two cycles in one year will appropriate twice as much surplus value as will a capital which can complete only one such cycle. The reduction of circulation time therefore provides a means of raising the rate of profit, without any increase in the rate of surplus value, while its increase will similarly reduce the rate of profit. This has obvious implications for the theory of the tendency for the rate of profit to fall, although Marx does not develop these implications here.

The analysis of the turnover of capital also introduces the distinction between fixed and circulating capital, which political economy confused with the quite different distinction between constant and variable capital. Fixed capital is investment in buildings, machines, etc., which last for longer than one turnover, while circulating capital is investment in labour power and raw materials which are immediately consumed in production.

Fixed capital has a twofold importance in the understanding of the tendency to crisis. First, fixed capital represents a portion of capital which is immobilised in a particular branch of production, and which can only be valorised over an extended period of time, and so is a barrier to the mobility of capital between branches of production in response to changes in relative values and consequently in the rate of profit in alternative employments. Second, investment in fixed capital is discontinuous. A capitalist has to accumulate the money required to pay for the investment over a particular period of time, which is then spent as a lump sum to buy machines, building etc. While the capitalist is accumulating money he is making sales without any corresponding purchases, when he makes his investment he is making purchases to which there are no immediately corresponding sales. This is the problem which Marx examined through his 'reproduction schemes'.

Marx saw the immobility of fixed capital as a part of the explanation of the periodicity of the cycle. We have seen that in his early works he believed that the duration of the cycle was about five to seven years, a view which he revised when the expected crisis did not strike in 1852 in favour of a normal duration of ten years. Marx first sought the key to the periodicity of the cycle in the turnover time of fixed capital in the *Grundrisse*, picking up on the ideas of Babbage, for which he sought confirmation from Engels.

Fixed Capital and the Periodicity of the Cycle

At the end of January 1858 Marx wrote to Engels that he had reached 'the circulation of capital — how it varies in various kinds of business, the effect of the same on profit and prices' (29.01.58, CW40, 256). In the course of this research Marx developed the idea that the cycle was connected with the replacement of fixed capital, and came upon Babbage's claim that the average reproduction time of machinery in England was five years, a figure which corresponded to Marx's earlier belief that the period of the cycle was five years, but not to the newly determined period of ten years. In the *Grundrisse* Marx noted Babbage's claimed average reproduction time of five years, adding that the 'real one' was 'hence perhaps ten years'. On this basis, he continued, 'there can be no doubt at all that the cycle through which industry has been passing in *plus ou moins* ten-year periods since the large-scale development of fixed capital, is linked with the *total reproduction phase of capital* determined in this way. We shall find other determining factors too, but this is one of them.' (CW29, 105)

Marx wrote to Engels to check, asking Engels how often machinery has to be replaced, doubting Babbage's five years and noting that 'the average period for the replacement of machinery is *one* important factor in explaining the multi-year cycle which had been a feature of industrial development ever since the consolidation of big industry' (02.03.58, CW40, 278). Engels replied at some length, arguing that Babbage's estimate was wrong, and even 'absurd' since nobody could afford to replace their machinery so frequently. Engels told Marx that it was normal to set aside 7 1/2% for depreciation, which implied a replacement cycle of thirteen years, although one can see twenty and thirty year old machines still working. Scrapping as a result of bankruptcies and breakdowns would shorten the period, so that Engels estimated a minimum of ten years as the length of the replacement period (04.03.58, CW40, 279–281).

Marx replied the next day with thanks. 'The figure of 13 years corresponds closely enough to the theory, since it establishes a *unit* for one epoch of industrial reproduction which *plus ou moins* coincides with the period in which major crises recur; needless to say their course is also determined by factors of a quite different kind, depending on their period of reproduction. For me the important thing is to discover, in the immediate material postulates of big industry, *one* factor that determines cycles' (05.03.58, CW40, 282).

In Volume Two of *Capital* Marx refers to this material foundation of the periodicity of the cycle once more, making it clear that what is in question is not the physical life of the machinery, but its 'moral depreciation' in the face of the 'constant revolutionizing of the means of production'. Marx continues to assume that the average duration of the cycle is ten years. 'The precise figure is not important here. The result is that the cycle of related turnovers, extending over a number of years, within which the capital is confined by its fixed component, is one of the material foundations for the periodic cycle [crisis] ... But a crisis is always the starting point of a large volume of new investment. It is also, therefore, if we consider the society as a whole, more or less a new material basis for the next turnover cycle' (CII, 264).

Later Marx fleshes out the argument in discussing an example of a boom which is provoked by an increase in investment. Capital is advanced to purchase means of production and means of subsistence, but it may be a considerable time before commodity equivalents come onto the market, so that for a period demand exceeds supply. This would create no problem in a communist society, which could plan in advance. 'In capitalist society, on the other hand, where any kind of social rationality asserts itself only *post festum*, major disturbances can and must occur constantly'. The demand for large-scale advances of capital, which may initially be stimulated by an easy money market, soon puts the money market under pressure. 'The other side of the coin is pressure on the society's available productive capital'. Prices rise, swindlers abound, overproduction is stimulated in branches in which production can be increased rapidly, and a speculative boom develops, which culminates in 'the inevitable crash' (CII, 390-1).

This part of the manuscript was written in 1870, at which time Marx still assumed, on the basis of the recurrence of crises in 1847, 1857 and 1867, that the period of the cycle was ten years. However, Marx did not regard this as a stable figure. In a letter to Engels in November 1864 Marx had noted that crises seemed to be gaining in frequency what they had lost in intensity (CW42, 19). In the French edition of *Capital*, which was revised after this part of the manuscript of Volume Two, Marx noted that the periods of boom, in which workers achieved higher wages, were becoming shorter (MEGA II.7, 553), and stressed that the period of the cycle was likely to shorten as the pace of technical progress increased. 'So far the period of these cycles has been ten or twelve years, but there is no reason to consider this a constant figure. On the contrary, one must infer from the laws of capitalist production, as we have just developed them, that it is variable

Fixed Capital and the Periodicity of the Cycle

and that the period of the cycles will gradually shorten' (MEGA, II.7, 557).

At this time the problem of the periodicity of crises was considerably exercising Marx. Since the late 1860s the neatness of the industrial cycle had broken down. While partial crises were becoming endemic, the general crisis never seemed to arrive. Although the relevant manuscripts have not been published, Marx wrote to Engels at the end of May 1873 about 'a problem which I have been wrestling with in private for a long time'. He had been examining 'tables which give prices, discount rate, etc. etc.'. 'I have tried several times — for the analysis of crises — to calculate these ups and downs as irregular curves, and thought (I still think that it is possible with enough tangible material) that I could determine the main laws of crises mathematically. Moore, as I say, considers the matter impracticable, and I have decided to give it up for the time being.' (31.05.73, CW44, 504)

Marx ended his Afterword to the Second German edition of Volume One of *Capital*, written in January 1873, with a prediction of a new crisis. 'The contradictions inherent in the movement of capitalist society impress themselves upon the practical bourgeois most strikingly in the changes of the periodic cycle, through which modern industry runs, and whose crowning point is the universal crisis. That crisis is once again approaching' (CI, 20), but during the following year his published writings and correspondence were once more preoccupied with the political impact not of an economic crisis, but of a European war, with its associated wave of political repression (e.g. CW45, 18, 30, 42).

In 1875 Marx wrote to Lavrov, drawing comfort from the increased frequency of crises : 'One truly remarkable phenomenon is the decrease in the number of years between general crises ... signs of its decrease are so palpable as to augur ill for the survival of the bourgeois world.' (18.06.75, CW45, 78)

Engels, on the other hand, seems to have had a somewhat different interpretation. In his own works he continued to refer to the ten year cycle well into the 1880s (CW45, 108–9 (1875); CW25, 464 (1876); CW24, 401, 412 (1881)).[9] In the 1875 French edition of *Capital* Engels added a note to the end of Marx's earlier Afterword to the Second German edition quoted above, which clearly distinguished between the

---
[9] In February 1886 Engels noted that in the 1840s it had seemed as though the cycle was 5 years, although it was actually ten, but since 1868 it has changed again (CW26, 404).

increasingly frequent partial crises, and the general explosion which was still awaited: 'Some time later the predicted crisis broke out in Austria, the United States and Germany. Many people erroneously believe that the general crisis has been discounted, so to speak, by these violent but partial explosions. On the contrary, it is tending to its apogee. England will be the seat of the central explosion, whose repercussions will be felt on the universal market' (MEGA II.7, 697).

Marx predicted this extension of the crisis to England in a note to the French edition of *Capital*. In 1878 he wrote to Danielson that 'the English crisis which I predicted on p. 351 of the French edition, note — has at last come to a head during the last few weeks' (15.11.78, CW45, 344), but it proved another damp squib, as Marx acknowledged in a letter to Danielson a few months later, in which he notes that however the crisis develops, 'it will pass over, like its predecessors, and initiate a new 'industrial cycle' with all its diversified phases' (10.04.79, CW45, 355).

By the mid 1880s the expected decennial general crisis had still not come, and Engels was clear that something had changed, but was not sure whether it was a matter of a lengthening of the cycle, or that the cycle had itself given way to general and permanent stagnation, albeit a stagnation which was bound ultimately to culminate in a great crisis. This theme recurs throughout Engels's writings in the last ten years of his life. 'A change has taken place here since the last major general crisis. The acute form of the periodic process, with its former ten-year cycle, appears to have given way to a more chronic, long drawn out, alternation between a relatively short and slight business improvement and a relatively long, indecisive depression — taking place in the various industrial countries at different times. But perhaps it is only a matter of a prolongation of the duration of the cycle. In the early years of world commerce, 1815–47, it can be shown that crises occurred about every five years; from 1847 to 1867 the cycle is clearly ten years; is it possible that we are now in the preparatory stage of a new world crash of unparalleled vehemence? Many things seem to point in this direction.' (CIII,477n)

The problem of the periodicity of the cycle would be a serious one, if Marx's theory of crisis was based on a theory of the investment cycle based on the replacement period of fixed capital, for it certainly was the case that by the 1870s the character of the cycle had changed. The industrial cycles of the middle of the nineteenth century had been dominated by one or two leading industrial sectors, particularly cotton

Fixed Capital and the Periodicity of the Cycle

and railways, and had been centred on Britain. As Marx and Engels realised, by the last quarter of the century capitalist production had extended to many more branches of production, and to many more centres of accumulation, one result being that the investment cycles in different countries and in different branches of production were no longer in phase with one another.[10] The diffusion of capitalist production had undermined any tendency to general crisis that might be based on the replacement cycle of fixed capital.

Quite apart from this difficulty, a theory which bases the periodicity of the cycle on the replacement period of fixed capital faces a fundamental theoretical problem, since the replacement period of fixed capital is itself determined by the periodicity of the cycle. As Marx noted, following Engels' advice, the machinery is physically capable of working for twenty or thirty years. Its retirement is determined not by its physical but by its 'moral' depreciation. One feature of the crisis is the massive devaluation of capital, and a corresponding addition to the 'moral depreciation' of fixed capital, which results in the widespread scrapping of plant and machinery. It is therefore the period of the crisis which determines the replacement period of fixed capital, and not the other way around. This means that 'the industrial cycle is of such a nature that the same circuit must periodically reproduce itself, once the first impulse has been given' (CIII, 477).

Although Marx referred to the replacement period of fixed capital as providing the 'material foundation' of the periodicity of the cycle, he did always acknowledge that the replacement period is only one factor underlying the periodicity of the crisis, and he never provided even a suggestion of an explanation for crises based on the replacement cycle. In fact the discussion in Volume Two of *Capital* develops in a quite different direction.[11]

---

[10] Engels added a note to Volume III of *Capital*, noting that by the 1890s the expansion of means of transportation and communication had made the world market a fact, producing challenges to the former English monopoly and more fields for investment of European surplus capital, 'so that it is far more widely distributed and local over-speculation may be more easily overcome. By means of all this, most of the old breeding-grounds of crises and opportunities for their development have been eliminated or strongly reduced', but only to be replaced by new factors which lead to an intensification of competition for world markets, the formation of monopolies, trusts and protective tariffs. 'But these protective tariffs are nothing but preparations for the ultimate general industrial war, which shall decide who has supremacy on the world-market. Thus every factor, which works against a repetition of the old crises, carries within itself the germ of a far more powerful future crisis' (CIII, 477n.).

[11] Although many Marxists, from Hilferding to Mandel, have attributed a fundamental role to the replacement of fixed capital in the cycle there is nothing specifically Marxist in such

Fixed Capital and the Problem of Reproduction

In Part III of volume II Marx moves beyond the consideration of the 'individual capital ... [as] an autonomous part of the social capital', to explore the ways in which 'the circuits of individual capitals are interlinked, they presuppose one another and condition one another, and it is precisely by being interlinked in this way that they constitute the movement of the total social capital' (CII, 429). He is still not looking at *particular* capitals, but at the 'collective capitalist', where 'the total capital appears as the share capital of all individual capitalists together' (CII, 509), nor is he looking at competition and credit, so it is not yet the time to develop the theory of crisis. Nevertheless the discussion is very relevant to the interpretation of Marx's crisis theory because it is focused on the problem of the realisation of the increased value embodied in the commodity product, which Marx had already discussed at length in the 1861–3 manuscripts.

In Part III Marx departs from the '*assumption* that the individual capitalist first converts the components of his capital into money by selling his commodity product, and can then transform this back into productive capital by repurchasing his elements of production on the commodity market. ...The immediate form in which the problem presents itself is this. How is the *capital* consumed in production replaced in its value out of the annual product, and how is the movement of this replacement intertwined with the consumption of surplus value by the capitalists and of wages by the workers?' (CII, 469)

Marx looks first at 'reproduction on a simple scale. Moreover, we assume not only that products are exchanged at their values, but also that no revolution in values takes place in the components of productive capital' (CII, 469). Thus Marx is not concerned yet with the concrete reality of capitalist reproduction, but at this stage at the conditions of *possibility* of such reproduction. Marx demonstrates this possibility through his 'reproduction schemes', a development of Quesnay's *tableau économique*, which shows the conditions of proportionality which must be met to permit the simple and expanded reproduction of capital.

---

an account, which was popular amongst bourgeois economists, such as Schumpeter, in the inter-war period. As Marx noted, even in his day 'a disproportionate production of fixed and circulating capital is a factor much favoured by the economists in their explanation of crises' (CII, 545). Keynesian theories of the investment cycle, which largely displaced theories of the replacement cycle, are quite different because they do not rest on the physical replacement of fixed capital.

Fixed Capital and the Problem of Reproduction

Marx first developed a simple reproduction scheme in the *Grundrisse* (CW28, 370–5), which was designed to address the problem of the realisation of surplus value through the sale of the increased product, in response to Proudhon's crude underconsumptionist thesis that the source of crisis lay in the existence of such a surplus. In that discussion Marx established that there is no problem in principle in realising the surplus value, the corresponding commodities being exchanged amongst the capitalists to serve as means of consumption and as additional means of production and labour power as the basis for the expansion of their capital. 'The valorisation consists in each capitalist exchanging his own product for a fractional part of the products of the other four, and this in such a way that a part of the surplus product is destined for the consumption of the capitalist, and a part is converted into surplus capital with which to set new labour in motion. The valorisation consists in the *real possibility* of greater valorisation — the production of new and larger values' (CW28, 371). In *Theories of Surplus Value* Marx reiterated this argument in his criticism of Smith and Malthus (TSV1, 106, 221–2; TSV2, 485).

Marx developed a much more elaborate version of the reproduction scheme towards the end of his 1861–3 manuscript (MEGA II, 3.6, 2243–80), of which he sent a copy to Engels for his comment in a letter of 6th July 1863. This adaptation of Quesnay's scheme developed out of Marx's critique of Adam Smith's neglect of constant capital in reducing the national product to the revenues of wages, rent and profit, ignoring that component which serves to replace the means of production used up during the year, and was the basis of the discussion of reproduction in Part Three of Volume Two of *Capital*. In the latter text Marx presents a much more extensive and systematic treatment of the proportional relations between the various branches of production which are necessary if reproduction is to be sustained, looking not only at the physical and value relationships between the branches of production, but also at the implications of these relationships for the circulation of money.

The problem of reproduction arises in relation to the realisation of the surplus value. We have already seen that surplus value is realised through the exchange of commodities between the capitalists, but this raises the question posed in the *Grundrisse*, where does the money come from to achieve this exchange? The capitalist throws more commodities into circulation than he originally withdrew, which means, from the opposite point of view, that he withdraws more money from circulation than he originally threw in. He originally threw a sum of money into circulation to buy means of production and labour power, but he ends the process with a sum of money which is greater to the extent of his realised surplus value. Where does this additional money come from? Marx argued that this is a false problem, for it is merely the other side of the problem of realisation of the surplus value, which is already resolved. 'The only requirement for the realisation of this higher value is that it should find an equivalent in circulation.' (CW33, 189).[12]

If the capitalists want to hoard their surplus value, rather than spend it on increased consumption and investment, they do so by buying gold, which means that gold production must be correspondingly increased.[13] In general their surplus value is not hoarded, but reinvested in buying labour power and means of production, in which case all that is required is a sufficient increase in the supply of money to meet the needs of increased circulation, so that, if we leave out credit money, there must be some gold production, but 'nothing more is necessary than that enough money should circulate in order to pay the commodity values' (CW33, 208).

In his consideration of monetary circulation in *Capital* Marx reiterates these arguments (CII, 404–13), concluding that '*the problem itself does not exist.* ... a definite sum of money is required to circulate the commodity value ... quite irrespective of how much or how little of this value accrues to the direct producers of these commodities. In as much as a problem does exist here, it coincides with the general problem: where does the sum of money needed in a country for the circulation of commodities come from' (CII, 407; c.f. 549–56). There *seems* to be a problem because the 'the capitalist class as a whole ... must itself cast into circulation the money needed to realise its surplus value', but this proposition 'is not only far from paradoxical, it is in fact a necessary condition of the overall mechanism' (CII, 497).

The transition from simple to expanded reproduction creates no additional difficulties, because it simply involves a transfer of productive resources from producing means of consumption to the production of

---

[12] As we have seen, Marazzi (1984) argues that this problem of the source of the additional money required to realise the surplus value lay at the heart of Rosa Luxemburg's underconsumptionist theory of crisis, which was based on Marx's reproduction schemes.

[13] Marx raised the problem of what will happen if capitalists want to increase their savings without there being any increase in gold production, asking to whom the corresponding commodities would be sold in this case, but consideration of this point is postponed (CW 33, 238).

Fixed Capital and the Problem of Reproduction

means of production (CII, 572–3),[14] so that all that is required is 'that the quantity of money existing in the country ... is sufficient both for active circulation and for the reserve hoards, — i.e. the same condition that ... has to be fulfilled for simple commodity circulation' (CII, 576), the only difference being that growing production requires a growing supply of the means of circulation. The issue is always the same: not 'where does the money come from?', but 'do equivalent commodities exist in the appropriate form?'

The principal problem which arises in considering the reproduction of capital as a whole is not that of the availability of money, but that of reconciling the proportionality of production with the existence of fixed capital. The problem is that fixed capital investment is discontinuous, so that the demand for new means of production varies from one year to another. In the case of simple reproduction Marx considers this problem in relation to the proportionality of the branches of production 'quite independent of the monetary relation' (CII, 543), and notes that there would be no problem if fixed investment occurred at a constant annual rate, so that the proportions between the branches of production would be constant year-by-year, but in any other circumstances the 'lumpiness' of fixed investment will create problems of disproportionality. In this case 'there would be a crisis — a crisis of production — despite reproduction on a constant scale' (CII, 543).

The deficiencies could be made good by increasing productivity, but this would still involve 'a shift of labour from one branch of production to another ... and any displacement of this kind would produce momentary dislocations'. Foreign trade could also help. 'But foreign trade, in so far as it does not just replace elements (and their value), only shifts the contradictions to a broader sphere, and gives them a wider orbit' (CII, 544). This kind of over-production would not create a problem in a planned economy, 'within capitalist society, however, it is an anarchic element' (CII, 545).

The problem so far is one of the anarchy of capitalist production, and the emergence of disproportionalities between the branches of production. However there is an additional problem raised by the existence of fixed capital. The capitalist accumulates money over a period of years, which he then spends as a lump sum in a fixed

---

[14] This way of looking at it can give rise to the idea that 'accumulation is achieved at the expense of consumption — ... an illusion that contradicts the essence of capitalist production, in as much as it assumes that the purpose and driving motive of this is consumption, and not the grabbing of surplus-value and its capitalization, i.e. accumulation' (CII, 579).

capital investment. This means there is a period in which money is being withdrawn from circulation, and so not used to purchase equivalent commodities, and then a point at which it is thrown back into circulation, without there being any equivalent production.[15]

If all capitalists were hoarding money in this way 'it seems impossible to explain where the buyers are to come from, since in this process — and it must be conceived as a general one, in as much as every individual capital may be simultaneously engaged in the act of accumulation — everyone wants to sell in order to hoard, and no one wants to buy'. The only solution, given such an absurd assumption, would be for there to be new gold production equal to the entire annual surplus product (CII, 567). However, in practice some capitalists are hoarding in anticipation of future investment, while others are disgorging their hoards to make new investment, and if the two sides match, reproduction can be sustained, although 'this balance exists only on the assumption that the values of the one-sided purchases and the one-sided sales cover each other' (CII, 570).

If this assumption is violated, and there is no *a priori* reason why it should hold, then barriers to realisation will arise as proportionality breaks down, and we find the coexistence of relative over-production in one department of production, and the accumulation of money in the other (CII, 578–9). This tendency to breakdown is a specifically capitalist phenomenon. What has happened is that money is no longer playing a role only as the means of circulation 'but also as money capital within the circulation sphere, and gives rise to certain conditions ... for the normal course of reproduction, ... which turn into an equal number of conditions for an abnormal course, possibilities of crisis, since, on the basis of the spontaneous pattern of this production, this balance is itself an accident ... The very complexity of the process provides many occasions for it to take an abnormal course.' (CII, 571)

The discussion of reproduction in Volume Two of *Capital* makes it clear that the relationship between fixed capital and the tendency to crisis is not a matter of the physical life of fixed capital, but of the

---

[15] Marx wrote to Engels about the problem of the reproduction of fixed capital in August 1867, recalling their correspondence of four years earlier, and asking what manufacturers do with the money they set aside to cover depreciation. Engels replied with two examples, in one of which the capitalist accumulates the depreciation fund in the form of savings, and spends it as a lump sum to replace the fixed capital after a certain period, and in the other the capitalist uses the money set aside for depreciation to renew a portion of the fixed capital every year (Marx to Engels 24.08.67. Engels to Marx, 26.08.67, 27.08.67).

disproportionalities between branches of production that arise as a result of the temporal unevenness of capital investment. Marx is clearly moving towards a theory of the investment cycle, in which a burst of investment in the boom stimulates inflation and disproportionalities, which in turn provoke speculation and monetary instability, while the crash sees a massive liquidation of fixed capital which eventually lays the foundation for recovery. However, Marx cannot take the analysis further at this stage, primarily because the problem of fixed capital and the investment cycle is linked to the problem of credit, which he has not yet considered. In the early stages of development of capitalist production the capitalist might withdraw money from circulation in the form of gold in order to accumulate a fund to replace fixed capital. However, the development of credit institutions allows the capitalist to deposit this fund in the bank, which can use it as the basis for extending credit to other capitalists. The relationship between depreciation and investment in fixed capital is therefore mediated through the credit system.

Credit and the Investment Cycle

We have seen that throughout his notebooks Marx repeatedly postpones consideration of crises until he reaches the analysis of competition and credit. In Volume III of *Capital* Marx turns to the process of capitalist production as a whole, as 'the synthesis of the processes of production and circulation' already examined in Volumes I and II. This is not simply a synthesis of the preceding material, but aims to 'locate and describe the concrete forms which grow out of the *movements of capital as a whole.* ...The various forms of capital, as evolved in this book, thus approach step by step the form which they assume on the surface of society, in the action of different capitals upon one another, in competition, and in the ordinary consciousness of the agents of production themselves' (CIII, 25). However, although Volume Three of *Capital* moves towards the analysis of competition, it does not actually get there, so that the detailed analysis of crisis is still postponed. The discussion of credit is equally rudimentary.

Despite the importance of credit in the crisis, theoretical discussion of credit in Marx's works is to be found only in asides in the *Grundrisse, Theories of Surplus Value,* and *Capital.* This is primarily because Marx did not regard credit as introducing any fundamentally new determinations of the process of capitalist production and accumulation. Throughout Volume Two of *Capital*, although Marx notes that the growth of credit 'increases ... the artificial character of the entire machinery and the chances of its normal course being disturbed' (CII, 576), he argues that 'it is important above all, however, to start by assuming metal circulation in its most simple original form, since in this way the flux or reflux, settlement of balances, in short all those aspects that appear in the credit system as consciously regulated processes, present themselves as existing independently of the credit system, and the thing appears in its spontaneous form, instead of the form of subsequent reflection' (CII, 576-7). Crises appear to the bourgeois economist to be features of the system of money and credit, but 'what appears as a crisis on the money market in actual fact expresses anomalies in the production and reproduction process itself' (CII, 393).

In the *Grundrisse* Marx generally assumed that the producer sold directly to the consumer, although in practice he knew that the productive capitalist sells to the commercial capitalist, who buys the commodity in anticipation of final sale, for credit. Credit accordingly suspends the barrier of the market. 'It appears to be a matter of chance for production based on capital, whether or not its essential condition, the continuity of the various processes which constitute the totality of its process, is fulfilled. The transcendence of this element of chance through capital itself is *credit*'. In this capacity credit is merely extending the role of money in separating the moments of purchase and sale, since 'money itself is a form for suspending the unevenness of the times required in different branches of production, to the extent that this obstructs exchange' (CW28, 459).

Credit solves the problem of realisation for the individual capitalist, but it cannot create a commodity equivalent where that does not already exist. Credit does not resolve the contradictions of the commodity form, it merely generalises them. 'Money transcends the barriers imposed by barter only by making them general, i.e. by entirely separating purchase and sale from one another. Later we shall see that *credit* likewise transcends these barriers to the valorisation of capital only by elevating them to their most general form, by positing the periods of overproduction and underproduction as two periods.' (CW29, 12)

In the same way it is credit that oils the wheels of competition, by promoting the free flow of capital between branches of production in accordance with divergences in the rate of profit. In this way each individual capital is re-constituted as a component part of the total social capital, the equalisation of the rate of profit allowing each to share in the gains of capital as a whole in proportion to the size of the capital employed.[16] '*Credit* therefore is the means by which the capital of the whole capitalist class is placed at the disposal of each sphere of production, not in proportion to the capital belonging to the capitalists in the given sphere but in proportion to their production requirements — whereas in competition the individual capitals appear to be independent of each other. Credit is both the result and the condition of capitalist production and this provides us with a convenient transition from the *competition between capitals* to *capital as credit.*' (TSV2, 211)

This is a particularly important function in those branches of production which require large capital outlays. 'Production in these branches is therefore dependent on the extent of the money-capital which the individual capitalist has at his disposal. This limit is overcome by the credit system and the forms of association related to, e.g., joint-stock companies' (CII, 433).

In credit 'one part of capital - in the form of moneyed capital, appears in fact to be the material common to the whole class and employed by it' (TSV3, 519), and so minimises the unproductive hoarding of capital. Credit concentrates the money hoards of the various capitalists in the bank and makes them active (CII, 569). 'The surplus product ... is ... absolutely unproductive in its monetary metamorphosis ... It is a "dead weight" on capitalist production. The attempt to make use of this surplus-value that is being hoarded up as virtual money capital, either for profit or for revenue, culminates in the credit system and "papers". In this way money capital maintains an enormous influence in another form on the course of the capitalist system of production and its prodigious development.' (CII, 574)

Credit benefits the individual capitalist, by reducing the circulation time of the productive capital, and it economises in the need for money by holding the money capital of the capitalist class as a whole in a common pool, but it also has an independent influence, overcoming the immediate barrier of the market, but only to generalise and intensify the crisis tendencies of capitalist accumulation. The expansion of

---

[16] 'The social character of capital is first promoted and wholly realised through the full development of the credit and banking system' etc (CIII, 593).

credit is therefore an expression of the tendency to overproduction, which it in turn reinforces, so that 'banking and credit thus become the most potent means of driving capitalist production beyond its own limits, and one of the most effective vehicles of crises and swindle' (CIII, 593).

'The whole *credit system*, and the over-trading, over-speculation, etc., connected with it, rest upon the necessity to extend the range of, and to overcome the barrier to, circulation and exchange. ...Thus e.g. Englishmen compelled to *lend* to foreign nations to have them as their customers.' (CW28, 343) The credit system arises 'out of the difficulty of employing capital ...profitably'. 'Over-production, the credit system, etc., are means by which capitalist production seeks to break through its own barriers and to produce over and above its own *limits*. Capitalist production, on the one hand, has this driving force; on the other hand, it only tolerates production commensurate with the profitable employment of existing capital. Hence crises arise, which simultaneously drive it onward and beyond [its own limits] and force it to put on seven-league boots, in order to reach a development of the productive forces which could only be achieved very slowly within its own limits.' (TSV3, 122)

In Volume Three of *Capital* Marx notes that the separation of merchant's capital increases the chances of overproduction, since

> under the modern credit system it disposes of a large portion of the total social money-capital, so that it can repeat its purchases even before it has definitely sold what has previously been purchased. ...In spite of its independent status, the movement of merchant's capital is never more than the movement of industrial capital within the sphere of circulation. But by virtue of its independent status it moves, within certain limits, independently of the bounds of the reproduction process and thereby even drives the latter beyond its bounds. This internal dependence and external independence push merchant's capital to a point where the internal connection is violently restored through a crisis. Hence the phenomenon that crises do not come to the surface, do not break out, in the retail business first, which deals with direct consumption, but in the spheres of wholesale trade, and of banking, which places the money-capital of society at the disposal of the former. (CIII, 299)

Marx argues that the ultimate limit of the stimulation of capital accumulation by the expansion of credit is set by the market for final

Credit and the Investment Cycle

consumption. The circulation of constant capital against constant capital 'is at first independent of individual consumption because it never enters the latter. But this consumption definitely limits it nevertheless, since constant capital is never produced for its own sake but solely because more of it is needed in spheres of production whose products go into individual consumption' (CIII, 299–300).

Credit performs various functions for the capitalist, but it does not add any new determinations. While inappropriate monetary and credit policies can certainly exacerbate a crisis, the monetary crisis is only the form of appearance of a crisis which has more fundamental roots. 'As long as the social character of labour appears as the *money-existence* of commodities, and thus as a *thing* external to actual production, money crises — independent of or as an intensification of actual crises — are inevitable.' (CIII, 504) The fundamental question is 'to what extent does the accumulation of capital in the form of loanable money-capital coincide with actual accumulation' (CIII, 482).

'It is clear that there is a shortage of means of payment during a period of crisis. The convertibility of bills of exchange replaces the metamorphosis of commodities themselves ... Ignorant and mistaken bank legislation, such as that of 1844-5, can intensify this money crisis. But no kind of bank legislation can eliminate a crisis. In a system of production, where the entire continuity of the reproduction process rests upon credit, a crisis must obviously occur ... when credit suddenly ceases and only cash payments have validity. At first glance, therefore, the whole crisis seems to be merely a credit and money crisis. And in fact it is only a question of the convertibility of bills of exchange into money. But the majority of these bills represent actual sales and purchases, whose extension far beyond the needs of society is, after all, the basis of the whole crisis', an extension which is exaggerated by all manner of swindles and speculation (CIII, 478).

Similarly, a monetary crisis may appear to be provoked by a crisis in the system of international payments, as an imbalance of trade provokes a drain on the reserves and a consequent contraction of the currency, but this is only an expression of an imbalance in the system of global production which is itself a symptom of a general overproduction. 'It should be noted in regard to imports and exports, that, one after another, all countries become involved in a crisis and that it then becomes evident that all of them, with few exceptions, have exported and imported too much, so that *they all have an unfavourable balance of payments*. The trouble, therefore, does not actually lie with the balance of payments. ... The balance of payments is in times of general crisis unfavourable to every nation, at least to every commercially developed nation, but always to each country in succession, as in volley firing.' (CIII, 479–81)

It appears that over-production has been stimulated by an overexpansion of credit, which has expanded the trade between capitalists beyond the level demanded by the consumers. This leads the bourgeois economists to see the phenomenon of overaccumulation and crisis as a monetary phenomenon, which can be controlled by a sufficiently rigourous monetary policy.

'The credit system appears as the main lever of over-production and over-speculation in commerce solely because the reproduction process, which is elastic by nature, is here forced to its extreme limits, and is so forced because a large part of the social capital is employed by people who do not own it and who consequently tackle things quite differently than the owner, who anxiously weighs the limitations of his private capital in so far as he handles it himself. This simply demonstrates the fact that the self-expansion of capital based on the contradictory nature of capitalist production permits an actual free development only up to a certain point, so that it constitutes an immanent fetter and barrier to production, which are continually broken through by the credit system.' (CIII, 431–2)

We return to the conclusion with which Marx began his exploration of crises in the *Grundrisse*. While a restrictive monetary policy might be able to curb the wildest excesses of speculation, it cannot contain the tendency to overaccumulation and crisis, which is the necessary form of the dynamics of capitalist accumulation.

9
Conclusion

The conclusions which we have to draw from our long exploration of Marx's theory of crisis are more methodological than substantive.

The most fundamental conclusion is that Marx did not have a theory of crisis, in the sense that such a theory has come to play a role within Marxism. The catastrophic crises that periodically disrupt accumulation are only the most superficial manifestations of the fundamental contradiction of the capitalist mode of production. However, the tendency to crisis is pervasive, since the competitive regulation of capital accumulation is not achieved by the smooth anticipation of market adjustments by omniscient capitalists, but by the process of overaccumulation and crisis, as the tendency to overproduction runs into the barrier of the limited market. In this sense Marx's theory of crisis lies at the heart of his critique of political economy, replacing the classical theory of competition with whose critique Marx and Engels began their explorations in political economy.

The problem of the Marxist theory of crisis was first raised by Bernstein's challenge to the orthodox Marxism of the Second International, when Bernstein insisted that Marx's economics did not lead to revolutionary conclusions, and in particular that it did not imply the inevitability of capitalist breakdown. The importance of Bernstein's critique was that Bernstein was not just a revisionist critic of Marxism. He, with Kautsky, was Engels's literary executor, the officially endorsed guardian of Marxist orthodoxy, so that his was a critique from within, a frank admission that Marxism had lost its revolutionary content.

Bernstein's critique was possible because the revolutionary content of Marx's theory had indeed been watered down, as Marx's ideas were integrated into other political and theoretical traditions. The reaction to Bernstein's apostasy was not to recover the revolutionary core of Marx's critique of capitalism, but to assert, or to attempt to prove, the inevitability of crisis. The revolutionary aspect of Marx's theory was thus detached from its core, and was condensed into the theory of crisis as the exceptional event, the culmination of history. At the same time Kautsky, Hilferding and Luxemburg laid the foundations for the reabsorption of Marx's economics back into the framework of bourgeois economic theory, so that Marxism no longer laid claim to the terrain of 'economics', but came to exist only in the shadowy world of 'political economy', or even, ghastly fate, of 'sociology'.

For Marx crises were not the ultimate truth of capitalism, nor were they the culmination of history. Crises were the superficial and transient expression of the most fundamental contradiction of the capitalist mode of production. But at the same time the tendency to crisis is inherent in every aspect of the everyday reality of capitalist social existence: 'Constant revolutionising of production, uninterrupted disturbance of all social conditions, everlasting uncertainty and agitation distinguish the bourgeois epoch from all earlier ones' (*Communist Manifesto*, CW6, 487). This turmoil is not something whose possibility economics has to prove, it is something whose actuality economics has to explain.

To insist that Marx had no theory of crisis is to insist that the focus of Marx's work is not the crisis as catastrophic event, but the inherent tendency to crisis that underlies the permanent instability of social existence under capitalism. From this perspective Marx is the first and the most radical theorist of the 'post-modern' condition, a condition whose novelty has only just struck the metropolitan capitalist intelligentsia, but which has afflicted the proletariat since the beginning of capitalism. However, Marx does not offer us a philosophical discourse on post-modernity, but a scientific account of the contradictory foundations of modern society.

The possibility of crisis is already inherent in the separation of purchase and sale and the development of money as means of payment, which are the distinguishing features of the circulation of the products of human labour as commodities. Production is no longer oriented directly to human need, but takes the alienated form of the production and circulation of commodities as values. However, there is no inherent reason why the regulation of production by the competitive interaction of supply and demand should not tend towards an equilibrium, while the exchange of commodities as values simply mediates the social relations between petty commodity producers, each producing in order to meet his or her own reproduction needs. If, like bourgeois economics, we develop our model of capitalism on the basis of an ideal characterisation of petty commodity production, it is not

Conclusion

surprising that we find that any crisis tendencies are purely accidental. It is equally unsurprising that we cannot explain the dynamic character of capitalism, except as a feature of the subjective motivation of the capitalist.

The distinctive feature of the capitalist system is not the market economy, but a system of production in which the production of things is subordinated to the production, appropriation and accumulation of surplus value. The transformation of the social relations of production from those of petty production to those of capitalist production involves a fundamental transformation in the dynamics of economic development, since it detaches the production of things from the need for the product. It is not simply that the motive of the capitalist is to produce values in order to appropriate a profit. The decisive point is that of the means by which the capitalist is able to appropriate a profit.

Once the capitalist has taken command of production, the characteristic way in which the capitalist appropriates a profit is not by responding to fluctuations in demand for the product, but by introducing new and more productive methods of production in order to reduce his costs below those of his competitors. The capitalist who is able to reduce his costs is not confined by the limits of his share of the market, but can expand his production without limit in the anticipation of undercutting his competitors. The tendency to expand production without limit is not just a matter of the subjective motivation of the capitalist, since it is imposed on every capitalist by the pressure of competition.

The tendency to overproduction cannot be checked by competition, since competition is not an external force imposed on each individual capitalist from without. Competition presupposes over-production, since capitalists only experience competitive pressure when the product is greater than the amount that can be sold at a price corresponding to the price of production. Competition is simply the form in which over-production is experienced by each individual capitalist. Thus competition is simultaneously the cause and the result of over-production, and in this sense is the superficial expression of the tendency to over-production which is inherent in the social form of capitalist production.

Ultimately the products of capital have to be sold to a final consumer, either as means of consumption or as means of production. It is only at this point that capitalist production comes up against the barrier of the market. However, the market does not constitute a limit to which production adapts itself, as capitalists respond to the pressure of competition by cutting back production. On the one hand, the pressure of competition itself presupposes over-production and so can only operate as a more or less effective counter-tendency to the tendency to overproduction. On the other hand, the limit which confronts the capitalist is not the limit of the market, but the limit of profitability. The capitalist will persist in expanding production for as long as he anticipates that he will be able to realise a profit, either by further reducing the cost of production, or by opening up new markets. The dynamism of the capitalist mode of production derives precisely from the fact that capitalist production is not confined within the limits of the market, but regards those limits as no more than a barrier to be overcome. The tendency to overproduction is therefore inseparable from the accumulation of capital, which necessarily takes the form of overaccumulation and crisis.

Overaccumulation and crisis is the normal form of capitalist accumulation which marks the development of every branch of capitalist production, as well as of the capitalist system as a whole. The driving force of capitalism is the tendency to develop the forces of production without limit. Within any particular branch of production competitive pressure increases as the tendency to overproduction confronts the limits of the market. As the price falls the producers face a fall in the realised rate of profit, compounded by the devaluation of their stocks of finished products and fixed capital, to which they can only respond by attempting to reduce their costs of production. This they do in the first instance by intensifying labour and extending the working day in order to increase the output of their existing plant, by forcing down wages, laying off workers, running down stocks of raw materials, and delaying payment to creditors and suppliers. In the longer term the only secure route to survival is to introduce new methods of production. However, these measures relieve the pressure on the individual capitalist only to exacerbate the pressure within the system as a whole, by increasing production on the one hand, and reducing expenditure, which ultimately translates into demand for other capitalists, on the other.

The attempt to relieve the pressure of competition simply intensifies the overaccumulation of capital, until the point at which the more backward capitalists are liquidated, with the devaluation of their capital, destruction of productive capacity, redundancy of workers and default on their debts. This liquidation may be sufficient to relieve the pressure on the other capitalists by removing surplus capacity and/or by freeing scarce raw materials and labour power for more productive use. On the other hand, it may precipitate a chain of defaults and a generalisation of the crisis, so that the crisis of overproduction in one branch of production precipitates a general crisis of overproduction.

The tendency for accumulation to take the form of overaccumulation and crisis is common to every branch of capitalist production. However, the tendency is realised unevenly in different branches of production. The primary determinant of the development of the forces of production in any particular branch of production is the opportunity to achieve a surplus profit by the introduction of new methods of production. At any particular time such opportunities are unevenly developed between the various branches of production, which therefore would tend to expand at different rates. However, the expansion of any one branch of production creates a market for all of the others. This means that when we consider the accumulation of capital as a whole we expect to find that the pace of accumulation is determined by the development of the more dynamic branches of production, which drag the less dynamic branches of production along behind them.[1]

Although the tendency to overproduction is equally characteristic of all branches of production, this tendency appears in the form of the uneven development of the various branches of production, with the more dynamic branches of production providing the driving force of accumulation, but at the same time being those in which the tendency to overproduction is most highly developed. Disproportionality is therefore the necessary form of capitalist development, as the expression of the tendency to overproduction that is the driving force of capitalist accumulation. However this does not mean that Marx's analysis of capitalism leads inexorably to a disproportionality theory of crisis, and indeed, although most of Marx's discussion, and virtually all his substantive examples, related to disproportionality, he never explicitly endorsed disproportionality as the ultimate cause of crises.

Marx devoted a great deal of space to discussing the relationship between disproportionality and general overproduction, without finally clarifying the issue to his own satisfaction. On the one hand, Marx clearly established that the distinction made by political economy between 'partial' and 'general' overproduction was spurious, since the

---

[1] I develop this interpretation more fully as the basis of an historical account of the development of capitalism in *Keynesianism, Monetarism and the Crisis of the State* (Clarke, 1988b).

latter was merely the generalisation of the former. On the other hand, Marx clearly established that provided that proportional relationships between the branches of production and the components of capital are maintained, then there is no reason why there should be a crisis of general overproduction. However this does not mean that disproportionality *necessarily* gives rise to a crisis of general overproduction. Nevertheless the disproportional and uneven development of capitalism makes capitalism vulnerable to general crisis.

For Marx disproportionality may be the proximate cause of the crisis, but it is not the ultimate cause. Whenever Marx had to characterise the ultimate cause of the crisis he tended to do so in what appear to be unambiguously underconsumptionist terms, pointing to the contradiction between the tendency to develop the productive forces without limit and the limited consumption power of the mass of the population. In his early work there is little doubt that Marx adhered to such an underconsumptionist theory of crisis, to which Engels remained attached for the whole of his life. However, as we have just noted, in his later manuscripts, although he endorsed Malthus and Sismondi against Ricardo, Marx was clear that the limited consumption of the workers could not be the cause of the crisis. However, the social form of capitalist production was the underlying condition for crises. On the one hand, the limited consumption power of the mass of the population corresponds to the growing mass of surplus value that has to be realised through the sale of the surplus product to other capitalists, as the means for the renewed accumulation of capital. This growing divorce of production from consumption therefore makes capitalism increasingly vulnerable to crisis. On the other hand, the subordination of the production of things to the production and appropriation of surplus value is the ultimate cause of all crises, since the crisis arises not when production has developed beyond the limits of consumption, but when it has developed beyond the limits of profitability.

> If we disregard 'sham transactions and speculations', 'a crisis could only be explained as the result of a disproportion in various branches of the economy, and as a result of a disproportion between the consumption of the capitalists and their accumulation. But as matters stand, the replacement of the capital invested in production depends largely upon the consuming power of the non-producing classes; while the consuming power of the workers is limited partly by the laws of wages, partly by the fact that they are

Conclusion

used only as long as they can be profitably employed by the capitalist class. The ultimate reason for all real crises always remains the poverty and restricted consumption of the masses as opposed to the drive of capitalist production to develop the productive forces as though only the absolute consuming-power of society constituted their limit.' (CIII, 472–3)

The debate that has dominated Marxism between disproportionality theories, underconsumptionist theories, and falling rate of profit theories of crisis has really been a red herring. A crisis arises when capitalists face a fall in their realised profit which can arise for all manner of reasons, but the precipitating cause of any particular crisis is inconsequential. Although all three aspects of disproportionality, underconsumptionist and the tendency for the rate of profit to fall play a role in determining the vulnerability of capitalism to crisis, the underlying cause of all crises remains the fundamental contradiction on which the capitalist mode of production is based, the contradiction between the production of things and the production of value, and the subordination of the former to the latter.

The focus of orthodox Marxism on general crises, as opposed to the permanently contradictory and crisis ridden character of capital accumulation, has equally proved a distraction. Although Marx and Engels bolstered their revolutionary faith by appealing to the inevitable crisis, in practice they quietly abandoned the illusion that the revolution would be precipitated by a general crisis when that of 1857 turned out to be a damp squib. By the time that Marx wrote the first volume of *Capital* the emphasis of his analysis of capitalism was on the secular tendencies of capitalist development, the tendency to the concentration and centralisation of capital, to the polarisation of wealth and poverty, the coexistence of overwork and unemployment, and to the increasing instability of social existence which underlay the development of the organised working class. The crisis is no longer a cataclysmic effect, it is a part of the normal pattern of capitalist accumulation, the pattern of overaccumulation and crisis that underlies the permanence of the class struggle as capitalists seek to resolve the crisis tendencies of accumulation at the expense of the working class.

Marx does not so much offer a theory of crisis as a fundamentally different foundation for the analysis of the capitalist economy from that on which bourgeois economics is built. This foundation is not provided by the labour theory of value, or the theory of surplus value, about which little has been said in this book. The foundation is provided by the investigation of the social form of capitalist production, which leads to a specific characterisation of the dynamics of the capitalist mode of production.[2]

The theory which Marx developed, if only in outline, is both theoretically and empirically more adequate to the reality of capitalist development than the model proposed by bourgeois economics. This is hardly surprising, since bourgeois economics tries to explain capitalism on the basis of a model which offers an abstract formalisation of the exchange relations appropriate to the social form of petty commodity production. Such a model represented a considerable scientific advance when it was proposed by Adam Smith in 1776. However, this model had been developed to its scientific limits by David Ricardo by the 1820s, since when it has owed its reproduction to nothing more than its ideological power. One hundred and fifty years ago Marx identified those limits, and provided a more adequate foundation on which to build a scientific understanding of the contradictory development of the capitalist mode of production. We should not overestimate the power of science, but nor should we estimate the power of ideology. The point may be to change the world, but in order to change it helps to understand it.

---

[2] It is the characterisation of the social form of capitalist production which defines the appropriateness of the labour theory of value and the theory of surplus value as the simplest mode of conceptualisation of the fundamental relationships of the capitalist mode of production (Clarke, 1991).

Bibliography

Aglietta, M. *Theory of Capitalist Regulation*, New Left Books, London, 1979.
Armstrong, P. Glyn, A. and Harrison, J. *Capitalism Since World War II*, Fontana, London, 1984.
Baran, P. and Sweezy, P. *Monopoly Capital*, Monthly Review Press, New York, 1966.
Bell, P. 'Marxist Theory, Class Struggle, and the Crisis of Capitalism' in Jesse Schwartz (ed.), 1977.
Boddy, R. and Crotty, J. 'Class Conflict and Macro Policy', *Review of Radical Political Economics*, 7, 1, 1975.
Bologna, S. 'Money and Crisis: Marx as Correspondent of the *New York Daily Tribune*, 1856–7', mimeo., Red Notes, London, n.d., and *Common Sense* 13 and 14.
Bowles, S. Gordon, D.M. and Weisskopf, T.E. *Beyond the Wasteland*, Verso, London, 1984.
Braverman, H. *Labour and Monopoly Capital*, Monthly Review Press, New York, 1974.
Charasov, G., *Das System des Marxismus*, Berlin, 1910.
Clarke, S. 'Overaccumulation, Class Struggle and the Regulation Approach', *Capital and Class*, 36, 1988a, 59–92.
Clarke, S. *Keynesianism, Monetarism and the Crisis of the State*, Edward Elgar, Aldershot, 1988b.
Clarke, S. 'The Basic Theory of Capitalism', *Capital and Class*, 37, 1989, 133–150.
Clarke, S. 'The Marxist Theory of Crisis', *Science and Society*, 54, 4, 442–67, 1990.
Clarke, S. *Marx, Marginalism and Modern Sociology*, Second Expanded Edition, Macmillan, Basingstoke, 1991.
Cliff, T. 'Perspective of the Permanent War Economy', *Socialist Review*, 1957
Cliff, T. *Russia - A Marxist Analysis*, Socialist Review, London, 1964.
Cogoy, M. 'Les théories néo-Marxistes, Marx et l'accumulation du Capital', *Les Temps Modernes*, 314–5, 1972
Cogoy, M. 'The fall in the Rate of Profit and the Theory of Accumulation' *Bulletin of the Conference of Socialist Economists*, Winter 1973.
Day, R. *The Crisis and the Crash*, New Left Books, London, 1981.

Dobb, M. *Capitalism Yesterday and Today*, Lawrence and Wishart, London, 1958.
Dobb, M. *Political Economy and Capitalism* (1937), RKP, London, 1940.
Eaton, J. *Marx Against Keynes*, Lawrence and Wishart, London, 1951.
Fine, B. and Harris, L. *Rereading Capital*, Columbia UP, NY, 1979.
Engels, F. *Anti-Dühring*, (AD) (1878), FLPH, Moscow, 1962
Gillman, J.M.*The Falling Rate of Profit*, New York, 1958.
Glyn, A. and Sutcliffe, B. *British Capitalism, Workers and the Profit Squeeze*, Penguin, Harmondsworth, 1972.
Grossman, H. *The Law of Accumulation and Breakdown of the Capitalist System* (1929), Pluto Press, London, 1992.
Guttsman, W.L. *The German Social Democratic Party, 1875–1933*, Allen and Unwin London, 1981.
Harrison, J. *Marxist Economics for Socialists*, Pluto, London, 1978.
Hilferding, R, *Finance Capital* (1910) (FC), Routledge and Kegan Paul, London, 1981.
Howard, D. ed. *Selected Political Writings of Rosa Luxemburg*, Monthly Review Press, New York, 1971.
Howard, M.C. and King, J.E. *A History of Marxian Economics*, Macmillan, 2 volumes, 1989 and 1992.
Itoh, M. *The Basic Theory of Capitalism*, Macmillan, London, 1988.
Itoh, M. *Value and Crisis*, Pluto, London and Monthly Review, New York, 1980.
Kühne, K. *Economics and Marxism*, 2 vols, Macmillan, London, 1979.
Kautsky, K. *The Class Struggle* (CC) (1892) Translated by William E Bohn, Charles H Kerr, Chicago, 1910.
Kautsky, K. *The Economic Doctrines of Karl Marx* (EDKM), NCLC Publishing Society, London, 1936.
Kidron, M. *Western Capitalism Since the War*, Penguin, Harmondsworth, 1970.
Lallier, A.G. *The Economics of Marx's Grundrisse*, Macmillan, London, 1989
Luxemburg, R. *The Accumulation of Capital* (1913) (AC),
Luxemburg, R. Social Reform or Revolution, (1899/1908), in Howard, ed. *Selected Political Writings*, 1971.
Mandel, E. *Late Capitalism* (1972), New Left Books, London, 1975.
Mandel, E. *Marxist Economic Theory*, 2 vols, Merlin, London, 1962.
Marazzi, B. C. *Money and Disequilibrium*, PhD Thesis, Citu University, London, 1984.
Marx, K. and Engels, F. *Collected Works* (CWnn), Progress, Moscow and Lawrence and Wishart, London, 1975–.
Marx, K. and Engels, F. *Karl Marx Friedrich Engels Gesamtausgabe* (MEGA), Dietz, Berlin, 1975–.
Marx, K. *Capital*, Vol. I (CI), FLPH, Moscow, 1965.
Marx, K. *Capital*, Vol. II (CII), Penguin, Harmondsworth, 1978.
Marx, K. *Capital*, Vol. III (CIII), FLPH, Moscow, 1972.

Marx, K. *Fondements de la Critique de l'Economie Politique*, 2 vols, Anthropos, Paris, 1968.
Marx, K. *Letters on Capital* Translated by Andrew Drummond, New Park, London, 1983.
Marx, K. *Theories of Surplus Value* (TSVn), 3 Vols, FLPH, Moscow, 1969.
Marx, K. and Engels, F. *Selected Correspondence*, Progress, Moscow, 1955.
Mattick P. *Marx and Keynes*, Merlin, London, 1969.
Nakatani, T. 'The law of falling rate of profit and the competitive battle: comment on Shaikh', *Cambridge Journal of Economics*, 4, 1, 1980
Okishio, N. 'Technical Change and the Rate of Profit', *Kobe University Economic Review*, 7, 1961.
Preiser, E. 'Das Wesen der marxschen Krisentheorie', in *Politische Oekonomie im 20. Jahrhundert*, Munich 1970.
Reuten, G. 'Accumulation of capital and the foundation of the tendency of the rate of profit to fall', *Cambridge Journal of Economics*, 15, 1991, 79–93.
Ricciardi, J. 'Reading Marx on the Role of Money and Finance in Economic Development', *Research in Political Economy*, 10, 1987, 61–81.
Rosdolsky, R. *The Making of Marx's Capital*, Pluto, London, 1977.
Schwartz, J., ed.*The Subtle Anatomy of Capitalism*, Goodyear, Santa Monica, 1977.
Shaikh, A. 'Political economy and capitalism: notes on Dobb's theory of crisis', *Cambridge Journal of Economics*, 2, 3, 1978.
Smith, A. *The Wealth of Nations*, Everyman edition, Dent, London, 1910, 2 vols.
Strachey, J. *The Coming Struggle for Power*, Gollancz, London, 1932.
Strachey, J. *The Nature of Capitalist Crises*, Gollancz, London, 1935.
Sweezy, P. *The Theory of Capitalist Development* (1942), Dobson, London, 1946.
Tudor, H. and J.M. *Marxism and Social Democracy: The Revisionist Debate, 1896-8*, Cambridge University Press, Cambridge, 1988.
Uchida, H. *Marx's Grundrisse and Hegel's Logic*, Routledge, London, 1988.
Vance, T. M. *The Permanent War Economy*, Independent Socialist Press, Berkeley, date
Weeks, J. *Capital and Exploitation*, Edward Arnold, London, 1981.
Wilson, J.D. 'A Note on Marx and the Trade Cycle', *Review of Economic Studies*, February, 1938.
Wright, E.O. 'Alternative Perspectives in the Marxist Theory of Accumulation and Crisis', in Jesse Schwartz, ed, 1977.
Yaffe, D. 'The Marxian Theory of Crisis, Capital and the State', *Bulletin of the Conference of Socialist Economists*, Winter 1972.

Index

Aglietta, M.,4, 58, 71
alienation,83, 129–30, 194
Armstrong, P., Glyn, A. and Harrison, J.,70
banks,40–1, 45–6, 51, 93, 98, 100–01, 104–6, 112–3, 115, 118, 120, 126, 169, 189, 273, 275, 277
Banking School,103–05
Baran, P.,6, 57
Bauer, O.,60, 67
Bazarov, V.,52
Bebel, A.,20, 29
Bell, P.,71
Bernstein, E.,4, 6, 10, 17, 21, 29–33, 38–41, 94, 279
Boddy R.,64
Bologna, S.,99
Bortkiewicz, L. von ,59
Boudin, L.,37
bourgeois economics,1, 8, 10, 13, 15, 42–4, 51–2, 62, 75, 88, 274, 278, 280, 285–6
Bowles, S., Gordon, D. and Weisskopf, T.,4
Braverman, H.,71
Bukharin, N.,37, 52
Bulgakov, S.,35, 55
business cycle,3, 26–8, 36, 38, 45, 47–8, 50, 60, 67, 75, 261

capital accumulation,26, 33, 54, 56, 59–61, 86, 140, 146, 160–1, 169, 174, 206, 210, 221, 240, 260, 276, 279, 285
centralisation of capital,18, 40, 59, 77, 86, 91, 172, 224–5, 235, 239, 242–3, 250, 255, 260, 285
Charasov, G.,60, 64
circulating capital,158, 161, 262, 268

circulation,26, 32, 46, 51–2, 56, 76, 95, 104, 106, 111, 119, 121–3, 125–30, 132, 134–6, 138–40, 144–6, 148, 152–4, 157–8, 167–9, 172–5, 179, 189–91, 193–201, 205, 207, 230, 233, 238, 244, 247, 261–3, 269–76, 280
Clarke, S.,8, 9, 13, 58, 71, 82, 104, 283, 286
class struggle,4, 7–9, 15, 16, 21–2, 25–6, 28, 64–5, 70–3, 86, 96, 172, 174, 244, 285
classical political economy,1, 12, 88, 138, 143, 168, 170
Cliff, T.,57
Cogoy, M.,63, 67
commercial capital,111, 169
commercial crisis,17, 27, 84, 97, 111, 124, 173
commodity capital, 104, 126, 155, 185, 191, 195, 207, 261
commodity form,168, 178, 194, 196, 274
competition,2, 24, 27, 33, 39, 41–7, 49, 54–5, 68, 77, 85–94, 101, 110, 122, 138, 141–5, 147, 151–7, 160, 167–8, 170–1, 175, 178, 210–13, 218, 224, 226, 229, 237, 239, 242, 247, 250–1, 255, 257–9, 267–8, 273–5, 279, 281–2
composition of capital,34, 45–8, 59, 61, 63, 65–71, 154, 158–66, 170–2, 174, 208–22, 232, 235, 241–44, 252, 254–60
concentration of capital,224, 226, 228, 231, 255
constant capital,155, 159, 172, 182, 211–5, 218, 238, 254, 269, 276–7
consumption,5, 7, 17–18, 24, 33–7, 39, 42, 44–5, 54–7,59–60, 75, 80, 85–6, 88, 104–05, 123, 128, 133, 135–6, 141, 144–7, 149–50, 152, 155–7, 170, 180, 181, 184–8, 190–1, 194, 204, 206, 210, 212, 225–7,

Index

229–30, 239, 254, 268–71, 276–7, 281, 284–5
contradiction,5, 10, 15, 18, 24, 30–2, 36, 38–9, 41, 59–60, 62, 74, 83, 98, 107–08, 117, 127, 131, 134, 136–7, 140–1, 143–60, 163, 168, 173–4, 178–86, 193, 195, 240, 242–3, 247, 249, 254, 279–80, 284–5
credit,27, 29–32, 35–6, 40, 46, 50–2, 62, 71, 98, 100– 6, 112, 114–8, 125–6, 152, 169, 173–5, 178, 182, 188–9, 192, 198–202, 205, 225–6, 231, 235, 238, 241–2, 255, 257– 61, 268, 270, 273–8
Croce, B.,59, 66-7
Currency School,104, 254
cycle,3, 20, 26–8, 36, 38, 40–2, 45–53, 58, 60, 62, 67, 71, 74–5, 77, 81, 94–6, 109–10, 154, 169, 182, 189, 239, 250, 253–4, 258–68
cyclical,3, 16, 18–19, 23–6, 28, 32, 36, 38, 46, 48, 54, 77–8, 80–1, 93, 206, 212, 240, 248, 258–9

Day, R.,9, 52, 58, 117
disproportionality,2, 5, 6, 9, 34–40, 42–3, 47–8, 52–3, 58, 61, 63, 71, 75, 105, 109, 111, 126, 128, 137–42, 144, 150–1, 153, 155–8, 166, 169–71, 174, 176, 178, 189–90, 203–5, 229, 239–40, 271, 283–5
division of labour,87, 89, 127, 135, 222
Dobb, M.,5, 50, 57, 62, 67, 69–70
Dühring,17–18, 34, 178

Eaton, J.,53, 62
Engels,5, 6, 9, 10–12, 15, 17–20, 23, 28, 35, 42–4, 49–50, 54, 68, 74–5, 77–86, 89–97, 99, 102–3, 109–10, 112– 124, 126, 128, 131, 141, 165, 167, 170, 173, 176–8, 184–5, 208–9, 246, 248–9, 285
exchange value,38, 106, 108, 127–31, 133, 139, 141, 144, 146, 179, 188, 190–1, 194, 197, 231
exchange,4, 18, 67, 71, 75–6, 78, 82–5, 91, 103, 106, 120, 122–3, 125–30, 132, 134, 136, 139, 148, 152–3, 155–7, 177–9, 190, 193–6, 198, 240, 249, 269, 274, 276–7, 280, 286

expanded reproduction,34, 46, 55–6, 61, 150, 158, 166, 169, 186, 198, 268, 270
financial crisis,51, 96, 98–9, 102, 114–5, 117, 120
Fine, B.,159
fixed capital,40–50, 66, 69, 108, 160, 162, 165, 225, 227, 231, 233, 238, 261–8, 272–3, 282
fluctuations,16, 18, 28, 38, 40–1, 79-81, 202, 222–3, 254, 281
forces of production,5, 18–19, 24, 30, 32, 36, 42, 49, 54, 56, 69, 71, 74–5, 84–9, 91, 93, 99, 107–8, 110–11, 131–2, 142–3, 146–7, 149, 151, 153, 156, 167–9, 173, 186, 189, 231–5, 242–3, 254, 258, 260, 282–3
general law of capitalist accumulation, 68, 160, 172, 178, 206–7, 214, 219, 221, 224, 236, 246, 251–2, 254
Gillman, J.,62
gold,2, 51–2, 98–100, 103, 106, 115, 129, 134, 189, 238, 270, 272–3
Guttsman, W.,29

Harrison, J.,60, 70
Hilferding, R.,6, 10, 37–53, 58–60, 69, 75, 77, 116, 267, 280
hoarding,189, 270, 272, 275
Howard, M. and King, J.,9, 25, 37, 59–60
Howard, D.,31

industrial capital,40–1, 45, 111, 276
industrial crisis,51, 100–01, 116, 266, 268, 273
industrial cycle,40–1, 48, 250, 253, 259, 265–7
investment cycle,42, 45, 47–50, 52, 266, 268, 273
Itoh, M.,70, 71, 145

Kautsky, K.,6, 10, 14–17, 21–30, 32, 37–39, 42, 46, 49, 54, 74–5, 77, 90, 111, 116, 144, 170, 177, 279–80
Keynes, J.M.,3, 50–2, 57, 61, 67, 174
Keynesian,3, 6, 26–7, 53, 57–8, 63, 64, 67, 268

Kidron, M.,58

labour market,46, 62, 70, 89, 254
Lallier, A.,145
Lapinsky,52
law of the tendency for the rate of profit to fall,5, 7, 15, 23, 45, 47–8, 58–72, 138, 149, 155, 158–66, 169–72, 177–8, 180, 207–17, 220–33, 236–7, 240–5, 252, 262, 285
Lenin, V.I.,9, 37, 55
Luxemburg, R.,4–5, 10, 14, 31, 32, 35, 37–8, 53–6, 58, 60, 67, 75, 154, 270, 280

machinery,18, 21, 47, 66, 86–9, 94, 153, 155, 159–60, 171, 182, 203, 215, 221, 238, 250, 257, 263–4, 267, 274
Malthus, T.,145, 180–6, 210, 220, 227, 269, 284
Mandel, E.,58, 60, 267
Marazzi, C.,56, 154, 270
Marshall, A.,50
means of payment,188, 194, 197–200, 249, 277, 280
merchant's capital,276
method,11, 31, 37, 42, 68–71, 151, 167, 172, 213
Mill, J.S.,81, 103, 197
money capital,51, 61, 168, 191, 272, 275
money crisis,199, 277
money form,104, 134, 167, 196
monopoly,2, 56, 70, 77, 130, 152, 241, 267
Moseley, O.,61

Nakatani, T.,69
necessary labour,132, 144, 145–49, 155, 162, 164, 169, 182, 218, 219
necessity of crisis,31, 48–50, 75, 171–2, 205–6, 260

Okishio, N.,69
overaccumulation,2, 5, 9, 39, 47, 52, 60–3, 67, 69–71, 74, 89, 100–12, 235–42, 253–6, 259–61, 278–83, 285
overproduction,1, 2, 5–7, 9, 17–19, 24–36, 39, 42–8, 51, 52, 58, 60–63, 69, 74, 77, 80, 84–93, 97–112, 116, 121–2, 131, 133, 138–40, 143–5, 149–58, 166, 169, 174–5, 179, 181, 185–93, 197, 199, 203–07, 210, 212, 226, 229–33, 239–42, 249, 250, 264, 274–84

Parvus,30–1
pauperisation,172, 178, 18, 251
petty commodity production, 168, 172, 280, 286
polarisation,7, 16, 18, 21, 23, 94, 178, 225, 228, 251, 260, 285
populism,17, 34
Preiser, E.,61, 67, 70
productive capital,46, 51, 140, 160, 264, 268, 275
productive labour,84, 182

rate of exploitation,23, 59–61, 65–8, 71, 208–10, 213–21, 232, 236, 253
rate of interest,2, 23, 46, 50–1, 61, 101, 173, 217, 226
rate of surplus value,34, 68, 149, 154, 161–4, 166, 168– 71, 173, 209, 211, 216–9, 221, 223, 228, 238, 241, 262
realisation,8, 34, 39, 55, 59–60, 62, 74, 84, 104, 133, 136, 139, 141, 145–51, 155, 157, 168–70, 180, 182–6, 193, 199– 201, 220, 229, 232, 261, 268–74
relations of production,34, 67, 75–6, 82, 91, 123, 126–7, 164, 183, 219, 281
relative surplus population,24, 159–60, 172, 182, 210, 217, 221, 224, 228, 243–4, 251, 254, 257, 260
relative surplus value,71, 86, 132, 135–6, 163, 167, 169, 177, 211, 216–7
rent,23, 78, 102, 108, 130, 165, 170, 182, 203, 210–11, 244, 269
reproduction schemes,34, 36, 54–5, 67, 151, 155–8, 262, 268–70
reserve army of labour,27, 60–2, 81, 182, 185, 236–7, 251, 253–4, 257–8, 260
Reuten, G.,69
revolution,4, 14, 18–19, 22, 28, 30–1, 79, 95–102, 112, 114, 116, 118, 174–5, 222, 245, 248, 251, 268, 285

Index

Ricardo, D.,13, 102, 107, 121–2, 130–1, 136, 139–40, 146, 150–2, 160–3, 170–1, 179–80, 182–4, 187, 190–5, 204, 209–12, 215–21, 227, 236, 241, 284, 286
Ricciardi, J.,99
Rodbertus, J.,17
Rosdolsky, R.,60, 145

Say's Law,133, 138–9, 190
Schmidt, F.,36–7
secular tendency,6, 16, 18, 21–30, 35–6, 38, 42, 46, 49–50, 54, 57–8, 62, 68, 74–5, 77, 93, 117, 138, 170–1, 178, 180, 208–14, 233, 235, 240, 242, 245, 248–50, 260
Shaikh, A.,69
simple reproduction,269, 271
Sismondi, S. de,121, 136, 180, 182–4, 186, 220, 284
Smith, A.,88, 104, 141, 170, 180, 182, 209–12, 218, 220, 269, 286
Stalin, J.,14
Strachey, J.,53, 61–2, 69, 70
supply and demand,1, 2, 17, 26, 40–3, 47, 78, 80, 81–5, 93, 127–8, 139–43, 219, 236, 251–3, 280
surplus product,24, 109, 136, 145, 155, 180, 186, 236, 269, 272, 275, 284
surplus labour,130, 133, 135, 141, 144–55, 157, 164, 167, 170, 174, 211, 218, 222
Sweezy, P.,6, 9, 25, 35–8, 56–8, 66, 70, 186

trade cycle,3, 26, 46, 50, 58, 60, 96
Tudor, H. and J.,30–3
Tugan-Baranowsky,34–5, 67, 68
turnover of capital,46–48, 172, 209, 215, 261–2

Uchida, H.,167
underconsumption,5–6, 17, 25, 35–9, 42, 45, 48, 53, 56– 60, 74, 75, 111, 166, 170, 176, 180, 186
unemployment,8, 63, 80, 118, 160, 210, 221, 223, 285
unproductive consumption,181–2
unproductive labour,180–1

use value,74, 84, 108, 131, 133–4, 139–40, 146, 150, 157, 173–4, 178–9, 188, 190–1, 195, 197, 212, 242, 247, 249

Varga, E.,6, 56, 62
variable capital,34, 65, 155, 159–61, 167, 211, 214, 217–9, 223, 262

wages,7, 17, 39, 46, 52, 55, 57, 59–65, 69–70, 78, 86, 89–90, 93–4, 96, 117, 121, 144, 146–7, 149, 152, 159–60, 162, 172, 182, 185, 209, 211, 248, 254, 256–7, 264, 268–9, 282, 284
waste,6, 24, 57
Weeks, J.,69, 71
Wilson, J.,60
working class,4–5, 7, 8, 15, 17–18, 22, 28, 34, 53, 61, 63–65, 72–3, 80–1, 85, 95–6, 105, 145–7, 173, 175–6, 185, 186, 206, 222, 245, 248–51, 285
world market,17, 20, 26, 28, 32, 90–1, 93, 98, 101, 105, 109, 112, 118, 122, 135–6, 143, 168, 179, 192, 203, 212, 250, 258, 260, 267
Wright, E.O.,58, 68

Yaffe, D.,67, 68